/Autodata Car Manual

D1133490

AUSTIN/MORRIS MINI
1962-88

This Autodata Car Manual is the only reference book needed for the care, repair and maintenance of your Austin/Morris Mini.

It has been researched and written by Autodata's team of experts with assistance and advice from a number of professional sources, and incorporates the know-how and tips which have been derived from practical experience of the Mini.

The manual starts with the care and maintenance which every Mini needs. The rest of the manual gives complete instructions for the repair and overhaul of the car.

Each chapter begins with an introduction, followed by a tools and equipment section. These sections will tell you if a job is particularly complex or requires special skills or tools and should be read before starting any task.

Published by Autodata Limited
St. Peter's Road, Maidenhead, Berkshire, SL6 7QU, England

Autodata would like to acknowledge the help of the following companies in the preparation of this car manual:

Austin Rover Group Limited
Champion Sparking Plug Co. Limited
Lex Mead (Maidenhead) Limited
Hella Limited
Henlys PLC, Staines, Middx.
Henlys (London) Ltd, High Wycombe, Bucks
Plastigauge Mfg. Co.
Sykes Pickavant Limited
Lucas Electrical
Unipart Group Limited
C.P. Witter Limited
Gunsons Colourplugs Limited

Autodata Car Manual for the Austin/Morris Mini

Compiled and written by Ivor Carroll & Graham Corby
Edited by Vic Willson & Bill Price

Published by Autodata Limited
St. Peter's Road, Maidenhead, Berkshire SL6 7QU. England

©**1988 Autodata Limited**

ACM 250

ISBN 0-85666-444-8

Printed in England by Page Bros. (Norwich) Limited

Introduction

The Autodata Repair Manual is designed to guide you through all the stages of repair of service jobs on your car – from a simple engine oil and filter change right through to the removal and overhaul of the engine.

MANUAL LAYOUT

Easy reference to the appropriate section dealing with the part of your car to be checked or repaired is provided by the Contents pages and the individual chapter headings. Each chapter contains easy-to-follow repair sequences together with clear line drawings, cross referenced with the text, showing what fits where. A comprehensive Index page at the end of the manual gives quick reference to components and assemblies.

MOT TEST

A special chapter is devoted to passing the MoT test, with cross reference to the other chapters concerned. Check over all the items detailed in this chapter before submitting your car for its MoT test to avoid any needless failure.

BASIC PROCEDURES

To make sure that you are able to carry out all maintenance and repair operations efficiently and safely, we have included a comprehensive chapter which outlines basic do's and don'ts when working on or around your car.

A section is included which contains a list of suggested hand tools and equipment which should be considered to be the basis of any home mechanics tool kit.

ROUTINE MAINTENANCE

The regular maintenance operations are contained in a complete chapter and are forwarded by a Service Schedule identifying all the maintenance items required and showing the appropriate service intervals.

To ensure that your car is set up to give maximum performance and economy, a comprehensive Tune-Up chapter follows the Routine Maintenance. From the information contained in both chapters you will be able to carry out all the regular maintenance and adjustment operations required to keep your car running as efficiently, economically and safely as possible.

TROUBLE SHOOTING

To assist you in correctly diagnosing faults a special Trouble Shooter is included at the end of each appropriate chapter. These Trouble Shooters provide details of symptoms and possible causes and will help in tracking down problems as and when they arise. In addition to these the BREAKDOWN & NON-START HINTS will give you all the advice necessary if your car fails to start or if you have the misfortune to breakdown by the roadside.

TECHNICAL DATA

Technical information required for specific operations is contained in the text throughout the manual, to make each section as complete and easy-to-follow as possible.

At the end of the manual a Technical Data section is provided to give a comprehensive listing of the technical specifications likely to be needed by the DIY motorist.

SPECIAL TOOLS

Certain repair jobs covered in the manual require the use of special tools not normally found in a DIY toolkit. When such tools are required we tell you at the beginning of each chapter. If the special tool is likely to be available from your local tool hire shop then we tell you. Equally, if the job can only be done with a tool which is unique to your make of car then we advise you.

SPECIALIST SERVICES

In some cases the non-availability of spare parts and the need for special tools means that the best solution is to fit an exchange or specialist overhauled component, we then give the procedure for removal and replacement of the unit.

The need for specialised equipment to carry out some operations will require you to take your car to your local garage or service centre. Wheel alignment, as an example, can be checked using DIY equipment, but a full front suspension geometry check can only be undertaken by a garage or tyre specialist having the necessary equipment. In such cases we advise you accordingly.

Contents

History & Identification

OCTOBER 1962

Mini 850 Super and DeLuxe models replaced by Super DeLuxe. New 850 Countryman Estate with all metal body introduced. Revised gearbox fitted on some models.

SEPTEMBER 1964

Hydrolastic suspension introduced on all Saloon models. All models now have revised gear change and gearbox, diaphragm type clutch, and twin leading shoe type front brakes.

OCTOBER 1965

Automatic transmission available as optional extra.

OCTOBER 1967

Mk 2 models introduced, with modified steering and brake hydraulics, larger rear window, restyled front grille and larger tail lights. Mini 1000 Super DeLuxe introduced with 998 cc engine and remote control gearchange. Countryman with wood trim and Traveller Estates. Automatic transmission optional on all models. Mini Van and Pickup have optional 998 cc engine.

AUGUST 1968

New all-synchromesh gearbox on all models, also revised internal door handle.

NOVEMBER 1969

'Mini' named as marque in own right. Mk 2 models replaced by ADO 20 series Saloons (Referred to as Mk 3). Wind-up windows, concealed door hinges, 'dry' rubber cone suspension. Negative earth polarity, mechanical fuel pump. Mk 2 Traveller, Countryman Estates discontinued. Saloons (except Clubman) now have 'dry' rubber cone suspension replacing Hydrolastic. Mini Clubman 998 cc Saloon and Estate introduced. 1275 GT with Clubman body, front disc brakes, and Rostyle wheels.

MAY 1974

New 'fresh air' type heater fitted, with revised carburation and manifolds on 850 models. 1275 GT has larger discs, 12 inch wheels, and larger fuel tank.

JANUARY 1973

Radial ply tyres and alternator now fitted as standard, with 'rod' change type gearbox.

OCTOBER 1975

1100 Clubman manual models introduced with 1098 cc engine. 1000 Clubman automatic models have 998 cc engines. Mini 1000 Special available in limited edition with reclining front seats and striped upholstery.

MAY 1976

Revised instrument panel and trim on all models which now have new ignition/steering column lock and twin stalk controls on steering column. New type sub-frame rubber mountings fitted.

AUGUST 1977

Revised interior. Mini 1000 has reclining front seats. Denovo tyres on 1275 GT. Tinted glass on Clubman.

JULY 1979

Mini 850 City introduced, low price version.

AUGUST 1979

Limited edition Mini 1100 Special introduced, with 1098 cc engine, metallic paintwork and high specification interior trim including centre console with clock.

OCTOBER 1979

Mini 1000 renamed Mini Super.

MAY 1980

New 'Quiet Minis' with redesigned soundproofing.

AUGUST 1980

Mini 850, Clubman 1100 and 1275 GT discontinued.

SEPTEMBER 1980

Mini Super redesignated Mini 1000 HL. Mini 1000 HL Estate introduced. Mini 1000 City introduced. Clubman Estate discontinued. Mini Van available with 848 cc or 998 cc engine, Mini Pickup with 998 cc engine only.

APRIL 1982

Mini 1000 HL Estate discontinued. Mini 1000 City E and HLE models launched with new 'A' Plus economy engine based on the Metro 1,0 engine.

OCTOBER 1982

Mini 1000 Mayfair introduced, replacing HLE.

OCTOBER 1983

Limited edition Mini Sprite introduced with alloy wheels, side stripes and special interior.

JULY 1984

Limited edition Silver Jubilee Mini 25 introduced, featuring 998 cc engine, front disc brakes and uprated rear brakes. Trim specification includes reclining seats with headrests and velvet upholstery. Tinted glass and twin door mirrors standard.

OCTOBER 1984

City and Mayfair models now have 12 in wheels, disc brakes, and wheel arch extensions. City has 'saw-tooth' design upholstery and Mayfair has 'chalk-stripe' velvet upholstery.

JUNE 1985

Limited edition Mini Ritz introduced with 998 cc engine. Specification includes alloy 12 in wheels and wheel arch extensions, Silver leaf metalic paintwork, side trim coachline with Ritz logo. The upholstery is colour co-ordinated in red, white and blue. A three spoke steering wheel, radio and rear seat belts are standard.

JANUARY 1986

Limited edition Mini Chelsea introduced with 998 cc engine. Specification includes alloy 12 in wheels and wheel arch extensions, Targa red paintwork, side trim coachline with Chelsea logo. The upholstery is grey cloth with red piping. A three spoke steering wheel, radio and tachometer are standard.

FEBRUARY 1986

Five millionth Mini produced.

JUNE 1986

Limited edition Mini Piccadilly introduced with similar mechanical specification to the City but with 'Piccadilly' autograph on seats, boot and coachline.

JANUARY 1987

Limited edition (only 1500 produced) Mini Park Lane introduced, with black paint finish, tinted glass, coffee/beige velvet with black sculptured velvet seat trim, radio/stereo cassette player and full width wheel trims.

MAY 1987

Limited edition Mini Advantage introduced, with Diamond White body colour, matching wheel trims and full length 'tennis net' side stripes with Advantage logo. Special grey interior trim with green pinstripes, push button radio and tachometer also included in specification.

FEBRUARY 1988

Limited edition Red Hot and Jet Black models introduced. Finished in red and black respectively, both trimmed in black velour with red piping. Special badges and decals, plus push-button radio as standard equipment.

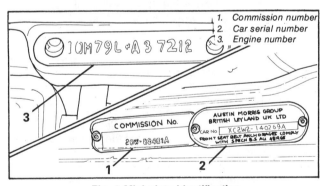

1. VIN plate
2. Engine number
3. Body number
4. Serial/Commission number

Fig. 1 Mini plate locations

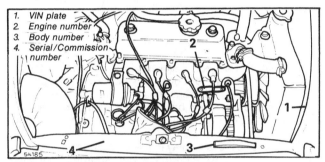

1. Commission number
2. Car serial number
3. Engine number

Fig. 2 Mini plate identification

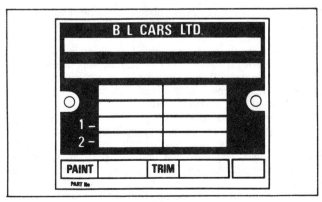

Fig. 3 VIN plate

COMMISSION, CAR & BODY NUMBERS
— 1 & 2, Fig.2

Before the introduction of the VIN number system, the car Serial and Commission numbers were used to identify the car and body. The Commission number is located on a plate on the bonnet locking panel, next to the car serial number.

The Commission number is explained as follows:
1 15 W 000101 A
1   Car series, 1 or 2
15   BL internal reference.
W   Body type, as detailed for VIN plate.
000101 Commission number
A   BL internal reference.

The car serial number is explained as follows:
A A W 7 – 000
A   Model marque:
A   Austin
M   Morris
A   Engine type.
W   Body type, as detailed for VIN plate.
3   Car series
–   Unless specification different from standard:
D   DeLuxe
L   LHD
S   Super DeLuxe
000 Serial number

ENGINE NUMBER — 3, Fig.2

The engine number is stamped on a plate rivetted to the engine block below the number 1 spark plug. The engine number should be used whenever obtaining mechanical components. Early cars have a code number stamped on the transmission casing.

The engine number code is explained as follows:
85 H 791 P H 101
85 Engine capacity code:
85 848 cc
99 998 cc
10 1098 cc
12 1275 cc
H   Transverse engine
791 Combination code detailing alternator, gearbox, etc.
P   Code for carburettor, distributor, crankcase ventilation system
H   Engine compression.
101 Engine serial number.

VIN PLATE — Fig.3

The VIN plate details the EEC type approval number, paint and trim codes, weight and loading codes and the Vehicle Identification Number. The plate is fitted to Saloons on the left-hand front inner wing panel. On Estate cars, the plate is on top of the panel. On Vans and Pick-up models the plate is on the front of the right-hand inner wing panel.

NOTE: Only very late models have a paint code number specified on the VIN plate. Prior to this, no paint code was marked on the body.

The VIN number is explained as follows:
SAX X A 1A 1 SAX World make identifying number.
X BL internal reference.

A	Engine capacity:	1A	Body type:		
K	848 cc	2W	2 door estate	U	Pickup
L	998 cc	2S	2 door saloon	1	Series
C	1098 cc	G	Van (Post Office)	1	1st series
		V	Van	2	Clubman

Pass the MoT

When your Mini is three years old, it must be submitted for its first MoT test. The car must then be tested annually to ensure that it is in a roadworthy condition. The test fee paid to the garage covers the cost of carrying out the inspection whether the car passes the test or fails, so it makes sense to carry out your own pre-test check of the car beforehand.

To pass the test, the car must meet the statutory requirements of condition relating basically to the lighting equipment, the steering and suspension, the braking system, wheels and tyres, seat belts, and general items such as the windscreen wipers and washers, the horn, the exhaust system and the condition of the car body at the load bearing points. Bear in mind that even a simple item like a brake light or one of the screen washers not working could 'fail' the car.

Obviously a DIY owner will not be able to examine the car to the same standard of inspection as an official tester, but by checking your car following our step-by-step guide below, you could avoid a needless 'fail' certificate.

If you work your way through the check guide and you find that certain components are faulty and overhaul or replacement is necessary, further information will be found on the pages referred to.

The following checks are separated into those operations carried out with the car on the ground and those for which it is necessary to have the car raised or the wheels free of the ground. For all checks related to the suspension and steering systems, refer to Fig.MoT:1.

CHECK GUIDE

CAR ON GROUND

Lighting Equipment .... Pages 36,169
Check that all external lights (including headlamp main and dipped beams) are working correctly and that none show signs of dimness due to corrosion of the reflector or bad electrical connections. The light lenses and reflectors must not be damaged or missing (even a small crack in a lens can constitute a 'fail') and all lights should be visible from a reasonable distance.

The direction indicators must flash at the correct rate – between one and two flashes per second – and the instrument panel 'tell-tale' light must also be functioning.

The headlamps must be correctly aligned so as not to dazzle other road users when on dipped beam.

Horn .... Page 176
Operate the horn and check that it makes a clear audible sound. If the horn is weak or inoperative, check the electrical connections at both the horn and the switch. Note that horns which sound two or more consecutive tones are not acceptable and will constitute an MoT fail.

Windscreen Wipers .... Pages 36,174
Operate the windscreen wipers and check that the blade clears the screen effectively without smearing. If smearing is evident this indicates worn blade rubbers. This test should be carried out with a wet windscreen.

Windscreen Washers .... Pages 36,176
Check that the screen washers operate correctly and that each jet of water strikes the screen towards the top of the glass area on both driver and passenger side. It is advisable to top up the washer reservoir just before taking the car to the MoT test in order to avoid the risk of running out of water during the test.

Note that in winter there is a risk of the washer fluid freezing, in which case it is advisable to add washer fluid to the reservoir.

Steering Wheel/Column/
Mechanism .... Pages 36,125-132
Check that the steering wheel is secure on the steering column by gripping the steering wheel at the 'quarter to three' position and trying to rock it sideways. Similarly, grip the wheel at the six o'clock position and try to move it up and down to check for wear of the steering column bearings (Fig.MoT:2). There should be no perceptible movement between the steering shaft and the outer column but allow for slight flexing of the column assembly as a whole.

Now check for excessive play in the steering mechanism by turning the steering wheel slightly but vigorously in each direction and note the amount of free-play (if any) before movement at the front road wheel. The maximum amount of free movement at the steering wheel rim should be ½ in.

Seat Belts .... Page 190
Check the condition of both front seat belts, looking for signs of fraying or damage to the belt fabric. Make sure that the belt anchorage points on the car body are secure and tight and check for corrosion around them.
NOTE:Some belt designs have part of the mechanism secured to the seat frame; in this case it is essential to verify that the seat anchorages are secure and, indeed that the seat frame itself is in sound condition. In fact, checking the security of the seats is advisable in all cars as it is a safety-related item. An MoT tester can fail a car for having a worn seat reclining mechanism, for instance, or for any fault that can allow the seat or any part of it to move involuntarily.

On inertia reel type belts, check that the belt locking mechanism is operating correctly by carrying out the following test:
1. Choose a length of dry, straight road which is traffic-free.
2. Sit in the driving seat and put the seat belt on; adjusting the belt to the correct length. It is important to sit in a normal relaxed position for the purposes of this test, and not to anticipate the retarding effect of applying the brakes.
3. Drive the car at a speed of 5 mph, check that there is no other moving vehicle behind and apply the footbrake sharply. The belt mechanism should lock instantly, preventing you being thrown forwards and it should unlock when the tension is released. It should also retract into the reel when the car has stopped.
NOTE:Some designs of inertia reel belt require manual assistance to retract.

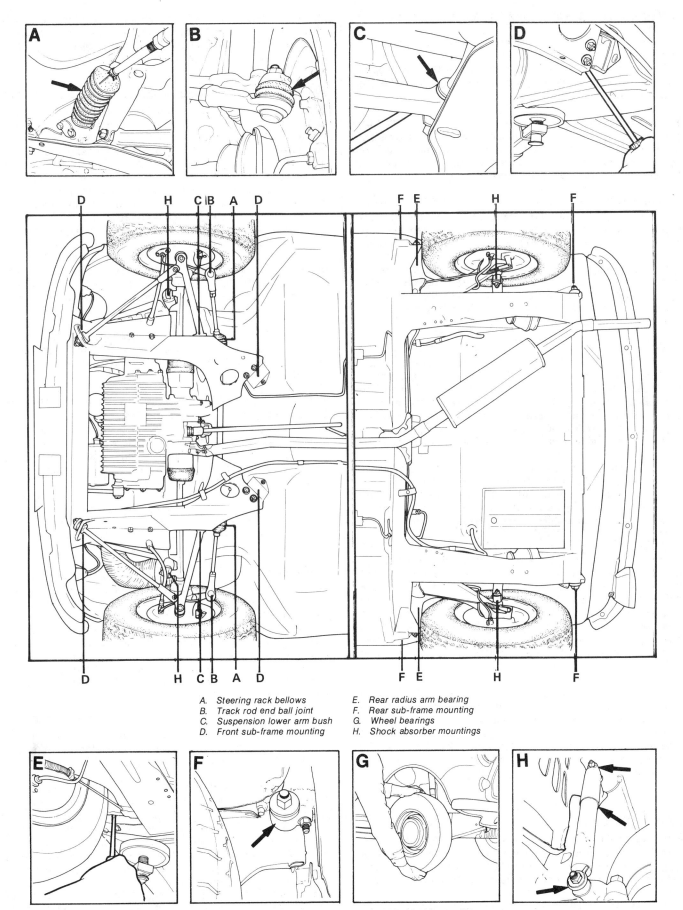

A. Steering rack bellows
B. Track rod end ball joint
C. Suspension lower arm bush
D. Front sub-frame mounting
E. Rear radius arm bearing
F. Rear sub-frame mounting
G. Wheel bearings
H. Shock absorber mountings

Fig. MoT:1 Front & rear underbody checking points

4. Repeat the test with an assistant testing the belt on the passenger's side.

If a belt fails to lock or retract then the inertia reel mechanism is faulty and must be renewed.

As a final check, make sure that the belt latches engage positively and that the belts cannot accidentally disengage due to a faulty latch mechanism.

Wheels & Tyres .... Page 36
Make sure that the tyres are all the same size and that they are of the type specified for the car. Check that all wheel nuts are correctly tightened and that the tyres are inflated to the correct pressure – this could affect the MoT brake test.

Shock Absorbers .... Pages 136,146
Check the operation of the shock absorbers (if fitted) by fully pressing down each corner of the car in turn and then releasing it. If the unit is in good condition, the corner of the car will spring up again and then settle in its normal 'at rest' position. If it rebounds down or continues bouncing, the shock absorber at that corner of the car is ineffective. On early Saloon models from 1964 to 1968 hydrolastic suspension was fitted and this operation is not necessary, although the trim height should be checked – see FRONT SUSPENSION.

Brakes .... Pages 34,153-166
Check the operation of the handbrake, making sure that it will hold the car stationary on a steep incline when fully applied and that the brakes do not 'stick' on after the brake is released. The handbrake ratchet should be felt to operate positively and should effectively hold the brake in the 'on' position even when the lever is pushed from side to side. Check that the handbrake lever does not travel excessively. Examine the fluid pipes and brake master cylinder in the engine compartment for leaks and also check that the brake servo – if fitted – is operating correctly. The operation of the servo can be checked as follows:

With the engine off, apply the brake pedal. Start the engine while still depressing the pedal – the action of the engine running should actuate the servo and the brake pedal should be felt to sink slightly underfoot.

Check the operation of the footbrake during a road test, making sure that the car stops without pulling to one side when braking both normally and heavily. Also make sure that the brake pedal does not 'pump up', (i.e. increase its resistance or 'hardness' as it is repeatedly depressed) as this is indicative of poor brake adjustment. If the brake pedal feels 'spongy' in use then suspect the presence of air in the hydraulic system. If the brake pedal tends to creep downwards under sustained pressure suspect deterioration of the seals in the master cylinder.

Exhaust System .... Pages 36,64
With the engine running and an assistant placing a gloved hand over the tailpipe (Fig.MoT:6) to partially pressurise the system, listen for the characteristic 'rasping' or 'fluttering' noise of a blowing exhaust along the length of the car, including under the bonnet. With the hand removed, listen to determine the effectiveness of the silencer.

CAR RAISED
Steering System .... Pages 125-132
Turn the front wheels from lock to lock and feel for stiffness or roughness in the steering system, also check that the wheels or tyres do not contact any part of the car body or flexible brake hoses.

Examine the condition of the steering rack bellows, looking for signs of split rubber or leakage of lubricant (Fig.MoT:1A). Check the tightness of the steering rack mountings and the steering linkage joints. With an assistant inside the car turning the steering wheel from side to side slowly, check the track rod end ball joints for excessive play (Fig.MoT:1B). Check the ball joint boots for leaks or splits.

Front Suspension Components ...... Pages 133-144
With the weight of the car on the wheels and a long bar positioned under each front wheel in turn, attempt to lift each wheel, at the same time looking and feeling for relative movement in the top and bottom suspension ball joints (Fig.MoT:3).

To check the condition of the lower suspension arm inner pivot bushes, position a suitable lever (i.e. a large screwdriver) between the inner end of the arm and its mountings (Fig.MoT:1C) and try to move the arm relative to the mounting. Check the tie-rod bushes at the front sub-frame by positioning a screwdriver between the rubber mountings and gently levering apart to check for wear. Excessive movement indicates deterioration of the bush while a slight, cushioned movement is acceptable and is due to the natural flexibility of the bush. Check that there is no side play in the arm – this can be caused by delamination of the bush or looseness of the arm pivot bolt. To check the front and rear subframe mountings, position a suitable bar or large screwdriver between the subframe and the mounting bracket (Fig.MoT:1D) and try to move the subframe relative to the mounting. Check all the suspension securing nuts and bolts for tightness.

Rear Suspension Components ...... Pages 145-152
Test the condition of the rear radius arm bearings by grasping the wheel at the 'quarter to three' position and rocking the wheel inwards and outwards, at the same time looking and feeling for movement in the radius arm bearings. Alternatively use a screwdriver between the radius arm and the subframe and carefully lever apart to check for wear (Fig.MoT:1E).

To check the condition of the front and rear subframe mountings, position a suitable bar or large screwdriver between the subframe mounting and the body (Fig.MoT:1F) and try to move the subframe relative to the mounting. Check all suspension securing nuts and bolts for tightness.

Wheel Bearings .... Pages 136, 145
At each wheel in turn, rotate the wheel slowly by hand and check for rough rotation, taking care not to mistake brake pad or shoe drag for roughness. A worn bearing will either be felt or heard as the wheel is turned. Grasp the wheel at the top and bottom, then rock it inwards and outwards to check for excessive play (Fig.MoT:1G). Excessive play is present if the wheel can be felt to rock about the stub axle, accompanied by a slight knocking. Very slight movement of the wheel relative to the stub axle is permissible.

Shock Absorbers .... Pages 136,146
Visually inspect the condition of the shock absorber units (if fitted) looking for signs of fluid leakage. Check the condition and security of the upper and lower mountings (Fig.MoT:1H).

Transmission Driveshafts .... Page 138
Check the transmission outer driveshaft joint boots, looking for signs of splitting or leakage of lubricant (Fig.MoT:4). Check the condition of the CV joints by trying to move the driveshaft and the joint outer body in opposite directions, looking for movement between the two. Under road test conditions a worn CV joint will be heard as a 'cracking' noise under acceleration when the steering is on lock.

Several different types of inner joint have been fitted to the Mini range. On early models with rubber coupling type joints secured with 'U' bolts, check that the four outer ends of the joint are not breaking up causing the inner metal part of the joint to

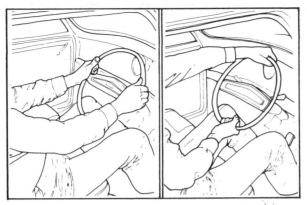

Fig. MoT:2 Checking steering column bush

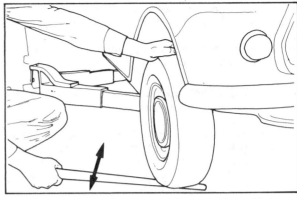

Fig. MoT:3 Checking top & bottom ball joints with bar

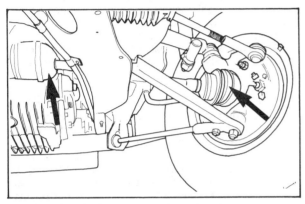

Fig. MoT:4 Checking driveshaft boots

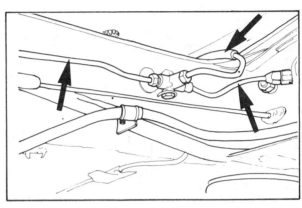

Fig. MoT:5 Checking brake pipes & hoses

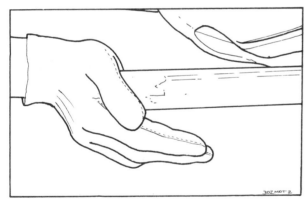

Fig. MoT:6 Checking exhaust system for leaks

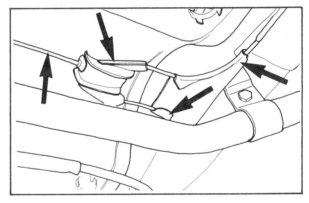

Fig. MoT:7 Checking handbrake cables & linkage

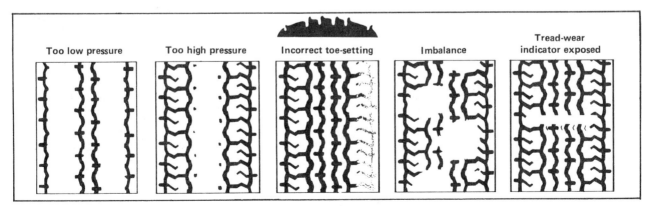

Too low pressure   Too high pressure   Incorrect toe-setting   Imbalance   Tread-wear indicator exposed

Fig. MoT:8 Examples of tyre tread wear

show through.

On automatic models fitted with needle roller universal joints check for wear in the joint by carefully levering between the yokes.

Later models are fitted with a CV type inner joint (similar to the outer joint) and should be checked in the same way.

Brake Pipes & Handbrake Linkage .. Pages 156,164

Examine all brake pipes and flexible hoses, front and rear, checking for leaks, heavy corrosion and perishing, cracks or splitting of the hose rubber (Fig.MoT:5). With the help of an assistant holding the footbrake pedal depressed, examine each rubber brake hose for swelling or 'ballooning'. Also check that the metal brake pipe securing clips are all in position. Inspect the condition of the handbrake cable(s) and linkage where exposed (Fig.MoT:7), looking for frayed cables and seized or worn linkages.

Exhaust System .... Pages 36,64

Examine the full length of the exhaust system, checking for serious corrosion weakness by tapping the pipe gently with a hammer. Make sure that the exhaust pipe connecting clamps and system mountings are in good condition and securely fitted and check for evidence of exhaust gas leakage, indicated by black, sooty deposits around the joints.

Wheels & Tyres .... Page 36

At each wheel in turn, check for excessive distortion of the wheel rim (caused by hitting the kerb) then examine the inner and outer walls of the tyre, looking for cuts, bulges or other damage, also the condition of the tread. Check the tyre 'mix' – steel and fabric belted radial ply tyres should not be fitted on the same axle.

Check the depth of tread, preferably with a proper tread depth gauge. In the UK the minimum legal requirement is that the tread is visible throughout the entire tread area and that the depth is at least 1 mm over three-quarters of the tread width. This makes provision for premature wear of the shoulder of the tyre but this wear must be in one uniform band around the circumference and the tread must still be visible. It is advisable to renew the tyre before this degree of wear is reached as roadholding and resistance to punctures will be reduced well before this. If you are unsure of the condition of the tyre then seek professional advice.

Abnormal tyre wear (Fig.MoT:8) may be caused by improper inflation pressures, wheel imbalance, misalignment of front or rear suspension, slack wheel bearings, distorted brake discs or mechanical irregularities such as worn or damaged suspension or steering joints. When rapid or uneven tyre wear becomes apparent, the cause should be established and dealt with as soon as possible.

Fins and feathering on the tyre tread surface are an indication of severe wheel misalignment. This condition takes the form of a sharp 'fin' on the edge of each pattern rib, and the position of this indicates the direction of misalignment. Fins on the outboard edges are caused by excessive toe-out, whereas fins on the inboard edges of the pattern ribs are caused by excessive toe-in.

Body Corrosion .... Page 190

Check the condition of the car body for any damage or corrosion likely to make the car unsafe, particularly at the important load bearing areas – the suspension and crossmember mounting points, the side sills and sub-frames (especially at the rear) as well as the seat belt anchorage points.

This completes the check of the car for the MoT test, and although this guide is based on the official MoT check list at the time of publication, it is only a guide and should be treated as such.

Breakdown & Non-Start Hints

IN AN EMERGENCY

Sooner or later everyone suffers the inconvenience of a breakdown on the road, or a non-start problem, however good or well maintained the car.

The motoring organisations have shown that over 50% of all breakdowns are caused by electrical problems and more breakdowns are reported during the winter months when the climate is damp and cold.

On the following pages you will find a trouble-shooter to assist you in making a quick and accurate diagnosis. With the help of the chart and the illustrated instructions you should be able to make a successful diagnosis and repair, or at least be able to give a breakdown service an accurate description of what has gone wrong.

SAFETY FIRST

Breakdowns always seem to happen when the car is in a difficult position on the road. Whether the problem arises on a motorway or a country lane the first priority must always be to ensure that the car and its occupants are moved to as safe a position as possible.

If the car is fitted with hazard flasher lamps it is good sense to switch them on as soon as possible. At night the car lights should be left on, with at least the sidelights lit.

Although it is not always possible, try to avoid stopping the car on a blind bend or over the brow of a hill. If you carry a warning triangle, make sure that you position it to give approaching traffic sufficient time to slow down. At night, use a warning lamp positioned to give as much warning as possible. Don't stand behind the vehicle in such a position that obscures the rear light.

Motorway breakdowns can be a frightening experience, particularly if the problem occurs when you are in the overtaking lane. If the car starts to behave strangely for any reason it is a sensible precaution to move into the slow lane as soon as is safely possible. You can then move safely onto the hard shoulder if necessary. Remember that you must not drive along the hard shoulder, so stay in the slow lane if you are attempting to make it to the next emergency phone. When you do stop on the hard shoulder make sure that you position the car as far to the left as possible . If you are carrying passengers, don't let them wander about on the hard shoulder, they should also be prevented from using the right hand doors on the car to avoid the possibility of collision with passing traffic.

WHATS THE PROBLEM ?

Once you have managed to get your car in to as safe a position as possible the next step is to diagnose what has gone wrong.

Try not to panic, think carefully about what happened as the symptons first appeared. This should help to give the first clue as to the most likely problem. For example, if the engine suddenly cuts out the most likely cause is an electrical fault whereas a fuel problem often starts with a power loss or hesitancy before cutting out.

With any non-start problem it is important to carry out your diagnosis in a logical sequence. The following two pages provide a Non-Start Trouble Shooter to help you determine the problem, followed by illustrated instructions showing how to carry out the checks safely and correctly. The problem may of course be something not related to the functioning of the engine and may be an electrical failure of the lighting system or windscreen wipers, or simply a puncture. For electrical fault diagnosis you should refer to ENGINE ELECTRICS or GENERAL ELECTRICS later in this manual.

CALLING FOR ASSISTANCE

If you are a unable to make a diagnosis and repair at the roadside then the next move must be to seek assistance.

At this point it is too late to start wishing you had joined one of the motoring organisations or recovery services. Your checks on the car should have at least identified some clues which will be useful to the garage or recovery service in deciding the type of assistance you require. Make sure that you know the full details of your car as this will help the breakdown service if spare parts are likely to be required. They will also need to know if your car is fitted with automatic transmission as this could affect the method of tow recovery should this be necessary. Also make a note of the location of your breakdown, using landmarks if necessary, particularly if you are in an area with which you are not familiar.

The next problem is to locate the nearest telephone. If you breakdown on a motorway the marker posts alongside the hard shoulder will indicate the direction to the nearest emergency telephone. On all other roads you will have to use a public telephone, or if you are a member of the AA or the RAC, the special emergency coin-operated phones.

The motorway telephones are linked to the police who will arrange for breakdown service with your motoring organisation or from one of the local garages operating a breakdown and recovery service. If you are making your own arrangements then use a garage you know or, if you are in an unfamiliar part of the country, a garage holding a franchise for your make of car.

BREAKDOWN SERVICE

Once you have made your emergency call to the motoring organisation, breakdown recovery service or local garage you must return to your car as quickly as possible. Breakdown service patrols are not permitted to work on unattended vehicles and are not going to be very amused if they have to await your return before they can start work. If you are a member of a motoring organisation, when a breakdown truck arrives, make sure that the driver has details of the breakdown from your organisation before you accept any offer of assistance. There are 'cowboy' breakdown services operating and they can prove to be very expensive!

Breakdowns at peak holiday periods or during the rush hour can mean that you could be in for a long wait until help arrives. If in the meantime you are able to cure the problem and continue your journey – do remember to advise the attending garage or organisation to prevent a wasted journey and possible delay to someone else.

ENGINE WILL NOT START

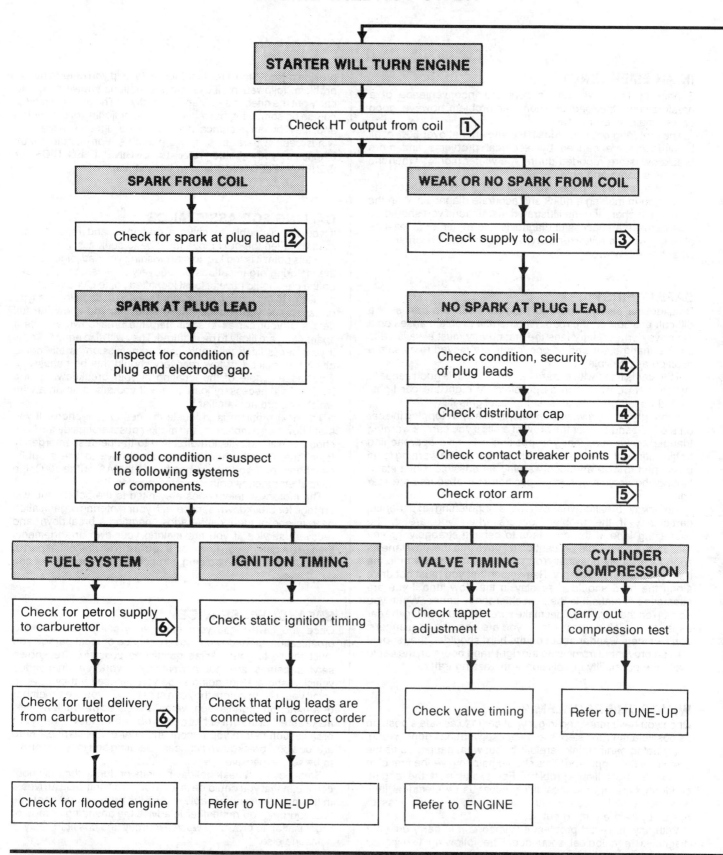

STARTER WILL TURN ENGINE

Check HT output from coil 1⟩

SPARK FROM COIL	**WEAK OR NO SPARK FROM COIL**
Check for spark at plug lead 2⟩	Check supply to coil 3⟩
SPARK AT PLUG LEAD	**NO SPARK AT PLUG LEAD**
Inspect for condition of plug and electrode gap.	Check condition, security of plug leads 4⟩
	Check distributor cap 4⟩
If good condition - suspect the following systems or components.	Check contact breaker points 5⟩
	Check rotor arm 5⟩

FUEL SYSTEM	**IGNITION TIMING**	**VALVE TIMING**	**CYLINDER COMPRESSION**
Check for petrol supply to carburettor 6⟩	Check static ignition timing	Check tappet adjustment	Carry out compression test
Check for fuel delivery from carburettor 6⟩	Check that plug leads are connected in correct order	Check valve timing	Refer to TUNE-UP
Check for flooded engine	Refer to TUNE-UP	Refer to ENGINE	

ENGINE WILL NOT START

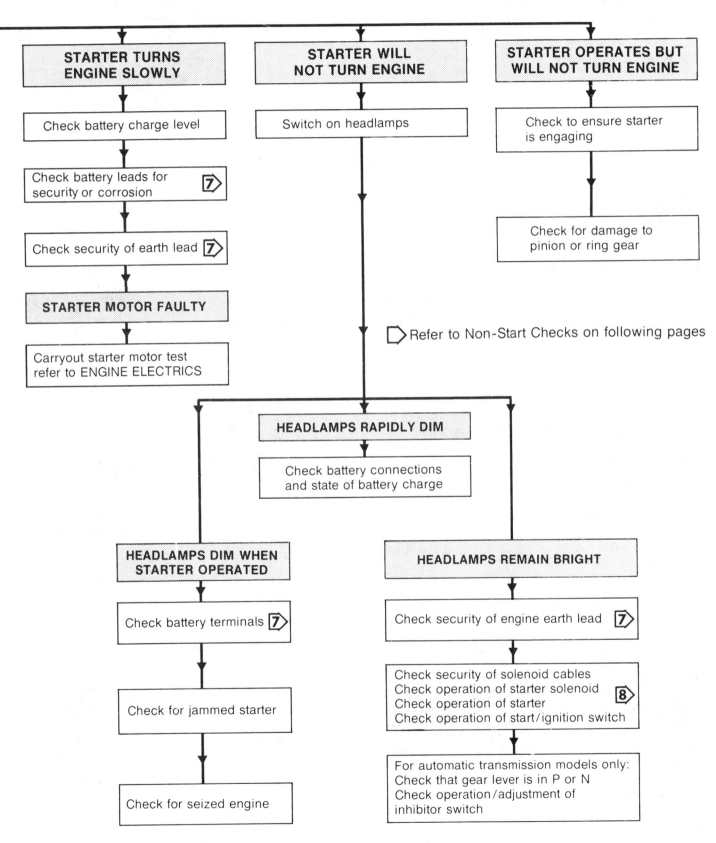

STARTER TURNS ENGINE SLOWLY

Check battery charge level

Check battery leads for security or corrosion 7⟩

Check security of earth lead 7⟩

STARTER MOTOR FAULTY

Carryout starter motor test refer to ENGINE ELECTRICS

STARTER WILL NOT TURN ENGINE

Switch on headlamps

⟩ Refer to Non-Start Checks on following pages

STARTER OPERATES BUT WILL NOT TURN ENGINE

Check to ensure starter is engaging

Check for damage to pinion or ring gear

HEADLAMPS RAPIDLY DIM

Check battery connections and state of battery charge

HEADLAMPS DIM WHEN STARTER OPERATED

Check battery terminals 7⟩

Check for jammed starter

Check for seized engine

HEADLAMPS REMAIN BRIGHT

Check security of engine earth lead 7⟩

Check security of solenoid cables
Check operation of starter solenoid 8⟩
Check operation of starter
Check operation of start/ignition switch

For automatic transmission models only:
Check that gear lever is in P or N
Check operation/adjustment of inhibitor switch

NON-START CHECKS

1️⃣ **Check spark from coil**

Pull the coil to distributor high tension (HT) lead from the top of the distributor cap and hold it about 3 mm from a good earth point on the engine while an assistant operates the starter motor. There should be a strong blue spark jumping across from the lead to earth if the coil is operating correctly.

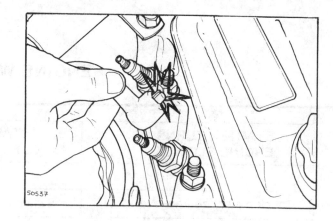

2️⃣ **Check spark at spark plug**

Carefully pull off one of the spark plug leads from the plug terminal. If you have a spare plug, in good condition, connect the plug lead to the spare plug and place the plug on a metal part of the engine which is not painted. Operate the starter and check that a strong spark is produced across the plug electrodes. If you do not have a spare plug then hold the end of the plug lead 3 mm from a good earth point on the engine and check for a strong spark.

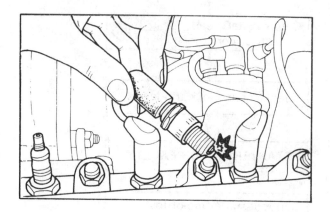

3️⃣ **Check electrical supply to coil**

This requires a test lamp with two leads and clips to check whether battery voltage is being supplied to the coil. Connect test leads between + terminal on the coil and a good earth. With the ignition on, the lamp will light brightly if there is supply to the coil. Disconnect the lead from the + terminal and reconnect to the - terminal. If the bulb again lights the primary winding in the coil is not broken and the coil should function.

NOTE:Ensure that the contact breaker points are open when carrying out this test.

4️⃣ **Check plug leads and distributor cap**

Pull off the moulded caps from the spark plugs and take off the distributor cap. Thoroughly wipe the plug caps and the H.T. leads with a clean, dry cloth. Check that the leads are not cracked or chafed. If the weather is damp, spray the leads and cap with water repellant spray. Clean the distributor cap inside and out and check that the electrodes are not badly eroded. Make sure that the carbon brush is in place in the centre of the cap and is not damaged, also that the spring is pushing the brush forward correctly.

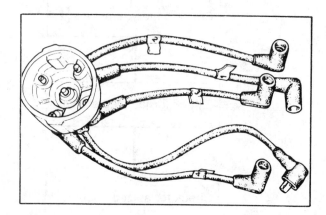

⑤ Check rotor arm and contact breaker

With the distributor cap removed, operate the starter and check that the rotor arm turns and the points open and close. Remove the rotor arm and check the tip is not excessively eroded. The tip can be cleaned with a fine file or abrasive paper if necessary. Check that the rotor arm has no hairline cracks and that it is not loose on the distributor spindle when refitted. Check the contact breaker points for excessive burning and pitting by levering apart with a screwdriver and ensure that the gap is correct when the heel of the moving contact is on the peak of the cam lobe. If a pip has built up or the points are burned or dirty they should be cleaned with a fine file or abrasive paper. If the points are badly burned or blue the condenser is the likely problem and should be replaced.

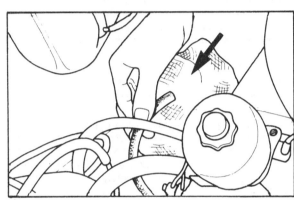

⑥ Check fuel supply

Remove the fuel filler cap from the fuel tank to release any vacuum build up, if there is a large rush of air the breather system (either the cap or the pipe) may be blocked. Disconnect the fuel feed pipe to the carburettor and direct it into a large transparent container to prevent fuel being spilt. Actuate the fuel pump by operating the starter motor or turning on the ignition on models with electric fuel pumps. Disconnect the leads to the coil during this test. If the supply is working, reconnect the pipe. Remove the air cleaner and check if the inside of the air intake is damp with fuel.

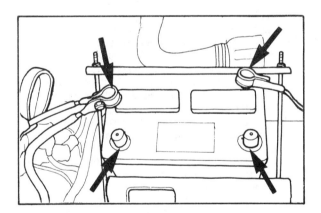

⑦ Check battery connections and engine earth

Check that the battery connections are tight and that there is no corrosion around the terminals. If one of the terminals gets hot whilst the starter is operating it is a sure sign that the terminal is loose. Check that the earth connection on the battery cable to the car body is making a good connection and that there is no corrosion between the terminal and the body. Clean up the contact area to bright metal if any rust is present. Similarly check both ends of the engine earth strap.

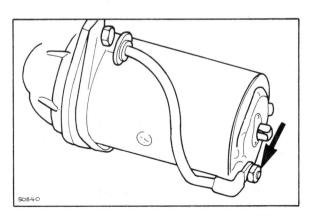

⑧ Check starter motor connections

Make sure that the heavy wiring between the battery and solenoid is in good condition and that the connections are clean and tight, making good electrical contact. When the ignition switch is turned to the start position the solenoid should click. Check the supply to the solenoid by disconnecting the heavy lead to the solenoid and connecting the end to a 12 volt test lamp which is in turn connected to a good earth. If the lamp lights brightly then there is a supply to the starter. Check solenoid contacts are closing by connecting a 12 volt test lamp across the two main solenoid connections. The lamp should light brightly, if not suspect the earth connection. When the ignition is turned to the start position the bulb should go out. If not the solenoid switch is faulty.

50540

Basic Procedures

SAFETY PRECAUTIONS .... [1]

Precautions with Engine Running

When working on or near the engine when it is running, make sure that you do not have any loose clothing or tools in close proximity to moving or very hot components (i.e. cooling fan and exhaust manifold).

If the engine is being run with the car in a garage or similar confined area, ensure adequate ventilation to prevent the accumulation of toxic exhaust gases.

The Electrical System

When working on any part of the car's electrical system the battery earth lead should be disconnected in order to avoid the risk of accidental short-circuits and possible fire damage.

Modern ignition systems operate at very high voltages and these high voltages can severely damage transistorised components such as a wrist watch if electrical contact is made. Wearers of heart pacemaker devices, therefore, should not at any time carry out work on ignition systems.

The Battery

The car's battery contains sulphuric acid which is highly corrosive and can damage both skin and clothing. If the battery case is found to be leaking, the battery should be removed from the car as soon as possible, taking care to avoid spillage on the paintwork. Both battery support tray and the adjacent bodywork should then be thoroughly washed with a solution of water and an alkali such as bicarbonate of soda or ammonia to neutralise and remove the acid. Wash the solution away with boiling water and, if necessary, repaint the affected area after thorough drying.

During charging, the battery cells give off hydrogen and oxygen. This mixture of gases is flammable and if ignited by a naked flame, a spark or a cigarette, an explosion can result. Always switch the battery charger off before disconnecting it from the battery terminals in order to prevent sparking.

Finally, never rest tools on the battery.

Brake Fluid

Brake fluid, apart from being poisonous, is corrosive and is a very effective paint stripper. Therefore, when topping up the brake reservoir or when disconnecting or bleeding the braking system, always have a thick cloth handy to catch any spilt fluid. Wrapping rags around hydraulic fluid reservoirs when topping up is a good idea but throw the rags away afterwards to prevent spreading the fluid.

If any fluid is accidentally spilt on the car's paintwork, it should be mopped up immediately and the affected area thoroughly washed with soapy water to remove all traces.

Cooling System

The car's cooling system operates under pressure to raise the boiling point of the coolant to allow the engine to run at a more efficient temperature. If the cooling system is suddenly depressurised when hot, i.e. by undoing the pressure cap, boiling coolant and steam will be ejected from the filler and severe scalding can result. If possible, the coolant level should be checked and topped up when the engine is cool. However, if it is necessary to do so with the engine hot then muffle the pressure cap first with a thick piece of rag and undo the cap slowly and gradually to relieve the pressure before removing it completely (Fig.1).

The anti-freeze used should be the correct type for the car, especially if the engine has aluminium components as these may corrode badly if the wrong anti-freeze is used. The safest type of anti-freeze is ethylene glycol and this should be chosen in preference to the less often used and flammable methanol type. If the anti-freeze you have is of the latter type then avoid any naked flame or spark in close proximity to the cooling system filler cap or overflow pipe as the vapour can ignite.

Fuel System

It is important to exercise extreme care when working on any part of the car's fuel system or indeed when handling petrol in general. Apart from being highly flammable, petrol is poisonous, toxic upon inhalation and very irritating to the skin. Swallowing petrol can cause internal irritation and even unconsciousness and we strongly recommend, therefore, that any siphoning be carried out using a purpose-built siphon and not by mouth. ALWAYS ensure adequate ventilation when handling petrol.

Petrol or petrol vapour does not require a naked flame to ignite it as the tiniest electric spark will suffice. The engine compartment contains electrical wiring, and an ignition system which are all sources of potential sparking. If work is being carried out, therefore, on any part of the fuel system, ALWAYS disconnect the battery earth lead first.

Because petrol evaporates rapidly it must not be stored in or drained into open trays, rather metal screw-top containers. For the same reason, never drain a car's fuel tank over an inspection pit as the lack of ventilation can lead to an accumulation of vapour in the pit.

Finally, if you have a tarmac driveway, do not allow any petrol to spill on to it as this can cause the tar to dissolve.

RAISING & SUPPORTING THE CAR .... [2]

Mini Saloon models are fitted with a single jacking point on each side of the car, and they are designed to be used with the jack supplied with the car. This jack is designed for wheel changing only and must not be utilised when carrying out repair work underneath the car.

When changing a wheel, make sure that the jack is placed on firm, level ground with the handbrake fully applied. The wheel directly opposite the one being removed should be securely chocked by placing bricks or wood blocks behind and in front of the wheel. Each jacking bracket has a locating socket on its underside which engages with the head of the jack (Fig.2). Remove the plastic cap in the locating hole by carefully levering out with screwdriver. If the plastic cap is missing make sure that the locating socket hole is not obstructed with dirt. Fit the jack

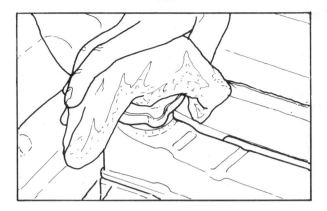

Fig. 1 Remove radiator cap using a cloth

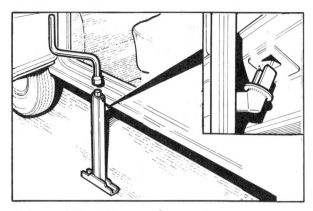

Fig. 2 Use wheel lift jack (Saloon)

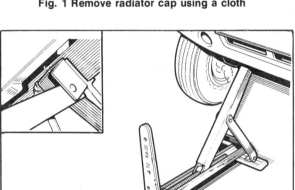

Fig. 3 Using wheel lift jack (front sub-frame)

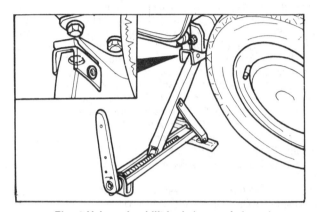

Fig. 4 Using wheel lift jack (rear sub-frame)

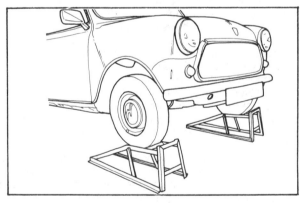

Fig. 5 Using wheel ramps when working beneath car

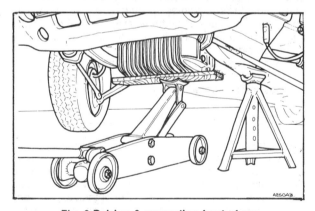

Fig. 6 Raising & supporting front of car

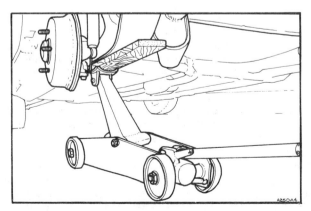

Fig. 7 Raising rear of car

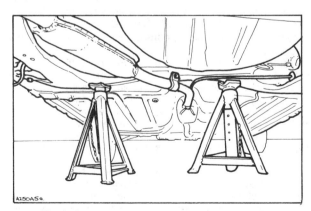

Fig. 8 Supporting rear of car with axle stands

head firmly into the locating socket and angle the jack outwards at the top (Fig.2). Remove the wheel trim (if fitted) and slacken the wheel nuts before raising the car. Do not lift the car any more than is necessary to clear the wheel from the ground.

All other models are fitted with individual wheel lift jacking points on the front and rear sub-frames. At the front these are located either side of the number plate (Fig.3). Position the jack with the tongue at the rear of the head under the front of the sub-frame. When in contact with the sub-frame the lifting arm should not touch the number plate. At the rear the lifting points are on the underside of the sub-frame suspension arm mounting. The jack head should butt against the edge of the sub-frame (Fig.4). Never rely on the jack alone except when changing a wheel, and even then, one wheel should be placed under the car to act as a cushion should the jack slip.

When carrying out work under the car it is necessary to have some form of safe lifting equipment to give sufficient working room underneath.

Drive-on ramps are inexpensive and practical although great care must be taken to align them properly and not to overshoot them (Fig.5). A useful tip to prevent ramps being pushed along the ground by the car's wheels is to wrap a long strip of carpet around the lower rung of each ramp. As the car's wheels drive over the carpet the ramps will be effectively held.

A variety of sturdy jacks are available; screw jacks, hydraulic bottle jacks and trolley jacks. The trolley type is the most desirable as it can usually provide the greatest amount of lift.

When lifting the front of the car, with both wheels free, position the trolley jack with a wooden spacer under the centre of the transmission casing (Fig.6). At the rear of the car, position the jack head with a wooden spacer under one of the sub-frame sides (Fig.7).

Having raised the car it is essential that it is supported on purpose-built axle stands and never on a pile of bricks or wooden blocks as these are usually unstable and bricks can even crumble under the weight of the car. Axle stands should be positioned under the sub-frames. At the front of the car position the stands under the sides of the frame at the back (Fig.6). At the rear of the car position the stands under the forward part of the frame on each side (Fig.8).

Finally, when the car is raised and supported and before anyone ventures beneath it, rock the car to check that the stands are securely located.

BASIC TOOLS & EQUIPMENT . . . . [3]

Before undertaking any work on your car, you will need a basic tool kit, the contents of which we detail within this section. In addition to these tools, many repair and maintenance operations will require certain tools which have specialised functions; it is often wiser to hire these rather than to purchase them as they may not be needed more than once or twice in the car's lifetime. Every chapter contains a section entitled Tools & Equipment, listing tools not contained within the 'basic' tool kit, together with a brief summary of what each tool is needed for.

The following is a list of tools considered necessary to form a basic tool kit:

- AF/Metric socket set
- AF/Metric combination ring and open-ended spanner set
- Torque wrench
- Selection of long and short flat-bladed screwdrivers
- Selection of long and short cross-head screwdrivers
- Feeler gauge set
- Ball pein hammer
- Soft-faced mallet
- Thin-nosed pliers
- Square-nosed pliers
- Wire cutters
- Self-locking grips
- Water pump pliers (grips)
- Adjustable wrench
- Junior hacksaw
- Hacksaw
- Electrical circuit testing lamp
- Inspection lamp
- Hydraulic or screw jack and axle stands
- Circlip pliers.

As well as these items an electric drill, a set of high speed steel drill bits and a centre punch find many uses, especially when fitting accessories.

GENERAL REPAIR PROCEDURES . . . . [4]
Spanners, Sockets & Fastenings

It may have been noticed that our recommendations for a basic tool kit include combined ring and open-ended spanners (combination spanners). This is because ring spanners and sockets are preferable as they provide a more secure purchase than open ended spanners or an adjustable wrench. There are, of course, occasions when an open-ended spanner is the only tool with which one can gain access to a nut or bolt head; thus the combination spanner provides an economical alternative to separate ring and open-ended spanner sets.

It must be stressed that it is very important to use a spanner or socket of the correct size when undoing or tightening nuts or bolts; very often a spanner or socket will seem to fit properly and yet slip round on the head when turned. The effect of a slipping spanner is that the head becomes rounded and difficult, if not impossible to grip. Your car is fitted with Metric and AF threaded nuts and bolts. Always check, therefore, that you have selected the correct spanners and sockets before working on the car and do not rely on tools appearing to fit.

In case you are ever in doubt as to which type are fitted, most of the larger diameter nuts and bolts have identification markings. Metric nuts and bolts have the letters ISO m or M embossed on the head or on one of the flats of the hexagon (Fig.9) whilst Unified bolts have a circular recess stamped in the upper surface of the bolt or alternatively a continuous line of circles indented on one of the flats of the hexagon (Fig.10).

Seized Nuts & Bolts

During dismantling operations, it is likely that some nuts and bolts will refuse to undo and there are various methods of freeing them. If a stubborn bolt is encountered, a liberal application of penetrating oil – allowed to soak in for a while – will often be sufficient to soften the corrosion that binds the threads together. After soaking with oil, a sharp hammer blow on the bolt head should be sufficient to jar the thread free. It should then be possible to unscrew the bolt normally.

A tool known as an impact driver (Fig.11) is also available which can be fitted with a socket or screwdriver bit holder. A hammer blow on the end of the tool provides both the impact necessary to jar the corroded thread loose and a turning action to unscrew the bolt at the same time.

If the methods described above prove insufficient to free a seized nut then more drastic methods will have to be employed, such as hacksawing through one side of the offending nut until it can be split without damaging the threads of the stud or bolt. An alternative to this method is to use a 'nut splitter' as shown in Fig.12.

This device consists of a very strong steel frame with a large chisel headed bolt incorporated in the arm of the tool.

Position the tool over the seized nut so that the chisel end bears on one of the flats of the nut, then progressively screw up the hexagon until the nut splits, allowing it to be easily removed.

Studs

Studs can be removed with a proprietary stud extractor tool (B,Fig.13) or alternatively by locking two nuts together on the threaded portion and then applying an unscrewing action to the lower nut (A,Fig.13). This will bear against the upper nut and so cause the stud itself to unscrew. If a stud breaks below the surface of the component, then the portion left in the stud hole can be removed with a screw extractor – a hardened tapered screw with a left-hand thread. After drilling a pilot hole in the remaining portion of stud, the extractor is screwed into the hole, biting home and causing the stud to unscrew (Fig.14).

Bushes

The removal and installation of rubber bushes in the suspension system very often causes problems but need not do so if the right approach is adopted. A simple way of removing a bush from its housing is to use a Rawlbolt as an extractor. This is a bolt with a sleeve around it which expands as the bolt is screwed in (Fig.15). The Rawlbolt is normally used for attaching

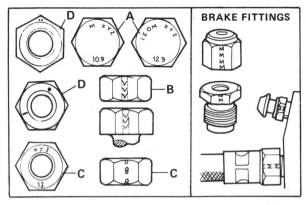

Fig. 9 Metric nut, bolt & brake fittings identifications

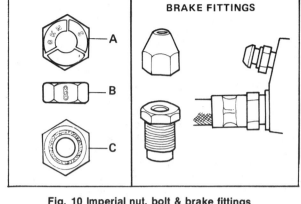

Fig. 10 Imperial nut, bolt & brake fittings

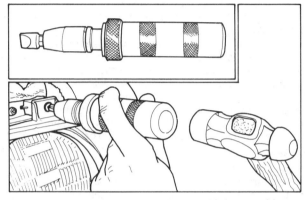

Fig. 11 Start stubborn nuts & bolts with impact driver

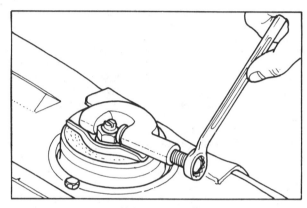

Fig. 12 Using a nut splitter

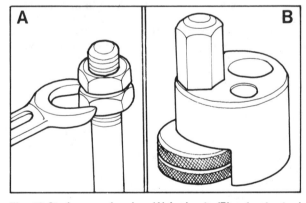

Fig. 13 Stud removal, using (A) locknuts (B) extractor tool

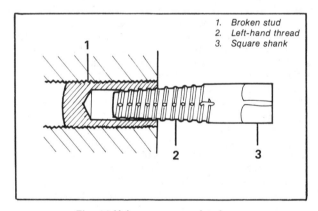

1. Broken stud
2. Left-hand thread
3. Square shank

Fig. 14 Using a screw extractor

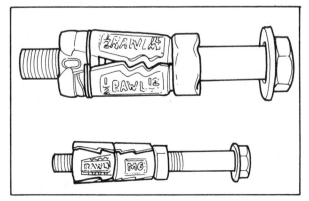

Fig. 15 Expanding masonary bolts (Rawlbolts)

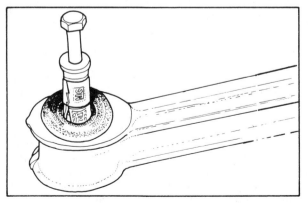

Fig. 16 Using masonary bolt to grip bush

items to masonry and can be bought in a hardware store. Use a Rawlbolt assembly which is of a slightly smaller diameter than the inside diameter of the bush and push the expanding sleeve fully into the bush without the bolt. As the bolt screws inwards it will expand the sleeve, causing it to grip the bush (Fig.16). The bolt can then be pulled out with a slide hammer or a suitably arranged lever.

Replacement bushes can be fitted using an arrangement of a long bolt, two washers, a nut and a tubular spacer. Referring to Fig.17 it can be seen that tightening the nut will draw the new bush evenly into position, while using a smaller washer under the head of the bolt and the large spacer on the other end is an alternative method of drawing the old bush out (Fig.18). Good results can also be achieved by using a socket against the rubber, a suitable spacer on the other side of the bush housing and a vice or G-clamp to press the bush either in or out (Fig.19). Before installing the new bush, clean the housing thoroughly to remove all traces of rubber and dirt then lubricate the outside of the bush and the inside of the housing with washing-up liquid. Note that a bush without a steel outer casing must be pressed fully home in one continuous movement as stopping it half way will make it very difficult to start again.

If a bush proves very difficult to remove then try heating up its housing with a blowlamp flame in order to help release the rubber from the metal or expand the housing away from the metal outer of the bush, depending on the type. If the bush is still reluctant to move, the rubber can be burned out with the blowlamp, and the metal outer (if it has one) can then be peeled back using a hammer and a small chisel. Alternatively, in stubborn cases, the bush can be sawn through by feeding the blade of a junior hacksaw through it, taking great care not to damage the bore of the housing.

Bearings

Replacing bearings can be a daunting task as the bearing tracks are often a very tight fit in their housings, or on shafts, with little visible means of gripping them or gaining access behind them. Close analysis, however, will always reveal a point of access and successful removal of the track then depends on the correct choice of tools. For example, a bearing inner track which is a tight fit on a shaft will always stand sufficiently proud of the shaft on one side to allow a cold chisel (Fig.20) or the jaws of a universal bearing puller to grip behind it.

In some cases, where bearings are particularly tight or difficult to gain access to, a special puller may be required (Fig.21). A bearing track within a housing such as a wheel hub also often stands sufficiently proud of the hub casting to permit contact from behind with a drift (Fig.22). Sometimes if the track is fitted up to a shoulder and it is no higher than the shoulder, two or three grooves are machined into the hub to allow points of contact with a drift. A bearing track or a bronze bush which is fitted into a blind hole can often be removed with the aid of a Rawlbolt as mentioned previously, using the end of the bolt to push against the bottom of the recess in order to draw the track/bush out. It must be remembered, however, that it is possible to select too wide a Rawlbolt and the effect of using this is that the bush is crushed against its housing and will not move at all. If the bearing bore is in an aluminium housing then take care not to crack the housing by using too much torque on the bolt.

An alternative method of removing bushes from blind holes is to use hydraulic force. Pack the hole with grease and insert a close fitting drift (Fig.23). Tapping on the end of the drift will create pressure behind the bush and force it from the housing.

If the bearing track is of a fairly wide diameter and is in a very shallow hole then it may be possible to lever it out with a large, flat screwdriver, alternating the position of the screwdriver around the track to keep the track and housing square.

If the bearing is a very tight fit in its housing, it may be necessary to shock the two components apart, using a slide hammer attached to a puller.

If removal of a bearing outer track proves difficult then heating the housing around it can help to free it. On steel or iron housings this can safely be done with a blowlamp flame but aluminium alloy castings should only be heated up by immersion in boiling water or by surrounding the area with hot, wet rags. A bearing track is best driven into position using a drift made of a relatively soft metal such as brass in order to reduce the likelihood of damage to either the track or the housing. It is imperative that the housing bore or the shaft is scrupulously clean before fitting a bearing to it as trapped dirt can not only damage surfaces but it can also prevent the correct seating of components.

When drifting a bearing or track into a recess where it cannot be seen if it is fully seated, listen for the difference in sound created by contact between the track and the shoulder as you tap the drift. The best way of ensuring that bearings are being drifted in squarely is to tap them in using a socket or a length of tubing between the mallet and the bearing. If the bearing is being fitted into a bore then the socket or length of tubing should be of a slightly smaller diameter than that of the outer track but not so much less that it can contact any other part of the bearing. If it is being fitted over a shaft then the socket or tubing should be of a slightly larger diameter than that of the inner track but not large enough to touch the rest of the bearing. If none of the methods mentioned proves successful then you can be sure that a special tool has been made for the particular application that you are dealing with. Quite often dealers are prepared to lend or hire special tools or will actually remove the bearings or tracks in question on their premises. Tool hire shops often carry automotive equipment and engineering works have a variety of equipment at their disposal with which to carry out the work.

Oil Seals

Replace oil seals by levering them out with a wide, flat screwdriver (Fig.24) or a tyre lever. Alternatively, screw a number of self-tapping screws into the seal and pull it out with pliers (Fig.25). Drive the new seal into position squarely and evenly, using wooden blocks, sockets or lengths of tubing of suitable diameter (Fig.26). Where there is a shoulder in the housing behind the oil seal then it should be tapped in up to this shoulder; where there is no shoulder tap the seal in until it is flush with the housing unless a setting depth is specified. If the seal passes over sharp components such as splines then cover these with tape first and grease the tape in order to prevent damage to the lip of the seal.

Joints & Gaskets

When separating mating components such as crankcase and cylinder head never insert screwdrivers or similar wedges between the joint faces to lever them apart; this can severely damage the mating surfaces (especially on aluminium castings) resulting in poor sealing when the engine is reassembled. Separate components by tapping sharply along the line of the joint with a soft faced hammer, the shock caused by the blows should be sufficient to break the seal. When reassembling always make sure that the mating faces are perfectly clean and free from any old sealing compound or gasket material.

When scraping gasket material off iron castings it is permissible to use a metal implement such as a wallpaper scraper, providing care is taken not to gouge or scratch the surface. Gasket material on aluminium castings, however, must never be scraped with metal implements as the aluminium is soft and the surface is very easily damaged. In this case it is best to make a scraper from a sharpened piece of hardwood or stiff plastic. Silicone rubber gasket substitute is easily peeled off while gasket jointing compound is best removed with a solvent such as methylated spirit or paint stripper.

Storing & Cleaning Components

It is a good idea to have a number of small tins, boxes, and polythene bags on hand during the overhaul and dismantling procedures to keep components together and clean, particularly if the engine is to remain in a dismantled state for any length of time. Label the collected parts clearly. Simple

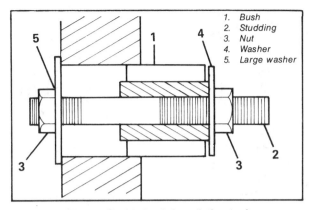

1. Bush
2. Studding
3. Nut
4. Washer
5. Large washer

Fig. 17 Simple bush installation tool

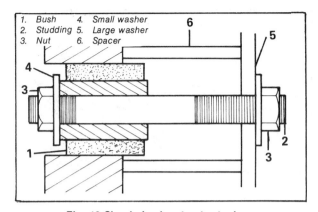

1. Bush
2. Studding
3. Nut
4. Small washer
5. Large washer
6. Spacer

Fig. 18 Simple bush extractor tool

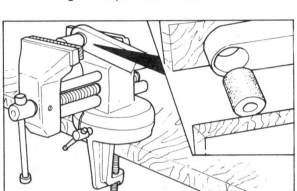

Fig. 19 Use a vice to press-fit bushes

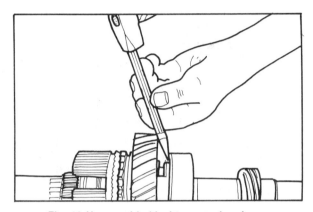

Fig. 20 Use a cold chisel to move bearings

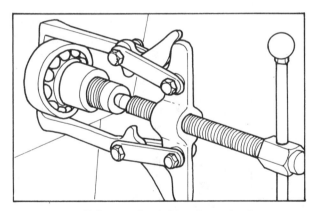

Fig. 21 Using a universal two legged puller

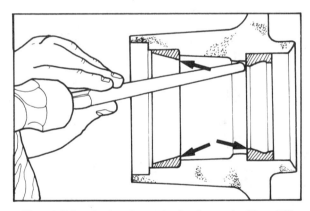

Fig. 22 Drive the bearing outer bushes out with a drift

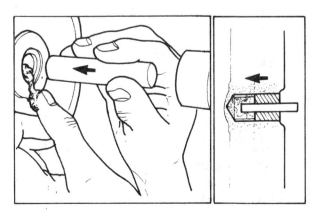

Fig. 23 Using hydraulic force to extract bush

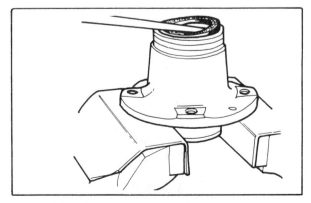

Fig. 24 Levering oil seal from housing

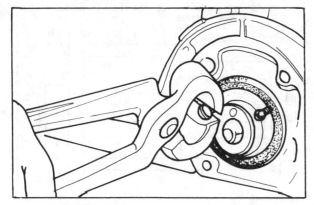

Fig. 25 Using self-tapping screw for extracting oil seal

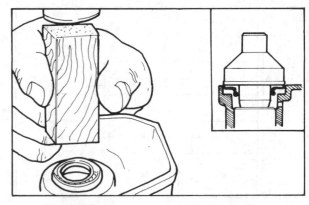

Fig. 26 Fit oil seals squarely in their bores

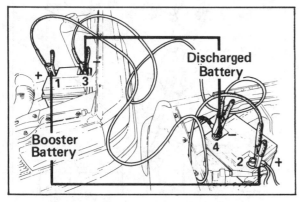

Fig. 27 The correct order of battery connection
for jump starting

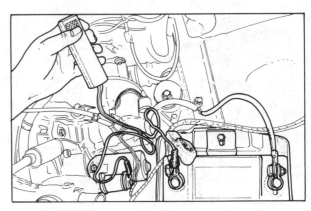

Fig. 28 Using remote switch to operate starter

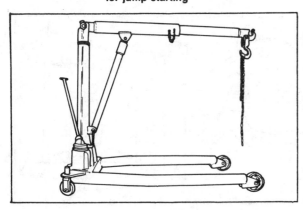

Fig. 29 Engine lifting crane

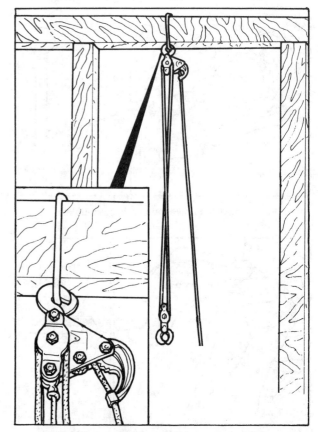

Fig. 31 Support garage roof beam by wedging
timber supports

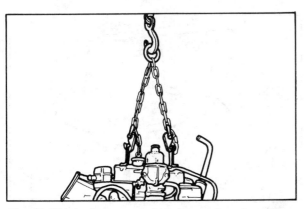

Fig. 30 Attach a rope or chain to the engine when lifting

sketches made during the dismantling procedure will also help jog the memory as to the correct assembly of parts when everything is put back together.

Before components can be inspected or refitted they should be cleaned thoroughly. A paraffin/petrol mixture is good for removing oil and grime but take care as the mixture is highly flammable – always use in a well ventilated area.

Before reassembly probe all bolt and stud holes with a piece of wire to make sure that there is no dirt lodged in them. Debris or swarf at the bottom of a blind stud hole can cause problems, as can fluids such as oil, water, petrol etc. This is because the presence of an obstruction can prevent a bolt from seating fully and can cause incorrect torque readings when tightening the bolt with a torque wrench. This can also damage the threads. If the thread is damaged it may be possible to run a tap of suitable size through the threaded hole but if the thread has been damaged beyond repair, the hole can be drilled oversize and a 'Helicoil' insert fitted. This job should be done by a specialist.

As a general rule whenever reassembling components, always renew all gaskets, oil seals, lockwashers, split pins and locknuts as it is false economy to skimp on such small but important articles.

BATTERY CHARGING & JUMP STARTING ... [5]
Battery Charging
If the battery is found to be in a low state of charge – see ROUTINE MAINTENANCE under Battery – then it should be recharged from an external battery charger, preferably with the battery removed from the car.

It is always preferable to slow-charge or 'trickle-charge' a battery as this reduces the risk of damage to the battery plates, provided that the electrolyte is at the proper level in all the cells. If the battery is in a state of complete discharge, charge it at a rate of between 4 and 5 amps for a minimum of 24 hours. A high-rate charger should only be used if the battery has been disconnected from the car's electrical system. Some types of 'maintenance-free' batteries, the lead-calcium type, for example, can be damaged by high-rate chargers.

A battery is in a fully charged condition when all the cells are gassing freely and there is no change in the correct specific gravity of the electrolyte over at least one hour. The vent plugs must be removed whilst charging, unless the battery is either of the 'maintenance-free' type or is fitted with an Autofill type cover, in which case the balls in the vent plugs are automatically displaced.
NOTE:The gases given off by the battery as it charges are hydrogen and oxygen, which, when combined are highly explosive. Any spark or naked flame will ignite the gases, causing an explosion.

When charging the battery, the following precautions should be taken:
1. Disconnect the leads to the battery terminals.
2. Check that the charger output voltage is the same as the nominal voltage of the battery.
3. The charger Positive (+) lead is connected to the Positive battery terminal.
4. The charger Negative (-) lead is connected to the Negative battery terminal.

Jump Starting
When jump starting using another car's battery, it is important that the jump leads be connected in the right order (Fig. 27): Positive (+) to Positive (+) and Negative (-) either to the Negative battery terminal or to a suitable earth point on the engine. Failure to connect the leads in the correct order can result in serious damage to the charging system and electrical components of either car. The following precautions must also be observed.
1. The booster battery must be of the same voltage as the car's battery.
2. The jump leads should be of sufficient capacity to carry a starting current of at least 300 amps.

3. The cable terminals must be clean and making good contact to avoid the cable overheating.
4. The cables should be connected one at a time between the discharged battery and the booster battery.
5. If the booster battery is installed in a car, run the engine of the car at a fast idle whilst the car with the discharged battery is being started. This will ensure sufficient alternator output to prevent the booster battery becoming rapidly discharged.
6. The engine speed of both cars should be reduced to 1000 rpm or below before disconnecting the jump leads in the exact reverse order of connection.

The car's own battery leads should never be disconnected while the engine is running.

TURNING THE CRANKSHAFT .... [6]
Several methods can be used to rotate the crankshaft for checking and adjusting the ignition timing, valve clearances or other operations dependent on the crankshaft position. Note that regardless of which method is used, the ignition should either be switched off or disconnected at one of the LT connections to the coil in order to prevent accidental firing of the engine when the crankshaft is turned. It is also advisable to remove all of the spark plugs in order to relieve the compression pressure – this will make the engine easier to turn. The easiest way to turn the crankshaft is to use a ring spanner or socket on the alternator/dynamo pulley nut.

An alternative method is to engage top gear, release the handbrake and push or pull the car forward to rotate the crankshaft. Make sure that the car is on level ground when doing this.

If space is limited, it is possible to turn the crankshaft by selecting top gear, raising one of the driving wheels clear of the ground and turning it in the normal direction of rotation so that it turns the engine with it.

This latter method, however, only applies to cars with a manual gearbox. On models with automatic transmission the torque converter prevents the crankshaft being driven round by the road wheels. In this case, the alternative is to actuate the starter motor in short bursts until the crankshaft is in the relevant position for the operation being undertaken. To make this task easier, it is possible to buy a switch which connects between the starter motor solenoid and the battery (Fig.28). This allows the user to actuate the starter motor from the engine compartment.

LIFTING THE ENGINE .... [7]
Some major repair operations will require the engine to be removed from the car and this will require some form of safe lifting equipment such as a pulley hoist. If the garage in which the job is being carried out has a sufficiently strong roof beam then the hoist can be suspended from this. If space allows, it is wise to strengthen the roof beam by supporting it at either end. This can be done by wedging in two upright timber struts as shown in Fig.31, remembering that a space allowance must be made between the sides of the car and the struts as the car body will rise as the engine weight is removed. If no beam is available then the alternative is either to attach the hoist to a portable gantry or to employ a hydraulic engine lifting crane. Both gantry and crane can be hired, if necessary, from most tool hire shops.

If lifting lugs are fitted to the engine then attach the hoist to these by means of a length of chain (Fig.30), tow-rope or a steel hawser. If no lifting lugs are fitted then it will be necessary to pass a tow-rope around the engine, ensuring that it supports the weight at suitable load bearing points such as mounting brackets, sump, and large projections in the crankcase and cylinder head castings. If the tow-rope is made of a natural material rather than man-made fibres then make sure that it has not been contaminated with oil as this can seriously weaken it.

When lifting an engine, always have somebody present in case an emergency situation arises and also to push the car away once the engine has been lifted high enough to clear the front panel.

Service Schedule

WEEKLY OR WHEN REFUELLING
- Check/top-up engine coolant
- Check/top engine oil
- Check/top up brake and clutch fluid
- Check tyre pressures, and condition, including spare
- Check operation of all lights and horn
- Check operation of wipers and washers
- Check/top-up battery electrolyte (except sealed type)
- Check/top-up windscreen washers

EVERY 3,000 MILES OR 3 MONTHS, WHICHEVER IS SOONER
As for weekly service, plus the following items:

ENGINE COMPARTMENT

NOTE:The following service items are carried out at 12,000 miles or 12 months on A plus cars, except for those marked with an asterisk * which should be carried out at 6,000 miles or 6 months

ENGINE COMPARTMENT
- Check tension and condition of generator drive belt (6,000 for 1982 on)
- Check fuel and clutch pipes for chafing, leaks and corrosion
- Check steering rack mountings and bellows
- Check front suspension joints for wear
- Check rear suspension joints for wear
- Check exhaust system for leaks and security*

CAR RAISED
- Adjust front and rear drum brakes*
- Check brake pipes, hoses and unions for leaks and damage
- Check driveshaft gaiters

CAR ON GROUND
- Check/top-up battery electrolyte (except sealed type)
- Check headlamp alignment
- Check front wheel alignment
- Check handbrake operation

EVERY 6,000 MILES OR 6 MONTHS, WHICHEVER IS SOONER
As for 3,000 mile service, plus the following items:

NOTE:Items marked with an asterisk * are normally carried out at 12,000 miles or 12 months on A plus cars

ENGINE COMPARTMENT
- Change engine oil and filter (Manual)*
- Change engine oil and filter (Automatic)
- Check/adjust clutch return stop
- Check cooling and heating hoses for leaks*
- Top-up carburettor piston damper
- Lubricate throttle linkage*
- Clean/adjust spark plugs*
- Check contact breaker points gap*
- Lubricate distributor*
- Check/adjust ignition timing*
- Check/Adjust engine idle speed and CO level*

CAR RAISED
- Check front brake pads and discs
- Check front brake shoes and drums*
- Lubricate suspension grease points
- Lubricate handbrake cables and guides

CAR ON GROUND
- Check steering comun clamp bolt*
- Clean and grease battery terminals*
- Check seatbelts and seats for condition and security*
- Lubricate locks, hinges and linkages*
- Road test, including brake efficiency test*

EVERY 12,000 MILES OR 12 MONTHS, WHICHEVER IS SOONER
As for 3,000 and 6,000 mile services, plus the following items:
NOTE:Items marked with an asterisk are normally carried out at 24,000 miles on 'A' Plus cars

ENGINE COMPARTMENT
- Check/adjust valve clearances
- Renew spark plugs
- Renew contact breaker points*
- Renew air filter element
- Check air intake control valve
- Check crankcase breather system
- Renew engine oil filler cap*
- Clean brake servo air filter
- Check brake servo hose

CAR RAISED
- Check rear brake shoes and drums

CAR ON GROUND
- Check fuel filler cap seal

EVERY 18,000 MILES OR 18 MONTHS, WHICHEVER IS SOONER
- Change brake fluid

EVERY 24,000 MILES OR 24 MONTHS, WHICHEVER IS SOONER
- Drain cooling system, flush and fill with fresh anti-freeze
- Renew generator drive belt

EVERY 36,000 MILES OR 36 MONTHS, WHICHEVER IS SOONER
- Change all fluid seals and brake hoses
- Change brake servo air filter

Routine Maintenance

INTRODUCTION . . . . [1]

The importance of regular servicing cannot be overemphasised – remember 'prevention is better than cure'. Carrying out the servicing yourself will not only save you money but also give you the opportunity to get to know your car.

The SERVICE SCHEDULE lists all the service checks and adjustments with the intervals at which they should be carried out. Cars which cover a low annual mileage should be serviced on a time basis instead of mileage. The sequence in which items are given has been arranged to give a reasonably logical order of working around the car. The underbonnet operations are given first, followed by the under car operations and then the items with the car on the ground. It is therefore recommended that this is followed where possible.

Apart from the necessary materials such as oils and filters, the most important requirement is time. If time is limited, the service can be split up into two or more sections and the remaining items carried out at a later date. The advantage of this is that the service can be spread out over a few weekends rather than carrying it all out in one go. In this way, there will be no need to hurry the job or miss out any items, as each is important in its own way, even if it is only a check or inspection.

Items listed in SERVICE SCHEDULE are covered in detail either in this or the next chapter. Certain items such as tyre and seat belt inspection are detailed in PASS THE MoT as they are of prime importance in the MoT test. For convenience, all items directly concerned with engine performance and economy, such as spark plugs and ignition timing are covered in TUNE-UP. This enables a complete engine tune to be carried out as a separate operation if required. The remainder of the routine maintenance checks and operations are contained in this chapter, although major overhaul operations are described in the relevant chapters.

Before starting work, familiarise yourself with the components in the engine compartment (Fig.A:1) and read through both of these two chapters carefully so that you are aware of the work entailed and the tools and parts required. All relevant data such as capacities and clearances, where not included in the text, can be found in TECHNICAL DATA at the end of this manual. Note that procedures apply to all models unless otherwise specified.

TOOLS & EQUIPMENT . . . . [2]

To successfully carry out your own routine servicing on your Mini you will need the basic tool kit detailed in BASIC PROCEDURES as well as the following more specialised items:

- Oil filter strap wrench – for the removal of the engine oil filter on manual transmission models from 1973 on.
- $^{15}/_{16}$in A/F socket – for removing the engine/transmission oil drain plug.
- Torque wrench – for accurate tightening of nuts and bolts.
- Battery hydrometer – for checking the state of charge of the battery.
- Brake adjusting spanner – for accurate adjustment of drum brakes.
- Anti-freeze hydrometer – for checking the concentration of anti-freeze in the cooling system.
- Grease gun – for lubricating the suspension arm pivots and balljoints.
- Tyre pressure gauge – to check the tyre pressures at least once a week.
- Oil can – for the general lubrication of door hinges etc.

With this tool kit and some safe car lifting equipment – see BASIC PROCEDURES – you will be able to complete all the periodic service items listed on the previous page.

ENGINE OIL & FILTER . . . . [3]

The Mini range has a combined lubrication system serving both the engine and gearbox/final drive unit.

Oil Level Check

It is essential that the oil level is maintained at the correct level. The oil level should be checked at least once a week, and always before a long run.

If the engine has been running, wait a few minutes after switching off to allow the oil to drain back into the sump for a correct reading. On automatic cars, run the engine first then allow to stand for 1 minute. The car must also be standing on level ground when checking the oil level. If an ignition shield is fitted, release the top fasteners and pull the shield forward to expose the oil level dipstick.

The dipstick on manual gearbox cars is located at the front of the engine (Fig.A:2), and on automatic transmission models, the dipstick is located at the top of the converter housing. The oil level should be maintained between the two marks on the dipstick, and must never be allowed to fall below the lower mark.

To check the oil level, remove the dipstick and wipe the end with a piece of clean tissue or lint-free cloth to remove the oil film. Reinsert the dipstick fully then withdraw it again to check the level.

If the level is low, remove the filler cap from the rocker cover (Fig.A:3) and top up with the recommended grade of oil given in

TECHNICAL DATA. Wait for a few minutes to allow the fresh oil to reach the sump before taking the dipstick reading. The level should not be above the upper mark. When correct, refit the oil filler cap.

Do not overfill as this may result in oil leaks and increased oil consumption.

Changing Engine Oil & Filter

The engine oil and filter should be changed at the recommended service intervals or more frequently under severe operating conditions. Some early cars have an amber oil filter warning light. If this light operates, it indicates that the filter is becoming clogged and both the oil and filter should be changed as soon as possible.

The most severe type of operation, and which gives rise to a sludge formation inside the engine, is light engine loading, slow engine speeds and short journeys where the engine never reaches normal operating temperature. High speeds over long distances are generally kinder to the engine. Modern multi-grade engine oils contain additives which help towards preventing sludge formation, but even these have certain limitations.

The oil should be changed when the engine is warm, after a run. The car need not be raised for this as there is sufficient clearance underneath for access to the drain plug. Place a suitable container under the engine oil drain plug. An old 5 litre oil can with one side cut out is ideal for this (Fig.A:4). The drain plug is located on the offside at the bottom of the transmission casing (Fig.A:4). Undo the drain plug and allow the oil to drain into the container. While the oil is draining, clean the plug and check the condition of the sealing washer. The drain plug incorporates a magnet to pick up any metal particles. Renew the sealing washer if the faces are damaged or it has been excessively flattened.

When the oil has completely drained, refit the plug and tighten it to the correct torque – see TECHNICAL DATA. Beware of overtightening the plug as difficulty may be met when draining the oil next time.

The oil filter on early manual gearbox cars is of the replaceable element type with a metal casing secured by a central bolt containing a disposable element (A,Fig.A:6). Late cars, from late 1973, have a screw-on disposable cartridge type filter (Fig.A:5). The two types of filter are not interchangeable.

All automatic models have a larger horizontally mounted replaceable element filter (B,Fig.A:6). Note that the filter is of a different specification to the element designed for manual transmission cars.

On most models it will be easier to replace the filter if the front grille is removed first – see BODY & FITTINGS. Place a suitable container under the filter to catch any oil spilt.

To remove the early and automatic transmission element type filter, release the casing by unscrewing the central bolt. Remove the assembly and discard the element. Wash the container in paraffin and dry it. Examine the bolt end sealing rings. If these are not a good fit on the bolt, new ones should be fitted. Using a sharp pointed tool such as a scriber or needle, pick out the filter casing sealing ring from the engine block. Clean the seal groove thoroughly to remove any oil and dirt, then fit the new sealing ring (supplied with the filter). Make sure the seal is fitted fully all the way round the groove. Fit a new element to the filter casing and refit the casing to the housing on the cylinder block. Start and tighten the retaining bolt – see TECHNICAL DATA ensuring that the lip of the bowl seats correctly on the seal.

On models with screw-on disposable cartridge filters it may be possible to unscrew the filter by hand, but if not, a strap or chain wrench will be required to release it (Fig.A:5). Unscrew the filter from the engine and discard it. Thoroughly clean the filter sealing flange on the engine block to remove all traces of oil and dirt.

Make sure the rubber sealing ring on the new filter is correctly located, and then apply a smear of clean engine oil to the sealing ring.

Screw the new filter into position until the sealing ring just contacts the mounting flange, then tighten a further ⅔ turn. Do NOT overtighten the filter as this may distort the sealing ring and give rise to leakage.

The engine oil should be added in two stages, after checking that the drain plug has been refitted. Measure out into a suitable container the oil quantity corresponding to the sump capacity given in TECHNICAL DATA. Pour the oil into the rocker cover filler hole taking care not to spill any over the engine.

Run the engine for a few minutes to circulate the oil, then stop the engine and check the dipstick level as described previously. Top-up the level to the upper mark on the dipstick as the new filter will have absorbed some of the new oil. Examine the oil filter seal for leaks.

NOTE:It is illegal to dispose of old oil by tipping it down the drain or burying it in the ground. Most local councils have a facility for oil disposal and use should be made of this. Alternatively, a local garage may be willing to dispose of the oil for you.

Oil Leaks

Check all joints on the engine which can be seen from above for oil leaks. Also check the underside of the engine for leaks at the following places: Oil drain plug, engine to transmission flange, oil filter and pump mounting flanges, fuel pump mounting (later models),tappet cover plates (where fitted), gear change oil seal and generally around the timing cover end of the engine especially at the crankshaft oil seal.

If any evidence of oil leakage is found, the area should be wiped clean, then the engine run to confirm the source. If the leak is serious, remedial action should taken as soon as possible – see ENGINE.

COOLING SYSTEM . . . . [4]
Cooling Level

The coolant level should be checked at least once a week and always before a long run. Check the level when the engine is cool. To top up the coolant level, press on the spring loaded pressure cap, turn the cap a quarter turn anti-clockwise and allow any pressure to escape. The cap can then be completely removed by pushing down and turning anti-clockwise. The coolant level should be just below the bottom of the filler neck (Fig.A:7).

Top up the level with a water/anti-freeze mixture in the correct proportions as described below, until the level is correct. Refit the pressure cap.

NOTE:If the level has fallen appreciably, check for signs of leakage.

Anti-Freeze

Anti-freeze has the ability to raise the boiling point and lower the freezing point of the coolant. It is recommended, therefore, that anti-freeze is used permanently in the system to afford maximum protection against freezing, overheating, corrosion and the formation of scale in the system. During the winter months an anti-freeze mixture MUST be used to protect the engine against frost damage. See TECHNICAL DATA for the correct anti-freeze specification.

Before filling the system with anti-freeze solution, inspect all hoses, hose connections and cooling system joints. After adding the anti-freeze, run the engine up to operating temperature and check for leaks. Attach a label to the front panel to record the date of filling.

The anti-freeze concentration in the system should be checked periodically and in any case before the beginning of the winter season or before travelling to a colder climate. The specific gravity of the coolant should be checked with a suitable hydrometer (Fig.A:8) and brought up to the required strength as necessary. The specific gravity of a 50% solution should be

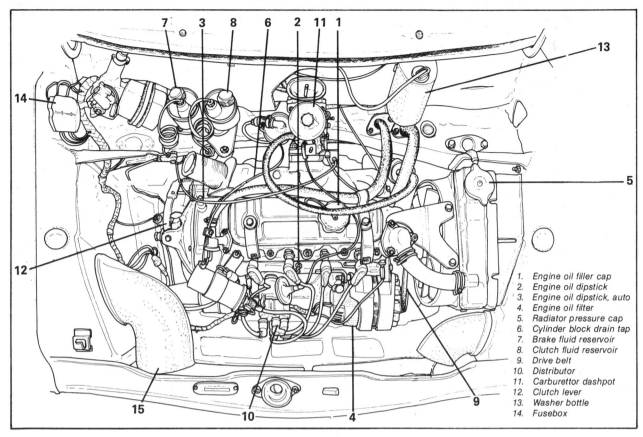

1. Engine oil filler cap
2. Engine oil dipstick
3. Engine oil dipstick, auto
4. Engine oil filter
5. Radiator pressure cap
6. Cylinder block drain tap
7. Brake fluid reservoir
8. Clutch fluid reservoir
9. Drive belt
10. Distributor
11. Carburettor dashpot
12. Clutch lever
13. Washer bottle
14. Fusebox

Fig. A:1 Engine compartment

Fig. A:2 Check engine oil level with dipstick

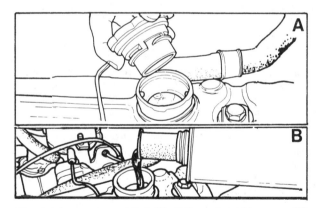

Fig. A:3 Remove cap (A) & fill oil through rocker cover (B)

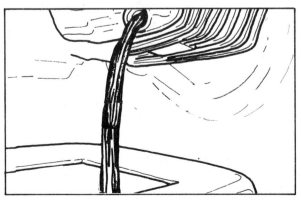

Fig. A:4 Drain engine oil into old can

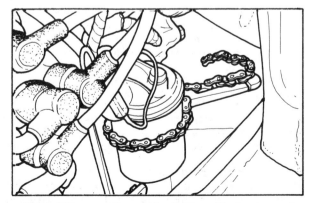

Fig. A:5 Remove disposable oil filter with strap wrench

1.073 providing no other additives are in the coolant.

The cooling system should be flushed and refilled with a fresh anti-freeze mixture every two years. Details of draining, flushing and refilling the system are given in COOLING SYSTEM.

Hoses — Checking Condition

The hoses, hose connections and system joints should be checked periodically for leaks before the coming of winter or when filling the system with anti-freeze.

Examine each hose in turn, looking for deterioration, indicated by cracks, separation of the layers, swelling or excessive softness of the rubber. Also inspect them for chafing or damage due to contact with other components. Check that the hose clips have not damaged the rubber beneath. Replace any suspect hoses.

Check that the hose clips are secure and in good condition. Tighten or replace as necessary – see COOLING SYSTEM.

BRAKE & CLUTCH FLUID LEVEL .... [5]

The brake and clutch fluid reservoirs are mounted on the engine compartment rear bulkhead. Early cars have metal reservoirs, and the fluid level should reach the bottom of the filler cap neck. Some early models have a metal brake reservoir with plastic extension and level marks. Later cars have a translucent plastic reservoir with a level mark moulded into the side (Fig.A:9).

If the fluid level falls excessively, or requires frequent topping up, this indicates a leak in the braking system, and steps should immediately be taken to establish the cause and deal with it.

If topping up is necessary, clean the area around the filler cap before unscrewing it. Use only the brake fluid specified in TECHNICAL DATA. Check that the vent hole in the filler cap is clear before refitting the cap. Do not overtighten the plastic caps.

The clutch level is topped up using the procedure as described for the brakes.

Any spilled brake fluid should be wiped up and washed away immediately with cold water as it can damage paintwork.

It is recommended that the fluid in the braking and clutch systems should be changed completely every 24,000 miles or 24 months. This is because the fluid absorbs moisture (hygroscopic) which lowers the boiling point of the fluid and could result in vapour locks with a consequential loss of braking. Moisture in the brake fluid can also promote premature failure of the system components by corrosion.

A brake fluid change can be carried out using the sequence detailed under Bleeding the Brakes in BRAKES. Repeating the operation until all the air bubbles are gone and the new clean fluid emerges from each of the bleed nipples in turn.

A clutch fluid change can be carried out using the sequence detailed in CLUTCH & GEARBOX.

CARBURETTOR DAMPER .... [6]

The action of the carburettor piston is controlled by an oil filled damper. This damper should be periodically checked and topped up as necessary. Unscrew the cap from the top of the suction chamber and withdraw the cap and piston. Top-up with clean engine oil to bring the level 13 mm (0.5 in) above the top of the hollow damper rod (Fig.A:10). Push the damper assembly back into position and screw the cap back into place.

AIR FILTER .... [7]

The air filter mounted within the air cleaner assembly should be replaced every 12,000 miles or yearly, whichever is sooner. If the car is used in dusty conditions it should be replaced more frequently.

The air cleaner is removed from the carburettor intake pipe by undoing the two wing nuts. Remove the air cleaner assembly and the sealing 'O' ring between the carburettor air intake and air cleaner casing. The lid is removed from the air cleaner body by levering apart with a screwdriver, starting at the moulded arrow (Fig.A:11). The lid can then be removed and the element withdrawn. Clean out the inside of the air cleaner body to remove any accumulation of dust and dirt.

Take care not to drop any dirt or debris down the carburettor intake. Fit a new element and push the cover back into place. Press the clips into place.

Early cars are fitted with a metal filter housing. The lid may be retained by one or two wing nuts. Position the air intake toward the exhaust manifold in winter, away from the manifold the rest of the year.

On later cars the air cleaner body should be a firm fit on the rubber sealing ring, also the heated air inlet pipe should be located on the air intake control valve and hot air box.

Check that the air temperature control valve is free to move. Examine the sealing foam and replace if necessary.

DRIVE BELT .... [8]
Drive Belt Tension

The dynamo/alternator water pump and cooling fan are driven by a 'V'-belt from the crankshaft pulley. It is important that the correct tension of the drive belt is maintained to ensure efficient operation of the electrical and cooling systems. Too great a tension will place excessive strain on the dynamo/alternator or water pump bearings, and cause undue wear on the belt.

To test the belt tension, press the belt down at a point mid-way between the dynamo/alternator and water pump pulleys (Fig.A:12) using firm thumb pressure. The belt should deflect (13 mm) 0.5 in. If retensioning of the belt is necessary, slacken the bottom mounting strap and upper pivot bolts (Fig.A:13). Lever the dynamo/alternator away from the engine, applying any force to the drive end bracket only, until the correct tension is obtained.

Tighten the adjustment bolts. Recheck the tension and readjust as necessary.

Drive Belt Replacement

Check the condition of the drive belt periodically and replace if excessively worn, stretched or frayed.

To replace the belt, proceed as for adjusting, but pivot the dynamo/alternator fully towards the engine, and detach the belt from the pulleys. Manoeuvre the belt between the fan blades and the right-hand top of the radiator cowling. On models with the sixteen bladed fan, feed the belt between the individual blade tips and the cut-outs in the cowling flange.

Fit the new belt and adjust the tension as described previously.

Run the engine at a fast idle for about 5 minutes, then recheck the belt tension. Do not attempt to lever a new belt onto the pulleys as this will damage both the belt and pulleys.
NOTE:The tension of a new belt should be rechecked after approximately 100 miles as it will stretch after initial use.

Dynamo Lubrication

On cars fitted with a dynamo, the rear bearing should be regularly lubricated. Add two or three drops of engine oil to the bearing through the central hole in the rear end bearing plate. Do not over-oil or the commutator may be contaminated. Alternators do not require lubrication.

BATTERY .... [9]

The battery in Saloon models is located in a well in the floor of the boot. In Estate cars the battery is below the rear seat cushion. In Vans and Pick-ups, the battery is behind the driver's seat.
NOTE:Cars built before October 1969 are of Positive (+)earth polarity, cars built after this date are of Negative (-) earth polarity.

Electrolyte Level

The level and charge of the battery electrolyte should be

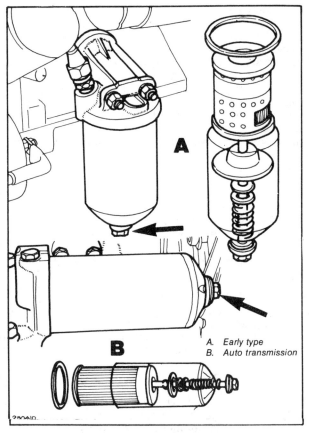

A. Early type
B. Auto transmission

Fig. A:6 Canister type oil filters

Fig. A:7 Top-up coolant level

Fig. A:8 Checking anti-freeze concentration
with coolant hydrometer

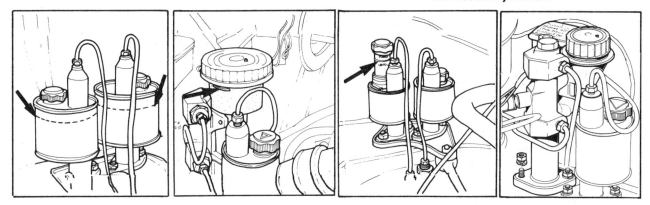

Fig. A:9 Check/top-up brake & clutch fluid reservoirs

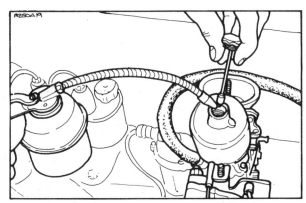

Fig. A:10 Top-up carburettor piston damper

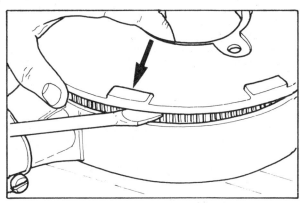

Fig. A:11 Air filter element replacement

checked periodically. If a refillable type battery is fitted (Fig.A:14), distilled (de-ionised) water should be added if the level in any cell is below the separators, or the bottom of the filling tube on trough filled batteries. In some cases the battery case is translucent to allow the level to be checked without the need for lifting the vent cover. Do not overfill the battery. Run the engine immediately after topping up the battery, especially in cold weather to ensure thorough mixing of the acid and the water and so prevent freezing.

If the battery is found to need frequent topping up, steps should be taken to find out the reason. For example, the battery may be receiving an excessive charge, in which case the charging system rate should be checked. If one cell in particular needs topping up more than the others, check the condition of the battery case. If there are signs of an electrolyte leak, the source should be traced and corrective action taken. *NOTE:The electrolyte level should not be topped up within half an hour of the battery being charged, other than by the car's own charging system, lest it floods.*

State of Charge
The state of charge of the battery can be determined by checking the specific gravity of the electrolyte in each cell with a hydrometer (Fig.A:14). This is a relatively inexpensive item and should be generally available from most accessory shops. The state of charge is indicated by reading the scale on the float. If a calibrated hydrometer is used, a specific gravity reading of at least 1.275 should be indicated if the battery is fully charged, or 1.120 if discharged.

After charging recheck the gravity after leaving the battery for about an hour. The procedure for charging the battery is given in BASIC PROCEDURES. If the reading is still low, the battery should be replaced.

Battery Connections
To ensure good electrical contact the battery terminals should be tight on the battery posts. If the battery posts or cable clamps are corroded, the cables should be disconnected and the terminals and posts cleaned with a soda solution and a wire brush. When reconnecting the clamps to the battery posts, a thin coating of petroleum jelly (not grease) should be applied. The battery earth strap and the engine earth strap should also be checked for proper connection and condition.

DISTRIBUTOR .... [10]
Distributor Lubrication (Fig.A:16)
The distributor may be made by Lucas or Ducellier, and should be lubricated whenever the contact breaker points are checked or replaced.

Remove the distributor cap after levering the spring clips with a screwdriver, then pull off the rotor arm.

If a Lucas distributor is fitted, lightly smear the cam face with grease. Do not oil the cam wiping pad. If the contact points are of the non-sliding type, see TUNE-UP grease the moving contact pivot post. In the centre of the cam is a felt pad which should be lubricated with a few drops of oil, also apply a few drops of oil to the governor mechanism through the base plate hole. When changing the points add a drop of oil to the base plate groove.

If a Ducellier distributor is fitted, lightly smear the cam face with grease. In the centre of the cam is a felt pad which should be lubricated with a few drops of oil. Turn the crankshaft, see BASIC PROCEDURES until the advance weights are visible through the base plate hole. Apply a drop of oil to the pivot post and rotate the crankshaft until the opposite post is visible.

After lubricating the various components, check that there is no lubricant on the contact breaker points. If so, wipe clean with methylated spirits.

CLUTCH ADJUSTMENT .... [11]
As wear of the clutch driven plate takes place, the clearance

between the clutch thrust ring and release bearing changes. To check the clearance on early models, disconnect the return spring from the lever, and measure the gap between the stop bolt and the clutch lever with a feeler gauge (Fig.A:15).

If the clearance is different from that specified in TECHNICAL DATA, reset the clearance. Adjust by slackening the stop bolt locknut and screw the bolt in or out as necessary to obtain the correct clearance. Tighten the locknut and recheck the gap. Refit the spring.

On later models fitted with a Verto clutch, this can be identified by a much shorter clutch release lever and a repositioned slave cylinder. The clutch can also be adjusted for wear by altering the clutch throw out stop – see CLUTCH & GEARBOX.

CRANKCASE VENTILATION .... [12]
The crankcase ventilation system on early models consists of a hose between the rocker cover and the air filter. On later models, the hose is connected between the oil separator cannister at the rear of the engine and the air filter casing (Fig.A:17).

The connecting hose should be inspected periodically for blockage and cleaned out as necessary, otherwise a pressure build-up in the crankcase can occur, causing oil leaks from the engine and an increase in oil consumption.

The air intake filter is incorporated in the oil filler cap, and the cap should be replaced every 12,000 miles (A,Fig.A:3).

DRIVESHAFTS .... [13]
Check both inner and outer driveshaft joint gaiters for signs of leakage or damage. If they are at all suspect they must be renewed. If a hole in the gaiter is not spotted quickly, the joint will rapidly deteriorate and need replacing, this operation is detailed in FRONT SUSPENSION. If wear of one or more of the joints is suspected then test the joint(s) as detailed in PASS THE MoT.

STEERING & SUSPENSION .... [14]
Ball Joints, Bushes & Gaiters
Check the steering, front suspension balljoints and rear suspension radius arms for excessive movement indicating wear. Check the steering balljoint gaiters and the steering rack bellows for splitting or leakage of lubricant. Any such damage will necessitate immediate attention for even a small tear can allow sufficient dirt and water to enter and cause wear of the joint or steering mechanism. Movement of the steering rack backwards and forwards can even assist the ingress of harmful dirt and water. Any split gaiters, therefore should be renewed as soon as possible – see STEERING or the relevant SUSPENSION chapters for the renewal procedure.

For full details of inspection of the steering and suspension systems for security, wear and general deterioration, see PASS THE MoT. Note that procedures for checking and adjusting the front wheel alignment are given in STEERING.

Hydrolastic Suspension
Saloon models built between September 1964 and October 1968 are fitted with Hydrolastic suspension. All other models are fitted with 'dry' or rubber cone suspension with hydraulic shock absorber units.

If Hydrolastic suspension is fitted, the displacer units act as springs and dampers. If the units are suspected of leaking, this will be shown by a difference in the trim height on each side. The trim height can be checked by measuring from the road wheel hub to the centre of the wheel arch above. A special pump is required to increase or decrease the pressure in the units. If the measurement is different from that specified in TECHNICAL DATA, have the system pressure checked and the trim height adjusted by an Austin/Rover dealer.

Fig. A:12 Check drive belt tension by hand

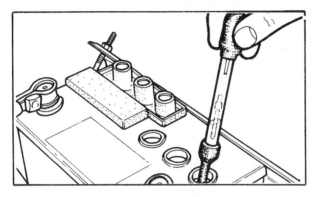

Fig. A:14 Check battery eletrolyte with hydrometer

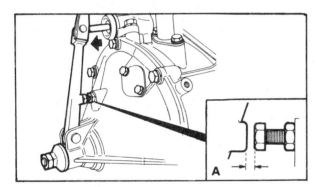

Fig. A:15 Check adjuster bolt & lock nut

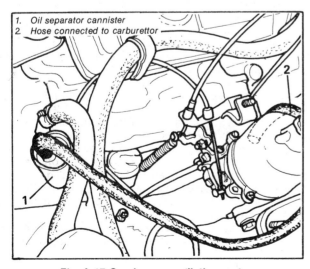

1. Oil separator cannister
2. Hose connected to carburettor

Fig. A:17 Crankcase ventilation system

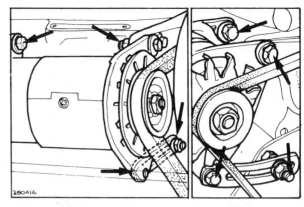

Fig. A:13 Dynamo/alternator pivot & tensioning bolts

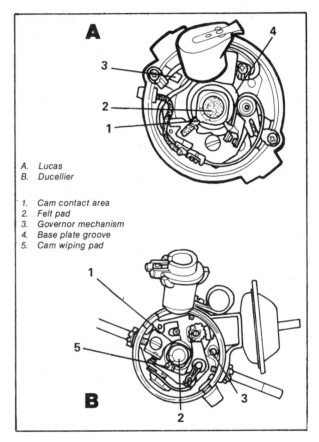

A.   Lucas
B.   Ducellier

1.   Cam contact area
2.   Felt pad
3.   Governor mechanism
4.   Base plate groove
5.   Cam wiping pad

Fig. A:16 Distributor lubrication

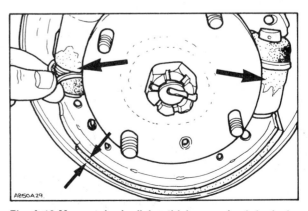

Fig. A:18 Measure brake lining thickness, check for leaks

BRAKES . . . . [15]

Front Brake Shoe Linings

The front brake shoe linings should be regularly checked for wear at the intervals recommended in SERVICE SCHEDULE.

Raise and support the front of the car – see BASIC PROCEDURES. The drum is secured by two crosshead screws. If these screws are rounded off, an impact screwdriver may be required to start them moving – see BASIC PROCEDURES. It may also be necessary to slacken the brake adjuster(s) to allow the drum to come off as described below.

Clean out the drum, shoes and backplate using a soft brush. Take care not to inhale any asbestos dust from the linings.

Inspect the shoe linings for wear. If the lining material has worn down to the minimum specified thickness – see TECHNICAL DATA, or will do so before the next check is called for, the brake shoes should be replaced as detailed in BRAKES. Measure the thickness of bonded linings; measure the depth to the rivet heads on riveted shoes (Fig.A:18).

Inspect the surface of the brake linings for oil, grease or brake fluid contamination. If present, the linings should be replaced once the cause has been established and dealt with. Inspect the wheel cylinders for signs of fluid leakage (Fig.A:18). If present, the cylinders should be overhauled immediately. Check the brake drum friction surfaces for scoring.

If the linings are satisfactory, make sure that enough lining material remains to allow the car to run until the next service check. Refit the brake drum in the reverse order of removal and then adjust the shoes as detailed below.

Rear Brake Shoe Linings

Checking the rear brake lining thickness is a similar operation to that detailed for the front shoes. A single adjuster is fitted.

To pull the drum away from the shoes, slacken the adjuster by turning anti-clockwise as viewed from behind the backplate. Remove the brake drum and check the linings and wheel cylinders as previously described. Refit the brake drum in the reverse order of removal and adjust the brakes as detailed below.

Front Brake Pads

1275 GT models are fitted with disc brakes at the front as are Mini 25 models and all models built from late 1984 on. Raise and support the front of the car – see BASIC PROCEDURES and remove the road wheels. The thickness of the pads can be checked by looking into the end of the caliper (Fig.A:20).

Measure the distance between the face of the pad backing plate and the contact face. When this distance is reduced to, or is approaching 3 mm (⅛ in) the pads should be replaced – see BRAKES.

NOTE:If one or more pads require replacement, both pads on both front brakes should be replaced as a set otherwise brake balance will be affected.

If the pads are not to be replaced, make sure that enough pad material remains to allow the car to run until the next scheduled service check.

Front Brake Adjustment - Early Single Leading Shoe Type

Early Mini models (pre Sept 1964) were fitted with leading and trailing shoe type front brakes, and these have a single square headed adjuster on each brake back plate which effects adjustment of both brake shoes (Fig.A:19).

Raise and support the front of the car – see BASIC PROCEDURES, turn the adjuster clockwise, viewed from behind the back plate, using a suitable spanner or brake key, until the drum is locked, but do NOT strain the adjuster. Back off the adjuster just sufficiently to allow the wheel to rotate freely without dragging or binding.

Spin the wheel in its normal direction of forward rotation, apply the foot brake hard to centralise the brake shoes, and recheck the adjustment.

Adjust the other front brake in a similar manner.

Front Brake Adjustment — Later Twin Leading Shoe Type

All later models with the exception of disc brake models, are equipped with the more efficient twin-leading shoe type front brakes. These have two square-headed adjusters, one for each shoe, on the backplate (Fig.A:19).

It should be noted that, due to the location of the upper adjuster behind the steering arm, it is difficult to get a proper brake spanner to fit on it and an open-ended spanner will probably by required to turn the adjuster. In this case, take great care to avoid rounding-off the corners of the adjuster if it is stiff.

Raise and support the front of the car – see BASIC PROCEDURES. Turn the adjuster in the same direction as the forward rotation of the wheel until the wheel is locked then back it off sufficiently to allow the wheel to rotate freely without dragging or binding.

Spin the wheel in its normal direction of forward rotation, apply the footbrake hard to centralise the shoe, and recheck the adjustment.

Repeat this operation with each adjuster on both front brakes.

Rear Brake Adjustment

The rear brakes are of the leading and trailing shoe type and a single square-headed adjuster (Fig.A:19), which effects adjustment of both brake shoes is provided at each backplate.

Raise and support the rear of the car – see BASIC PROCEDURES, adjust the rear brakes in a similar manner to that described previously for the single leading shoe type front brakes. Ensure that the handbrake is fully released before attempting to adjust the brakes.

Handbrake

The handbrake is correctly adjusted when it operates efficiently on the third notch of the ratchet. Braking effect should be equal on both rear wheels and it should just be possible to turn them by heavy hand pressure.

Free play in the handbrake linkage is normally taken up automatically when the rear brakes are adjusted. However, if even with the rear brakes correctly adjusted the handbrake does not hold properly, it can be adjusted as follows:

First, raise and support the rear of the car – see BASIC PROCEDURES, check that the cable or cables, dependent on model year, are operating both rear brakes properly and are not seized or stiff at the pivot sections on the radius arms or in the cable guide channels (A,Fig.A:22). Also check that the handbrake levers at the backplate are operating freely (B,Fig.A:22). Lubricate all pivot points (Fig.A:22).

With the handbrake lever pulled on to the third notch on the ratchet, adjust the cables on early models at the lever trunnion immediately behind the handbrake lever (A,Fig.A:21). Screw the adjusting nuts along the cables until the correct braking effect is achieved at each rear wheel.

On later models, a single primary cable linkage with a compensator bracket is used (B,Fig.A:21), and only a single adjustment point is provided. If unequal braking effect is obtained, check that the cable is free to slide through the guide channels at the front of the rear subframe, also that the radius arm pivots are free.

After adjusting the handbrake, release the lever then check that both rear wheels turn freely without dragging or binding.

Hoses, Pipes & Seals

A visual check of the flexible hoses and rigid brake pipes should

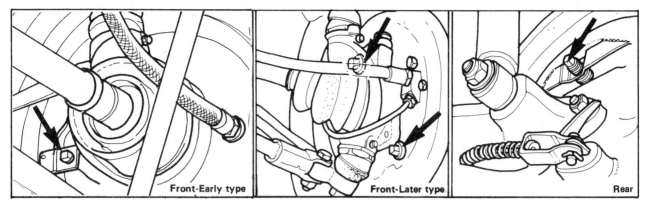

Fig. A:19 Front & rear brake shoe adjusters

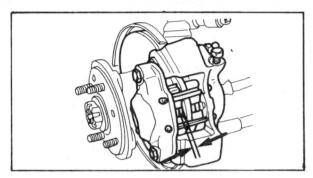

Fig. A:20 Check brake pad thickness in front calipers

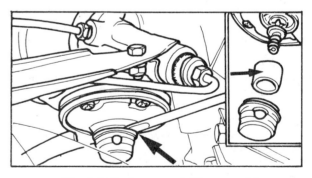

Fig. A:21 Handbrake cable adjustment

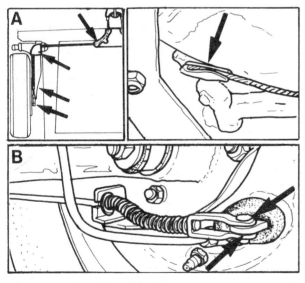

Fig. A:22 Handbrake cable lubrication points

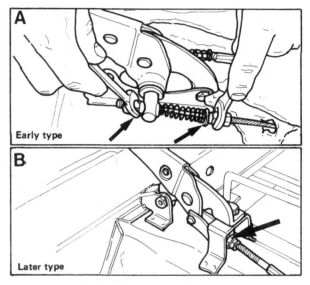

Fig. A:23 Brake servo air filter assembly

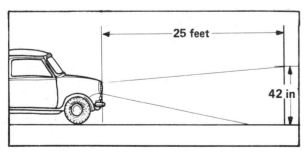

Fig. A:24 Headlamp alignment main beam height setting

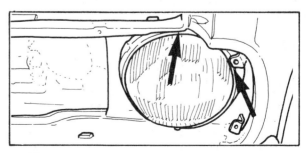

Fig. A:25 Headlamp alignment adjustment screws

be carried out every time the car is off the ground for any reason. Look for leaks, damage, chafing and corrosion – see PASS THE MoT for further details. Any component which is suspect should be changed immediately – refer to BRAKES.

As preventative maintenance, all fluid seals in the braking system should be replaced every 3 years or 36,000 miles. If any leakage is discovered, all seals in the system should be replaced as a safety measure. At the same time, the working surfaces of the pistons and bores of the master cylinder, wheel cylinders and calipers should be examined and new parts fitted where required.   The procedures for replacing the brake seals in the various hydraulic components are detailed in BRAKES.

Brake Servo Filter — Replacement
A brake servo unit is fitted as standard equipment only on 1275 GT models up to 1974. The only periodic maintenance required is attention to the servo air filter.

The filter element is located under the plastic dome on the underside of the servo unit cylinder (Fig.A:23). The filter should be removed for cleaning every 12,000 miles (12 months), and replaced every 36,000 miles (36 months).

To remove the filter, lever the dome off the valve cover with a screwdriver and lift out the filter. Clean the filter element with a low-pressure air line. Do NOT use cleaning fluid or lubricant of any description on the filter.

When refitting the filter element, ensure that the air valve spring is securely located onto the valve. Snap fit the plastic dome onto the valve cover.

WHEELS & TYRES ....[16]
Tyre Pressures
The tyres should be checked and adjusted to the recommended pressures where necessary at least once a week. Check the pressures when the tyres are cold as tyre pressures may increase by as much as 0,4 bar (6 lb/in²) when hot. The recommended inflation pressures are given in TECHNICAL DATA. The spare tyre should be set at the higher specified pressure and adjusted as necessary after fitting.

Incorrect inflation pressures will cause abnormal tyre wear and may result in premature failure. When checking pressures ensure that the dust caps are refitted to the valves as, apart from keeping out dirt, they also provide a secondary seal to the valve.

The tightness of the wheel securing nuts should be checked at the same time as the tyre pressures.

Tyre Inspection
The tyres should be checked periodically for wear or damage. Full details of tyre inspection are given in PASS THE MoT.

Wheel Balancing
Imbalance of the road wheels may cause axle tramp, vibration in the steering or abnormal tyre wear. To obtain maximum ride comfort and tyre life, the balance of the road wheels should be checked periodically. Since specialised knowledge and equipment are required for this operation, the work should be entrusted to an authorised Austin/Rover dealer or tyre specialist.

EXHAUST SYSTEM ....[17]

The exhaust system should be checked periodically for leaks and security. It is a good idea to spend a few minutes examining the system whenever work is being carried out under the car, always ensuring that the car is supported safely – see BASIC PROCEDURES.

Check the alignment of the system to ensure that none of the mounting points are under strain. Inspect the exhaust pipes and silencer boxes for damage, corrosion or signs of exhaust gases blowing. Refer to PASS THE MoT for further details of the exhaust system inspection. Exhaust system replacement is dealt with in ENGINE.

LIGHTS & INSTRUMENTS ....[18]
The lamps, horn and indicators should be checked periodically to ensure that they are functioning correctly. The function of the instruments is best checked under road test conditions. Bulb replacement procedure is described in GENERAL ELECTRICS.

Headlamp Alignment
Headlamp alignment is usually carried out in a garage using optical beam setting equipment, to which the DIY owner is unlikely to have access. For MoT purposes, it is advisable that the alignment be adjusted by a garage for complete accuracy, however, it is possible to achieve a satisfactory setting by adjusting as follows:

The headlamps should be aligned so that, when on dipped beam, they will not dazzle a person standing more than 7,5 metres (25 feet) from the front of the car (with the car in its normal laden state but not carrying any extra weight). Check this as follows:

Find a straight wall which has a stretch of LEVEL ground before it. Position the car about 7,5 meters (25 feet) from the wall (Fig.A:24). Covering each headlamp in turn, set the beam height and direction by turning the adjuster screws with a screwdriver (Fig.A:25). Note that on some models it will be necessary to remove the headlamp surround.

WINDSCREEN WIPERS & WASHERS ....[19]
Wiper Blades
The wiping speeds and park position of the wiper blades as well as the condition of the blades and rubbers should be checked periodically.

Blades which are contaminated with insect or oil deposits should be removed and cleaned with a hard brush and detergent solution. Worn blades will cause streaks and unsatisfactory cleaning of the glass. The wiping edge of the blades must not be cracked or torn. Wear of the blades will increase under conditions of dust, air pollution and when used on a frozen or dry screen.

New blades should be fitted at least once a year according to condition. The wiper blades are retained on the arms by locating dimples (Fig.A:26). Depress the spring lever on the underside of the blade to free the lower dimple. Tilt the blade away from the arm and pull the blade up and off. Push the new blade into position until it locates.

Washer Reservoir Top-up
The windscreen washer reservoir should be checked and topped up weekly or more often if in regular use. The reservoir is mounted on the engine compartment bulkhead on the passenger's side (Fig.A:27).

The reservoir should be filled with a mixture of water and washer fluid. This will improve the washing action as well as stopping the fluid freezing in cold weather. Do not use any other fluid such as anti-freeze.

GENERAL LUBRICATION & BODY ....[20]
Suspension Lubrication
The front and rear suspension joints should be regularly lubricated. On the front suspension, grease nipples are provided at the top and bottom of the swivel hub and at the upper arm pivot. Raise and support the front of the car – see BASIC PROCEDURES, remove each wheel in turn. Clean the nipple heads and push a grease gun filled with a suitable good quality grease onto the swivel hub nipples (Fig.A:28). Pump the grease gun until the old grease is seen to emerge from under the rubber cap on each joint. If the joint is dry, turn the wheel from lock to lock after each stroke of the gun. A grease nipple is also

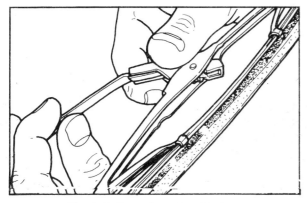
Fig. A:26 Removing wiper blade

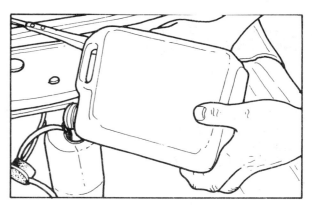
Fig. A:27 Windscreen washer reservoir

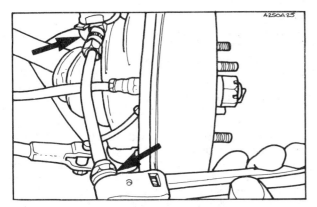
Fig. A:28 Lubricate front hub upper & lower swivels

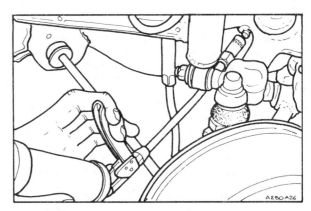
Fig. A:29 Lubricate front upper arm pivot

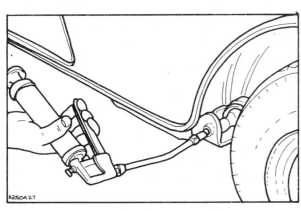
Fig. A:30 Lubricate rear arm pivot

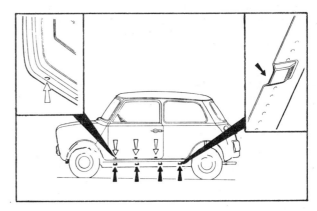
Fig. A:31 Regularly clean out body & door drain holes

fitted at each suspension arm inner pivot and should be pumped with grease until it is seen to exude from the end of the pivot (Fig.A:29).

The rear suspension trailing arms can be lubricated with the wheels on the ground. The nipples are located at the outer end of the radius arm pivot shafts (Fig.A:30). Clean the nipple heads and pump the grease gun until excess grease appears from the bush at the inner end of the shaft.

Locks, Hinges & Linkages

All hinges and locks should be regularly lubricated to prevent wear and possible seizure. Use a pump type oil can containing engine oil. Put a few drops onto each door hinge and latch, tailgate hinge and bonnet hinge and retaining strap pivots. Grease the tailgate latch. Wipe up any excess oil to prevent staining and dripping.

The lock barrels in the doors and tailgate should be lubricated

by dipping the key in lock-lube oil or graphite powder and inserting it into the lock. Do not attempt to lubricate the steering column lock.

Gearchange Mechanism

On early cars with remote control gearchange, a grease nipple is fitted at the front of the remote control housing at the rear of the engine, on the right-hand side of the gearchange shaft. This should be greased at major services.

Body Drain Holes

The drain holes in the body and doors should be checked periodically to ensure that they are clear. There are four drain slots in the outer sill panel on each side of the car, and three in the bottom of each door (Fig.A:31). Use a piece of wire to probe the apertures and remove any obstruction.

Tune-Up

INTRODUCTION . . . . [1]

Difficult starting, poor performance and excessive fuel consumption are some of the problems associated with an engine which is badly worn or out of tune. This is why at every major service the various relevant components of the engine should be checked and adjusted as specified in SERVICE SCHEDULE.

Engine tune-up has been deliberately presented as a separate chapter independent of ROUTINE MAINTENANCE so that if any problems occur between services the engine can be attended to on its own.

The following checks and adjustments have been arranged in logical sequence and it is advised that they be followed in the order given when carrying out a complete engine tune-up.

Often it is the condition or adjustment of only one component which is at fault, for example the ignition timing or idle adjustment, and consequently it will not be necessary to carry out a complete engine tune-up. However, it is usually only by a process of elimination that the fault can be traced and rectified. To assist in pin-pointing the source of any trouble a NON-START TROUBLE SHOOTER is included at the front of this book.

The various service and maintenance operations on the engine should be checked according to the time or mileage intervals given in SERVICE SCHEDULE.

TOOLS & EQUIPMENT . . . . [2]

In addition to the tools listed under Basic Tools & Equipment in BASIC PROCEDURES, the following tools will be required to carry out the operations contained in this chapter:

- A spark plug spanner or socket – for removing the spark plugs.
- Compression tester – for determining the state of wear of the cylinder bores, piston rings and valves.
- Dwell meter, such as Gunson's Autoranger or Testune – necessary for the accurate setting of contact breaker points.
- Tachometer (rev-counter), such as Gunson's Autoranger or Testune – to determine the exact engine speed when checking and adjusting the ignition timing or carburettor settings.
- Stroboscopic timing light – for checking ignition and the operation of the distributor vacuum advance mechanism.
- Special tool 18G 1308 – for carrying out adjustments on the Ducellier distributor. However, this tool is not essential.
- Exhaust gas analyser, such as Gunson's Gastester – for determining the CO (carbon monoxide) content level in the exhaust gases when checking the carburettor settings.

As an exhaust gas analyser is an expensive instrument it may be preferable either to hire one or to leave the mixture adjustment to your Austin/Rover dealer.

SPARK PLUGS . . . . [3]
Inspection

The spark plugs should be removed and checked periodically as recommended in SERVICE SCHEDULE.

When disconnecting the HT leads from the plugs, grasp the moulded cap and pull it off the plug. Do not pull on the plug lead itself, otherwise the core inside the lead may be damaged. The plug leads are not always marked with the plug number as standard, so if no markings are visible it is advisable to number the leads before removal. This is most effectively achieved using short lengths of tape attached to each lead. No.1 cylinder is situated at the radiator end of the engine.

Blow or brush any dirt away from around the plug recesses before attempting to remove the plugs from the cylinder head. This will prevent the possibility of any foreign matter entering the combustion chambers as the plugs are removed.

Use a proper spark plug socket or spanner to remove the spark plugs, (Fig.B:1) taking great care to avoid damaging the white porcelain insulator on the plug during removal.

Inspect the condition of the centre electrode and insulator nose, also the outer earth electrode of each plug, as this can give a good indication as to the general state of the engine. Typical examples of spark plug conditions are shown in Fig.B:3.

Electrode Gap (Fig.B:2)

Spark plugs which are in good condition and with low mileage can be cleaned, preferably with a proper sandblast cleaner, however, a stiff wire brush will do. Hold the spark plug with the electrode end facing downwards whilst brushing the electrode surfaces to avoid any particles of dirt or carbon lodging between the insulator nose and the outer shell of the plug. File the end of the centre electrode square with a points file if necessary.

Check the electrode gap with a gap setting gauge or feeler gauges. The correct gap is specified in TECHNICAL DATA.

If necessary, adjust the gap by bending the outer electrode slightly, using pliers. Make sure that the outer electrode is aligned with the centre electrode, again by bending it slightly with pliers.

When fitting new spark plugs, check and adjust the electrode gap before installation in the engine. Also, make sure that the replacements are of the correct grade and type for the engine – see TECHNICAL DATA.

Apply a few drops of clean engine oil to the plug threads before fitting. Do NOT overtighten the plugs when installing them – this is most important. The plugs should be screwed in by hand until finger-tight, followed by a maximum of a quarter turn with a plug spanner.

COMPRESSION CHECK . . . . [4]

Valuable time can be wasted trying to tune an engine which is badly worn. This is particularly applicable in the case of an

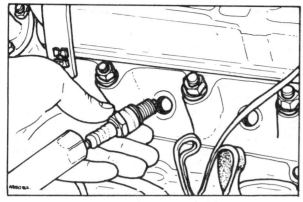

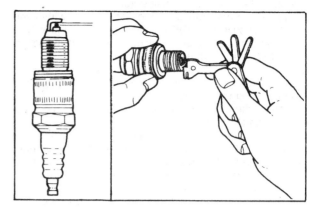

Fig. B:1 Remove spark plug with a socket or a spanner

Fig. B:2 Check & adjust spark plug electrode gap

1. NORMAL – If all plugs are lightly coated with tan or grey deposits and electrode wear is normal, good engine and ignition condition is indicated. Plugs can be cleaned, re-gapped and refitted, replace at mileage shown in Service Schedule.

2. HEAVY DEPOSITS – White or yellow deposits on the electrodes and plug shell, which are easily flaked off, are usually the result of fuel or oil additives. These change the chemical nature of the deposit to minimise misfire. Re-use plug after cleaning.

3. CARBON FOULING – Deposit has dry black appearance. May be corrected by using next hotter grade of plug. First check for sticking valves or damaged ignition leads (if only one or two plugs are affected): clogged air filter or a faulty choke.

4. OIL FOULING – Black wet deposits resulting from plug short circuiting due to excessive oil entering combustion chamber. In high mileage engines the piston rings, valve guides or cylinder bores may be excessively worn. Hotter plugs can temporarily cure problem but severe cases require engine overhaul.

5. OVERHEATING – White or blistered insulator nose and badly eroded electrodes indicates hotter than normal operating temperatures. Engine overheating or incorrectly set ignition timing may be cause. If individual plugs overheat check for coolant blockage, worn distributor parts or manifold leaks. Replace affected plugs.

Fig. B:3 Typical spark plug conditions

6. PRE-IGNITION – Electrodes melted, probably caused by excessive temperatures resulting in pre-ignition. This could result in engine damage. Check ignition timing, intake manifold for air leaks, distributor for worn parts, and possible causes of overheating. Make sure that plug is of correct heat range. Plug must be renewed.

engine which has covered a considerable mileage.

The engine compression pressures should be within the specifications given in TECHNICAL DATA or the engine will not run or idle smoothly, neither will it be working at maximum efficiency. Carry out the check as follows:

1. Run the engine until it attains normal operating temperature, then switch off and remove the spark plugs and leads as described previously.

2. Disconnect the LT (low tension) lead from the + (positive) terminal on the ignition coil.

3. Screw or push the compression tester into one of the spark plug holes, (Fig.B:4) and, with an assistant inside the car, hold the accelerator pedal fully down and crank the engine on the starter. Continue cranking the engine for a few revolutions until the tester needle stops moving.

4. Note the tester gauge reading on paper alongside the cylinder number.

5. Remove the compression tester and repeat the compression testing operation on the remaining cylinders in turn, noting the readings.

6. Now compare the readings with each other. If all the readings are within 10% of each other, then the cylinder bores and pistons can be considered to be in good order.

If one or two cylinder readings are lower than the others, the cause could be due to either the valves/head gasket, or the pistons/cylinder bores. Either cause can be confirmed by repeating the compression test on the suspect cylinders, only this time adding a small amount of engine oil to the cylinder beforehand. This is called the 'wet' test as opposed to the 'dry' test previously. If the 'wet' test causes the compression reading to rise substantially, then the cause is likely to be due to the piston or cylinder bore. If, on the other hand, the reading remains the same, then it is likely that the cause is due to the head gasket or valves not sealing properly.

If this is the case, refer to ENGINE, which will detail how the faults can be rectified.

VALVE CLEARANCES .... [5]

The valve clearances should be checked and adjusted at every 12,000 mile service interval or if you have reason to suspect that the valve clearances are the cause of excessive noise or loss of power (or after the cylinder head has been disturbed). This job can be done quite easily after the rocker cover has been removed, remembering that both valves and cylinders are numbered from the front of the engine – No.1 piston being at the radiator end.

The procedure for adjusting the valves (engine cold) is as follows:

1. Remove the rocker cover by disconnecting the vacuum advance pipe from the carburettor and removing the fixing nuts and pulling it clear (Fig.B:5). The cover may be stuck by the gasket so take care not to damage it as it is lifted off or a new gasket will be needed.

2. Rotate the engine – see BASIC PROCEDURES in the normal direction of rotation (clockwise as seen from the front of the crankshaft pulley end of the engine).

3. Rotate the engine until valve number 8 is in the fully open position. Check the clearance on valve No.1. Slide an appropriate size feeler gauge between the rocker arm pad and the valve stem – see TECHNICAL DATA for the specified gap. If the clearance is correct, the feeler gauge should be a neat sliding fit.

4. If the gap is found to be either excessive or too small, the clearance should be adjusted by loosening the locknut with a ring spanner, turning the adjuster with a screwdriver until the correct clearance is obtained (Fig.B:6). When the clearance is correct, hold the adjuster in place with the screwdriver and tighten the locknut with the ring spanner. Recheck the clearance after tightening the locknut.

5. Repeat the adjustment operation for the other valves. If the order given below is followed, crankshaft rotation will be reduced to a minimum.

Check No. 1 valve with .... No. 8 valve fully open
Check No. 3 valve with ....No. 6 valve fully open
Check No. 5 valve with ....No. 4 valve fully open
Check No. 2 valve with ....No. 7 valve fully open
Check No. 8 valve with ....No. 1 valve fully open
Check No. 6 valve with ....No. 3 valve fully open
Check No. 4 valve with ....No. 5 valve fully open
Check No. 7 valve with ....No. 2 valve fully open

6. When all the clearances are correct, replace the rocker cover and new gasket (if required) to the cylinder head with the oil filler cap nearest to the pulley end of the engine. Tighten the cover bolts firmly but take care not to overtighten them. Refit the distributor vacuum advance pipe.

DISTRIBUTOR .... [6]

The distributor fitted to your Mini may be of Lucas or Ducellier manufacture. Two different types of Lucas distributor are used on Mini models; the 25D4 type and the 45D4, the latter being the more recent fitment.

As the distributor is mounted on the front of the engine block behind the air intake grille, access is slightly limited on non-Clubman models. It is advisable, therefore, to unscrew and remove the grille when working on the distributor fitted to these models. Some models also have a plastic ignition shield over the distributor and leads and this is easily removed by releasing the three twist fasteners and lifting the shield off.

Before purchasing replacement parts, check the distributor manufacturer. The maker's name and type number will be marked on the side of the body and on the cap. Note, however, that Lucas parts are also available for the Ducellier unit.

Contact Breaker Points Inspection

The condition of the contact breaker points can be inspected after removing the distributor cap and the rotor arm. The distributor cap is retained by spring clips which are best undone by prising them away from the cap with a screwdriver. The rotor arm is a push-fit on the distributor shaft.

If the points are badly burned, or if excessive metal transfer has taken place, (i.e. from one contact to the other) the points should be replaced. Metal transfer is considered excessive when the metal build-up or 'pip' on one of the points is clearly visible.

If the points are badly burned or bluish in colour, this is an indication that the condenser unit is probably defective and it should be replaced at the same time as the points.

In most cases it is probably better to fit new points rather than attempt to clean up the existing set with a nail file or emery board; this measure being best reserved for emergency breakdown situations.

Checking the Points Setting

The contact breaker points setting can be checked either by measuring the gap with feeler gauges, or by measuring the dwell angle with a dwell meter. It is recommended that a dwell meter be used in preference to feeler gauges as this will both simplify the procedure and ensure accurate adjustment. Using a dwell meter eliminates the need to remove either the distributor cap or the rotor arm in order to check the setting, and it is particularly useful when checking the setting of used points which have formed a 'pip'. Relatively inexpensive units are available from most motor accessory shops and in many cases a tachometer (rev-counter) function is also incorporated in the unit.

To check the contact breaker points gap using feeler gauges, proceed as follows:

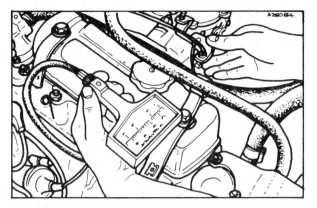

Fig. B:4 Checking cylinder compression pressure with gauge

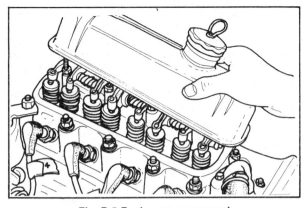

Fig. B:5 Rocker cover removal

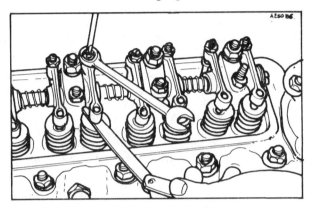

Fig. B:6 Valve clearance adjustment

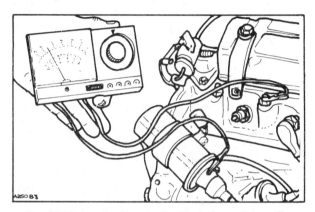

Fig. B:7 Using dwell meter to check the points setting

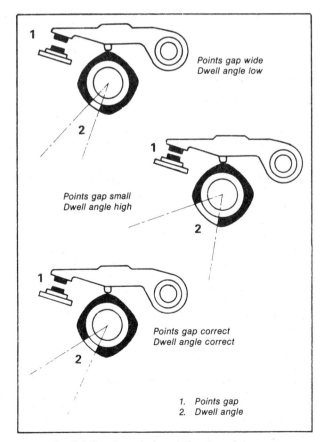

Fig. B:8 Dwell angle in relation to points gap

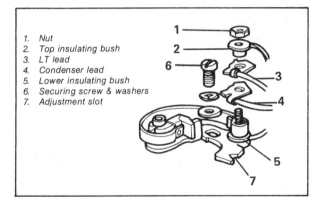

1. Nut
2. Top insulating bush
3. LT lead
4. Condenser lead
5. Lower insulating bush
6. Securing screw & washers
7. Adjustment slot

Fig. B:9 24D4 type contact breaker points

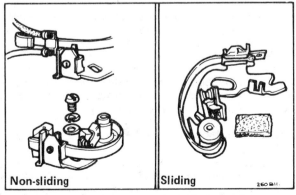

Fig. B:10 45D4 type contact breaker points

Turn the crankshaft in the normal direction of rotation (clockwise) – see BASIC PROCEDURES until the contact breaker heel is bearing directly on the peak of a cam and the contacts are fully open. Pass the correct thickness feeler gauge blade between the points (Fig.B:11). If the gap is correct, the blade will be a tight but free sliding fit between the points without moving the breaker arm. If the gap is too large or too small, then proceed with adjustment as detailed in the following section. See TECHNICAL DATA for gap specification.

NOTE:When measuring used contact points where a slight 'pip' has formed on the face of one contact, the gap measurement should be made outside the formation in order to achieve the correct reading (this can be done more accurately with a dwell meter).

Check the contact breaker points setting with a dwell meter as follows:

On later Negative earth models (late '69 on), the meter should be connected with the red (positive) lead to the LT terminal on the ignition coil (the terminal which connects to the side of the distributor); and the black (negative) lead to any suitable earth point on the car (scrape away any paint or dirt, if necessary) – see Fig.B:7.

NOTE:On pre '69 models with a Postive earth electrical system, the dwell meter connections described should be in the reverse order.

Run the engine at idle speed and observe the dwell angle reading on the meter. See TECHNICAL DATA for the correct dwell angle specifications. The dwell angle of the points is the angle of points closure; the wider the points gap the smaller will be the dwell angle and vice-versa (Fig.B:8).

As a check on the distributor condition, make a second dwell angle reading with the engine speed increased to about 2,000 rpm. The needle of the dwell meter should then not deviate from the previous figure by more than 1° either way. A larger deviation indicates that the distributor shaft or bearings are worn.

Points Adjustment — General

If the points have just been replaced, set the points gap initially to that specified in TECHNICAL DATA using feeler gauges. With new points it is better to set the points gap at the higher specified limit, or the dwell angle at the lower limit, as the points gap will reduce (angle will increase) as the points rubbing block beds in.

When the dwell angle has been adjusted, the ignition timing must be checked and reset if necessary, as detailed in the appropriate section in this chapter.

Points Adjustment — Lucas 25D4 Distributor (Fig.B:11)

Unclip the distributor cap and remove the rotor arm. Slacken the contact breaker plate securing screw slightly and insert the blade of a screwdriver into the notched hole in the baseplate. Twist the screwdriver clockwise to decrease the gap or anti-clockwise to increase it.

The feeler gauge blade(s) should be a neat sliding fit between the contacts (Fig.B:11). Tighten the securing screw and recheck the gap. If a dwell meter is available, connect it as detailed previously and (with distributor cap and rotor arm still removed) crank the engine using the starter motor. Note the reading of the dwell meter. If the reading is incorrect, adjust the gap accordingly and recheck. If it is within limits, refit the rotor arm and the cap then check the dwell angle again with the engine running at idle speed, as detailed previously.

Contact Set Replacement — Lucas 25D4 Distributor (Fig.B:11)

Remove the cap and rotor arm. Undo and remove the nut from the top of the terminal post and lift off the top insulating bush and both electrical leads (Fig.B:9). Remove the screw, spring and plain washer securing the contact set to the baseplate and lift out the contact set. Take great care to ensure that none of the

components are dropped down inside the distributor body.

If this happens the distributor base plate must be removed to retrieve them.

Before installing the new contact set, clean out the inside of the distributor thoroughly. Wipe the contact surface on the breaker cam, also the contact faces of the points on the new set as these are normally coated with preservative. Methylated spirits is ideal for this purpose. Do not use petrol as this is oil-based.

Position the new contact set on the baseplate and secure with the locking screw and washers. Tighten the screw only lightly at this stage. Locate the condenser and LT lead terminals onto the top insulating bush, then fit the bush over the terminal post so that the terminals make contact with the breaker arm spring. Refit the retaining nut and tighten securely. Ensure that the lead terminals are properly positioned so that they are insulated from the terminal post.

Lubricate the distributor cam, cam spindle and points pivot as detailed in ROUTINE MAINTENANCE under Distributor.

Check that the contact faces of the fixed and moving contacts are parallel to each other, aligning them correctly if necessary using thin-nosed pliers.

Points Adjustment — Lucas 45D4 Distributor (Fig.B:11)

The contact breaker points adjustment procedure is the same as detailed previously for the Lucas 25D4 distributor but turn the screwdriver clockwise to increase the gap and anti-clockwise to decrease it. Instead of a hole in the baseplate, there is a notch in the breaker plate and corresponding pips on the baseplate – these should be used as the screwdriver levering point when adjusting.

Contact Set Replacement — Lucas 45D4 Distributor

The contact breaker points on the 45D4 distributor are similar to those fitted to the 25D4 but the procedure for replacement is slightly different as the condenser and LT lead are connected to the set by means of a common terminal plate (Fig.B:10). To release the plate, press the breaker arm spring away from the insulating block and unclip the plate from the hooked end of the spring.

When reconnecting the terminal plate, slide it into the end of the spring, then position the spring on the insulated block between the two locating shoulders.

On models with sliding contact breaker points make sure that the locating fork is fitted over the base plate peg, fit the securing screw and washers and adjust the points gap as previously described.

Points Adjustment — Ducellier Distributor (Fig.B:11)

Adjustment of the Ducellier points is made easier by using BL tool No.18G 1308 although this tool is not essential.

Turn the crankshaft in its normal direction of rotation (clockwise) – see BASIC PROCEDURES until the contact breaker heel rests upon a cam peak and the contacts are fully open. Slacken the locking screw on the points assembly. The position of the lower contact plate can be adjusted either by the special tool, or by levering with a screwdriver (Fig.B:13). Set the gap to the figure specified in TECHNICAL DATA (the feeler blade should be a tight but free sliding fit Fig.B:11), and then tighten the locking screw.

With the vacuum line disconnected and the engine running at idle speed, check the dwell angle. Readjust the gap as necessary.

Check the dwell angle with the engine running at 2,000 rpm; the angle should be within the tolerance given in TECHNICAL DATA. If the angle is outside the specified limits, the distributor is faulty. With the engine running at 2,000 rpm and the vacuum pipe reconnected, the dwell angle should still be within tolerance. If not, adjust the dwell variation by rotating the serrated cam pivot post. Either use the special service tool or a

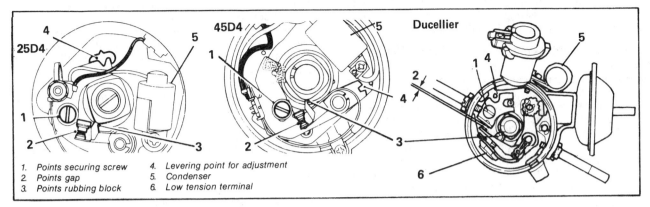

25D4

45D4

Ducellier

1. Points securing screw
2. Points gap
3. Points rubbing block
4. Levering point for adjustment
5. Condenser
6. Low tension terminal

Fig. B:11 Distributor contact points adjustment & replacement

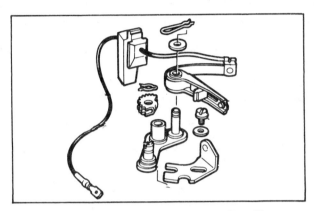

Fig. B:12 Details of contact set — Ducellier

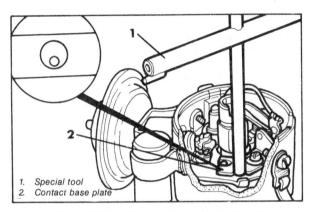

1. Special tool
2. Contact base plate

Fig. B:13 Ducellier points gap adjustment

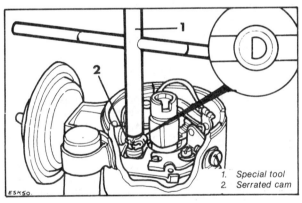

1. Special tool
2. Serrated cam

Fig. B:14 Ducellier dwell variation adjustment

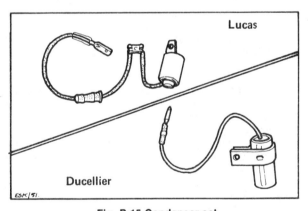

Lucas

Ducellier

Fig. B:15 Condenser set

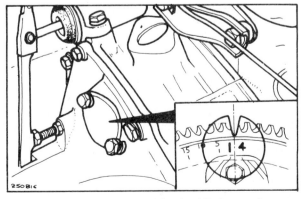

Fig. B:16 Location of flywheel timing marks (manual models)

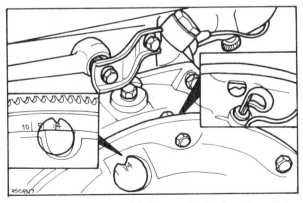

Fig. B:17 Location of timing marks (early automatic)

pair of fine-nosed pliers (Fig.B:14). After altering the dwell variation, recheck the dwell angle at idle. It may be necessary to check and reset the ignition timing afterwards.

Contact Set Replacement — Ducellier Distributor (Fig.B:12)

Remove the distributor cap and rotor arm, pull the low tension lead connector from the coil and pull the condenser lead from the bottom of the low tension lead rubber block. Pull the low tension lead rubber block distributor housing. Remove the spring clip from the moving contact pivot post. Remove the washer and lift the moving contact from the pivot. Undo the screw holding the fixed contact plate and withdraw the plate.

Fit the new assembly in the reverse order of removal and set the contact breaker points gap as previously described.

Condenser (Fig.B:15)

If the contact points are badly burned, pitted, or bluish in colour, this is an indication that the condenser is probably defective. This will show itself as a weak spark, probably resulting in misfiring and lack of power.

The condenser is best checked by substituting if for a known good one.

As the condenser is a relatively inexpensive item it should be replaced if in any way suspect.

To change the condenser on the Lucas distributor, remove the distributor cap and disconnect the low tension lead from the points spring clip, and from the wiring harness outside the distributor on the 45D4 distributor. Remove the screw securing the condenser to the base plate and remove the condenser. On 45D4 type distributors manoeuvre the low tension lead through the hole in the side of the distributor. Refit the distributor in the reverse order of removal making sure that the condenser earth lead is reconnected when replacing the the condenser securing screw.

To change the condenser on the Ducellier distributor, pull the low tension lead from the bottom of the rubber connector in the distributor housing. Remove the retaining screw securing the condenser to the distributor housing and withdraw the condenser. Refit the condenser in the reverse order of removal.

Distributor Advance Mechanism Check

The operation of the distributor advance mechanism may be checked using a strobe timing light aimed at the flywheel or crankshaft pulley timing marks.

As the throttle is gradually opened, the timing marks on the flywheel or crankshaft pulley (Figs.B:16, B:17, B:18 & B:19) should appear to move smoothly away from the fixed timing mark, against the direction of engine rotation. As the throttle is closed, the mark will move back to its original position. If the timing marks suddenly leap away from each other it indicates that the advance weights are binding. If the timing marks waver, this indicates that the advance weight springs are weak or broken or possibly that the distributor shaft bearings are worn.

The advance mechanism can be examined by removing the contact breaker baseplate. In many cases, cleaning and lubricating the mechanism can cure the problem.

Vacuum Advance Mechanism Check

A simple method of checking the operation of the vacuum advance mechanism is to detach the vacuum pipe from the carburettor and apply suction to it with the mouth while checking that the mechanism partially rotates the contact breaker baseplate. When the suction is released, the baseplate should snap smartly back to its original position.

If the baseplate seems sluggish on return, it could be that the vacuum advance unit is worn or that the return spring is weak or broken.

Distributor Cap, Rotor Arm, Coil, HT Leads

Thoroughly clean the distributor cap, inside and out with a clean cloth, paying particular attention to the spaces between the metal electrodes (Fig.B:20). Check that the electrodes are not excessively eroded and that there are no signs of 'tracking' (etched hairline zig-zag cracks) on the surface of the cap. Also check that the small carbon brush inside the centre of the cap is undamaged.

Similarly, clean the rotor arm and look for damage or excessive erosion of the electrode. Check that the rotor is a neat fit on the distributor shaft without excessive side play.

Clean the outside of the ignition coil tower and check for signs of damage or 'tracking' as detailed for the distributor cap.

Wipe all oil and dirt from the HT (High Tension) and LT (Low Tension) leads, and check them for signs of cracking, chafing or any other damage. Ensure that all ignition leads are securely and correctly connected and that the moisture caps at each end of the leads are firmly in place.

IGNITION TIMING . . . . [7]

The contact breaker points gap or dwell angle must be correctly set before attempting to check or adjust the ignition timing. Conversely, the ignition setting should be checked after cleaning, renewing or resetting the contact breaker points.

Static Check

During this procedure the crankshaft will have to be turned – see BASIC PROCEDURES under Turning the Crankshaft. Crankshaft rotation is clockwise, viewed from the radiator end of the engine.

It will make rotation of the crankshaft easier if the spark plugs are first removed from the engine.

On early models, remove the cover plate from the inspection hole in the clutch housing (rubber plug from the converter end cover on automatic transmission models) to allow observation of the timing scale on the flywheel or torque converter (Figs.B:16,B:17 & B:19). A mirror will be required to enable the timing marks to be seen.

It should be noted that later models have a timing scale situated on the timing cover adjacent to the crankshaft pulley (Fig.B:18).

Remove the distributor cap and connect a 12 volt test lamp between the distributor LT terminal and a good earthing point.

Rotate the crankshaft in its normal direction of rotation (clockwise) until the rotor arm is pointing approximately midway between the No.2 and No.1 segments in the distributor cap. The rotor arm rotation is anti-clockwise viewed from above.

With the ignition switched on, rotate the crankshaft slowly until the test lamp just lights, indicating that the points have opened. This gives the firing point for No.1 cylinder. If the ignition setting is correct, the appropriate mark on the timing scale will now be aligned with the reference pointer in the inspection hole or the crankshaft pulley notch – see TECHNICAL DATA for the specified ignition settings.

The setting can be checked by gently pressing the rotor arm in the opposite direction to its normal rotation, when the test lamp should go out until the arm is released again.

If the timing setting is incorrect, it should be adjusted as described below.

Adjustment

The 25D4 type distributor is fitted with an ignition timing adjusting device and if only a small correction is required, this can be achieved by rotating the knurled adjuster nut on the end of the vacuum unit spindle (Fig.B:21). One graduation on the vernier scale is equal to about 5° of crankshaft movement (fifty five clicks of the adjuster nut). Turn the adjuster nut in the direction of the cast 'A' to advance the timing, or in the direction of the cast 'R' to retard the timing.

If a large correction is required the complete distributor body must be turned to obtain the correct setting. This is the method which must be used with the 45D4 and Ducellier type

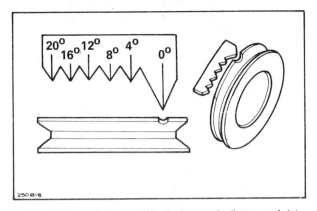

Fig. B:18 Crankshaft pulley timing scale (later models)

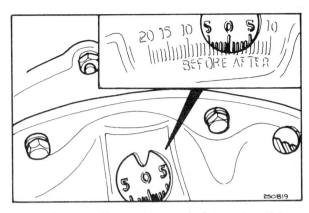

Fig. B:19 Location of timing scale (later automatic)

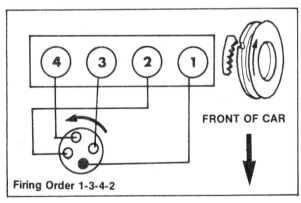

Fig. B:20 Checking distributor cap & electrodes

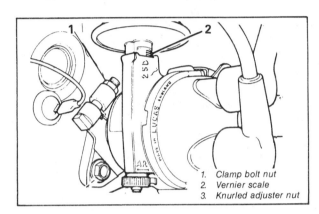

1. Clamp bolt nut
2. Vernier scale
3. Knurled adjuster nut

Fig. B:21 Ignition timing adjustment (25D4 shown)

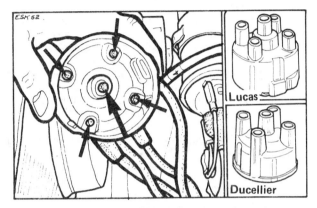

FRONT OF CAR

Firing Order 1-3-4-2

Fig. B:22 Firing order & distributor rotation

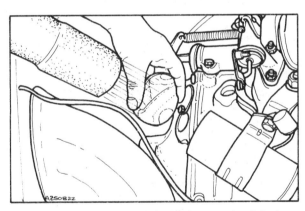

Fig. B:23 Using a strobe light & mirror to check timing

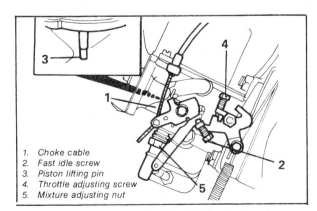

1. Choke cable
2. Fast idle screw
3. Piston lifting pin
4. Throttle adjusting screw
5. Mixture adjusting nut

Fig. B:24 Carburettor idle & CO adjustments
— HS2 carburettor

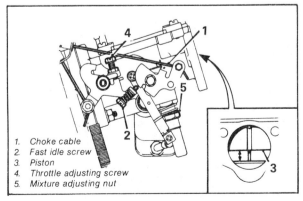

1. Choke cable
2. Fast idle screw
3. Piston
4. Throttle adjusting screw
5. Mixture adjusting nut

Fig. B:25 Carburettor idle & CO adjustments
— HS4 carburettor

distributors as they do not have an adjuster nut. In the case of the 25D4 unit, first turn the knurled adjuster nut until the vernier scale is in the central position.

Turn the crankshaft until the correct mark on the timing scale is aligned with the pointer in the inspection hole or the crankshaft pulley notch. Slacken the distributor clamp bolt nut (Fig.B:21) and rotate the distributor body anti-clockwise past the point where the test lamp illuminates, then carefully rotate it back clockwise until the lamp just goes out. Tighten the clamp bolt without disturbing the body setting. Finally, recheck the setting as described above.

Dynamic Check

If possible the ignition timing should be checked with the engine running using a stroboscopic timing light as this will ensure optimum engine performance and economy. With later models, it really is essential that the ignition be set dynamically. The timing light should be used in accordance with the equipment manufacturer's instructions.

There are several types of dynamic timing light available. The light may be powered by dry batteries, directly from the car battery or from the mains. A pick-up is connected to the No.1 HT lead (Fig.B:22). When a high voltage is sent through this lead (i.e. to fire the plug) a signal is picked up and causes the timing light to flash. The light is aimed at the timing marks and as this happens many times a second, the timing mark and scale are stroboscopically illuminated at the point of ignition (Fig.B:23). It will make observation of the timing mark and scale easier if the notch on the pulley (or flywheel mark) and the appropriate pointer on the timing cover scale (or clutch housing) are highlighted with white paint before carrying out the check.

Note that the distributor vacuum advance pipe should be removed during the check. The engine should be running at the specified check speed, given in TECHNICAL DATA. A tachometer (rev-counter) may be needed to achieve this if the car is not already equipped with one as part of the fascia instrumentation.

If adjustment is required, proceed as described previously for the static check. Rotate the distributor body clockwise to advace the setting, or anti-clockwise to retard it.

CARBURETTOR ADJUSTMENT .... [8]

NOTE: The carburettor should be the last part of the engine tune-up to be attempted as the settings will be affected by the tune of the rest of the engine. See TECHNICAL DATA for details of carburettor settings and FUEL SYSTEM for overhaul details.

Some later Mini models are equipped with special emission carburettors which have plastic seals fitted at the adjustment points to render them 'tamperproof'. The purpose of this is to prevent unqualified persons from making adjustments which could increase emissions above a pre-determined level, either through lack of understanding or unsuitable measuring equipment.

These seals must be destroyed in order to gain access to the idle speed screw and/or mixture adjusting nut. The idle speed screw is sealed by a small plastic push-fit plug, and the mixture adjusting nut by a two-piece snap-fit plastic cover. With these carburettors it is advised that no attempt be made to remove the sealing plugs or covers or alter the settings of the sealed adjusters.

On carburettors of the conventional type, without seals, the idle adjustment is carried out in the normal manner.

Idle Speed & CO Level (Figs.B:24 & B:25)

Prepare the engine for carburettor checking and adjustments as follows:

1. Check that all other engine functions (compression, spark plugs, valve clearances, dwell angle and ignition timing) are correctly adjusted within specification.
2. The carburettor oil damper level should be correct – see ROUTINE MAINTENANCE.

3. The engine should be at its normal temperature. Ensure this by either running the engine for at least 15 minutes or drive the car for at least 5 miles.
4. Remove the air cleaner assembly and ensure that all electrical components (lights, radio, heater etc) are turned off.
5. Check that the throttle moves freely without signs of sticking and returns fully when released.
6. Check that the choke control knob returns fully when it is pushed fully home. Also check that the knob has about 2 mm (1/16 in) free-play before it starts to pull on the carburettor lever.
7. Check that a small clearance exists between the end of the fast idle screw and the fast idle cam.
8. Raise the carburettor piston and check that it falls freely onto the carburettor bridge with a distinct metallic 'click', when released. The piston can be raised for this purpose either with the piston lifting pin at the side of the carburettor, or directly with a finger at the air intake. If the piston fails to fall freely, the piston should be cleaned and the jet on early models centred as detailed in FUEL SYSTEM.
9. On models with automatic transmission, move the selector into the 'N' position and fully apply the handbrake.
10. A tachometer (rev-counter) and CO meter should be fitted in accordance with the manufacturers intructions.
11. Temporarily increase the engine speed to approximately 2,500 rpm, and maintain this speed for about half a minute to clear the inlet manifold of excess fuel. Repeat this procedure at three minute intervals if the remainder of the adjustments cannot be completed within this period of time.
12. Check the idle speed and adjust if necessary by turning the throttle adjusting screw (Fig.B:24 & B:25). The idle speed specification is given in TECHNICAL DATA.
13. If the engine will not run smoothly at idle speed, it will be necessary to adjust the idle mixture level. Looking from above the carburettor, turn the adjusting nut clockwise to enrichen or anti-clockwise to weaken the mixture (Fig.B:24 & B:25). Turn the nut either way and check whether the engine speed rises or falls. Adjust, the screw until the engine speed is at its highest. Then turn the nut anti-clockwise until the engine speed just starts to fall. Reset the idle speed by adjusting the throttle stop screw.
14. The mixture strength can be checked by lifting the piston approximately 0,8 mm (1/8 in) with the lifting pin.
a) If the engine speed momentarily increases very slightly, the mixture is correct.
b) If the engine speed increases, and continues to do so, the mixture is too rich.
c) If the engine speed decreases or the engine stalls, the mixture strength is too weak.
15. When the mixture is correct, the exhaust note should be regular and even. If it is irregular, with a splashy type of misfire and colourless exhaust, the mixture is too weak. If there is a regular or rhythmical type of misfire in the exhaust beat, together with a blackish exhaust, then the mixture is too rich.
16. If an exhaust gas analyser is available connect it in accordance with the manufacturer's instructions and check that the reading is within the specified limits – see TECHNICAL DATA. If the reading falls outside the specified limits, reset the jet adjusting nut by the minimum amount necessary to bring the reading just within the limits. If more than half a turn of the adjusting nut is required, the carburettor should be removed for servicing.

Fast Idle Speed

To check the fast-idle speed, pull out the choke knob until the linkage is just about to move the mixture jet and lock the knob in this position. The fast idle speed is specified in TECHNICAL DATA. If adjustment is necessary, turn the fast-idle screw until the correct fast-idle speed is obtained. Push the choke knob fully in and check that a clearance exists between the end of the fast-idle screw and the fast-idle cam.

Engine

INTRODUCTION .... [1]

Due to the relatively inaccessible installation of the power unit in the Mini, few repair operations can be easily and successfully carried out while the unit is still in the car. The obvious exception is any work concerning the cylinder head, although the timing cover, timing chain and gears can also be replaced with the engine in-situ, but only with difficulty due to the side mounting position of the radiator.

Clutch replacement can be carried out once the right-hand end of the engine/transmission unit has been raised, and involves removal of the clutch cover and the flywheel assembly to gain access.

Once the power unit has been lifted out of the car it is a relatively simple job to separate the engine from the gearbox casing. The clutch cover, clutch and flywheel assembly and flywheel housing however, must first be removed.

The basic 'A' series engine in various capacities, ranging from the original 848 cc to 1275 cc, has undergone various detail changes over the years, but is essentially the same today as it was in 1959 when the Mini was introduced.

From April 1982 all Minis are fitted with an improved version of the basic engine known as the 'A plus' (which is also used in the Metro range), but the overhaul procedures are very similar and any detail differences are noted in the text.

TOOLS & EQUIPMENT .... [2]

Some operations require the use of special tools that you will probably not possess. Whenever possible, a practical alternative using easily obtainable tools is given. Sometimes however, a DIY solution is not possible and in such cases it will be necessary to either obtain the recommended special tool or have the work carried out by your Austin/Rover dealer or a local auto engineer. They will have the facilities and knowledge to carry out the job satisfactorily.

In addition to the normal tool kit as described in BASIC PROCEDURES the following items will be required for specific jobs when overhauling some of the engine components.

- Universal valve spring compressor – for valve removal.
- Electric drill and wire brushes – for cleaning carbon from the valves and combustion chambers.
- Valve grinding tool – for grinding in the valves.
- Valve seat cutting tools – for refacing the valve seats if badly burnt.
- Suitable lengths of tubing – for installation of oil seals.
- Piston ring compressor clamp – for fitting the pistons to their cylinder bores.
- Flywheel remover – for removing the clutch/flywheel.
- Dial test indicator gauge – for checking crankshaft end float and flywheel run-out etc.
- Internal and external micrometers – for checking the bearing diameters and cylinder bores.

On 1275 GT engines, special equipment is needed to separate the pistons from the conrods if new pistons are to be fitted. We recommend that this job should be carried out by the piston supplier, an auto engineer or an Austin/Rover dealer who will have the necessary special equipment.

Due to the confined underbonnet space, especially on non Clubman/1275 GT models, the power unit must be angled during the removal operation and a special lifting attachment is available to facilitate this. However a much cheaper alternative is to bend an Austin/Rover engine lifting 'eye' (Part number 12A 1968) through approximately 30°, and attach it to the central cylinder head stud at the front of the engine. As the engine is lifted it will hang naturally at the correct angle, enabling the edge of the transmission casing to the lifted over the subframe at the front, and ensuring that the differential housing does not become caught at the back of the engine compartment.

CYLINDER HEAD .... [3]

Removal

1. Disconnect the earth strap from the battery.
2. Remove the bonnet, after first marking the fitted position of the hinges to facilitate alignment when refitting.
3. Drain the cooling system by removing the cylinder block drain plug (if fitted) or disconnecting the bottom hose at the radiator.
Note:Early models may have a drain plug in the bottom of the radiator.
4. Disconnect the HT leads from the plugs, after suitably labelling them to ensure correct positioning on reassembly. Also disconnect the lead from the water temperature gauge sender unit at the thermostat housing.
5. Disconnect the breather hose (where fitted) from the rocker cover, and remove the air cleaner assembly.
6. Disconnect the distributor vacuum pipe, fuel hose and engine breather pipe (where fitted) from the carburettor. On automatic models, also disconnect the kick-down linkage rod from the carburettor.
7. Disconnect the throttle return spring from the carburettor. Remove the two nuts securing the carburettor to the inlet manifold, detach the carburettor from the studs and place it to one side. Where a cable abutment plate is fitted between the carburettor and the inlet manifold, the plate should be removed with the carburettor.
8. Remove the two nuts securing the heater water control valve, detach the valve and place it to one side with the hose and cable still attached.
9. Remove the nuts securing the radiator upper support bracket to the thermostat housing, and the bolts securing it to the radiator cowl, and remove the bracket (Fig.C:2).
10. Slacken the clip securing the small by-pass hose to the cylinder head connection, this is located on the underside of the

cylinder head, above the water pump (Fig.C:2).

11. Remove the two nuts, together with their cup washers and seals, retaining the rocker cover, and lift off the cover and gasket.

12. On 1275 GT models, remove the additional securing bolt 'A' and nut 'B' at the ends of the cylinder head (Fig.C:3).

13. Remove the cylinder head and rocker shaft pedestal nuts, releasing them evenly until the valve spring load on the rocker shaft assembly is released.

14. On models where the ignition coil mounting bracket is attached to one of the cylinder head studs, remove the coil and place to one side.

15. Lift off the rocker shaft assembly (Fig.C:4) then withdraw the pushrods, keeping them in their installed order.

16. Disconnect the radiator top hose from the thermostat housing.

17. Lift off the cylinder head, complete with the exhaust manifold. If difficulty is encountered in removing the head, tap each side of the head with a hide-faced mallet to free it.

18. Remove the cylinder head gasket and discard it.

Dismantling

1. Unscrew the spark plugs from the cylinder head.

2. Remove the inlet and exhaust manifolds, together with the hot air intake box (Fig.C:5).

3. Remove the water outlet housing and lift out the thermostat from the recess in the head (Fig.C:5).

4. Remove all carbon deposits from the combustion chambers, valve heads and valve ports using a suitable scraper, such as a screwdriver, and a wire brush. Take care to avoid damaging the machined surface of the cylinder head.

5. Similarly, clean all deposits from the cylinder block face and piston crowns, but leave a ring of carbon around the outside of each piston and the top of each bore. Ensure that carbon particles are not allowed to enter the oil or water ways in the block. This can be prevented by plugging the passages with small pieces of cloth while the carbon is being removed.

6. At each valve in turn, remove the spring clip from the collets (early models only). Compress the valve spring, using a suitable spring compressor tool (Fig.C:6) and extract the two split tapered collets from around the valve stem. Take care to ensure the valve stem is not damaged by the spring retainer when pressing it down. Release the compressor tool and remove the spring retainer, shroud (early models only) and valve spring (Fig.C:7). Remove the rubber oil seal (where fitted) from the valve stem and withdraw the valve from the cylinder head. Suitably mark the valve and associated components to identify their position in the cylinder head.

7. To dismantle the rocker assembly, remove the shaft locating screw from the No.2 rocker shaft bracket. Remove the split pins from each end of the rocker shaft, and slide the washers, springs, rocker arms and support brackets off the shaft (Figs.C:8 and C:9). Note the relative position of the components for reassembly. If necessary, the blanking plug can be unscrewed from the front end of the shaft to enable the oilways of the shaft to be cleaned out.

Inspection & Overhaul — Valves

Clean the valves and seatings and examine them for signs of pitting, burning or other damage.

A simple method of removing carbon from the valves is to insert the valve stem in the chuck of an electric drill and, using as slow a speed as possible, scrape the deposits off with a file or screwdriver. The valve can then be finished off with emery cloth.

Inspect the valve face and edges for pits, grooves, scores, or other damage. Valves in reasonable condition may be resurfaced on a valve grinding machine, but only sufficient metal to true up the face should be removed. If the thickness of the valve head is reduced to 0,5 mm (0.020 in) or less after grinding, then the valve should be discarded as it will run too hot in use.

Examine the valve stem for excessive or abnormal wear, and renew the valve if necessary.

If the valves are in poor condition, they should be renewed.

Valve Guides

Check the stem to guide clearance of each valve in turn in its respective guide. Raise the valve slightly from its seat and rock the head from side to side, as shown in Fig.C:10. If the movement across the seat is excessive, this indicates a worn guide and / or valve stem. Repeat the check using a new valve. If the movement is still excessive, the guide is worn and should be replaced.

Remove the old guide by drifting it downwards into the combustion chamber (A,Fig.C:11). Ensure the bore in the cylinder head is clean, then drive the new guide into position in the head so that its top end protrudes the specified distance above the machined face of the valve spring seating (B,Fig.C:11) – see TECHNICAL DATA. The inlet valve guide must be fitted with the largest chamfer at the top, and the exhaust guide with the counterbore at the bottom.

NOTE:The valve seats should be recut after fitting new valve guides to ensure the seat is concentric with the guide bore.

Valve Seats

Inspect the seating surface on each valve seat in the cylinder head for signs of pitting, burning or wear. Where necessary, the seat can be recut as long as the seat width and correction angle are maintained.

The seating surface must be recut when fitting a new valve, or after fitting a new valve guide.

Sets of hand operated valve seat cutters are readily available from most DIY motorist tool stockists and include a 'pilot' which is inserted in the valve guide to centralise the cutter.

Valve Grinding

Place the head, supported on wood blocks, upside down or on a work bench, then grind in each valve(including new valves) to its respective seat by hand, using a valve grinding tool as follows:

1. Smear a quantity of 'course' or 'fine' grinding paste (depending on the condition of the seat) around the valve seat, making sure that the paste does not contact the valve guide bore. Lubricate the valve stem with a smear of clean engine oil.

2. Attach the suction pad of a valve grinding tool to the head end of the valve and then insert the valve into its respective guide.

3. Grind in the valve by rotating the grinding tool handle between the palms of the hands, backwards and forwards (Fig.C:12) while applying slight pressure on the valve.

4. Periodically, lift out the valve, apply fresh grinding paste, then turn the handle by a few degrees and repeat the grinding procedure.

5. Continue grinding until a continuous matt grey ring is visible right round the contact area of both the valve and seat head. If any pitting is still visible within this grey ring the grinding process should be continued.

When a satisfactory result has been achieved, clean all traces of grinding paste from the seat and valve – this is very important.

6. Repeat the grinding procedure for the remaining valves.

NOTE:It may take at least 10 minutes of continuous grinding to produce a satisfactory seat between the valve and the seat.

Valve Springs

Inspect the valve springs, spring top caps and cotters for wear and damage and replace any suspect parts. Check the springs for squareness using a steel square rule on a flat surface. Revolve the spring slowly and observe the clearance between the top coil and the square (A,Fig.C:13). If the out of square is excessive, the spring should be replaced.

Replace the spring as a matter of course if the car has covered a high mileage, as springs eventually weaken (B,Fig.C:13). The free spring height is given in TECHNICAL DATA. If the height is less than specified the springs should be replaced as a set.

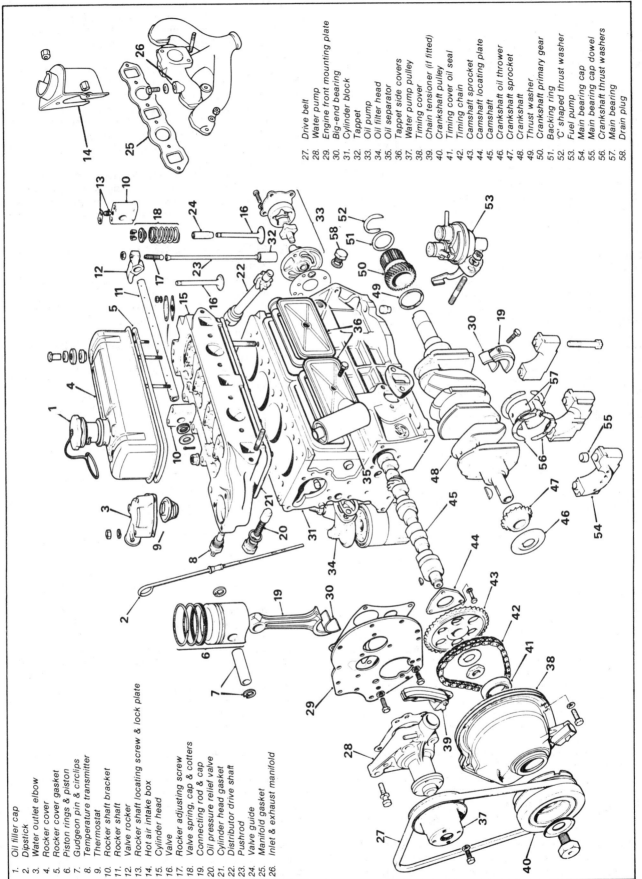

1. Oil filler cap
2. Dipstick
3. Water outlet elbow
4. Rocker cover
5. Rocker cover gasket
6. Piston rings & piston
7. Gudgeon pin & circlips
8. Temperature transmitter
9. Thermostat
10. Rocker shaft bracket
11. Rocker shaft
12. Valve rocker
13. Rocker shaft locating screw & lock plate
14. Hot air intake box
15. Cylinder head
16. Valve
17. Rocker adjusting screw
18. Valve spring, cap & cotters
19. Connecting rod & cap
20. Oil pressure relief valve
21. Cylinder head gasket
22. Distributor drive shaft
23. Pushrod
24. Valve guide
25. Manifold gasket
26. Inlet & exhaust manifold

27. Drive belt
28. Water pump
29. Engine front mounting plate
30. Big-end bearing
31. Cylinder block
32. Tappet
33. Oil pump
34. Oil filter head
35. Oil separator
36. Tappet side covers
37. Water pump pulley
38. Timing cover
39. Chain tensioner (if fitted)
40. Crankshaft pulley
41. Timing cover oil seal
42. Timing chain
43. Camshaft sprocket
44. Camshaft locating plate
45. Camshaft
46. Crankshaft oil thrower
47. Crankshaft sprocket
48. Crankshaft
49. Thrust washer
50. Crankshaft primary gear
51. Backing ring
52. 'C' shaped thrust washer
53. Fuel pump
54. Main bearing cap
55. Main bearing cap dowel
56. Crankshaft thrust washers
57. Main bearing
58. Drain plug

Fig. C:1 Exploded view of engine components — 998 cc engine

Ensure that the replacement springs are the correct rating for the engine.

Rocker Assembly

Inspect the bearing surface on the rocker shaft and the bushes in the rocker arms for wear. Two types of rocker arm are used; a pressed-steel type and a forged type. If the latter type is fitted, the arm can be rebushed if worn, but the pressed-steel type must be replaced as an assembly. The installation of the new bushes should be left to a specialist auto engineers as they must be burnish-reamed to size after fitting.

Inspect the contact pad at the valve end of each rocker arm for indications of scuffing or excessive or abnormal wear. If the pad is grooved, replace the arm. Do NOT attempt to true the surface by grinding. Check that all oil passages are clear. Replace any damaged or worn adjusting screws or locknuts.

Inspect each push rod for straightness. If bent, the push rod must be replaced – do NOT attempt to straighten it. Also inspect the ends of the rods for nicks, grooves or signs of excessive wear.

Reassembly

Reassemble the cylinder head in the reverse order of dismantling, with special attention to the following points:
1. Assemble the rocker shaft assembly in the reverse order of dismantling. The plugged end of the shaft must be located at the front of the engine. On 1275 GT models ensure that a shim is fitted behind the No.2 (tapped) rocker shaft bracket, and another in front of the No.3 rocker shaft bracket (Fig.C:9). Shims must also be fitted on either side of the No.1 and No.8 (end) rocker arms. On all other models, ensure that the double coil spring washers are fitted at either end of the rocker shaft (Fig.C:8).
2. Lubricate the valve guides and valves with clean engine oil before installing the valves in their original fitted position.
3. Fit new valve stem oil seals over the valve stem and onto the valve guide, where applicable. Lubricate the seal with oil to make fitting easier. On very early models with the valve spring shroud and collet spring, the oil seal is located on the valve stem at the bottom of the collet groove (Fig.C:7).
4. Ensure that the valve stem is not damaged by the spring retainer when compressing the valve spring, and that the split tapered collets engage correctly in the valve stem and spring retainer when the spring is released. Refit the spring clip to the collet, where applicable.
5. Use new gaskets when refitting the manifolds and water outlet housing.

Installation

Installation is a reversal of the removal procedure, with special attention to the following points.
1. Ensure that all joint surfaces, especially the mating surfaces of the cylinder head and block, are perfectly clean and free from old gasket material.
2. If the cylinder head was removed to replace a leaking or blown head gasket, check the mating faces on both the head and block for distortion before reassembly.
3. Use new gaskets where appropriate. A cylinder head gasket set should be obtained, as this will contain all the necessary gaskets.
4. Do not use grease or jointing compound of any type on the cylinder head gasket when fitting.
5. Ensure the head gasket is correctly positioned. The gasket is normally marked 'TOP' and 'FRONT'.
6. Ensure that the pushrods are installed in their original positions. Dip the ends of the rods in clean engine oil prior to installing them.
7. When fitting the rocker shaft assembly, ensure that the rocker arm adjusting screws locate correctly in the cupped end of their respective push rods. If any work has been carried out on the valves (e.g. recutting the valve seats) the rocker arm adjusting screws should be released slightly before installing the rocker shaft assembly. Lubricate the rocker assembly with

clean engine oil.
8. Tighten the cylinder head and rocker shaft pedestal nuts evenly, following the sequence shown in Fig.C:3. The cylinder head nuts and rocker pedestal nuts should be tightened to 50% of their specified torque and then to the full torque figure – see TECHNICAL DATA.
9. On models which have the ignition coil bracket attached to one of the cylinder head studs, do not forget to refit the bracket before fitting and tightening the head nuts.
10. On 1275 GT models, the additional securing bolt 'A' and nut 'B' must be tightened last. These should be tightened to their specified torque – see TECHNICAL DATA.
11. Check the valve clearances, as described in TUNE-UP and adjust if necessary.
12. When installation is complete, refill the cooling system, then run the engine and check for oil, water or exhaust leaks.
13. Finally, with the engine at normal operating temperature, check the ignition timing and engine idle settings as detailed in TUNE-UP.

TIMING COVER OIL SEAL .... [4]
Replacement

Tell-tale streaks of oil around the timing cover and pulley at the front of the engine are a sure sign that the crankshaft/cover seal is leaking. Replacing the seal is quite straightforward once the timing cover has been removed.
1. Disconect the battery earth lead.
2. Remove the radiator as described in COOLING SYSTEM.
3. Slacken the dynamo/alternator mounting bolts, release the fan belt tension and remove the fan belt – see ROUTINE MAINTENANCE.
4. Remove the front retaining bolts and detach the fan blades and drive pulley from the water pump hub.
5. Remove the starter motor by undoing the bolts attaching it to the flywheel housing. The purpose of this is to be able to wedge the flywheel and prevent the crankshaft turning when undoing and tightening the front pulley bolt.
6. Bend back the locking washer tab, wedge a screwdriver or other suitable tool between the flywheel ring gear teeth and the starter motor aperture, then undo the crankshaft pulley retaining bolt using a suitable socket or wrench (Fig.C:14).
7. Carefully lever the pulley off the crankshaft.
8. On 1275 GT models, disconnect the engine breather hose from the timing cover.
9. Remove the bolts securing the timing cover flange to the engine front plate and detach the timing cover and gasket (Fig.C:14).
10. Carefully lever the old oil seal from the cover housing and check that the housing is clean and undamaged.
11. Lubricate the bore and outside diameter of the new seal with grease and press the seal squarely into place in the cover. It should be possible to press the seal in by hand, but if necessary the seal can be driven home by bearing on the metal outside diameter of the seal (Fig.C:15). In this case the timing cover should be firmly supported around the seal location to avoid distorting the cover.
12. Ensure that the mating faces on both the timing cover and engine front plate are clean and free of old gasket material.
13. Locate a new gasket on the face on the engine front plate, using grease to hold it in position.
14. Ensure that the oil thrower on the crankshaft is fitted with the face marked 'F' away from the engine. On early type engines the thrower is unmarked and should be fitted with its concave face away from the engine.
15. Refit the timing cover and centralise the oil seal using the crankshaft pulley. It will avoid damage to the new seal if the sealing lips are first lubricated with oil or grease.
16. Fit and tighten the cover retaining bolts, then fit the crankshaft pulley bolt with a new lock washer. Tighten the pulley bolt to its specified torque – see TECHNICAL DATA and secure by bending over the lock washer tab.

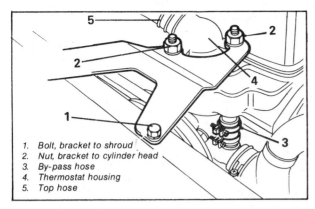

1. Bolt, bracket to shroud
2. Nut, bracket to cylinder head
3. By-pass hose
4. Thermostat housing
5. Top hose

Fig. C:2 Radiator bracket & by-pass hose removal

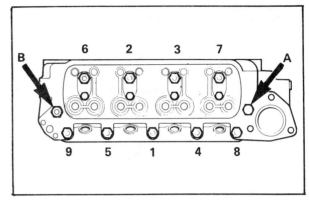

Fig. C:3 Cylinder head nut tightening sequence

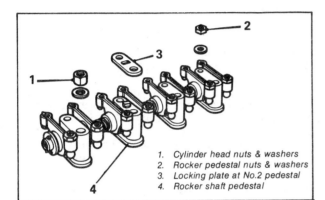

1. Cylinder head nuts & washers
2. Rocker pedestal nuts & washers
3. Locking plate at No.2 pedestal
4. Rocker shaft pedestal

Fig. C:4 Details of rocker shaft assembly

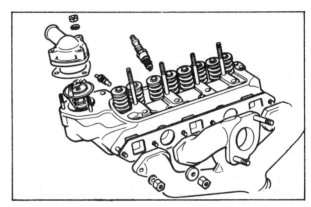

Fig. C:5 Removing thermostat & exhaust manifold

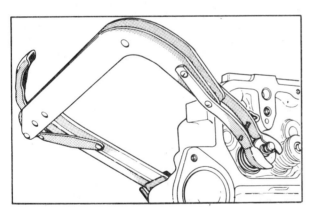

Fig. C:6 Using a valve spring compressor tool

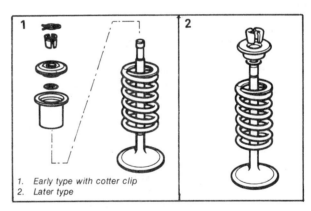

1. Early type with cotter clip
2. Later type

Fig. C:7 Exploded view of valve & spring

1. Split pins
2. Plain washers
3. Double coil spring washers
4. Shaft locating screw
5. Screw locating hole

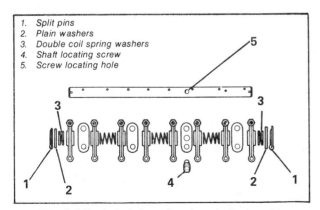

Fig. C:8 Exploded view of rocker shaft assembly

1. Split pins
2. Plain washers
3. Shim washers
4. Shaft locating screw
5. Screw locating hole

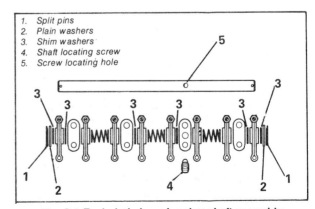

Fig. C:9 Exploded view of rocker shaft assembly — 1275 GT

17. Refit the fan belt and adjust the belt tension as described in ROUTINE MAINTENANCE.
18. Finally, refit the radiator and refill the cooling system – see COOLING SYSTEM.

TIMING CHAIN & TENSIONER .... [5]
Removal
1. Remove the timing cover as detailed in the previous section, and detach the oil thrower from the crankshaft.
2. Rotate the engine until the timing marks are aligned as shown in Fig.C:16.
3. Unscrew the camshaft sprocket retaining nut, making sure that the sprocket alignment marks are still in-line.
4. On late type 'A' Plus engines remove the timing chain tensioner (B,Fig.C:17), and then gently lever off the crankshaft and camshaft sprockets together with the timing chain. This is best done by easing each sprocket forward a fraction at a time with suitable small levers.

Installation
If moved, turn the crankshaft to bring the keyway to the top (TDC position) and the camshaft to bring the keyway to approximately the 2 o'clock position (Fig.C:16).

Engines not fitted with a blade type chain tensioner have two rubber tensioner rings fitted in slots around the camshaft sprocket. These should be replaced before installing the new chain.

Assemble the sprockets in the timing chain with their alignment marks opposite each other. Keeping the sprockets in this position fit the sprocket on the crankshaft then rotate the camshaft as necessary to align the key with the keyway in the sprocket. Push both gears as far onto the shafts as they will go, and secure the camshaft sprocket with the lock washer and nut.

Check the alignment of the sprockets by placing a straight-edge across the teeth of both gears and measuring the gap between the straight-edge and the crankshaft sprocket with feeler gauges (Fig.C:18). Adjust, if necessary, by altering the thickness of the shim pack behind the crankshaft sprocket. The key must be removed from the crankshaft keyway to allow the shims to be removed.

On late type engines refit the timing chain tensioner. Using a slight pressure, press the tensioner against the chain before tightening the bolts. Refit the oil thrower and timing cover as detailed in the previous section.

ENGINE MOUNTINGS .... [6]
Left-hand Side
To replace the left-hand engine mounting the radiator must first be removed as detailed in COOLING SYSTEM.

Support the engine assembly with a jack placed under the sump using a piece of wood to spread the load. Remove the two long through-bolts securing the mounting bracket to the gearbox casing (Fig.C:19). Remove the two nuts and bolts securing the mounting to the subframe.

On models with the one-piece radiator cowl, if the cowl was left in position on the car, remove the two bolts securing the bottom of the cowl to the engine mounting bracket and lift the cowl out of the engine compartment.

Remove the engine mounting bracket assembly, complete with the engine mounting. The mounting can now be unbolted from the bracket, and the new mounting fitted in its place.

Refit the mounting bracket assembly and radiator in the car, following the reverse sequence of removal.

Right-Hand Side
To replace the right-hand engine mounting, support the engine using a jack and a piece of wood to spread the load. Remove the two bolts securing the mounting to the subframe, then raise the engine further to allow access to the three bolts securing the mounting to the clutch housing. Fit the new mounting in the reverse order of removal (Fig.C:20).

OIL PUMP & RELIEF VALVE .... [7]
Oil Pump Removal
1. Remove the flywheel housing as detailed later in this chapter, or the torque convertor and convertor housing on automatic transmission models – see AUTOMATIC TRANMISSION.
2. On automatic models lever the main feed oil pipe from between the oil pump and the transmission casing (Fig.C:23).
3. Knock back the locking plate tabs and remove the pump retaining bolts or socket headed screws on automatic models and locking plate. The pump can now be withdrawn together with its gasket (Figs.C:21, C:22 & C:23).
4. On automatic and 1275 GT models, the pump is of the 'star-drive' type and the splined coupling will either be removed with the pump or left in the end of the camshaft. In the latter case, the coupling can be easily withdrawn if required. Other models have a 'pin-drive' type pump and no separate coupling is used.

Pump Overhaul
1. Remove the pump cover retaining screw, pull the pump cover from its two locating dowels and lift out the pump rotors.
2. Clean the pump components and fit the rotors to the pump body, ensuring that the outer rotor is fitted chamfer downwards.
3. Using a feeler gauge – see Fig.C:24, check the rotor lobe clearance 'A', outer rotor to body diametrical clearance 'B' and inner rotor to outer rotor endfloat 'C'. If any of these clearances are outside the specified limits given in TECHNICAL DATA, or if there is damage to components, replace the pump. If the clearances and component condition are satisfactory, reassemble the pump in the reverse order dismantling.

Installation
Install the pump in the reverse order of removing. Use a new gasket and locking plate. Ensure that the gasket is fitted correctly so that the holes align with the pump inlet and delivery ports. Tighten the bolts to the specified torque – see TECHNICAL DATA – before tapping over the locking plate tabs.

On models with the 'pin-drive' type pump, align the slot in the end of the pump drive shaft with the pin on the camshaft before positioning the pump on the cylinder block. Ensure the pin engages correctly with the camshaft.

On automatic and 1275 GT models, fit the coupling on the pump drive spindle before positioning the pump on the cylinder block. Again ensure that the coupling engages correctly with the camshaft.

Check that the oil seals on and in the oil feed pipe are in good condition, and renew if necessary (Fig.C:23).

Pressure Relief Valve
1. The oil pressure relief valve is located directly above the starter motor and adjacent to the distributor (A,Fig.C:25).
2. Remove the valve by unscrewing the valve cap and withdrawing the spring and valve from the engine block (B,Fig.C:25).
3. Check the condition of the valve, looking for pitting or other signs of damage which would prevent it from working properly. Check the valve spring for signs of breakage, also its free length – see TECHNICAL DATA. If the valve is worn or damaged, or if the valve spring length is less than that specified, the parts should be replaced.
NOTE:Do not attempt to stretch a valve spring.
4. Clean the valve seat inside the engine block, and lubricate the valve components before refitting them in the reverse order of removal. Tighten the cap to the correct torque – see TECHNICAL DATA.

ENGINE REMOVAL & INSTALLATION .... [8]
Removal — Manual Transmission (Fig.C:26)
1. Disconnect the earth strap from the battery.
2. Remove the bonnet, after first marking the fitted position of the hinges to facilitate alignment when refitting. On some

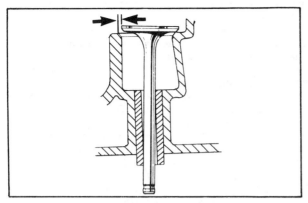

Fig. C:10 Checking valve stem & guide wear

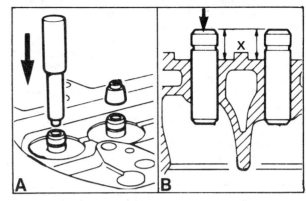

Fig. C:11 Replacing the valve guides

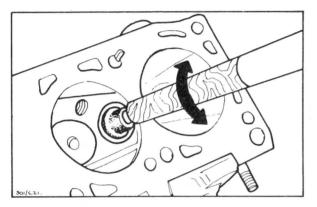

Fig. C:12 Method of grinding in valves

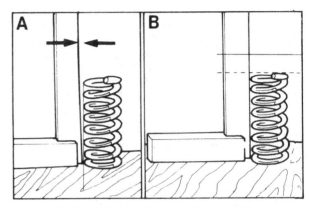

Fig. C:13 Checking valve spring condition

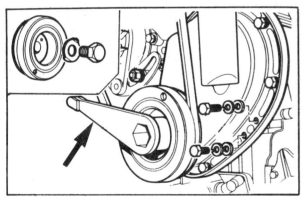

Fig. C:14 Removing the timing chain cover

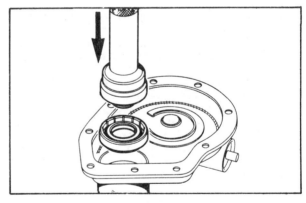

Fig. C:15 Method of fitting timing cover oil seal

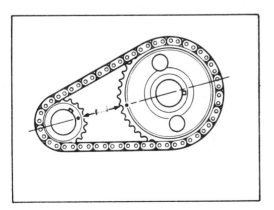

Fig. C:16 Timing sprocket marks aligned

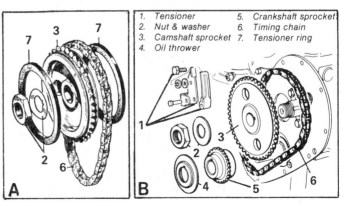

1. Tensioner
2. Nut & washer
3. Camshaft sprocket
4. Oil thrower
5. Crankshaft sprocket
6. Timing chain
7. Tensioner ring

Fig. C:17 Exploded view of timing chain & sprockets
(A) early type (B) late type

models it will also be necessary to remove the front grille to obtain access to some of the engine components. The grille is secured in position by self-tapping screws.

3. Where fitted, release the heater air intake tube from the front grille and wing valance and secure it clear of the engine. Some later models have a plastic air intake assembly at the right-hand front wing valance and this should be removed after releasing the flexible pipe from beneath the wing.

4. Where the horn is mounted on the bonnet locking platform, disconnect and remove the horn.

5. Drain the cooling system by removing the cylinder block drain plug (if fitted) or by disconnecting the bottom hose at the radiator – see COOLING SYSTEM.

6. Where required, remove the sump plug and drain the oil out of the engine/transmission unit.

7. Disconnect the heater hose from the adaptor on the radiator bottom hose. Detach the heater water control valve from the rear of the cylinder head and secure it clear of the engine with the hose and cable still attached.

8. Remove the air cleaner assembly. Disconnect the distributor vacuum pipe, fuel supply hose and engine breather pipe (where fitted) from the carburettor. Disconnect the throttle return spring from the carburettor. Remove the carburettor and position it to one side with the throttle and choke cables still attached. Where a cable abutment plate is fitted between the carburettor and the inlet manifold, the plate should be removed with the carburettor.

9. Remove the windscreen washer bottle and bracket, if necessary.

10. Disconnect the exhaust down pipe from the exhaust manifold flange.

11. On early 1275 GT models which have a brake servo unit, disconnect the servo unit vacuum pipe and detach the servo from the right-hand wing valance. It should not be necessary to disconnect the brake pipes as these can be carefully bent to position the unit out of the way once the pipe securing clip has been detached.

12. Disconnect the clutch operating lever return spring at the slave cylinder and detach the slave cylinder from the flywheel housing. It is not necessary to disconnect the hydraulic hose. Suspend the cylinder from a suitable point on the bulkhead.

13. Remove the ignition shield from the front of the engine, where fitted. Disconnect the HT leads from the spark plugs and ignition coil and remove the distributor cap and rotor arm. This avoids the possibility of damage to the cap or arm while the engine is being removed. Label the plug leads with their respective cylinder numbers to facilitate reassembly.

14. Disconnect the starter cable from the starter motor. Where the starter solenoid is mounted on the flywheel housing, detach the solenoid and place it in some suitable position out of the way.

15. Disconnect all other electrical connections from the engine (coil, temperature sender, oil pressure switch, etc). Label the leads if necessary to ensure correct connection on reassembly.

16. Disconnect the engine earth strap from the engine; normally attached to one of the clutch cover bolts at the flywheel housing, or the engine tie-rod on later models.

17. Disconnect the oil pressure gauge pipe, where fitted.

18. Disconnect the engine tie-rod from the rear of the cylinder block and swing it clear or remove it completely.

19. On models with a centrally situated speedometer, disconnect the speedo cable from the rear of the instrument. On other models, the cable must be disconnected from the transmission casing once the power unit has been partially raised.

20. On models with a mechanical fuel pump, disconnect the fuel supply pipe from the pump inlet. Plug the pipe end to prevent loss of fuel.

21. Raise and support the front of the car as described in BASIC PROCEDURES.

22. Detach the exhaust pipe support bracket from the final drive unit casing. Secure the pipe against the bulkhead and out of the way.

23. On early models without the remote control type gearchange, remove the hexagon plug and withdraw the anti-rattle spring and plunger from the gearbox extension. From inside the car, remove the two bolts securing the gear lever retaining plate and pull the lever out of the casing into the car.

24. On models with the early extension housing type remote control gear change – see CLUTCH & GEARBOX; from underneath the car, remove the four bolts securing the gear change extension to the transmission casing and separate the extension housing from the final drive unit casing. It will allow sufficient clearance if the extension housing is merely allowed to hang down under the car. Retain the halfmoon rubber plug fitted at the extension housing mating face.

25. On later models with rod type remote control gearchange, drift out the roll-pin securing the remote control extension rod to the selector shaft and separate the extension rod from the selector shaft. Remove the through-bolt securing the remote control steady rod fork to the final drive unit housing and release the steady rod.

26. On later models, detach the engine lower tie-rod from the rear of the gearbox casing and swing the tie-rod clear of the power unit.

27. On early models with the rubber coupling type drive shafts, disconnect the drive shafts from the final drive unit by removing the coupling 'U' bolts.

28. On later models with the offset sphere type inboard joint on the drive shaft, disconnect both drive shafts from the final drive unit housing as detailed in FRONT SUSPENSION. This involves removing the road wheel, disconnecting the track rod end from the steering arm and separating the upper swivel joint ball pin from the upper suspension arm. The drive shafts can then be withdrawn from the inboard joints, then reconnect the swivel joints and track rods and refit the road wheels.

29. Remove the stands and lower the car back onto its wheels.

30. Attach a suitable lift bracket to the engine. The most common type attaches to two of the cylinder head studs at the front edge of the engine and obviates the need for removing the rocker cover which some other types of lifting bracket require. As an alternative, an angled lifting 'eye' can be used – see Tools & Equipment at the beginning of this chapter.

31. Support the weight of the engine with lifting tackle – see BASIC PROCEDURES and then remove the bolts and nuts securing the engine mountings to the subframe at each end of the power unit.

32. Lift the engine sufficiently to ensure that the drive shafts are properly disengaged from the final drive unit housing.

33. At this point, if the speedometer cable has not already been disconnected, it can now be unscrewed from the drive housing on the transmission casing.

34. Carefully lift the engine/transmission unit, complete with the radiator assembly, out of the engine compartment. Where a two position lifting bracket is being used, the straight lift position should now be used instead of the angled-lift one which should have been used to clear the final drive unit of the bulkhead.

Installation

Installation is basically a reversal of the removal procedure, but special attention should be paid to the following points:

1. Where appropriate, reconnect the speedo cable to the drive housing on the transmission casing while the transmission unit is only partially lowered into the engine compartment. If this operation is left till later it will be much more difficult.

2. On models without the remote control type gearchange, pull the gear lever up into the car before the engine/transmission unit is lowered into position.

3. On models with the offset sphere type inboard drive shaft joints, ensure the drive shafts are positioned clear of the inboard joints while lowering the engine/transmission unit into position.

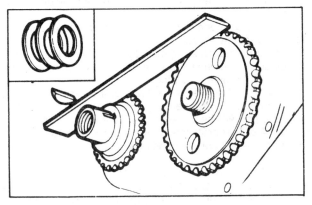

Fig. C:18 Checking/adjusting timing sprocket alignment

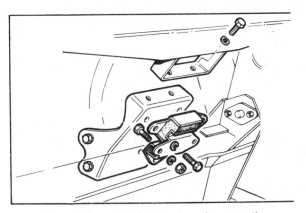

Fig. C:19 Removing left-hand engine mounting

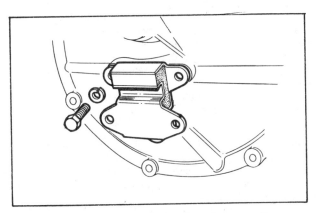

Fig. C:20 Removing right-hand engine mounting

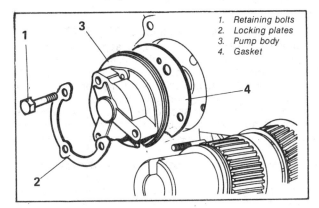

1. Retaining bolts
2. Locking plates
3. Pump body
4. Gasket

Fig. C:21 Removing oil pump assembly —
848, 998 & 1098

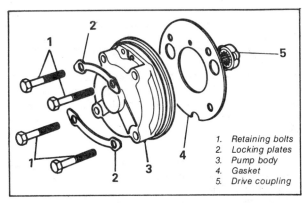

1. Retaining bolts
2. Locking plates
3. Pump body
4. Gasket
5. Drive coupling

Fig. C:22 Removing oil pump assembly — 1275 GT

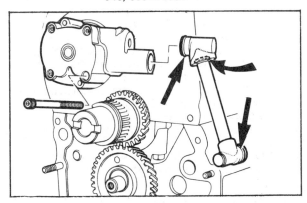

Fig. C:23 Removing oil pump — automatic

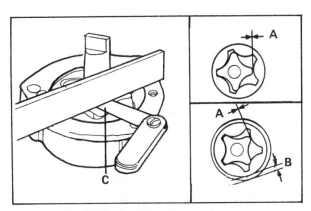

Fig. C:24 Checking oil pump for wear

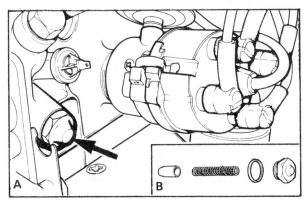

Fig. C:25 Oil pressure relief valve & components

When assembling the drive shafts to the inboard joints the circlip in the end of the shaft must be compressed and the drive shaft pushed smartly into the joint to lock it in position. Reconnect the upper swivel joint and track rod end and refit the road wheel.

4. On models with the earlier rubber coupling type drive shafts, keep the sliding joints pushed well on to the drive shaft splines while the rubber couplings are moved into position at the final drive unit flanges.

5. On models with the early type remote control gearchange, ensure the half-moon rubber plug is correctly located between the extension housing and the transmission casing when reconnecting the extension housing. Also ensure that the gearchange rod on the transmission engages correctly with the primary shaft in the extension housing.

6. When installation is complete, refill the cooling system, and engine/transmission unit where required. Start the engine and check for oil, water, fuel or exhaust leaks.

7. Finally, check the ignition and idle settings and adjust if necessary.

Removal — Automatic Transmission (Fig.C:27)

The subsequent items in this section apply specifically to models fitted with automatic transmission. In most cases, in the interests of brevity and simplicity, only the variations in procedure from the equivalent operations for the manual transmission models are given, and back-reference to the relevant previous headings should be made where indicated.

The engine and transmission unit is removed in a similar manner to that described previously for manual transmission models.

In this case, however, obviously no clutch slave cylinder will be fitted.

The kickdown linkage control rod must be disconnected from the carburettor throttle lever before the carburettor can be removed (Fig.C:27).

Instead of the manual gearchange assembly, the gear selector cable must be disconnected at the transmission. To do this, first remove the cover plate (or rubber sleeve on early models) from the bell-crank arm. Slacken the locknut at the selector cable fork and remove the fork, locknut, both rubber ferrules and the sleeve (where fitted) from the cable. Remove the cable front adjusting nut from the outer cable and pull the cable clear of the bracket or abutment on the transmission (Fig.C:28).

The driveshafts in this case have a universal-jointed flange at the inboard end and this locates on studs in the final drive unit flange. The flanges are secured by four self-locking nuts (4,Fig.C:27).

When lifting out the power unit, raise it only sufficiently at first to release the drive shafts from the studs on the drive flanges.

Installation

When installing the power unit, lower it into the engine compartment to a position where the drive shaft flanges can be engaged on the studs on the final drive unit flanges and screw the nuts on loosely. Tighten the nuts fully once the power unit is lowered into position.

After reconnecting the gear selector cable, it must be adjusted as detailed in AUTOMATIC TRANSMISSION.

Also, after reconnecting the kickdown linkage control rod, the linkage setting should be checked and adjusted if necessary.

FLYWHEEL HOUSING . . . . [9]

The flywheel housing can be detached from the engine/transmission unit while the power unit is still installed in the car, but is more easily performed once the engine/transmission unit has been removed.

Replacement procedures for the 1st motion shaft bearing and idler gear bearing are detailed in CLUTCH & GEARBOX.

Removal

1. Detach the flywheel and clutch assembly, following the relevant steps given under the appropriate heading in CLUTCH & GEARBOX. The engine oil must also be drained out of the power unit.

2. On 1275 GT models, unbolt the engine breather from the top of the flywheel housing.

3. Unbolt the clutch slave cylinder from the flywheel housing and place to one side out of the way. It is not necessary to disconnect the hydraulic pipe.

4. Fit tape or foil over the splines of the crankshaft primary gear to protect the flywheel housing oil seal as the housing is removed. This will be unnecessary if the seal is to be renewed anyway. A proper protector sleeve is available as a special tool, but the makeshift solution above will do the same job if some care is used.

5. Knock back the locking plate tabs and remove the flywheel housing securing bolts and nuts (Fig.C:29). Note the respective positions of the nuts and bolts to ensure correct fitment on reassembly.

6. Withdraw the flywheel housing from the engine/transmission unit. It may be necessary to tap the housing free as it is located by two dowels on the transmission casing. Remove the housing gasket.

7. The needle bearing of the idler gear shaft and the outer race of the gearbox input shaft roller bearing will come away with the flywheel housing.

8. Withdraw the 'C' shaped thrust washer locating the primary gear on the crankshaft, and slide off the backing ring, primary gear and inner thrust washer (Fig.C:30).

Inspection & Overhaul — Primary Gear Oil Seal

The primary gear oil seal in the flywheel housing should be renewed if it shows any signs of wear, damage or oil leakage. If the engine has covered a high mileage, a new seal should be fitted as a matter of course.

Lever the oil seal out of its location in the housing, taking great care to avoid damaging the housing bore.

Lubricate the new seal with grease or engine oil and press it into position in the housing. The proper seal installer tool is shown in Fig.C:31, but it should be possible to press the seal into position by hand or by tapping it carefully on its outer edge. In this latter case, support the underside of the housing beneath the seal aperture while installing the seal.

It should be noted that the flywheel housing oil seal can be renewed while the housing is still in position on the engine/transmission unit. The procedure for this operation is fully detailed under the appropriate heading in CLUTCH & GEARBOX.

Installation

1. Ensure that the mating faces on the flywheel housing, cylinder block and transmission casing are clean and free from old gasket material.

2. If the idler gear or idler gear thrust washers have been changed, it will be necessary to check the idler gear endfloat and adjust if necessary as detailed in CLUTCH & GEARBOX.

3. If the crankshaft primary gear or thrust washers have been changed, the gear endfloat should be checked and adjusted, if needed, as detailed in CLUTCH & GEARBOX. It should be noted that the primary gear endfloat can be checked with the flywheel housing in or out of position on the engine/transmission unit – see CLUTCH & GEARBOX Fig.G:28. If the flywheel housing is in position and the primary end float requires adjustment the flywheel housing oil seal must be removed together with the primary gear to change the front thrust washer. A new housing oil seal must be fitted on reassembly.

4. Fit the primary gear front thrust washer onto the crankshaft with its chamfered side against the crankshaft register (Fig.C:30). Fit the primary gear and backing washer and secure in position with the 'C' shaped thrust washer.

5. Fit the protector sleeve or tape over the primary gear splines to protect the flywheel housing oil seal.

6. Two pilot bars, made up and screwed into the two bottom

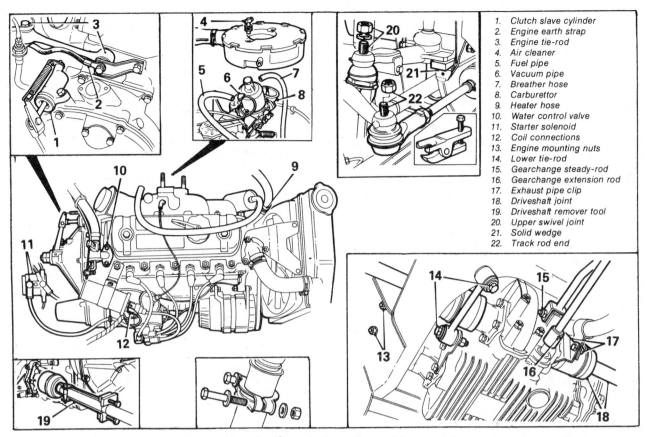

1. Clutch slave cylinder
2. Engine earth strap
3. Engine tie-rod
4. Air cleaner
5. Fuel pipe
6. Vacuum pipe
7. Breather hose
8. Carburettor
9. Heater hose
10. Water control valve
11. Starter solenoid
12. Coil connections
13. Engine mounting nuts
14. Lower tie-rod
15. Gearchange steady-rod
16. Gearchange extension rod
17. Exhaust pipe clip
18. Driveshaft joint
19. Driveshaft remover tool
20. Upper swivel joint
21. Solid wedge
22. Track rod end

Fig. C:26 Remove engine transmission unit — rod type gearchange

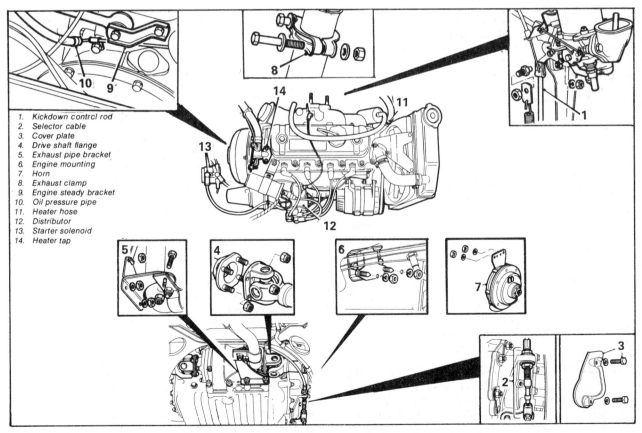

1. Kickdown control rod
2. Selector cable
3. Cover plate
4. Drive shaft flange
5. Exhaust pipe bracket
6. Engine mounting
7. Horn
8. Exhaust clamp
9. Engine steady bracket
10. Oil pressure pipe
11. Heater hose
12. Distributor
13. Starter solenoid
14. Heater tap

Fig. C:27 Removing engine & transmission unit — automatic

tapped holes in cylinder block, will help locate the flywheel housing in position and take the weight off the primary gear oil seal.

7. Pack the transmission input shaft bearing rollers with high melting point grease to help prevent them tilting as the flywheel housing is refitted. Also ensure that the idler gear thrust washer is correctly in position on the end of the idle gear shaft (5,Fig.C:30).

8. Position a new housing gasket on the engine/transmission face and ensure that both locating dowels are fully in their holes.

9. Lubricate the primary gear oil seal and fit the flywheel housing into position. Tap it fully home onto the locating dowels, then remove the two pilot bars if used.

10. Secure the housing in position with the retaining nuts and bolts, using new locking plates. Ensure that the bolts are refitted in their original locations – this is most important as the oil gallery in the cylinder block may be damaged if a long bolt is fitted in the right-hand upper position.

11. Tighten the flywheel housing nuts and bolts to their specified torque – see TECHNICAL DATA – then secure with the locking plate tabs.

12. On 1275 GT models, refit the engine breather to the flywheel housing.

13. Refit the clutch/flywheel assembly as detailed in CLUTCH & GEARBOX.

14. Finally, refill the engine/transmission unit with oil as detailed in ROUTINE MAINTENANCE.

TRANSMISSION UNIT — MANUAL .... [10]
Separating Engine From Gearbox (Fig.C:32)
With the engine/transmission unit removed from the car, remove the clutch cover, the flywheel and clutch assembly and the flywheel housing, following the relevant steps given under the appropriate headings previously. It should be noted that the engine oil must be drained from the power unit during removal.

If required, the crankshaft primary gear can be removed from the end of the crankshaft, together with its thrust washers.

Remove the bolts securing the radiator to the left-hand engine mounting bracket and detach the radiator assembly.

If required, remove the oil filter cartridge or filter bowl from the filter head.

Remove all the nuts, bolts and spring washers securing the engine to the transmission casing, then lift the engine to separate it from the transmission unit.

Remove the gaskets and oil way sealing ring from the joint faces, and the oil seal from the front main bearing cap.

Installation
Installation is basically a reversal of the removal procedure.

Ensure that the joint faces on both the crankcase and transmission casing are clean and free from old gasket material before fitting new gaskets on the transmission casing. Fit a new oil feed 'O' ring seal (8,Fig.C:32) correctly in place at the oil feed hole on the transmission casing flange – this is most important.

Lubricate the new oil sealing strip before fitting it in position at the engine front main bearing.

Lower the engine onto the transmission unit and fit and tighten the securing bolts and nuts.

If a replacement transmission unit is being fitted, it will be necessary to check the idler gear endfloat before finally assembling the flywheel housing to the unit. The primary gear assembly must be removed from the crankshaft for this operation – see CLUTCH & GEARBOX.

TRANSMISSION UNIT — AUTOMATIC ..... [11]
Once the engine/transmission unit has been removed from the car, remove the oil filter assembly and the starter motor.

Remove the torque convertor and torque convertor housing – see AUTOMATIC TRANSMISSION.

Remove all the nuts, bolts and spring washers securing the engine to the transmission casing, then lift the engine to separate it from the transmission unit.

Remove the gaskets, oil way sealing ring, 'O' ring seals for the oil pump pipe to gearbox casing and front main bearing cap seal.

Installation
Installation is basically a reversal of the removal procedure.

Ensure that the joint faces on both the crankcase and transmission casing are clean and free from old gasket material before fitting new gaskets on the tranmission casing. Fit a new oil way sealing ring and place correctly at the feed hole in the transmission casing flange. Fit new 'O' rings to the oil pump feed pipe, lubricate the new sealing strip before fitting it in position at the engine front main bearing cap.

Lower the engine onto the transmission unit and fit and tighten the securing bolts and nuts.

ENGINE OVERHAUL .... [12]
Make sure that the engine oil has been drained beforehand, then remove the clutch and flywheel housing, or the torque converter and converter housing on automatic models as described previously. Note that a small quantity of engine oil may drain from the bottom of the gearbox when the clutch or converter housing is removed.

Unscrew and remove all the bolts around the gearbox flange attaching it to the engine block. Carefully lift the engine off the gearbox and place it on its side on wood blocks for protection.

Crankshaft, Conrods & Pistons
1. Remove the cylinder head following the relevant steps given under the appropriate section previously.

2. Turn the cylinder block so that it is resting on its side, on wood blocks.

3. On all engines, except 1275 GT, remove the side covers and withdraw the cam followers from the engine block before turning the block on its side. Place the followers in removal order.

4. For each piston and connecting rod in turn:
a) Turn the crankshaft as necessary to bring the connecting rod to the bottom of its travel.
b) Check that the rod and big-end bearing cap are suitably marked with their respective cylinder numbers.
c) On 1275 GT engines, release the multi-sided nuts securing the big-end cap (B,Fig.C:33). Tap the ends of the studs with the handle of a hammer, or similar, to release the bearing cap and detach the cap together with its bearing shell.
d) On all other engines, unscrew the cap retaining bolts two or three turns (A,Fig.C:33). Tap the bolts to release the big-end bearing cap, then completely remove the bolts and locking plate and detach the cap together with its bearing shell.
e) Push the piston and connecting rod assembly up the cylinder bore and carefully withdraw it from the top of the block. *NOTE:In most cases, the bore will have a wear ridge and the pistons or rings may foul on this ridge at the top of the bore and so prevent the piston from being removed. If this is the case, ease the piston or rings past the ridge using strips of thin feeler gauge inserted down the bore.*
f) If required, remove the bearing shells from the cap and rod. Suitably identify the shells with their respective locations if they are to be re-used.

5. Remove the timing cover and the timing chain and gears as detailed previously.

6. Remove the generator/alternator adjusting link bracket.

7. Remove the three bolts securing the camshaft locating plate and lift off the plate. Remove the retaining screws and detach the engine mounting plate from the front face of the cylinder block (29,Fig.C:1).

8. Withdraw the 'C' shaped thrust washer locating the crankshaft primary gear and slide the backing ring, primary gear and front thrust washer off the rear end of the crankshaft.

9. Check that the main bearing caps are suitably marked with

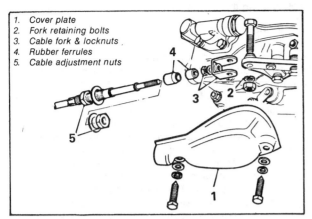

1. Cover plate
2. Fork retaining bolts
3. Cable fork & locknuts
4. Rubber ferrules
5. Cable adjustment nuts

Fig. C:28 Selector cable components — automatic

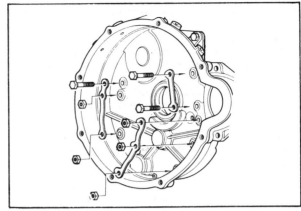

Fig. C:29 Removing flywheel housing

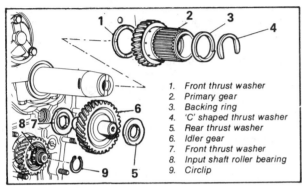

1. Front thrust washer
2. Primary gear
3. Backing ring
4. 'C' shaped thrust washer
5. Rear thrust washer
6. Idler gear
7. Front thrust washer
8. Input shaft roller bearing
9. Circlip

Fig. C:30 Exploded view of primary gear train

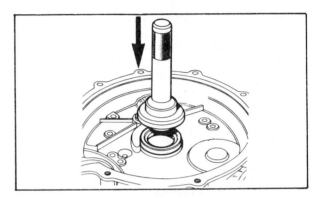

Fig. C:31 Installing flywheel housing oil seal

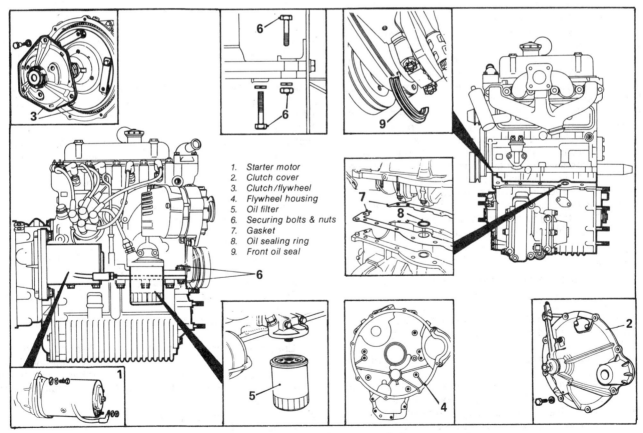

1. Starter motor
2. Clutch cover
3. Clutch/flywheel
4. Flywheel housing
5. Oil filter
6. Securing bolts & nuts
7. Gasket
8. Oil sealing ring
9. Front oil seal

Fig. C:32 Separating engine from transmission — manual

their respective locations.

10. Release the cap retaining bolts and detach the three main bearing caps together with their bearing shells. The bottom halves of the crankshaft thrust washers will be removed with the centre main bearing cap (Fig.C:36).

11. Carefully lift the crankshaft out of the crankcase.

12. Remove the remaining halves of the thrust washers from each side of the centre main bearing.

13. Remove the upper bearing shells from their locations in the crankcase. Identify the bearing shells and thrust washers if they are to be re-used.

Inspection and Overhaul

NOTE:The components of the cylinder head assembly have already been dealt with under Cylinder Head.

Pistons

Three different methods of retaining the piston pin are used depending on application,and each requires a different dismantling technique. In each case, ensure that the cylinder number and the relationship of the piston to the connecting rod is suitably marked before dismantling as big-end offset may be positioned either at the front or at the rear of the assembly, depending on the location of the rod in the engine.

On 848 cc models the piston pin is clamped in the connecting rod small end by a clamp bolt. To remove the piston pin, hold the pin in a vice between two plugs to avoid damaging the piston, and unscrew the clamp bolt. Push out the piston pin and separate the piston from the connecting rod.

998 cc and 1098 cc models have fully-floating piston pins which are located in the piston by a circlip at each end (Fig.C:34). Mark the piston and pin before dismantling to ensure that the pin is refitted in the same side of the piston from which it was removed. Remove the circlips and press out the piston pin by hand. It may be necessary to expand the piston by immersing it in hot water to enable the pin to be removed.

On 1275 GT models, the piston pin is a press fit in the connecting rod small end, and only the interference fit of the pin in the small end retains it in position. The piston pin can sometimes be driven out using a suitable drift, but there is a real danger that the piston may be damaged or distorted during this operation. It is best to have the pin pressed out and refitted by an Austin/Rover dealer or auto engineer who will have the proper tools to carry out this job. As before, the piston and pin should be suitably marked before dismantling.

The 848 cc, 998 cc and 1098 cc pistons have the piston pin bore offset in relation to the centre-line of the piston. When installed in the engine, the offset must be towards the camshaft side and therefore it is essential that the pistons are correctly fitted to their respective connecting rods. The word 'FRONT' or arrow head symbol on the piston crown must be towards the front of the engine, and the number stamped on the connecting rod and cap facing towards the camshaft side of the engine.

The 1275 GT pistons do not have an offset piston pin bore but the piston will normally still have the front side marked for ease of fitment.

Piston Rings

It is recommended that new piston rings be fitted as a matter of course when overhauling the engine.

Where new rings are being installed in a used cylinder, the glaze must first be removed from the cylinder wall. A proper glaze breaker tool should ideally be used for this purpose, but in its absence fine emery cloth can be used instead. In this latter case, ensure that all traces of abrasive are cleaned off the cylinder walls when the job is completed.

Before fitting the rings to the pistons, check the end-gap of each piston in its respective cylinder bore with the feeler gauges (Fig.C:35). Use an inverted piston to position the ring squarely in the bore. If the gap is outside the specified limits, try another ring set.

Also check the fit of each ring in its respective piston groove.

The ring should seat easily in the groove and be able to rotate freely around the circumference of the groove without binding.

Connecting Rods

In the 848 cc, 998 cc and 1098 cc engine, the connecting rod big-end is split at 45°, but the big-end bosses on alternate rods are offset to different sides of the assembly in relation to the rod centre line. The odd pair of rods have the offset to the rear and the even pair have it to the front (Fig.C:37). The connecting rod assemblies for No.1 and No.3 cylinders are identical and are interchangeable when new, as are those for the No.2 and No.4 cylinders. However, when refitting used parts it is essential that they should be fitted in their original positions.

These rods, once installed in the engine, must be located with the big-end split angled upwards towards the camshaft side of the engine (A,Fig.C:33). The stamped number on the rod and cap, where present, should also face towards the camshaft. With the clamped-type rod, the small end clamp bolt should also be on the camshaft side of the assembly.

In the 1275 GT engine, the connecting rod bosses are also offset, but, as the big-end is split horizontally, all the rods are similar and interchangeable. Where the rods are numbered, this is normally marked on the camshaft side of the assembly (B,Fig.C:33).

The connecting rods used in the 1098 cc engine differ from the others in that they have a bronze bush fitted at the small end, and this can be replaced if worn or damaged (Fig.C:34). All the others have a plain small end. The old bush must be pressed out and a new one pressed in, then the bush reamed to size. This job is best left to a specialist who will have the proper equipment to carry out the work.

Crankshaft

Inspect each bearing journal for signs of scratches, grooves or other damage.

The diameter of each journal should be measured in at least four places with an accurate micrometer to determine taper, ovality or undersize. If wear is excessive or if any of the journal surfaces are severely marked, the crankshaft should be reground or replaced. If any journals will not clean up within the minimum specified regrind diameter, the crankshaft must be replaced.

Main & Big-end Bearings & Thrust Washers

The bearing surface of each bearing shell should be inspected carefully for signs of chips, pitting or excessive wear. The bearing base may be visible, but this does not necessarily mean that the bearing is excessively worn. It is not necessary to fit new bearing shells in this case unless the bearing clearance is outside the specified limits.

Check the clearance of bearings which appear to be satisfactory, as described below.

Inspect the thrust washer halves in a similar manner to the bearing shells and replace if worn or damaged.

Bearing Clearances

The procedure given below is for checking the main bearing clearances, but the big-end bearings can be checked in a similar manner using Plastigauge.

NOTE:Plastigauge is the trade name for an accurately calibrated plastic filament measuring strip. It is available from Plastigauge Manufacturing Co. Hewarts Lane, Bognor Regis, Sussex. PO21 3DR.

1. Ensure that the crankshaft surface, bearing shells and bearing caps are perfectly clean and free from oil and dirt.

2. Fit the upper halves of the bearing shells into their locations in the crankcase, then carefully lower the crankshaft into place in the crankcase.

3. Fit the lower half of the shell into the cap of the bearing being measured.

4. Place a piece of Plastigauge across the full width of the crankshaft journal and about 6 mm ¼ in off-centre (Fig.C:38).

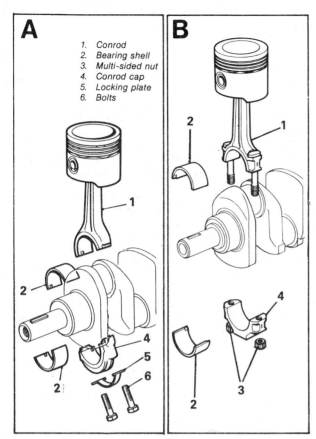

A

1. Conrod
2. Bearing shell
3. Multi-sided nut
4. Conrod cap
5. Locking plate
6. Bolts

B

Fig. C:33 Conrod, piston & big-end assembly

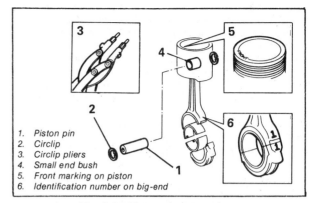

1. Piston pin
2. Circlip
3. Circlip pliers
4. Small end bush
5. Front marking on piston
6. Identification number on big-end

Fig. C:34 Piston pin removal

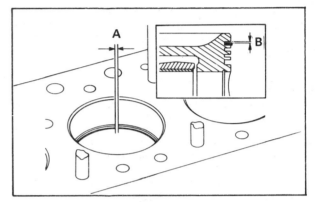

Fig. C:35 Checking piston ring gap (A) & groove clearance (B)

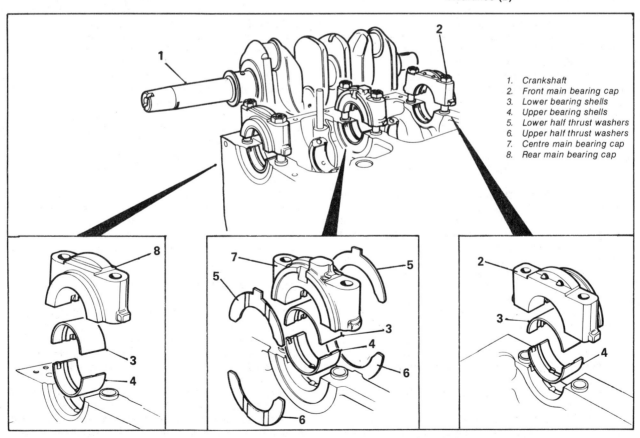

1. Crankshaft
2. Front main bearing cap
3. Lower bearing shells
4. Upper bearing shells
5. Lower half thrust washers
6. Upper half thrust washers
7. Centre main bearing cap
8. Rear main bearing cap

Fig. C:36 Details of crankshaft main bearing installation

5. Plastigauge is available in five different diameters, but in most cases the small diameter pack, size A, for the range between 0,025-0,175 mm (0.001-0.007 in) will suffice.

6. Install the main bearing cap and tighten the cap bolts to their normal specified torque – see TECHNICAL DATA. None of the remaining bearing caps must be fitted during this procedure. Each bearing must be measured individually.

7. Release the cap bolts and remove the bearing cap. Note that the crankshaft must not be moved while the Plastigauge is in position.

8. Measure the width of the compressed plastic filament, using the scale provided on the Plastigauge pack (Fig.C:39). The widest point will give the minimum clearance and the narrowest point the maximum clearance. The difference between the two readings will therefore give the taper on the journal.

9. To check the journal for ovality, clean all traces of Plastigauge material from both the journal and bearing shell. Rotate the crankshaft a quarter of a turn and repeat the measuring procedure. The difference between the two readings will indicate the out-of-round of the journal.

10. When measurement is completed, clean all Plastigauge material off both bearing shell and crankshaft journal. This is most important.

Installation

1. Install the crankshaft in the reverse order of removal, with special attention to the following points:

a) Ensure all oilways in the crankshaft are clear. This can be done by blowing out the passages with an air line, but in some cases it may be necessary to probe the passages with a piece of wire.

b) If the original bearing shells are being re-used, ensure that they are refitted in their original locations.

c) Ensure that the locating tag on each bearing shell correctly engages the corresponding notch in the crankcase or bearing cap.

d) Fit the half thrust washers on each side of the main bearing and cap with the oil grooves facing away from the bearing housing (Fig.C:36). The tab on the lower washers must locate in the slot on the centre main bearing cap.

e) Ensure that all the bearing surfaces are perfectly clean, then lubricate the bearing surfaces with clean engine oil before assembly.

f) Ensure that the bearing caps are refitted in their correct positions, indicated by the identification marks made previously.

g) Tighten the cap bolts evenly to their specified torque – see TECHNICAL DATA, then check that the crankshaft rotates freely and smoothly.

2. Check the crankshaft endfloat using either a dial gauge or feeler gauges. In the former case, locate the dial gauge with the stylus in contact with the machined surface of the crankshaft throw, then lever the crankshaft fully forward and zero the dial gauge. Lever the crankshaft in the opposite direction and note the gauge reading. If the endfloat exceeds the specified limits detailed in TECHNICAL DATA, rectify by selecting and fitting new thrust washers of the required thickness. If feeler gauges are being used, measure the clearance between the thrust washers and the crankshaft face with the crankshaft face pushed fully in one direction.

3. If the pistons were separated from their connecting rods, they should now be reassembled, noting the following points:

a) When fitting used parts it is essential that they be refitted in their original positions.

b) The cylinder number on the piston should match that on the connecting rod and cap.

c) The 'FRONT' or arrow head marking on the piston crown must be positioned to the front, and the number stamped on the connecting rod and cap must be to the left-hand side (camshaft side) of the assembly (Fig.C:34).

d) Check that the big-end boss has the correct offset. The odd (1 and 3) pair of rods have the offset towards the rear of the engine, and the even (2 and 4) pair have it towards the front (Fig.C:37).

e) Apply a light coat of graphited oil to the piston pin and the bosses in the piston and connecting rod, then fit the piston pin. The pin should be a thumb push-fit at normal room temperature (20°C).

f) Tighten the small end clamp bolt, or secure the pin in the piston with the two retaining circlips, as appropriate. In the latter case ensure that both circlips seal correctly in their grooves.

g) On 1275 GT models the piston pin is an interference fit in the connecting rod small end and must be pressed into place. This operation is best left to an Austin/Rover dealer or specialist who will have the proper equipment to carry out the job.

4. Assemble the piston rings on the piston, following the instructions supplied with the new rings. The rings must be fitted from the top of the piston. The rings will normally be marked 'TOP' on one face, and this side should face towards the piston crown (Figs.C:40 & C:41). Service rings for use in worn bores normally have a stepped top ring to avoid the wear ridge at the top of the bore. It is most important that these rings be fitted with the stepped portion uppermost, otherwise breakage of the rings will result when the engine is run. Where possible, proper piston ring pliers should be used to expand the rings when fitting them as this will eliminate the possibility of ring breakage or damage to the piston.

5. For each piston and connecting rod assembly in turn:

a) Lubricate the cylinder bore and piston rings liberally with clean engine oil.

b) Install the piston assembly in its correct respective bore with 'FRONT' or arrow head mark on the piston crown pointing towards the front of the block.

c) Position the piston rings so that their gaps are spaced out equally on the non-thrust side of the piston.

d) Compress the piston ring using a proper ring compressor tool. Do NOT attempt to fit the pistons by hand otherwise breakage of the rings may result. Carefully tap the piston into the cylinder bore, using the handle end of a hammer, until the piston crown is slightly below the top of the cylinder. Take great care to avoid the connecting rod hitting the crankshaft journal.

e) Fit the bearing shells dry in the connecting rod and caps, ensuring that the locating tag on each shell correctly engages the corresponding notch in the bearing housing.

f) Coat the crankshaft journal and bearings liberally with engine oil, then pull the connecting rod assembly down firmly onto the crankpin and fit the cap to the rod.

g) Check that the identification numbers on the cap and rod match, and are on the same side of the assembly (A and B, Fig.C:33).

h) On 1275 GT models, ensure that the cap is correctly located, then fit the two multi-sided nuts and tighten to their specified torque – see TECHNICAL DATA.

i) On 848, 998 and 1098 cc models, fit the big-end cap bolts with a new locking plate and tighten to their specified torque – see TECHNICAL DATA. Tap over the locking plate tabs to secure (A,Fig.C:33).

j) Check that the connecting rod has sufficient endfloat on the crank-pin.

6. Refit the adaptor plate to the front face of the cylinder block, using a new gasket, and tighten the securing screws (Fig.C:1).

7. Refit the camshaft locating plate, with the white metal side towards the camshaft journal, and secure with the three bolts.

8. Refit the dynamo/alternator adjusting link bracket on the cylinder block.

9. Reassemble the timing chain and sprockets, and the timing cover as detailed under the appropriate heading previously.

10. Refit the crankshaft primary gear assembly, and check and adjust the gear endfloat, if necessary, as detailed in CLUTCH & GEARBOX or AUTOMATIC TRANSMISSION.

11. Refit the cylinder head assembly, noting the points given

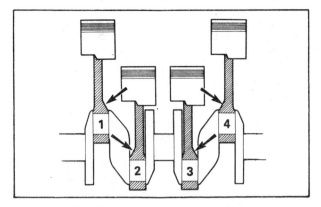

Fig. C:37 Conrod offset alignment

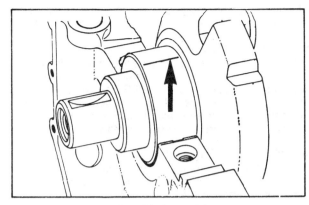

Fig. C:38 Correct position of Plastigauge on bearing journal

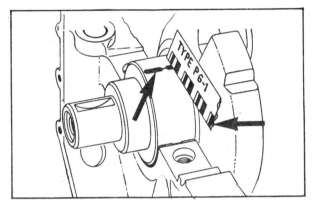

Fig. C:39 Measure width of compressed Plastigauge

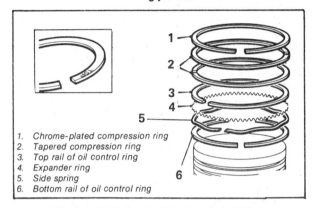

1. Chrome-plated compression ring
2. Tapered compression ring
3. Top rail of oil control ring
4. Expander ring
5. Side spring
6. Bottom rail of oil control ring

Fig. C:40 Details of piston ring installation

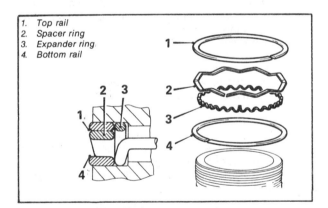

1. Top rail
2. Spacer ring
3. Expander ring
4. Bottom rail

Fig. C:41 Details of piston ring installation — 1275 GT

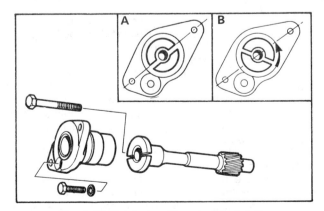

Fig. C:42 Distributor drive shaft installation

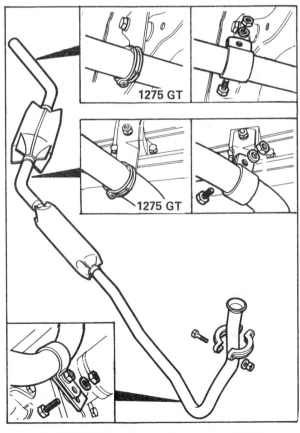

Fig. C:43 Details of exhaust system installation

under Cylinder Head.

12. Finally, assemble the engine to the transmission casing and refit the power unit in the car in the reverse order of removal.

Camshaft & Cam Followers

On all types of engine, the engine/gearbox unit must be removed from the car before the camshaft can be removed. However, on all engines, except 1275 GT, two detachable side covers on the fuel pump side of the engine block enable the cam followers to be removed separately from the camshaft once the rocker shaft and pushrods has been removed.

Camshaft Removal (Fig.C:1)

1. Remove the engine and gearbox assembly.
2. Remove the rocker shaft and push-rods, store the rods in their fitted order. Remove the engine side-covers, withdraw the cam followers and store them in their fitted order.
3. Remove the distributor, and then the distributor drive shaft by screwing a 5/16 bolt approximately 90 mm (3.5 in) long into the drive shaft and withdraw the shaft (Fig.C:42). Remove the fuel pump.
4. Remove the timing chain tensioner (if fitted), chain and sprockets, remove the camshaft locating plate and withdraw the camshaft from the engine.
5. If the camshaft bearings are to be replaced it will be necessary to strip the engine completely due to the possibility of swarf entering the engine when the bearings are being removed or refitted.
NOTE:Camshaft bearing replacement must be done by an Austin/Rover dealer or auto engineer as special tools are needed to ensure correct fitting and alignment.

Camshaft Removal — 1275 GT Engine

1. Remove the engine and gearbox assembly. Separate the engine from the gearbox as detailed previously.
2. Remove the rocker shaft and pushrods, store the pushrods in their fitted order. Remove the distributor, distributor drive shaft as detailed above and the fuel pump. Remove the timing cover, timing chain and sprockets.
3. Turn the engine upside down and support it on wood blocks. This will allow the cam followers to move away from the camshaft lobes and journals, thus making it possible to withdraw the camshaft.
4. Remove the camshaft locating plate and withdraw camshaft from the engine block, taking care to avoid damaging the cam bearings with the cam lobes.
5. If the camshaft bearings are to be replaced it will be necessary to strip the engine completely due to the possibility of swarf entering the engine when the bearings are being removed or fitted.
NOTE:Camshaft bearing replacement must be done by an Austin/Rover dealer or auto engineer as special tools are needed to ensure correct fitting and alignment.
6. Extract the cam followers and store them in their fitted order for examination.

Camshaft & Follower — Inspection

Clean the camshaft and followers in petrol or other suitable solvent, then inspect all the wearing parts, making sure that the followers are kept in their removal order at all times.

Camshaft lobe wear characteristics may result in very slight pitting in the general area of the lobe tip, but this is not detrimental to the operation of the camshaft (if the pitting is slight) and the camshaft need not therefore be replaced until the wear is such that the lobe lift loss exceeds 0,127 mm (0.005 in).

Check the teeth of the distributor drive gear and the oil pump drive at the end of the shaft for wear or damage indicated by bright marks. The camshaft runs in three bearings in the engine block. If one or more of the bearings are found to be outside the bearing clearance specified in TECHNICAL DATA, all three bearings should be replaced. This is a job that should be done by a local auto engineering firm with specialist line boring equipment to ensure correct alignment.

Check the cam followers for wear or scoring on the sides indicating oil starvation or seizure. If the follower face is heavily pitted the follower should be replaced. New cam followers must ALWAYS be fitted with a new camshaft.

Installation

Temporarily install the camshaft and fit the locating plate and chain sprocket. Use a feeler gauge to measure the clearance between the sprocket and the plate. If the clearance is outside the specified limits – see TECHNICAL DATA, a new locating plate should be fitted.

Install the camshaft and the followers in the reverse order of removal and refer to the Timing Chain & Tensioner, Cylinder Head and Engine Overhaul sections of this chapter for details of refitting these items.

To install the distributor drive shaft, No.1 piston must be on TDC (top dead centre) on its compression stroke. Turn the crankshaft until the engine timing marks are in the 1/4 or 'O' position – see TUNE-UP, and No.7 & 8 cylinder valves are in the rocking position. If No. 1 & 2 valves are rocking, then rotate the crankshaft one complete turn until the slot in the pulley and the timing marks are aligned again.

With the selected bolt screwed into the distributor drive shaft as previously described, enter the shaft into the block while holding the bolt, the large segment should be uppermost and the initial fitting is shown in B,Fig.C:42. As the shaft engages into the camshaft it will turn anti-clockwise and the fitted position is correct when the top edge of the offset slot is aligned with the the centre line of the two retaining studs (A,Fig.C:42).

EXHAUST SYSTEM . . . . [13]

The exhaust system should be examined periodically to check for corrosion and leaks – see PASS the MoT.

The system may be in one unit or consist of a separate front down pipe and a rear section including intermediate and rear silencers plus the tailpipe.

When either part of the system requires replacement, it may be as well to replace the complete system from manifold to tailpipe. A used section should only be reused if it is basically sound and undamaged. Remember that an exhaust system corrodes from the inside outwards as the hot corrosive gases attack the inside of the pipe. Therefore, when a pipe appears to have only surface rust on the outside, it could be that the pipe will only have a short life left before leakage. As corrosion takes place throughout the length of the exhaust system, examine each section very carefully to check how much requires replacement. It may well prove that fitting a complete system will be a greater economy.

Replacement — Complete System (Fig.C:43)

1. Raise and support the front and rear of the car – see BASIC PROCEDURES.
2. From inside the engine compartment, remove the air cleaner and remove the exhaust manifold to pipe flange clamp.
3. Undo the nut and bolt securing the front down pipe clamp to the transmission casing.
4. Disconnect the exhaust pipe from the intermediate mounting. 1275 GT models have a wire clip and other models have a nut and bolt, which must be removed.
5. Disconnect the tailpipe from the rear mounting. 1275 GT models have a wire clip and other models have a nut and bolt, which must be removed.
6. The exhaust system can now be manoeuvred out from under the car.
7. Install the exhaust system in the reverse order of removal, ensuring that the manifold clamp is tightened before the transmission casing bracket on the down pipe. A smear of exhaust sealing compound on the taper face of the manifold will help to prevent leaks.

Engine Problems

FAULT	CAUSE	ACTION
Noisy tappet (with correct clearance	☐ Worn rocker or shaft. ☐ Worn cam follower tappet.	▦ Replace rockers or shaft. ▦ Fit new follower/tappet.
Lack of compression	☐ Worn valve/seats. ☐ Faulty head gasket. ☐ Worn pistons, rings and bores.	▦ Regrind valves or recut seats. ▦ Fit new gasket. ▦ Fit new rings or pistons and rings and rebore. If engine badly worn then recondition engine.
Blue smoke from exhaust	☐ Worn valve guides/stems. ☐ Worn pistons/rings and/or bores. ☐ Engine oil overfilled. ☐ Blocked crankcase breather.	▦ Renew guides/valves. ▦ Renew pistons/rings and/or re-bore. ▦ Reduce oil level. ▦ Check crankcase breather.
Piston slap	☐ Worn pistons/rings and/or bores. ☐ Thrust side of piston facing wrong direction. ☐ Piston rings stuck in grooves.	▦ Renew pistons/rings and/or rebore. ▦ Reverse piston direction. ▦ Clean rings and grooves.
Big-end knock (heavy knocking)	☐ Insufficient oil pressure. ☐ Worn big-end bearing(s). ☐ Big-end bearing cap(s) loose.	▦ Check oil pressure and rectify. ▦ Renew bearing shells and regrind crankshaft if necessary. ▦ Inspect bearings, tighten cap(s).
Mains rumble	☐ Worn main bearing(s).	▦ Renew bearing shells and regrind crankshaft if necessary.
Camshaft knock	☐ Cam(s) and/or follower(s) worn.	▦ Renew camshaft and/or follower(s).
Idle speed drops when clutch pedal depressed. Movement at crank pulley	☐ Excessive crankshaft endfloat.	▦ Renew crankshaft thrust washers.
Clattering from front of engine	☐ Worn or slack timing chain.	▦ Renew chain and/or check tensioner.
Small-end knock (light knocking)	☐ Worn small-end bearing.	▦ Renew bearing or piston and piston pin.
Low oil pressure	☐ Lack of oil or oil too thin. ☐ Worn oil pump. ☐ Blocked oil pick-up strainer. ☐ Faulty pressure-relief valve. ☐ Blocked oil filter. ☐ Excessive wear in crankshaft journals.	▦ Top-up renew oil. ▦ Fit new pump. ▦ Clean strainer. ▦ Fit new relief valve. ▦ Fit new filter. ▦ Overhaul engine.
Oil leaks	☐ Crankshaft oil seals worn. ☐ Sump gaskets/seals damaged/worn. ☐ Rocker/camshaft cover gasket damaged. ☐ Camshaft oil seal worn. ☐ Oil filter loose. ☐ Blocked crankcase breather.	▦ Renew seals. ▦ Renew gaskets/seals. ▦ Renew gasket. ▦ Renew seal. ▦ Tighten filter. ▦ Check breather.

Engine Electrics

INTRODUCTION .... [1]

The engine electrics comprise three main systems: the starting, charging and ignition circuits. Apart from these three main circuits, there are additional circuits for monitoring the state of the engine, coolant temperature and engine oil pressure etc, depending on the model. These latter components are dealt with in GENERAL ELECTRICS.

The starter motor is of the inertia type on all early models and pre-engaged on later models. The starter motor is of Lucas manufacture. Overhaul of the starter motor is quite straightforward but should be limited to brush replacement (one of the most common faults) and pinion replacement. On the inertia type, a special Bendix compressor tool will be needed to remove the pinion – this can be hired or bought quite cheaply. The solenoid on pre-engaged starter motors can be replaced but cannot be overhauled. Otherwise, an exchange unit should be obtained as the most convenient solution for a badly worn or faulty unit. This will have the added advantage that it will be covered by a warranty.

The charging system uses either a dynamo (pre 1973 model year) or an alternator. The alternator may be one of two different types the main difference being that the early type has an externally mounted voltage regulator and the later type has a voltage regulator mounted integrally within the alternator rear housing.

The charging system can be checked as described in the relevant section of this chapter, however if there are any doubts about the results an auto-electrician should be consulted. Only replacement of the brushes and regulator are covered, as any further overhaul is not really an economic proposition due to the high cost of the parts compared with the more reasonable value that an exchange alternator unit offers.

Many charging problems come from a lack of battery maintenance and reference should be made to ROUTINE MAINTENANCE for details of battery maintenance and to BASIC PROCEDURES for charging procedure.

The ignition system is of the conventional coil and contact-breaker type using a distributor of either Lucas or Ducellier manufacture.
NOTE:The battery earth lead should always be disconnected before carrying out any work on the electrical system, to avoid any chance of damage due to short circuits.

Minis built prior to 1970 model year have a Positive (+) earth electrical system and those built after this date have a Negative (-) earth system. Care must be taken to observe the polarity whenever components are being tested or replaced.

It should be noted that modern car ignition systems operate at high voltages and wearers of surgically implanted pacemaker devices should not be in close proximity to ignition circuits or diagnostic equipment.

TOOLS & EQUIPMENT .... [2]

Other than those tools listed under Basic Tools & Equipment in BASIC PROCEDURES, the following items will be required in order to successfully carry out all the operations detailed within this chapter.
- A test lamp and small jump leads – to solve continuity and earthing problems – a test lamp can be made using a 12 volt bulb and some pieces of wire soldered to the terminals and some clips or probes attached to the free ends of the wires.
- A multi-meter – this meter should have voltage, amperage and resistance scales for testing the alternator and starter motor.
- Soldering iron and solder – for renewing starter motor field brushes.
- Bendix spring compressing clamp – for removal and installation of the drive pinion on the inertia type starter motor.
- Two legged puller – for refitting the pinion retaining collar on pre-engaged type starter motors.

Other useful tools will be a small electricians screwdriver and a small pair of long nosed pliers.

CIRCUIT TESTING PROCEDURES .... [3]
Dynamo System
1. Check that the generator drive belt is correctly adjusted. The battery should be in good condition and its terminals clean and tight, also the leads and connections in the rest of the charging circuit should be clean and making good contact.
2. Disconnect both leads ('D' and 'F') from the rear of the dynamo and connect a voltmeter between a good earth point and the 'D' terminal (the large one) on the rear of the dynamo. Start the engine and gently increase its speed to about 2500-3500 rpm. At this speed, the voltmeter reading should be between 2 and 3 volts.

If the reading is outside these limits, check the brushes condition first. If the brushes are in good order, a replacement dynamo is probably needed.

With the voltmeter still connected to the 'D' terminal, connect an ammeter between the two dynamo 'D' and 'F' terminals. Start the engine and increase its speed until the voltmeter reads 12 volts; the ammeter should then read not more than 2 amperes. If the ammeter reading is more or less than 2 amperes, a replacement dynamo is probably needed.

3. If the above tests show that the dynamo and its connections are apparently in order, then any fault will probably be with the voltage regulator unit. Adjustment of the regulator unit is not really a DIY proposition as special tools and conditions are necessary apart from the economics involved – a replacement unit is the cheapest and most convenient solution.

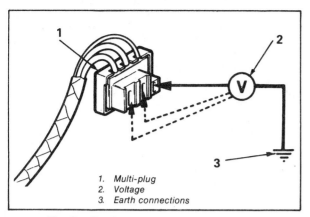

1. Multi-plug
2. Voltage
3. Earth connections

Fig. D:1 Testing alternator wiring harness

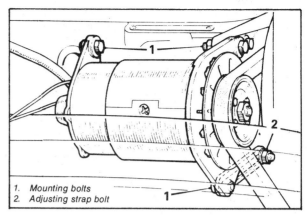

1. Mounting bolts
2. Adjusting strap bolt

Fig. D:2 Layout of dynamo mounting

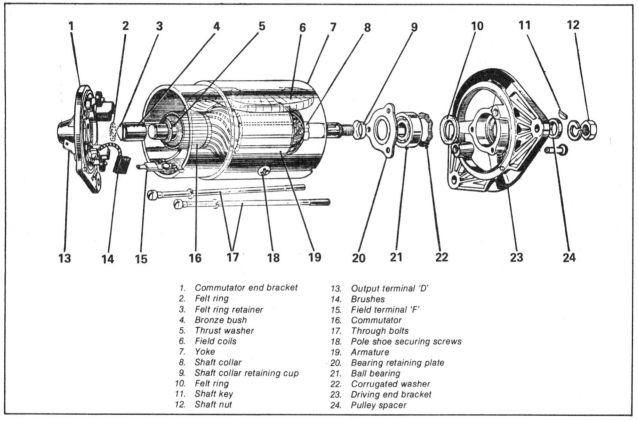

1. Commutator end bracket
2. Felt ring
3. Felt ring retainer
4. Bronze bush
5. Thrust washer
6. Field coils
7. Yoke
8. Shaft collar
9. Shaft collar retaining cup
10. Felt ring
11. Shaft key
12. Shaft nut
13. Output terminal 'D'
14. Brushes
15. Field terminal 'F'
16. Commutator
17. Through bolts
18. Pole shoe securing screws
19. Armature
20. Bearing retaining plate
21. Ball bearing
22. Corrugated washer
23. Driving end bracket
24. Pulley spacer

Fig. D:3 Exploded view of dynamo — Lucas C40

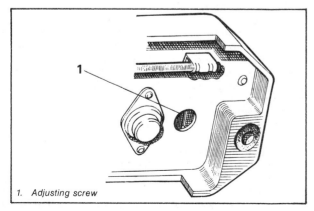

1. Adjusting screw

Fig. D:4 Voltage regulator — Lucas 4TR

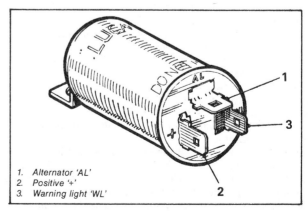

1. Alternator 'AL'
2. Positive '+'
3. Warning light 'WL'

Fig. D:5 Warning light control unit — Lucas 3AW

Alternator System

1. Check that the alternator drive belt is correctly adjusted. The battery should be in good condition and its terminals clean and tight, also the connections and leads in the rest of the charging system should be clean and making good contact.
2. Disconnect the cable plug from the rear of the alternator, then connect the negative side of a voltmeter to a good earth and switch the ignition on. Connect the other voltmeter lead to each of the disconnected alternator cables in turn. If a battery voltage is not recorded at the 'Brown' and 'Yellow' 'IND' cable, then check the warning light circuit and the bulb (Fig.D:1).
3. If a battery voltage is not recorded at the main charging lead, check the wiring and the connections between the battery and the alternator.
4. If all is well, reconnect the alternator cables and then disconnect the 'Brown' cable on the starter motor solenoid. Connect an ammeter between the 'Brown' cable and the terminal on the starter solenoid, also connect a voltmeter between the battery terminals.

If, with the engine idling, the ammeter reads zero, then the alternator is probably at fault. If the ammeter reads less than 10 amperes and the voltmeter reads between 13.6 and 14.4 volts, with the battery in a low state of charge, then suspect the alternator. If the ammeter reads more or less than 10 amperes and the voltmeter more or less than 13.6 volts, then suspect the voltage regulator.
5. Most faults allied to the charging system are usually due to either worn brushes or to a defective voltage regulator.

Replacement of both the brushes and the integral regulator unit on alternators is detailed under the appropriate headings. If anything more involved such as the rectifier diodes, slip rings, bearings etc., are faulty then it is recommended that any repairs are given to an auto electrical specialist or an exchange unit obtained.

In most cases, the latter will be found to be the most economical and convenient solution rather than attempt to obtain parts and repair an alternator or dynamo.

It should be noted that with an alternator, the battery should ALWAYS be disconnected before starting work on the charging system to avoid any possibility of damage to the semi-conductor devices in the rectifier and diode units.

Ignition System Test

NOTE:The following tests are for Negative (-) earth systems, but can be applied to Positive (+) earth systems if the reference to Positive (+) and Negative (-), in the text, are reversed.
1. Check coil supply.

Ensure that the distributor contact points are closed. Connect a voltmeter between the coil positive terminal and a good earth. Switch on the ignition. The meter will register approximately 12V if the supply line is in order.
a) A zero reading indicates a fault in the circuit up to the coil, or possibly a short-circuit. Disconnect and check the voltage at the lead. If the meter reads battery voltage the supply line is in order. Therefore renew the coil.
b) A reading of battery voltage indicates an open circuit further on. Proceed to test 2.
2. Check coil primary windings.

Connect a voltmeter between the coil negative terminal and a good earth. Open the distributor contact points and switch on the ignition. Meter will read battery voltage if the primary winding is satisfactory.

A zero reading may indicate an open-circuit primary winding, short-circuit condenser, or that the contact breaker line is earthed. Disconnect the lead from the coil negative terminal and check the voltage at that terminal. A zero reading indicates a faulty coil; a reading of battery voltage indicates a fault in the condenser or C.B. line. Trace and rectify the fault, then proceed to test 3.

3. Check the distributor contacts and C.B. earth.

With the voltmeter still connected between the coil negative terminal and a good earth, close the distributor contact points and switch on the ignition. The meter should read practically zero (0.2V max.) if the circuit is satisfactory.

A high reading indicates a poor C.B. earth or dirty contact points. Clean or renew the contact points, check the distributor earth wire, base plate fixing screws and distributor body to engine block connection. Proceed to test 4.
4. Check coil secondary winding.

Disconnect the coil H.T. cable from the distributor, and hold the free end approximately 6,5 mm (0.25 in) from a good earth. Switch on the ignition and flick open the contact points. A good H.T. spark between the cable end and earth indicates that the circuit is satisfactory.

No spark probably indicates that either the H.T. cable is faulty, or the condenser is defective. Otherwise proceed to test 5.
5. Check the condenser.

Test the condenser by substitution if suitable test equipment is unavailable. Fit a known good condenser, hold the free end of the H.T. cable approximately 6,5 mm (0.25 in) from a good earth and with the ignition switch on, flick open the contact points.

If a good H.T. spark is produced, the original condenser is faulty. No spark indicates that the coil secondary winding is defective. Rectify the fault, proceed to text 6.
6. Check the rotor arm insulation.

Hold the free end of the H.T. cable approximately 3 mm (0.125 in) from the rotor arm electrode. With the ignition switched on, flick open the contact points. No spark, or a very faint spark indicates that the rotor arm insulation is satisfactory. Proceed to test 7.
7. Check H.T. cables and distributor cover.
a) Check that the H.T. cables are clean, remove any oil and grease deposits as necessary. Cables which are perished or have splits in the insulation should be removed.
b) The distributor cover should be clean inside and out; check for signs of tracking and cracks. The H.T. carbon brush should move freely against the spring pressure in its holder; ensure that the brush makes contact with the rotor: Renew the cover if necessary for any of the above faults.
c) Excessive carbon deposits on the distributor cap electrodes must be removed; if the electrodes are badly pitted, the cap should be renewed.
8. Check distributor dwell and ignition timing.

Using suitable test equipment check, and adjust if necessary, the distributor contact-breaker dwell and ignition timing as described in TUNE-UP.

Starter Motor Test

NOTE:The following tests are for Negative(-) earth systems, but can be applied to Positive (+) earth systems if the references to Positive (+) and Negative (-),in the text are reversed.
1. Check battery voltage on load.

To ensure the engine will not start, disconnect the low-tension lead from the coil negative terminal. Connect a voltmeter across the battery and operate the starter. The voltmeter reading should not be less than 10.0V. A low reading probably indicates that the battery is discharged. Repeat the test with a well-charged substitute battery of equivalent capacity. If low readings are still obtained, the starter or circuit is taking too much current. Proceed to test 2.
2. Check starter voltage on load.

Connect a voltmeter between the starter main terminal and earth (commutator-end bracket). With the coil lead disconnected, operate the starter. If the voltmeter reading is not more than 0.5V below that recorded in test 1, the starter circuit is satisfactory.

If, however, a reading of more than 0.5V below that recorded in test 1 is obtained, a high resistance in the circuit is indicated. Proceed to test 3.

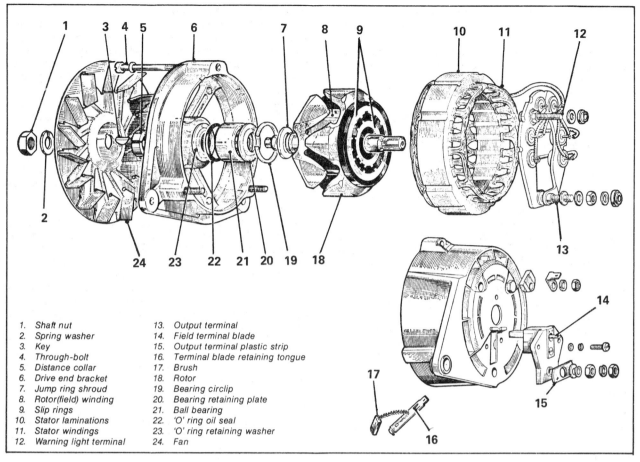

1. Shaft nut	13. Output terminal
2. Spring washer	14. Field terminal blade
3. Key	15. Output terminal plastic strip
4. Through-bolt	16. Terminal blade retaining tongue
5. Distance collar	17. Brush
6. Drive end bracket	18. Rotor
7. Jump ring shroud	19. Bearing circlip
8. Rotor(field) winding	20. Bearing retaining plate
9. Slip rings	21. Ball bearing
10. Stator laminations	22. 'O' ring oil seal
11. Stator windings	23. 'O' ring retaining washer
12. Warning light terminal	24. Fan

Fig. D:6 Exploded view of alternator — Lucas 11AC

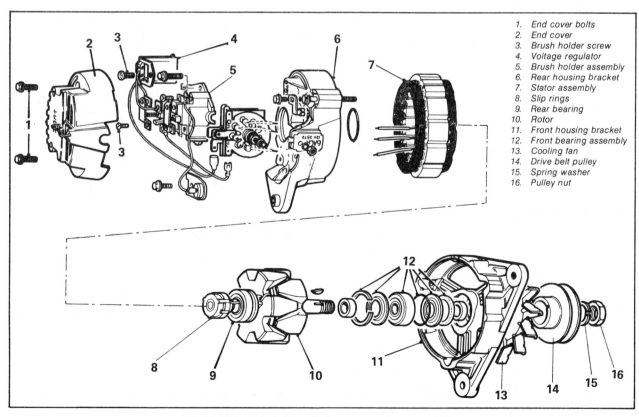

1. End cover bolts
2. End cover
3. Brush holder screw
4. Voltage regulator
5. Brush holder assembly
6. Rear housing bracket
7. Stator assembly
8. Slip rings
9. Rear bearing
10. Rotor
11. Front housing bracket
12. Front bearing assembly
13. Cooling fan
14. Drive belt pulley
15. Spring washer
16. Pulley nut

Fig. D:7 Exploded view of alternator — Lucas 16ACR

3. Check voltage drop on the insulated line.

Connect a voltmeter between the starter main terminal and the battery positive terminal. The meter will indicate battery voltage.

With the coil lead disconnected, operate the starter; the voltmeter reading should be practically zero. A high reading indicates a high resistance in the starter circuit. All insulated connections at the battery, solenoid switch and starter should be checked. Proceed to test 4.

4. Check voltage drop across the starter solenoid.

Connect a voltmeter across the starter solenoid switch main terminals. The meter will indicate battery voltage.

With the coil lead disconnected, operate the starter; the voltmeter reading should be practically zero. A zero or fractional reading indicates that the starter solenoid is satisfactory and the fault is elsewhere in the circuit, battery to solenoid, solenoid to starter cable. Rectify the fault and proceed to test 5.

5. Check voltage drop on the earth line.

Connect a voltmeter between the battery negative terminal and the starter earth (commutator-end bracket). With the coil lead disconnected, operate the starter; the voltmeter reading should be practically zero.

If the meter reading is high, clean and tighten all earth connections, starter to engine, battery to body and the engine to body bonding strap.

NOTE:*If after carrying out all the above tests and establishing that the battery and circuit are satisfactory, but that the battery voltage on load is still below 10V, remove and overhaul the starter.*

DYNAMO . . . . [4]
Replacement (Fig.D:2)

Dynamo removal is a straight-forward operation and is merely a matter of disconnecting the two leads from the rear of the unit and removing the mounting bolts. The unit can then be lifted away from the engine.

When installing the dynamo, set the drive belt tension so that a free-play of approximately 13 mm (½ in) exists at the midway point along the longest belt run.

If a replacement unit has been fitted, it should be 'polarised' before reconnecting the leads to the two terminals. To do this, connect a short lead between the two terminals on the dynamo and connect another longer lead to one of the terminals. At the starter solenoid, touch the other end of the long lead to the large battery feed terminal (opposite terminal to starter lead attachment) several times. The dynamo will now be correctly polarised to suit the electrical system. Remove the temporary leads and connect up the two dynamo leads to the large and small terminal respectively on the rear of the unit.

Brushes

Most faults associated with the dynamo are normally due either to the brushes or the rear bearing. In the latter case, excessive wear at the rear bearing bush allows the armature shaft to run eccentrically and touch the field coils, in which case the complete unit is best exchanged. This condition is easily identified as excessive side movement at the rear end of the shaft when the drive pulley is moved side-to-side.

To examine the brushes, unscrew the two through-bolts at the rear end bracket and withdraw the end bracket from the dynamo yoke (1,Fig.D:3).

Check the condition and length of the two carbon brushes in the end bracket, and the condition of the surface on the commutator. If the brushes are worn to or are approaching their minimum length of 6 mm (¼ in), they should be renewed.

To renew the brushes, detach the old brush leads from the holders on the end bracket by removing the screw and lock washer. Note the positions of the terminal tags before disconnecting the leads. Ensure that the replacement brushes are of the correct type and length. Secure the new brushes in position on the end bracket.

Inspect the contact surface on the commutator for signs of wear, burning or blackening of the segments. The latter indicates a short circuit. An open circuit will cause burned spots between the segments. Ideally the commutator surface should be smooth with a dark grey colour. If blackened or dirty, it can be cleaned up with a petrol moistened cloth. Slight imperfections can be removed with fine glass paper – not emery cloth. Use the glass paper over the whole surface of the commutator.

If the commutator is grooved, scored, pitted or badly worn, it must be skimmed down or replaced.

Fit each brush into its holder in turn and check for freedom of movement. If a brush sticks, it can usually be freed by cleaning both the brush and the holder with a petrol-moistened cloth, or by lightly polishing the sides of the brush with a smooth file.

Locate the brush springs on the side of each brush to hold them in the raised position. Check that the fibre thrust washer is in position on the end of the armature shaft, then refit the commutator end bracket. Ensure that the locating pip on the end bracket correctly engages the notch in the dynamo yoke. Fit the two through-bolts and tighten securely.

Release the brushes onto the commutator by inserting a thin screwdriver through the ventilation hole in the end bracket adjacent to the brush holders and gently levering up the spring end on to the top of the brush.

Before refitting the dynamo on the car, add one or two drops of light oil to the rear bearing through the hole in the centre of the end bracket. Do not over-lubricate the bearing otherwise oil may be thrown onto the brush gear in use.

Overhaul (Fig.D:3)

If any repair work, other than replacing the brushes, is necessary it will probably be more economical and convenient to have the dynamo repaired by an electrical specialist, or to exchange it for a replacement unit.

If the unit is being exchanged, it will be necessary to remove the drive pulley as this will not normally be supplied with the new unit. After removing the pulley nut, the pulley can be levered off the keyed shaft, but care should be taken to avoid damaging the rim of the pulley.

Voltage Regulator

A two-bobbin voltage control regulator – Lucas type RB106/2 – is used to control the generator output and this is mounted in the engine compartment bulkhead. If there is a charging fault and the dynamo is found to be working satisfactorily then it is likely that the regulator is at fault. Rather than attempt to clean or adjust the unit it is advised that the unit be exchanged at your local Austin/Rover dealer accessory shop or auto-electrician. Unless completely overhauled (requiring special tools and meters), it is likely that any adjustment would only be a temporary cure.

Removal & Installation

1. Disconnect the battery earth lead.
2. Remove the leads from the regulator, noting all of the various connections.
3. Unscrew two screws securing the unit to the engine compartment bulkhead.
4. Replace the regulator and secure it with two screws.
5. Reconnect the leads in the same positions as on removal.
6. Reconnect the battery.

ALTERNATOR . . . . [5]

Two different types of Lucas alternator are used on Mini models; the 11AC alternator and the later 16 ACR unit, and these can be identified from the illustrations in Fig.D:6 & D:7.

The 11AC type was used on early models which had a

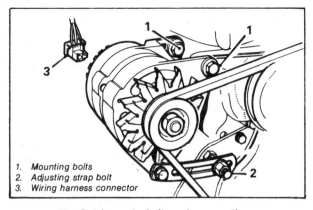

1. Mounting bolts
2. Adjusting strap bolt
3. Wiring harness connector

Fig. D:8 Layout of alternator mountings

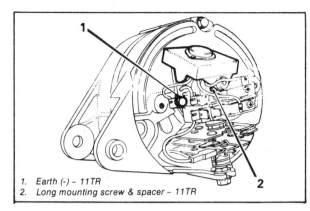

1. Earth (-) – 11TR
2. Long mounting screw & spacer – 11TR

Fig. D:9 Voltage regulator connections — 11TR

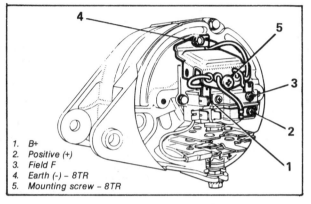

1. B+
2. Positive (+)
3. Field F
4. Earth (-) – 8TR
5. Mounting screw – 8TR

Fig. D:10 Voltage regulator connections — 8TR

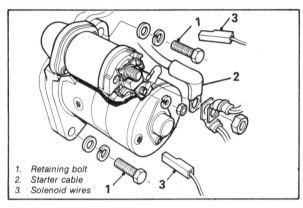

1. Retaining bolt
2. Starter cable
3. Solenoid wires

Fig. D:11 Starter motor removal (pre-engaged type)

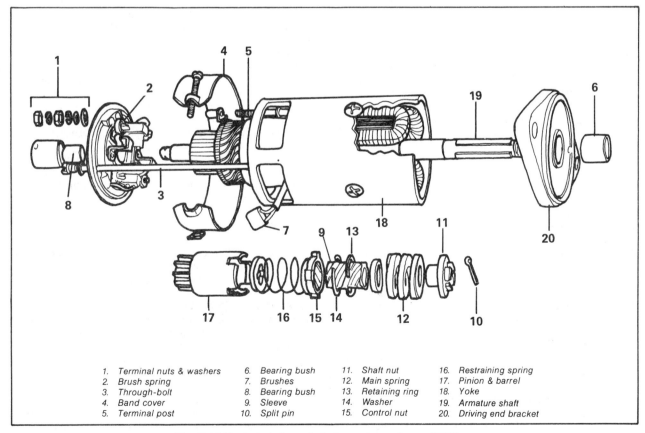

1. Terminal nuts & washers	6. Bearing bush	11. Shaft nut	16. Restraining spring
2. Brush spring	7. Brushes	12. Main spring	17. Pinion & barrel
3. Through-bolt	8. Bearing bush	13. Retaining ring	18. Yoke
4. Band cover	9. Sleeve	14. Washer	19. Armature shaft
5. Terminal post	10. Split pin	15. Control nut	20. Driving end bracket

Fig. D:12 Exploded view of starter motor — Lucas M35G

positive earth electrical system, but this was superseded by the 16 ACR type coincident with the adoption of negative earth in approximately October 1969. They differ mainly in that the later type has an integral voltage regulator incorporated in the rear end of the unit, whereas the 11AC type has a separate control unit. The 16 ACR type also has the slip rings mounted behind the rear motor shaft bearing outside the slip ring end bracket.

It should be noted that the 16 ACR unit cannot be used on the earlier models with positive earth, as this type of alternator can only be used with a negative earth system.

Most faults allied to the alternator charging system are due either to worn or damaged brushes, or a defective regulator. Replacement of both the brushes and the regulator unit is detailed under the appropriate headings below. If anything more involved, such as the rectifier diodes, slip rings, bearings, etc., is at fault, it is recommended that the alternator be given to an electrical specialist for repair, or an exchange unit obtained. In most cases this will be found to be the most economical and convenient solution rather than attempt to obtain replacement parts and repair it.

It should be noted that the battery should ALWAYS be disconnected before starting work on the charging system to avoid the possibility of damage to the semi-conductor devices in the alternator.

11AC Type (Fig.D:6)

The 11AC alternator charging circuit includes an alternator control unit, a field isolating relay and a warning light control unit (Fig.D:5). The electronic control unit is a Lucas 4TR type and is mounted remotely from the alternator. The voltage output is adjustable by means of a potentiometer adjuster at the rear of the control unit, but is not recommended that this be attempted without proper equipment and knowledge (Fig.D:4).

The Lucas 6RA field isolating relay acts to de-energise the alternator field windings when the engine is stationary by disconnecting the supply from the rotor field immediately the ignition is switched off. If the contacts inside the relay fail to close when the ignition is switched on, the alternator will not generate.

The warning light control unit is a thermally operated relay and is electrically connected to the centre point of one pair of diodes in the alternator. It enables a warning light to be used to indicate that the alternator is charging when the engine is running at normal speed. It should be noted that the 3AW control unit is externally similar to the FL5 type indicator flasher unit and thus is identified by a distinctive green label applied to the aluminium case of the unit. These two types of unit cannot and must not be interchanged.

Replacement (Fig.D:8)

Removal and installation of the alternator is a straight-forward operation, similar to that described for the dynamo previously. However, in this case it is most important that the battery is disconnected before starting work on the alternator as the alternator main feed cable is live at all times. Do not reconnect the battery until installation is complete and all leads have been properly reconnected.

It should be noted that 'polarisation' of the alternator is not necessary and in fact, if carried out, will probably cause damage to some of the semi-conductor devices in the charging circuit.

Brushes Removal (Fig.D:6)

1. Remove the nuts, washers and insulating pieces from the output terminal (B) at the rear of the alternator. Remove the two brush box retaining screws and withdraw the brush box assembly from the rear end bracket. Take care not to lose the two washers fitted between the brush box moulding and the end bracket as these must be refitted in their original locations on reassembly.
2. To remove the brushes from the brush box, close up the retaining tongue at the base of each field terminal blade and withdraw the brush, spring and terminal assembly from the brush box.
3. Check the brushes for wear. The brush length when new is 16 mm (⅝ in). If worn to, or approaching the wear limit of 8 mm (³⁄₁₆ in) the brush assemblies should be renewed. New brush assemblies are supplied complete with their spring and 'Lucar' field terminal blade.
4. It should be noted that the brush which bears on the inner slip ring is always connected to the positive side of the electrical system, since the lower linear speed of the inner slip ring results in reduced mechanical wear and helps to offset the higher rate of electrical wear peculiar to the positive connected brush.

Brushes Replacement

1. If the original brush assemblies are to be re-used, clean them with a cloth moistened in petrol or white spirit, then dry thoroughly.
2. Check the brushes for freedom of movement in their holders. If necessary lightly polish the brush sides on a smooth file, then clean off and refit.
3. To reassemble the brushes to their holders, push each brush complete with its spring and terminal blade into its holder until the tongue on the terminal blade registers in the brush box. To ensure the terminal blades are properly retained, the tongue should be levered up with a small screwdriver to make an angle of about 30° with the terminal blade.
4. Before refitting the brush box assembly, inspect the slip rings for any signs of damage or contamination. The surface of the rings should be smooth and free from oil or other matter. The easiest way of removing surface dirt from the slip rings is to press a petrol-moistened cloth through the hole in the end bracket and hold it in contact with the slip ring surface while rotating the pulley.
5. If more serious contamination or damage is evident on the ring surface, the alternator must be partially dismantled to gain access. In this case the drive pulley and fan must first be removed to allow the three through-bolts to be unscrewed. The alignment of the end brackets and stator should be marked so that they may be reassembled in the correct angular relation to each other. The drive end bracket and rotor can then be separated from the stator and slip ring end bracket to allow inspection of the slip rings.
6. The surface of the slip rings can be cleaned using very fine glass paper but on no account must emery cloth or similar abrasive be used. If badly scored, pitted or burned, the complete rotor assembly must be renewed.
7. When inspection is completed, refit the brush box assembly to the slip ring end bracket and secure with the two retaining screws. Assemble the insulating pieces, washers and nuts on the output terminal.

Overhaul

If any repair work, other than replacing the brushes, is necessary it will probably be more economical and convenient to have the alternator repaired by an electrical specialist, or to exchange it for a replacement unit.

16 ACR Type (Fig.D:7)

In the 16 ACR alternator charging circuit, all the electrical components of the charging system are incorporated in the alternator. These include the control unit (voltage regulator) and the rectifier pack, which are mounted on the rear of the alternator under the black plastic cover.

Several modifications have been made to the internal components of the 16 ACR alternator since its introduction. These mainly affect the voltage control unit which may be an 8TR, 11TR or 14TR on later models, but the termination is also different on later units, as improvements to the internal wiring have resulted in the elimination of the 'battery sensing' wire and

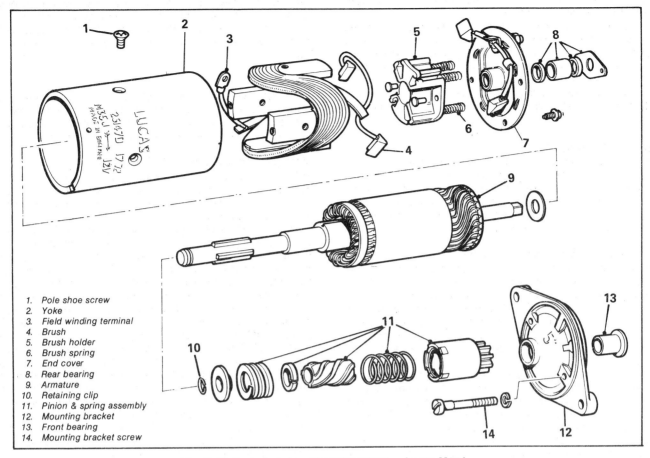

1. Pole shoe screw
2. Yoke
3. Field winding terminal
4. Brush
5. Brush holder
6. Brush spring
7. End cover
8. Rear bearing
9. Armature
10. Retaining clip
11. Pinion & spring assembly
12. Mounting bracket
13. Front bearing
14. Mounting bracket screw

Fig. D:13 Exploded view of starter motor — Lucas M35J

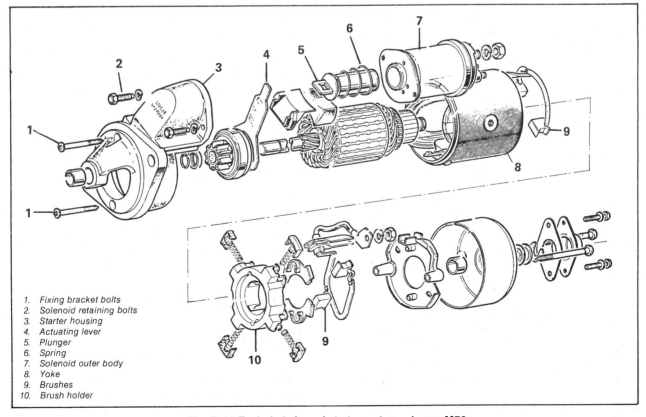

1. Fixing bracket bolts
2. Solenoid retaining bolts
3. Starter housing
4. Actuating lever
5. Plunger
6. Spring
7. Solenoid outer body
8. Yoke
9. Brushes
10. Brush holder

Fig. D:14 Exploded view of starter motor — Lucas M79

the separate earth wire used on previous units. The alternator now earths through the unit casing.

These later units have a single connector block with two leads to it, whereas earlier alternators have two connector blocks. Details of the wiring conversion necessary when fitting a later unit as a replacement for the earlier type are given under the appropriate heading below.

It should be noted that the 16 ACR alternator is suitable only for fitment to vehicles which have a negative earth electrical system.

Replacement (Fig.D:8)

Removal and installation is carried out in a similar manner to that described for the 11AC alternator previously.

Where a replacement unit with European termination is being fitted in place of an earlier type, the alternator wiring will have to be modified to suit and reference should be made to the heading below for details.

Conversion to European Termination

Later alternators have only one connector block at the rear instead of the two used on earlier units. This is due to improvements in the internal wiring which have resulted in the elimination of the 'battery sensing' wire (B+) and the separate earth wire (-) used on previous units. The connector block incorporates only two leads; one is the alternator main feed wire (+) and the other is the connection to the charge warning indicator light (IND).

Earlier units have a two-way connector and an L-shaped three-way connector. These connector blocks can only be fitted one way round. The two-way connector block incorporates connections for the alternator main output lead (+) and the unit earth (-). The three-way connector block incorporates connections for the battery sensing lead (B+) and the charge warning light lead (IND) and a short link lead between the 'IND' connection and the third position in the connector block.

When fitting a later unit in place of an early type one, the alternator wiring must be converted to suit the new connections. The use of the proper Lucas Plug conversion kit 54960402 is recommended.

1. First, disconnect the battery. Cut off all the leads from the existing plugs after noting, or preferably labelling them with their respective locations. Solder on the two new Lucar connectors supplied with the kit to the alternator main feed wire (+) and the charge warning light wire (IND). The large Lucar connector goes on the main feed wire, and the small connector on the 'IND' lead. Push first the small Lucar connector into its location in the European termination plug, then the large main lead connector into the adjacent slot in the plug, and snap on the plug cover. Connect the plug to the alternator and secure with the clip.
2. Discard the link wire and tape back separately the other leads from the original alternator. Finally, reconnect the battery.
3. Check the new brushes for freedom of movement in their holders. Clean any brush which is stiff with a petrol-moistened cloth, or by lightly polishing the brush sides on a smooth file if necessary.
4. Inspect the surface of the slip rings on the end of the rotor. If there is any evidence of roughness or burning this can usually be cleaned off with very fine glass paper, but on no account must emery cloth or similar abrasive be used. If the surface is badly scored, pitted or burned, the slip ring assembly on the rotor must be renewed.
5. Before refitting the brush box, clean off any dirt which may have collected around the slip ring end bracket or the apertures in the plastic end cover.
6. Check that the brushes are correctly positioned in their holders, then locate the brush box assembly on the slip ring end bracket and secure with the retaining screws. Ensure that the

regulator earth lead is also secured by one of the screws. Where applicable, refit the surge protection diode in position on the end bracket. Reconnect the brush box lead (and regulator lead, where applicable) to the rectifier pack. Finally, refit the end cover.

Overhaul

If any repair work, other than replacing the brushes or regulator unit is necessary it will probably be more economical and convenient to have the alternator repaired by an electrical specialist, or to exchange it for a replacement unit.

Voltage Regulator (Figs.D:9 & D:10)

Remove the black plastic cover from the rear of the alternator. This is secured by two retaining screws with either cross heads or hexagon heads. In the latter case a small box spanner or socket will be required to release them.

Identify the type of regulator fitted. The early 8TR type has two short mounting screws, one securing it along with the earth lead to the end bracket and the other securing it to the top of the brush box assembly (Fig.D:10). The 11TR type is secured by a single longer screw to the top of the brush box moulding only, and in this case a spacer is fitted between the brush box and the regulator flange. The earth lead is secured by one of the brush box mounting screws (Fig.D:9). Both of these units have four connecting leads. The later 14TR type regulator is similar to the 11TR type but has only two leads, one an earth lead secured by one of the brush box mounting screws. The regulator field connection in this case is by a flat connecting link between the regulator mounting screw and the adjacent brush assembly. Again an insulating spacer is fitted at the mounting screw.

Carefully note the respective positions of the leads before disconnecting them. Disconnect the wiring connectors from the top of the brush box, and from the brush box securing screw, where applicable. Remove the screw (or screws – 8TR) securing the regulator and withdraw the unit. With the 14TR type it may be necessary to slacken the field link retaining screw to allow the field link to be moved aside. Where fitted, retain the small plastic spacer fitted between the regulator and brush box at the retaining screw.

Position the new regulator on the brush box moulding and secure it in position. On 11TR and 14TR units, ensure that the plastic spacer is correctly fitted,and on the 14TR unit also the connecting link. Reconnect the regulator leads to the positions noted previously. Refit the rear cover.

Brushes

The slip ring brushes are located in the brush box at the rear of the alternator and can be easily replaced if worn or damaged. First remove the alternator rear cover as described above for removing the regulator.

Remove the four screws securing the two brush retaining plates and withdraw the brush assemblies from the brush box moulding (Fig.D:7). Note the respective positions of the leads secured by brush plate screws before disconnecting them. With the 14TR type regulator, it may be necessary to slacken the regulator mounting screws to allow the field connecting link to be moved aside.

Fit the new brush assemblies into the brush box and secure the retaining plates in position with the securing screws. Ensure that the various terminals are located as before at the screws. Refit the end cover.

Alternatively, the complete brush box assembly, together with the regulator unit can be removed from the slip ring end bracket. This will allow inspection of the slip rings and the brush holders.

Where a surge protection diode is fitted, first remove the screw securing the diode to the slip ring end bracket. The diode is then removed with the brush box assembly.

Disconnect the brush box lead (and regulator lead, where applicable) from the rectifier pack. Note the terminal to which

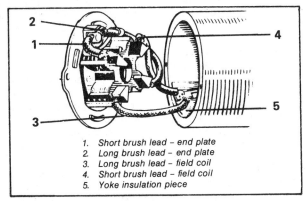

1. Short brush lead – end plate
2. Long brush lead – end plate
3. Long brush lead – field coil
4. Short brush lead – field coil
5. Yoke insulation piece

Fig. D:15 Removing end plate from starter motor — M35J shown

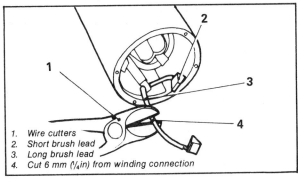

1. Wire cutters
2. Short brush lead
3. Long brush lead
4. Cut 6 mm (¼in) from winding connection

Fig. D:16 Replacing field winding brushes

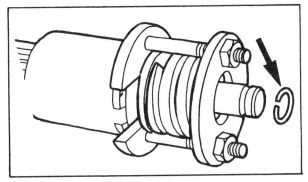

Fig. D:17 Using Bendix spring compressor tool — M35J inertia starter

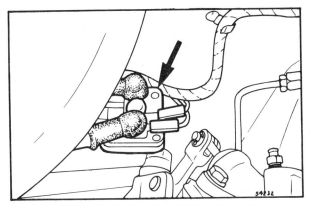

Fig. D:18 Starter solenoid (inertia type)

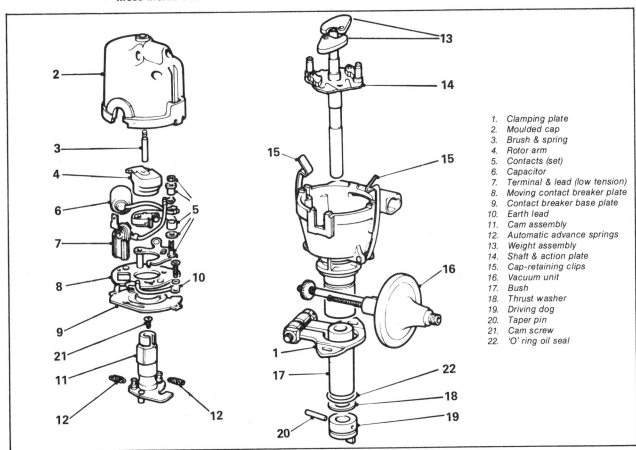

1. Clamping plate
2. Moulded cap
3. Brush & spring
4. Rotor arm
5. Contacts (set)
6. Capacitor
7. Terminal & lead (low tension)
8. Moving contact breaker plate
9. Contact breaker base plate
10. Earth lead
11. Cam assembly
12. Automatic advance springs
13. Weight assembly
14. Shaft & action plate
15. Cap-retaining clips
16. Vacuum unit
17. Bush
18. Thrust washer
19. Driving dog
20. Taper pin
21. Cam screw
22. 'O' ring oil seal

Fig. D:19 Exploded view of distributor — Lucas 25D4

the lead was connected for reassembly. Remove the screws securing the brush box and regulator to the slip ring end bracket and lift off the complete assembly. Note that the regulator earth lead is also secured by one of these screws.

Inspect the brushes for wear. With the brushes in the free position, measure the amount by which they protrude beyond the brush box moulding. The brush length when new is 13 mm (½ in). If the amount protruding is worn to or approaching the wear limit of 6 mm (¼ in), the brush assemblies should be renewed.

Remove the old brush assemblies from the brush box and fit the new ones as detailed above.

STARTER MOTOR .... [6]

Three types of starter motor have been fitted to the Mini range and these are the Lucas M35G and M35J inertia type starter motors (Fig.D:12 & D:13), the latter being the later fitment. On later '86-on Mini's, a Lucas M79 type pre-engaged type is fitted (Fig.D:14).

Although the Lucas M35G or a M35J type look externally similar, apart from the brush cover band on the M35G type, they differ mainly in two respects. The M35G type has a peripheral contact commutator on which the brushes bear from the side, whereas the M35J has a face-type commutator where the brushes bear on the end face. In the M35J unit, the field windings are earthed to the starter yoke but the brush box assembly and the commutator end plate brushes are fully insulated. The end terminal post is connected directly to the end plate brushes. The M35G field windings are insulated from the yoke and incorporate the field terminal post, but the end plate brushes are earthed directly to the end plate.

Replacement (Fig.D:11)
1. Disconnect the battery earth lead. This is very important on pre-engaged type starter motors as the thick supply wire to the starter from the battery is live at all times.
2. Disconnect the horn wires, undo the horn bracket retaining bolts and remove the horn and bracket.
3. On inertia type starter motors, remove the nut from the terminal on the end of the starter motor and disconnect the starter cable. On pre-engaged type starters pull the leads from the solenoid and remove the solenoid main terminal securing nut.
4. Remove the two bolts (lower one first) retaining the starter motor to the engine and withdraw the starter motor from its location.

Install the starter motor in the reverse order of removal.

Brush Replacement - M35G Starter (Fig.D:12)

A good indication of the brush condition can be obtained by inspecting the brushes through the apertures in the starter body, sliding away the cover band. If the brushes are damaged or worn so that they no longer make good contact on the commutator, they should be renewed as a set.

The brushes can be further inspected by lifting the brush springs, using a piece of hooked wire, and withdrawing them from their holders on the commutator end plate.

If the brushes are to be replaced, remove the nuts, washers and insulation bush from the field terminal post at the end plate. Unscrew the two through-bolts and withdraw the end plate from the starter body.

Inspect the contact surface on the outside of the commutator for any signs of wear, burning or other damage. If the surface is blackened or dirty, it should be wiped clean with a petrol-moistened cloth. Slight imperfections can be removed with fine glass paper, but emery cloth or similar abrasive must not be used. If the commutator is grooved, scored or badly worn, it should be skimmed or replaced.

To renew the earthed brushes on the commutator end plate,

unsolder the flexible lead from the terminal eyelet adjacent to the brush holder. Open the eyelet, then insert the replacement brush lead, squeeze the eyelet closed and resolder the connection.

To renew the insulated brushes on the field coils, cut the existing brush leads approximately 6 mm (¼ in) from the field coil connection. Clean the ends of the copper leads still attached to the field coils and solder the new brush leads to them. Note that the insulated brushes have longer leads than the earthed brushes, and also have a braided covering.

Check the new brushes for freedom of movement in their respective holders. Ease them if necessary by cleaning both the brushes and holders with a petrol-moistened cloth, or by polishing the sides of the brushes lightly with a fine file.

Check that the insulator band is fitted between the starter body and the end of the field coils, and that the insulating bush for the field terminal post is also fitted to the commutator end plate. Also check that the thrust washer is in place in the end of the armature shaft.

Pass the field brushes out through the apertures in the starter body. Fit the earthed brushes in their respective holders in the end plate and locate the brush springs on the side of each brush to hold them in the raised position. Assemble the end plate to the starter body, ensuring that the locating dowel on the plate correctly engages the notch in the yoke. Fit the through-bolts and tighten securely. Assemble the insulation bush, washers and nuts on the field terminal post.

Lift the brush springs and fit the field brushes into their respective holders. Press the brushes down into the commutator, then lift the brush springs into position on top of the brushes. Refit the brush cover band over the brush apertures and tighten the clamp screw to secure.

Brushes Replacement — M35J Starter (Fig.D:13)
In this case the commutator end plate must be removed to allow inspection of the brushes as inspection apertures are not provided.
1. Remove the two retaining screws and withdraw the commutator end plate from the starter yoke (Fig.D:13). Withdraw the two field brushes from the brush box on the end plate and separate the end plate from the yoke.
2. Inspect the brushes for wear or damage. Brushes which are worn to, or are approaching the wear limit of 10 mm (⅜ in) must be renewed as a set.
3. Inspect the contact surface on the end of the commutator for any signs of scoring, burning or other damage. If the surface is grooved or badly scored, the commutator should be skimmed or replaced. If the surface is merely blackened or dirty it can be cleaned with a petrol-moistened cloth, or fine glass paper, but emery cloth or similar abrasive must not be used for this purpose.
4. If the brushes on the commutator end plate are to be renewed, these are supplied attached to a new terminal post. Withdraw both brushes from their holders, then remove the nuts, washers and insulation sleeve from the terminal post and withdraw the terminal post and remove the insulation piece. Install the new brushes and terminal post in the reverse order of removing. Ensure that the insulation piece and sleeve are correctly located. Retain the longer brush lead under the clip on the end plate.
5. If the field winding brushes are to be renewed, these are supplied attached to a common lead. Cut the old brush leads approximately 6 mm (¼ in) from their joint on the field windings (Fig.D:16). Clean the leads still attached to the joint and solder the common lead of the new brushes to them. Do not attempt to solder directly to the field winding strip as this may be made of aluminium.
6. Check the brushes for freedom of movement in their respective holders. Any brushes which are stiff should be cleaned with a petrol-moistened cloth, or eased by lightly

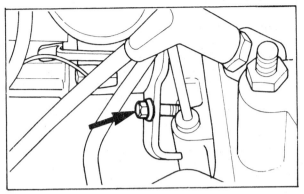

Fig. D:20 Distributor removal 'C' clamp type

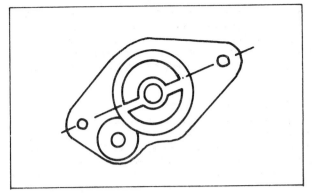

Fig. D:21 Distributor drive slot off-set

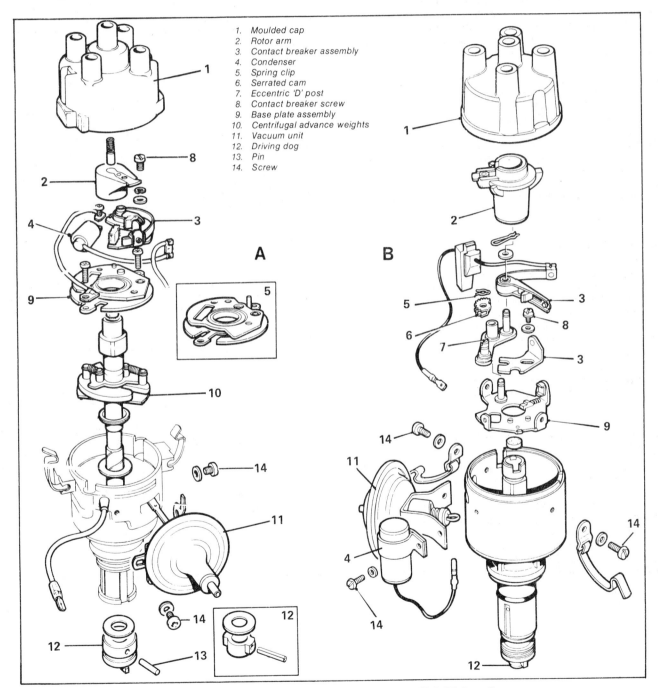

1. Moulded cap
2. Rotor arm
3. Contact breaker assembly
4. Condenser
5. Spring clip
6. Serrated cam
7. Eccentric 'D' post
8. Contact breaker screw
9. Base plate assembly
10. Centrifugal advance weights
11. Vacuum unit
12. Driving dog
13. Pin
14. Screw

A

B

Fig. D:22 Exploded view of distributor (A) Lucas 45D & (B) Ducellier

polishing the sides of the brush with a fine file.

7.   Install the two commutator end brushes and the two field winding brushes in their respective holders on the brush box. Check that the thrust washer is in position on the end of the armature shaft, then assemble the commutator end plate to the starter yoke. Secure the end plate with the two retaining screws.

Drive Pinion — Inertia Type

If difficulty is experienced with the starter motor pinion not meshing correctly with the flywheel ring gear, it may be that the drive assembly requires cleaning. The pinion and barrel assembly should move freely on the screwed sleeve. If there is dirt or other foreign matter on the sleeve it should be washed off with paraffin. Do not use grease or oil on the drive assembly as this would attract dirt.

To replace the drive pinion assembly, compress the main drive spring using a suitable clamping device (e.g. Bendix Spring Compressor Tool) (Fig.D:17) and remove the retaining clip from its groove at the end of the armature shaft. Release the clamping device and remove the spring cup, drive spring, thrust washer and drive pinion assembly from the shaft. It may be necessary to depress the pinion assembly and turn it slightly to disengage it from the shaft splines.

It should be noted that, if the screwed sleeve is worn or damaged, it is essential that it is renewed together with the barrel and pinion.

Fit the new pinion assembly on the armature shaft, with the pinion teeth towards the starter body. Assemble the thrust washer, drive spring and spring seat on the shaft, compress the drive spring and fit the retaining clip. Ensure that the clip is correctly seated in the shaft groove once the spring is released.

Solenoid Replacement — M79 Pre-engaged Starter (Fig.D:14)

1.   Remove the starter motor as previously described.
2.   Disconnect the connecting lead from the starter solenoid.
3.   Remove the two solenoid retaining bolts and pull the solenoid outer body away from the starter housing.
4.   Remove the solenoid spring and unhook the solenoid plunger from the operating lever inside the starter housing..
5.   To refit the solenoid, locate the solenoid plunger onto the lever inside the drive end housing. Refit the spring and guide the solenoid outer housing over the plunger. Refit the two retaining bolts and reconnect the connecting lead to the solenoid.

Solenoid Replacement — M35G & M35J Inertia Starter (Fig.D:18)

The starter solenoid on inertia type starter motors is of the remote type and is fitted to the inner wing panel adjacent to the clutch cover.

To remove the solenoid disconnect the battery earth lead. Pull back the terminal rubber covers, unscrew the terminal nuts and detach the cables from the solenoid. Note the position of the three smaller wires on the solenoid before disconnecting them, unscrew the two retaining screws and remove the solenoid.

Install the solenoid in the reverse order of removal.

DISTRIBUTOR .... [7]

Removal (Figs.D:19 & D:20)

1.   Disconnect the battery earth lead, rotate the crankshaft – see BASIC PROCEDURES, until No.1 piston is on TDC (top dead centre) on its compression stroke. See TUNE-UP for the correct timing marks. Check that No.1 is on the correct stroke by taking off the distributor cap and making sure that the rotor arm is pointing towards the No.1 plug lead segment. If it is not then turn the crankshaft through one revolution until the rotor arm aligns with the relevant segment.
2.   Where fitted, remove the distributor shield from the bonnet lock platform. On Clubman and 1275 GT models release the three clips and remove the ignition shield from the three brackets on the front of the engine.
3.   Disconnect the HT leads from the spark plugs and the ignition coil. If necessary, label the spark plug leads with their respective cylinder numbers to ensure correct fitment on reassembly. Remove the distributor cap from the distributor body.
4.   Disconnect the distributor low tension lead from the terminal blade on the distributor body (25D4 distributor) or from the 'Lucar' connector on 45D4 and Ducellier types. Disconnect the vacuum pipe from the vacuum control unit on the distributor.
5.   Mark the distributor housing to the cylinder block for installation reference.

On models with the clamp plate type, slacken one of the clamp plate retaining bolts securing the clamp plate to the cylinder block (1,Fig.D:19), slacken the clamp plate through bolt and remove the distributor noting the position of the rotor arm and vacuum unit angle for reassembly.

On models with the 'C' plate type fitting (Fig.D:20), undo the 'C' clamp retaining bolt and noting the position of the rotor arm and angle of the vacuum unit for reassembly, withdraw the distributor.

Installation

1.   Ensure that No.1 piston is at the TDC (top dead centre) compression stroke and position the distributor in its bore in the cylinder block with the vacuum unit and rotor arm in the same position as noted previously when removing.
NOTE:The slots in the drive gear and the lugs on the drive dog are off set and can only engage each other in one position (Fig.D:21).
2.   The rotor arm should now be aligned with the No.1 segment in the distributor cap. Check the reference mark at the base of the distributor and align if necessary. Tighten the distributor clamp bolt(s) finger-tight at this stage.
3.   Refit the distributor cap and HT leads and reconnect the LT lead and vacuum pipe. Reconnect the battery earth lead.
4.   Check and if necessary, adjust the dwell angle and ignition timing dynamically with a strobe light as detailed in TUNE-UP.

Distributor Overhaul (Figs.D:19 & D:22)

In most cases of wear or damage to the main components of the distributor (distributor shaft, cam assembly, advance mechanism, bearings etc.) it will probably be more economical and convenient to exchange the complete distributor, rather than attempt to overhaul or repair it. This will be particularly applicable if the unit has been in use over a long period.

Engine Electrical Problems

FAULT	CAUSE	ACTION
STARTER		
Starter doesn't turn (lights dim).	☐ Battery flat or worn. ☐ Bad connection in battery circuit (i.e. terminals loose, engine earth strap corroded).	■ Charge or replace battery. ■ Check all feed and earth connections.
Starter doesn't turn (lights stay bright).	☐ Faulty ignition switch or connections. ☐ Faulty starter solenoid or connections. ☐ Broken starter circuit. ☐ Faulty starter motor.	■ Check connections/replace switch. ■ Check connections/replace solenoid. ■ Trace break and repair. ■ Repair or replace starter.
Solenoid switch chatters	☐ Flat battery.	■ Charge or replace battery.
Starter draws excessive current	☐ Armature bearings worn or seized.	■ Replace bearings or starter motor.
Noisy starter operation	☐ Armature bearings worn.	■ Replace bearings or starter motor.
CHARGING CIRCUIT		
Alternator not charging	☐ Broken or slipping drive belt. ☐ Alternator brushes worn or dirty. ☐ Poor connections to alternator/regulator.	■ Replace drive belt. ■ Replace alternator brushes. ■ Trace faulty connection and repair.

IGNITION SYSTEM (CONTACT BREAKER TYPE)

Engine Fails to Start: *Close contact breaker points and check for:*

FAULT	CAUSE	ACTION
Low or no voltage at coil positive terminal (ignition on)	☐ Open or short circuit in coil circuit.	■ Proceed to next test.
No voltage at coil lead (disconnected from coil)	☐ Open circuit or short in wiring to coil.	■ Reconnect or replace wiring.
Engine fails to start, but battery voltage at coil	☐ Open circuit primary coil winding. ☐ Short circuit condenser. ☐ Contact breaker lines earthed.	■ Check coil primary windings. ■ Replace condenser. ■ Replace or insulate lead.
High voltage reading (over 0.2V max) between coil negative and earth (contact points closed)	☐ Poor C.B. earth. ☐ Dirty contact breaker points.	■ Clean earth connections. ■ Clean or renew CB points.
Poor or no spark between coil HT lead and earth when contacts flicked open	☐ Faulty HT lead. ☐ Faulty condenser.	■ Replace HT lead. ■ Check or replace condenser.
Poor or no spark between coil HT lead and earth) when contacts flicked open (with known good condenser)	☐ Coil secondary winding faulty.	■ Replace coil.

Cooling System

INTRODUCTION .... [1]

The cooling system is a pressurised, partially sealed assembly comprising radiator, water pump, thermostat, engine water jacket and the interior heater matrix.

Coolant is circulated through the system by an impellor type water pump mounted at the front of the engine block, and driven by a 'V' belt from the crankshaft pulley.

The radiator is of the vertical flow type, incorporating a header tank at the top, and is pressurised to approximately 0,91 bar (13 lb/in^2) – pre '74, or 1,0 bar (15 lb/in^2) – '74 on models. The radiator filler cap incorporates an expansion valve and a vacuum valve (Fig.E:2). The expansion valve allows coolant to escape through the overflow pipe if the system is overfilled or overheats. The vacuum valve allows air into the system as the coolant contracts when cooling down.

The thermostat, which is a temperature sensitive water valve, is located in the top hose elbow at the front of the cylinder head. When the engine is cold the thermostat should be closed and therefore the flow of water by-passes the radiator with the result that the engine rapidly reaches normal running temperature.

As the temperature rises, the valve progressively opens allowing the coolant to flow through the radiator.

The Mini is unusual in that the radiator is mounted at the side of the engine with the fan blowing air through it, rather than sucking as in the more normal arrangement with a front mounted radiator.

Access to the radiator and water pump is rather limited due to the lack of underbonnet space, but providing the procedures described in this chapter are followed no particular problems should arise.

TOOLS & EQUIPMENT .... [2]

Few special tools are required for the repair or maintenance of the cooling system. The normal DIY tool kit consisting of various screwdrivers, spanners and sockets etc will be quite adequate for most of the operations described in this chapter – see BASIC PROCEDURES.

However the following items of equipment will be necessary for certain operations.
- Hydrometer – for checking the anti-freeze content.
- Thermometer – for checking the thermostat.
- Drain tray – to collect the coolant when draining the cooling system.

DRAINING & REFILLING .... [3]
Draining
1. Set the heater control to hot.
2. If the car has been run recently, take great care when removing the radiator cap since considerable pressure can build up in the cooling system, causing steam and scalding hot water to be ejected on removal of the cap. To prevent accidental injury, muffle the cap with a heavy cloth and unscrew it slowly to release the pressure in the system. When satisfied that all pressure in the system has been released, remove the cap fully.
3. Place suitable containers beneath the cylinder block drain plug (if fitted) (situated at the rear of the engine block adjacent to the clutch or converter housing (Fig.E:1) and the lower radiator hose at the radiator or radiator drain-plug (if fitted). If the coolant is to be reused, make sure the containers are clean.
4. Open the cylinder block drain plug and release the clip holding the bottom radiator hose to the radiator bottom tank connection. Depending on the position of the clip, it can be undone either by using a long screwdriver from above and behind the engine, or through the access hole in the inner wing panel. To reach the latter, raise and support the front of the car – see BASIC PROCEDURES, raise and remove the passenger – side (near-side) road wheel. Pull the hose free and allow the coolant to drain into the containers.
NOTE:If the cooling system is to be left drained for any period of time, it is advisable to leave a reminder on the vehicle to prevent it being run in this condition.

Flushing
Ideally this operation should be carried out every two years and it involves back flushing the radiator and cylinder block with a high-pressure water hose. The procedure is as follows:
1. Remove the radiator as described later in this chapter.
2. Turn the radiator upside down, position the hose in the bottom hose neck and back flush the unit until all sludge and deposits have been removed. Flush any accumulations of dirt, leaves, etc from the outside fins of the radiator.
3. Remove the thermostat housing and thermostat as described later in this chapter.
4. Insert the high pressure hose in the thermostat location and back flush the cylinder block until all sludge and deposits have been removed.
5. Refit the thermostat housing using a new gasket.
6. Refit the radiator and reconnect the radiator hoses.
7. Refill the cooling system.

Refilling
NOTE:On no account fill or top up the cooling system with plain water. Always top up with the correct solution of anti-freeze (or corrosion inhibitor).
1. Make sure all hose connections are tight and that the heater controls are set to 'hot'.
2. Refill the system with coolant, making sure it is a solution of water and anti-freeze or water and corrosion inhibitor. The anti-freeze or corrosion inhibitor should be diluted in accordance with the maker's instructions and poured into the system slowly through the radiator filler neck. Pouring it slowly will allow much of the air in the system to escape. Top up the system to the

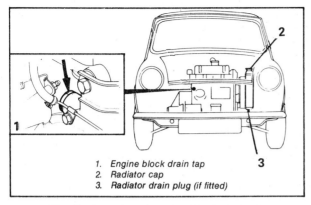

1. Engine block drain tap
2. Radiator cap
3. Radiator drain plug (if fitted)

Fig. E:1 Location of engine block drain plug

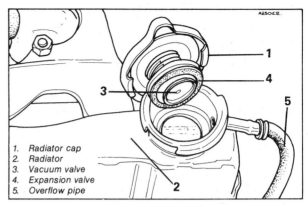

1. Radiator cap
2. Radiator
3. Vacuum valve
4. Expansion valve
5. Overflow pipe

Fig. E:2 Radiator cap & valves

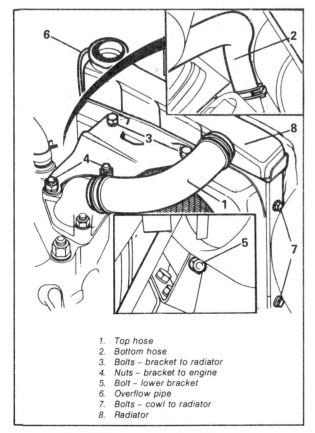

Fig. E:3 Test hose condition by feel

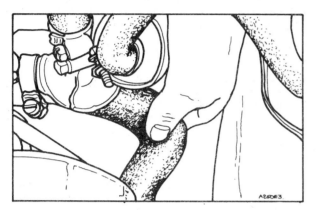

Fig. E:4 Hose clip types

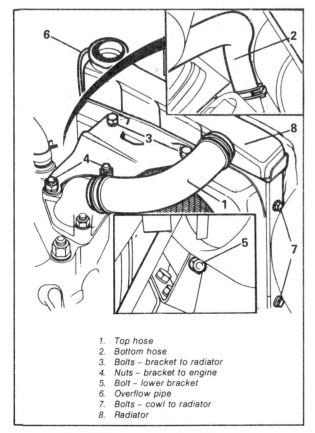

1. Top hose
2. Bottom hose
3. Bolts – bracket to radiator
4. Nuts – bracket to engine
5. Bolt – lower bracket
6. Overflow pipe
7. Bolts – cowl to radiator
8. Radiator

Fig. E:5 Removing radiator & hoses

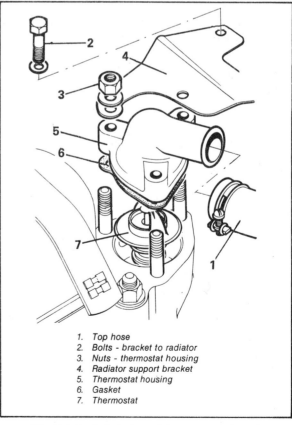

1. Top hose
2. Bolts - bracket to radiator
3. Nuts - thermostat housing
4. Radiator support bracket
5. Thermostat housing
6. Gasket
7. Thermostat

Fig. E:6 Exploded view of thermostat & housing

bottom of the filler neck and replace the filler cap (Fig.E:2).

3.   Run the engine for a short while to allow the coolant to circulate and to ensure that all air is expelled from the system.

4.   Stop the engine and recheck the level of coolant in the radiator. If necessary, top up again. Refit the filler cap and run the engine again. Top up once more if necessary.

NOTE:Take care when removing the radiator cap after running the engine, muffling it with a heavy rag and allow the pressure in the system to escape before removing the cap fully.

Topping Up

The coolant in the system should only be topped up with a water and anti-freeze or water and corrosion inhibitor solution to match that in the system. Topping up with plain water will further dilute the solution and will reduce the effects of either.

When checking the coolant level make sure the engine is cold.

Anti-freeze

Where protection against freezing is required, the system should be filled with a solution of at least 30% anti-freeze and always topped up with a solution of similar strength. The quantity of anti-freeze to be added when filling the system can be calculated from the cooling system capacity specified in TECHNICAL DATA.

When refilling the system with a fresh water and anti-freeze mixture, it may be mixed in one of two ways; either by mixing the exact quantity of coolant for the system in a large container and then pouring it into the system, or by partially filling the system with plain water pouring in the exact amount of anti-freeze and then finally topping up with water. In the latter case, the engine should be run for a while to thoroughly mix the water/anti-freeze solution. The anti-freeze contains a corrosion inhibitor so its strength should be maintained throughout the year. Its specific gravity should be checked periodically. It should be 1.044 for a 30% solution and 1.073 for a 50% solution.

An 'all season' type anti-freeze should be used and changed every two years. If it is necessary to drain the system for any reason during that period, collect the water/anti-freeze solution in clean containers so that it may be reused.

HOSES & CLIPS .... [4]
Checking

The cooling system hoses should be checked periodically – particularly before the beginning of winter – to ensure that they are in good condition and that the clips are secure.

Examine each hose carefully for cracks; particularly on the bends, separation of the layers, swelling or excessive softness of the rubber. Also inspect them for damage, especially chafing due to contact with other components.

Deterioration of the hose rubber is best detected by pinching the hose and looking to see if the surface shows signs of cracking. You can often tell by the feel if a hose is deteriorating because it will be soft and soggy (Fig.E:3).

Where wire clips have been used (Fig.E:4) engine heat will gradually cause the rubber to mould to the shape of the clip, effectively cutting into the hose and becoming a potential sourse of leaks. A tell tale sign of this effect is for the end of the hose to spread out. It may be possible to replace the wire clips with the worm drive type and reuse the hoses, but if there is any doubt about their condition they should be replaced.

The presence of anti-freeze in the coolant makes the location of leaks much easier, as the bright colour of anti-freeze will leave stains. If the cooling system is usually topped up with hard water, the deposits will be white.

Hose Replacement

Changing a hose can sometimes present problems. Access to the hoses on the Mini is generally good, but the bottom hose attachment to the radiator is difficult to reach. Before attempting to remove a hose, ensure that the cooling system is depressurised and that the coolant level is below the relevant hose connection. See the Draining & Refilling, section. Removal and refitting will be easier if the engine has cooled.

The clips fitted to the hoses may be of several types (Fig.E:4). Hose clips fitted during assembly of the car are mainly of the wire type, with a slotted screw to tighten or loosen them (2,Fig.E:4).

Whenever it is necessary to replace any of the clips the proprietary type of worm drive clip will make a very satisfactory substitute for the original.

There is no real substitute for brute force when it comes to shifting a hose that stubbornly adheres to its connecting stub – waggling, pulling and twisting will usually do the trick. However care must be taken with the radiator connections where excessive force could cause the connecting stubs to break away. To ease fitting the new hose, clean the connecting stub to remove any corrosion and then smear the end of the hose with a little grease or petroleum jelly. Position the clip on the hose before pushing it fully onto the stub and then tighten the clip.

RADIATOR .... [5]
Removal (Fig.E:5)

1.   Easier access to the radiator will be provided if the bonnet is first removed. In this case, mark the fitted position of the hinges to facilitate alignment on installation.

2.   Drain the cooling system by removing the cylinder block drain plug (if fitted) and/or disconnecting the bottom hose at the radiator.

3.   Disconnect the top and bottom hose from the radiator, if not already done. Also pull off the overflow pipe. On models with the one-piece radiator cowling, the bottom hose must be completely removed.

4.   Remove the two nuts securing the radiator upper support bracket to the cylinder head, and the two bolts securing the bracket to the radiator cowl, and remove the bracket.

5.   Remove the long through-bolt or the two retaining bolts securing the radiator lower support bracket to the engine mounting (see insert on illustration).

6.   On models with the two-piece cowling, remove the six screws securing the radiator to the cowling and lift out the top half of the cowling. Bend back the bottom hose to the outside of the lower cowling and lift out the radiator.

7.   On models with the one-piece cowling, remove the four screws securing the radiator to the cowling and lift out the radiator and cowling.

Installation

Install the radiator in the reverse order of removing. Finally, refill the cooling system and check for water leaks.

THERMOSTAT .... [6]
Replacement (Fig.E:6)

The thermostat is located under the water outlet elbow at the radiator end of the cylinder head and is easily replaced.

1.   Drain the cooling system sufficiently to bring the coolant level below that of the water outlet housing.

2.   Disconnect the radiator top hose from the water outlet elbow. Remove the two bolts securing the radiator upper support bracket to the radiator cowling. Remove the nuts securing the water outlet elbow to the cylinder head, and lift off the radiator support bracket.

3.   Remove the water outlet elbow together with its gasket and lift the thermostat from its location in the cylinder head.

4.   Clean all old gasket material from the mating faces on the outlet elbow and the cylinder head before installing the new thermostat. Also ensure the thermostat seating in the head is clean.

5.   Install the thermostat with the coil spring side positioned downwards into the head recess. The radiator side of the

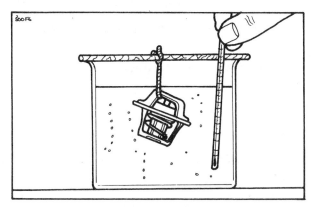

Fig. E:7 Thermostat test in hot water

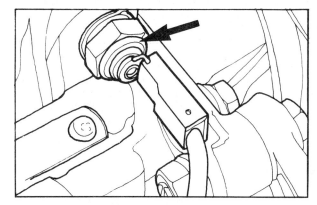

Fig. E:8 Location of temperature gauge sender unit

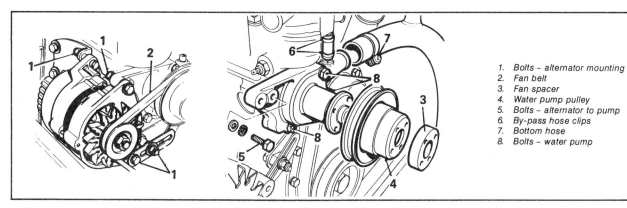

Fig. E:9 Layout of water pump & hose connections

1. Bolts – alternator mounting
2. Fan belt
3. Fan spacer
4. Water pump pulley
5. Bolts – alternator to pump
6. By-pass hose clips
7. Bottom hose
8. Bolts – water pump

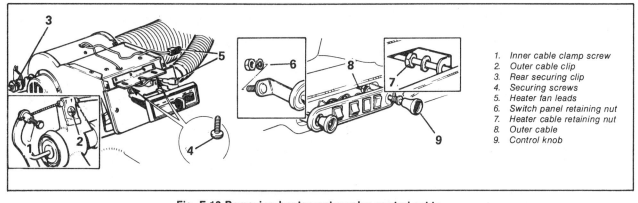

Fig. E:10 Removing heater water valve control cable

1. Inner cable clamp screw
2. Outer cable clip
3. Rear securing clip
4. Securing screws
5. Heater fan leads
6. Switch panel retaining nut
7. Heater cable retaining nut
8. Outer cable
9. Control knob

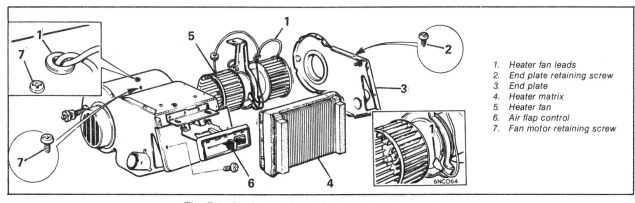

Fig. E:11 Exploded view of heater unit components

1. Heater fan leads
2. End plate retaining screw
3. End plate
4. Heater matrix
5. Heater fan
6. Air flap control
7. Fan motor retaining screw

thermostat is normally marked on the top flange. It is important that the thermostat be correctly positioned in the engine, otherwise overheating will result.

6.   Position a new gasket on the cylinder head face and locate the water outlet elbow over the thermostat. Fit the radiator support bracket in position and secure the bracket and outlet elbow with the three nuts and spring washers. Attach the bracket to the radiator cowling with the two bolts.

7.   Reconnect the radiator top hose and top up the system. Run the engine up to normal operating temperature and check for leaks. Recheck the coolant level once the engine has cooled down.

Testing (Fig.E:7)

The thermostat is a relatively inexpensive item and should be replaced if thought suspect. The operation of the thermostat can be checked, – see TECHNICAL DATA for details of operating temperature.

If a thermostat is found to be stuck in the open position after being removed from a cold engine, it is faulty and must be renewed.

1.   Suspend the thermostat in a suitable container full of water so that it does not touch the sides or bottom (Fig.E:7).

2.   Gradually heat the water, checking the temperature frequently with an accurate thermometer.

3.   If the thermostat does not open at the correct temperature, refuses to open fully, or does not open at all, replace it with a new unit.

TEMPERATURE GAUGE SENDER UNIT ...... [7]
Replacement (Fig.E:8)

If the water temperature gauge is not working or is giving an incorrect reading, it can be checked quite simply by disconnecting the wire from the sender unit and touching the wire terminal against a good earth point on the engine with the ignition ON. The gauge should now read HOT, indicating that the wiring and the gauge are operating correctly and the sender unit is faulty. If the gauge needle does not move, then check the wiring and renew the gauge if necessary.

The sender unit can be replaced very easily by partially draining the cooling system then unscrewing the old unit and screwing in the new one.

Finally top-up the coolant level and run the engine to check the gauge operation.

WATER PUMP .... [8]
Removal (Fig.E:9)

1.   Drain the cooling system and remove the radiator as described previously.

2.   Slacken the dynamo/alternator mounting bolts, press the dynamo/alternator towards the engine and detach the fan belt from the pulleys.

3.   Remove the four retaining bolts and detach the cooling fan, spacer and drive pulley from the water pump hub.

4.   Remove the two top pivot bolts and swing the dynamo/alternator outwards away from the mounting flange on the water pump.

5.   Slacken the clips on the small by-pass hose between the water pump and the underside of the cylinder head, and disconnect the hose.

6.   Disconnect the radiator bottom hose from the pump inlet.

7.   Remove the four bolts securing the water pump to the cylinder block face and detach the pump together with its gasket.

Installation

8.   Clean all old gasket material from the mating face on the cylinder block (and pump, if the original is to be refitted).

9.   Position a new gasket on the cylinder block face, using grease to retain it in position.

10.   Locate the water pump on the engine and secure with the four retaining bolts.

11.   Reconnect the by-pass hose and radiator bottom hose to the pump.

12.   Assemble the drive pulley, spacer and cooling fan to the pump hub, then fit the fan belt and adjust the tension as detailed in ROUTINE MAINTENANCE.

13.   Finally, install the radiator and refill the cooling system as previously described.

14.   When installation is complete, run the engine up to normal operating temperature and check for leaks.

HEATER CONTROLS & MATRIX .... [9]

The flow of water through the heater is controlled by a cable operated valve mounted on the cylinder head. The cable terminates in a push/pull or sliding control knob mounted on the right-hand side of the switch panel inside the car.

Replacement — Control Cable (Fig.E:10)

1.   Disconnect the battery earth lead.

2.   Slacken the inner cable clamp screw and the outer cable securing clip at the water valve on the cylinder head, and pull the cable free.

3.   Undo the two securing screws located below the parcel shelf and slacken the rear securing nut. Lower the heater assembly for access.

4.   Disconnect the heater blower motor switch wire from the switch terminals.

5.   Undo the two switch panel retaining nuts (6,Fig.E:10) and ease the switch panel from the parcel tray edge.

6.   Undo the cable securing nut at the rear of the panel, and remove it together with the 'shakeproof' washer.

7.   Pull the complete cable through the switch panel and remove it from the car.

Installation

Install the cable in the reverse order of removal, ensuring that the grommet is correctly positioned where the cable passes through the bulkhead.

Removal - Heater Assembly (Fig.E:10)

1.   Drain the cooling system as described previously. Remove the front carpet and position a washing up bowl or similar container under the heater casing to collect any coolant remaining in the heater. Disconnect the hoses and allow the coolant to drain into the bowl.

2.   Undo the two cross head screws (4,Fig.E:10) which are accessible from below the parcel tray, behind the switch panel. This will allow the heater assembly to swing down and rest against the bulkhead.

3.   Pull off the air trunking, demister pipes and blower motor wiring.

4.   Slacken the securing nut (3,Fig.E:10) and lift out the heater assembly.

Removal — Heater Matrix (Fig.E:11)

1.   Remove the heater assembly as described previously.

2.   Disconnect the wiring from the heater fan motor switch terminals.

3.   Undo the three retaining screws and remove the heater control mounting bracket.

4.   Undo the nine cross-head screws holding the right-hand end plate to the main heater casing.

5.   The heater matrix can now be lifted from the casing.

Installation

Install the matrix in the reverse order of removal, ensuring that the air deflector flap is correctly engaged on its hinge pins before finally screwing the casing end plate in position.

Cooling System Problems

FAULT	CAUSE	ACTION
Loss of coolant	☐ Leaks.	■ Locate and repair.
	☐ Damaged radiator or heater matrix.	■ Repair or replace radiator or matrix.
	☐ Damaged cylinder head gasket.	■ Replace gasket. Check engine oil and refill as necessary.
	☐ Cracked cylinder block.	■ Replace cylinder block.
	☐ Cracked cylinder head.	■ Replace cylinder head.
	☐ Loose cylinder head.	■ Tighten cylinder head.
Poor circulation	☐ Restriction in system.	■ Check hoses for kinking.
		■ Clear the system of rust and sludge.
	☐ Insufficient coolant.	■ Replenish.
	☐ Inoperative water pump.	■ Replace water pump.
	☐ Loose drive belt.	■ Adjust/replace belt.
	☐ Thermostat not opening.	■ Replace thermostat.
	☐ Air lock in system.	■ Refill system following. procedure in text.
Corrosion	☐ Insufficient anti-freeze.	■ Add anti-freeze.
	☐ Infrequent flushing and changing of coolant.	■ Flush thoroughly at least every two years.
Overheating	☐ Inoperative thermostat.	■ Replace thermostat.
	☐ Radiator fins obstructed.	■ Clean fins.
	☐ Incorrect engine tune.	■ Tune engine.
	☐ Inoperative water pump.	■ Replace.
	☐ Loose drive belt.	■ Adjust tension.
	☐ Restricted radiator.	■ Flush radiator.
Inaccurate temperature gauge reading	☐ Faulty gauge or sender unit.	■ Replace temperature gauge or sender unit.
Overcooling	☐ Inoperative or incorrect grade thermostat	■ Replace thermostat.

Fuel System

INTRODUCTION . . . . [1]

All Mini models have a conventional fuel system which basically comprises the carburettor, fuel pump and fuel tank.

The carburettor on all models is an SU type, an HS2 on early models, and an HS4 on later models and all automatic transmission variants.

Cars built before 1970 model year, with positive earth electrical systems, have an electric fuel pump mounted on the lower passenger-side (near-side) flange of the rear sub frame, in a rather exposed position. Later cars are fitted with a mechanical fuel pump mounted on the rear face of the engine block and driven from the camshaft.

The fuel tank on Saloon versions is mounted inside the boot on the passenger-side (near-side) and on Estate, Van and Pick-up models it is mounted below the rear floor area.

To minimise the risk of fire when working on the fuel system, ALWAYS disconnect the battery earth lead first and select a well ventilated area when carrying out repairs. Avoid working in a confined place such as a closed garage where petrol fumes could build up.

Keep all components as clean as possible and clean the area around any components or connections before removing them. Use new gaskets, sealing rings, hoses, clips etc., where required.

Note that the carburettor adjustment procedures for the idle speed and mixture are described in TUNE-UP.

TOOLS & EQUIPMENT . . . . [2]

Other than those tools listed under Basic Tools & Equipment in BASIC PROCEDURES, the following special tools will be required to carry out the operations detailed in this chapter.
- Vacuum pump – for checking the fuel pump.
- Tool No.18G 1119 – for removing and replacing the crankcase seal on mechanical fuel pumps.

AIR CLEANER . . . . [3]

Several different types of air cleaner unit have been used on the Mini range and all of them are easy to remove and install. All types have a paper element type filter. Details of the filter replacement are given in ROUTINE MAINTENANCE.

Air Cleaner Replacement — Early Models (Fig.F:1)
1. Undo the central wing nut and lift off the air cleaner assembly.
2. Disconnect the engine breather hose (2,Fig.F:1), if fitted.
3. Lever off the lid for access to the filter element.
4. Install in the reverse order of removal, ensuring that the rubber seal is in position between the air cleaner casing and the carburettor and before finally tightening the wing nut, position the air intake tube in either the 'summer' position (A,Fig.F:1) or

the 'winter' position (B,Fig.F:1). In the 'winter' position, warm air is drawn from the exhaust manifold to prevent the carburettor icing-up.

Air Cleaner Replacement — Later Models (Figs.F:2 & F:3)
1. Undo the two wing nuts securing the plastic air cleaner assembly to the carburettor adaptor.
2. Lift the assembly away from the engine and withdraw the air intake tube from the hot air box at the exhaust manifold (Fig.F:2) or pull the trunking from the air intake valve (Fig.F:3), whichever is applicable.
3. Insert a screwdriver in the moulded slots around the edge of the air cleaner casing and lever off the lid for access to the filter element.
4. Assemble the casing with the moulded arrow in line with the locating lug on the main casing.
5. Install the assembly in the reverse order of removal, ensuring the rubber sealing ring is in position between the casing and the carburettor adaptor.
6. If the air intake tube is not fitted with a flap valve, position the tube as described previously for early models.
7. If the air intake tube is fitted with a flap valve check the position of the flap with the engine cold. The flap should be closed and if it is pressed down and released it should spring back to the closed position again. Check also that the edge of the flap is sealing tightly against the valve casing.

FUEL PUMP . . . . [4]
Replacement — Electric Type

Early Mini models, up to the adoption of negative earth electrical system in October 1969, used either the SU SP or AUF 201 type fuel pump. The two types of pump are of similar construction, differing only in respect of the pump body which incorporates the inlet and outlet nozzles, filter and fuel valves. The AUF 201 pump can be identified by the two plastic nozzles retained by a clamp plate on the end of the pump body.

The three main sources of trouble with these types of pumps are the contact breaker points, fuel valve and diaphragm. Another common fault is air leakage into the fuel lines, particularly on the inlet side of the pump, causing a constant 'ticking' of the pump without proper fuel delivery when the ignition is switched on.

The pump is best removed from its location at the rear sub-frame for inspection, and this is a straight-forward operation. However, when refitting the pump, ensure that the outlet is located at the top. The outlet must be vertically above the inlet port with the outlet nozzles horizontal (Fig.F:4).

Overhaul (Fig.F:5)
1.First remove the end cover and inspect the contact points. The end cover is normally sealed with tape and a rubber band

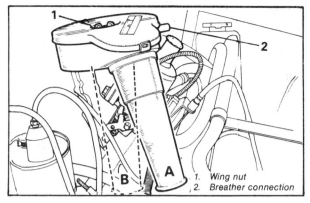

Fig. F:1 Air cleaner — early models

1. Wing nut
2. Breather connection

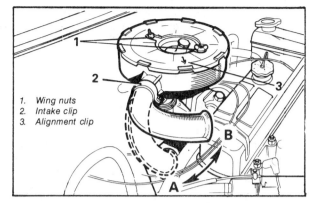

1. Wing nuts
2. Intake clip
3. Alignment clip

Fig. F:2 Air cleaner without valve — later models

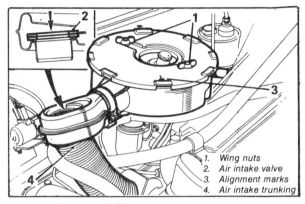

1. Wing nuts
2. Air intake valve
3. Alignment marks
4. Air intake trunking

Fig. F:3 Air cleaner with valve — later models

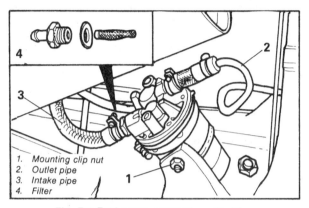

1. Mounting clip nut
2. Outlet pipe
3. Intake pipe
4. Filter

Fig. F:4 Fuel pump removal — electric

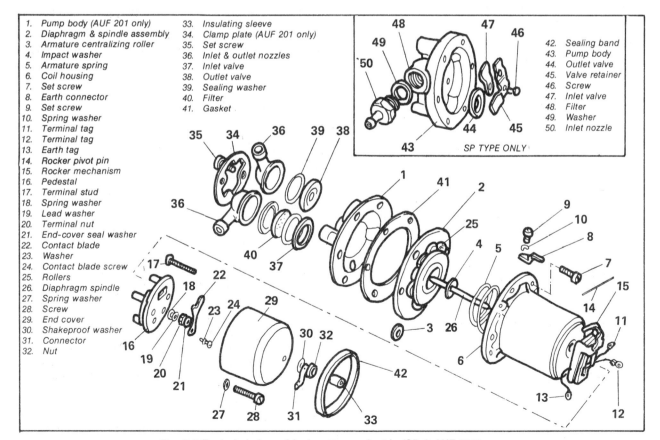

1. Pump body (AUF 201 only)
2. Diaphragm & spindle assembly
3. Armature centralizing roller
4. Impact washer
5. Armature spring
6. Coil housing
7. Set screw
8. Earth connector
9. Set screw
10. Spring washer
11. Terminal tag
12. Terminal tag
13. Earth tag
14. Rocker pivot pin
15. Rocker mechanism
16. Pedestal
17. Terminal stud
18. Spring washer
19. Lead washer
20. Terminal nut
21. End-cover seal washer
22. Contact blade
23. Washer
24. Contact blade screw
25. Rollers
26. Diaphragm spindle
27. Spring washer
28. Screw
29. End cover
30. Shakeproof washer
31. Connector
32. Nut

33. Insulating sleeve
34. Clamp plate (AUF 201 only)
35. Set screw
36. Inlet & outlet nozzles
37. Inlet valve
38. Outlet valve
39. Sealing washer
40. Filter
41. Gasket

42. Sealing band
43. Pump body
44. Outlet valve
45. Valve retainer
46. Screw
47. Inlet valve
48. Filter
49. Washer
50. Inlet nozzle

SP TYPE ONLY

Fig. F:5 Exploded view of fuel pump — electric (SP & AUF 201)

around the joint and these must be removed.

2.   Next remove the nut, Lucas connector and star washer from the end terminal screw and take off the Bakelite end cover. The points can then be inspected after slackening the screw securing the spring blade and withdrawing the blade which is slotted at its fixed end. The blade retaining screw also secures the long coil lead and need not be completely removed at this time.

3.   Examine the two sets of contact points for signs of burning or pitting. If either is evident, the brass rocker assembly and spring blade must be removed and replaced.

4.   To inspect the diaphragm which is located between the coil housing and the pump body, first mark the relative positions of the housing and body to ensure correct reassembly; also note or mark the position of the earth screw hole in the housing in relation to the pump body. Remove the six securing screws and separate the pump body from the coil housing and diaphragm. The neoprene diaphragm can now be examined after carefully peeling back the plastic protective sheet. If either the diaphragm or plastic sheet show signs of damage or deterioration, the diaphragm assembly must be replaced. The diaphragm and central spindle are serviced only as a unit and no attempt should be made to separate them.

5.   Reassemble the pump components in the reverse order of dismantling and check that the contact spring blade is resting against the ridge on the pedestal mounting (Fig.F:6), when the outer rocker assembly is pressed into the coil housing.

6.   Check the gap between the outer rocker and the coil housing, which should be 1,8 mm (0.070 in). When the outer rocker is released, the spring blade should be deflected away from the pedestal ridge. If this is not the case, gently bend the contact blade to achieve the correct setting.

Replacement — Mechanical Type

With the change to negative earth electrical system in October 1969, the electrical type fuel pump was replaced with a mechanical one, mounted at the rear of the engine block and driven by an eccentric on the camshaft. Early models will be fitted with the 700 series type pump which has a detachable domed cover for access to the fuel filter screen. However, some later models are fitted with the 800 series type which is a sealed unit and in this case no maintenance or overhaul is possible.

The mechanical pump installation is shown in Fig.F:7, but removal is a difficult task while the engine is installed in the car, and it will be necessary to remove some surrounding components to gain access to the unit. On some models it is difficult even to find enough room to remove the top cover to allow the filter screen to be cleaned. When refitting the pump, always ensure that the total thickness of the pump insulating block with its two gaskets remains unaltered (1,Fig.F:7).

The main sources of trouble with the mechanical type pump are the fuel valves and the diaphragm, but as stated previously, these can be serviced only on the 700 series pump.

Pump Output Test

The pump can be tested either by using a gauge reading for a vacuum of 63,5 cm (25 in) hg to 1,05 kg/sq cm (16 lb/in²) pressure, or without a gauge by simply blocking the inlet and outlet tubes as described below. For both of these tests, the pump will have to be removed from the engine.

If any of the tests described below give unsatisfactory results, the pump should be overhauled or replaced as applicable.

Testing — With Gauge

1.   Connect the gauge to the inlet nozzle of the pump.

2.   Operate the pump rocker lever by hand through three full strokes.

3.   The minimum vacuum reading should not drop more than 50 mm (2 in) Hg in 15 seconds.

4.   Disconnect the gauge hose from the inlet and connect it to

the outlet nozzle of the pump.

5.   Again, operate the pump rocker lever through two full strokes.

6.   The pressure reading should not drop more than 0,04 kg/sq cm (0.5 lb/in²) in 15 seconds.

Testing — Without Gauge

A reasonable indication of the condition of the pump can be obtained by the following test which does not require any special equipment.

1.   Block the inlet nozzle of the pump with a finger and operate the pump rocker lever by hand through three full strokes.

2.   Release the finger and listen for a noise caused by air being sucked into the pump chamber.

3.   Cover the outlet nozzle of the pump with a finger and depress the rocker lever fully.

4.   The lever should not return within 15 seconds.

Dismantling

The SU type AUF 800 mechanical fuel pump is a sealed unit and cannot be dismantled for repair. If it is faulty it must be replaced.

It is possible, however, to dismantle the AUF 700 type pump (Fig.F:8).

1.   Wipe the dirt from the outside of the pump and mark across the outlet cover and upper and lower body sections, so the alignment will not be altered on reassembly.

2.   Remove the filter by lifting off the outlet cover, and retain the sealing washer.

3.   Extract the upper body screws, securing the two halves of the pump together.

4.   Lift out the combined inlet/outlet valve.

5.   Withdraw the insert from the outlet cover.

6.   Drive the rocker lever pivot pin out using a hammer and thin parallel punch while holding the lever and diaphragm against spring pressure. The rocker lever and spring are now free.

7.   Lubricate the crankcase seal to ease the passage of the spindle stirrup through it, and withdraw the diaphragm spring assembly.

8.   If the crankcase seal is to be replaced, the old seal and the retaining cup will have to be extracted with tool No.18G 1119, screwing it in, in order to withdraw the cup from the lower body.

Reassembly

Reassemble the pump in the reverse order of dismantling, noting the following points:

a)   Use the special tool again to refit the retaining cup (if removed).

b)   Make sure there are no sharp edges on the diaphragm spindle and stirrup. Oil and refit, position the stirrup slot by the rocker lever ready for engagement.

c)   Ensure that the inlet/outlet valve groove locates in the housing and that the fine edge of the inlet valve contacts is seating evenly.

d)   Align the holes in the lower body with those in the diaphragm, push down the rocker to flatten the diaphragm and loosely fit the short screws.

e)   Assemble the outlet cover, sealing washer and filter and tighten all the screws down evenly.

THROTTLE CABLE . . . . [5]
Replacement (Fig.F:9)

Detach the throttle return spring from the throttle lever and its abutment bracket. Slacken the clamp nut to release the cable at the throttle lever, then withdraw the cable from the abutment bracket.

At the throttle pedal, release the nipple end from the slot in the top of the pedal lever and push the cable through the bulkhead into the engine compartment. Remove the rubber clips securing the cable to the heater hose, and withdraw the cable assembly.

Fit the new cable in the reverse sequence. Ensure that the

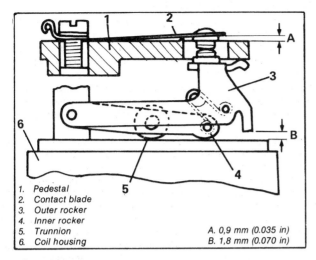

1. Pedestal
2. Contact blade
3. Outer rocker
4. Inner rocker
5. Trunnion
6. Coil housing

A. 0,9 mm (0.035 in)
B. 1,8 mm (0.070 in)

Fig. F:6 Fuel pump contact assembly — electric

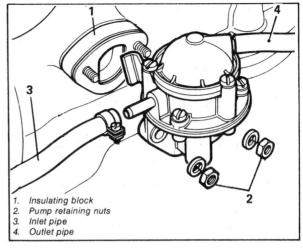

1. Insulating block
2. Pump retaining nuts
3. Inlet pipe
4. Outlet pipe

Fig. F:7 Removing fuel pump — mechanical

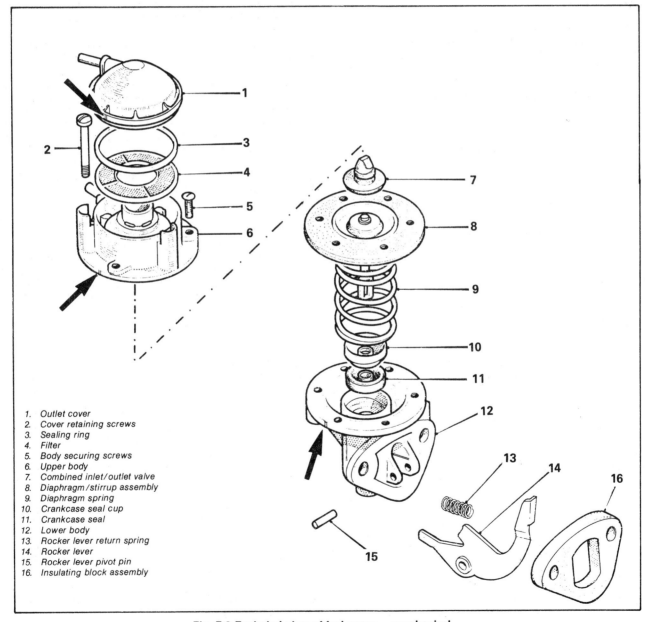

1. Outlet cover
2. Cover retaining screws
3. Sealing ring
4. Filter
5. Body securing screws
6. Upper body
7. Combined inlet/outlet valve
8. Diaphragm/stirrup assembly
9. Diaphragm spring
10. Crankcase seal cup
11. Crankcase seal
12. Lower body
13. Rocker lever return spring
14. Rocker lever
15. Rocker lever pivot pin
16. Insulating block assembly

Fig. F:8 Exploded view of fuel pump — mechanical

throttle pedal has approximately 4 mm (⅛in) free movement before it begins to open the throttle.

CHOKE CABLE .... [6]
Replacement (Figs.F:9 & F:10)
1. Remove the air cleaner assembly to allow access. Detach the clip securing the choke cable to the abutment bracket, then slacken the clamp screw at the cable trunnion and disconnect the cable from the carburettor.
2. Working inside the car, remove the screws securing the heater assembly under the parcel shelf, and lower the heater to gain access to the rear side of the switch panel. Disconnect the lead from the heater switch. Remove the nuts securing the switch panel and pull the panel forward. Remove the locking nut and washer securing the choke outer cable to the switch panel. Pull the complete cable assembly through the bulkhead grommet and withdraw it from the switch panel.
3. Install the new cable in the reverse order of removal, ensuring that the cable has 2 mm (¹/₁₆in) free movement before it starts to pull on the fast idle cam lever.

CARBURETTOR .... [7]

Most Mini models are fitted with an SU type HS4 carburettor, the exceptions being early 850/1000 models with manual transmission up to 1974. These latter cars are equipped with an HS2 carburettor. Although both types are of similar design, they differ mainly in respect of the position of the float chamber and the throttle lever assembly which are on opposite sides for the two types.

Idle Adjustment
The procedure for adjusting the carburettor idle speed is fully described in TUNE-UP.

Removal & Installation
1. Unscrew the wing nut or wing nuts on the air cleaner lid and lift the air cleaner assembly off the carburettor air intake duct. On some models it may be necessary to first disconnect the engine breather hose and/or the connector pipe from the air temperature control valve flange.
2. Disconnect and plug the fuel feed hose from the float chamber, also the engine breather hose from the carburettor adaptor (where applicable) and the distributor vacuum advance pipe (Fig.F.9).
3. Disconnect the throttle return spring from the throttle lever and its abutment bracket, then disconnect the throttle cable. On models with automatic transmission, it will also be necessary to disconnect the fork end of the kick-down control rod from the throttle lever. Disconnect the choke cable.
4. Remove the two nuts and spring washers securing the carburettor to the inlet manifold studs and lift off the carburettor assembly complete with the cable abutment plate.
5. If required, the air intake duct can now be detached from the carburettor intake.
6. Installation is a simple reversal of the removal procedure. Use new gaskets between the manifold face, abutment plate and carburettor flange if they have been damaged during removal.
7. When reconnecting the choke cable, allow approximately 2 mm (¹/₁₆in) free movement before the cable starts to pull on the fast idle cam lever. The throttle pedal should also have approximately 3 mm (1/8 in) of free movement before the throttle starts to open.
8. When installation is complete, check the idle and mixture settings as described in TUNE-UP.
9. On automatic models, check the adjustment of the kick-down control linkage as described in AUTOMATIC TRANSMISSION.

Cleaning the Float Chamber
On some models it may first be necessary to remove the air cleaner to gain access to the float chamber.
1. Disconnect and plug the fuel feed pipe from the float chamber lid. Mark the relative positions of the float chamber lid and body to ensure correct alignment on reassembly. Remove the three screws securing the lid to the float chamber body and detach the lid assembly, together with its gasket (Fig.F:11). Retain the part number tag fitted to one of the retaining screws.
2. Clean any sediment from the float chamber — this can best be done by soaking up the fuel in the chamber with a suitable absorbent lint-free cloth or tissue paper, then blowing any remaining sediment out of the chamber with an air line.
3. If required, the fuel float can be removed and the fuel needle withdrawn from its housing to check its condition. Hold the float hinge pin at its serrated end when withdrawing it. Examine the fuel needle for wear i.e. small ridges or grooves on the seat end of the needle. Also check that the spring-loaded plunger on the opposite end operates freely (later type needles only). Renew the needle valve and seating if worn. The seating is a screw fit in the float chamber lid.
4. Reassemble the components in the reverse order of dismantling. The fuel needle is inserted, tapered-end first, into its seating.
5. On early models which have a brass or nylon float with a metal float lever, the float level setting should be checked as follows:
6. With the float chamber lid held upside-down, insert a drill or gauge rod of suitable diameter between the hinged lever and the machined lip of the float chamber lid (Fig.F:12). The end of the lever should just rest on the rod when the needle is on its seating. Use an 8 mm (⁵/₁₆in) diameter rod for the brass float, and a 3 mm (⅛in) diameter rod with the nylon float.
7. If adjustment is necessary, this should be carried out at the point where the end of the lever meets the shank. Do NOT bend the shank, which must be perfectly flat and at right-angles to the needle when on its seating.

Cleaning Piston & Suction Chamber
A sticking piston will inhibit acceleration and smooth running. This can be checked by removing the piston damper from the top of the suction chamber then raising the piston with the lifting pin or a finger inserted into the carburettor intake. The piston should move up quite freely when raised, and fall back smartly when released.

If sticking does occur, the whole assembly should be removed and cleaned as follows:
1. Remove the air cleaner assembly and mark the position of the suction chamber in relation to the carburettor body to ensure correct alignment on reassembly. Thoroughly clean the outside of the suction chamber and the adjacent surface on the carburettor body.
2. Remove the damper from the top of the suction chamber. Remove the three securing screws and lift off the suction chamber. Remove the piston spring. Carefully lift the piston assembly and jet needle (Fig.F:14) out of the carburettor body, and empty the oil from the hollow in the end of the piston rod.
3. Carefully clean all fuel deposits, etc., from the inside of the suction chamber and the two diameters of the piston, using petrol, or preferably methylated spirit, then wipe the components dry. Do NOT use abrasives to clean these items.
4. The operation of the suction chamber and piston can be checked as follows if required: Plug the transfer holes in the bottom of the piston with rubber plugs or plasticine (Fig.F:13). Insert the piston fully into the suction chamber and refit the damper assembly. Secure a large flat washer to one of the suction chamber fixing holes with a screw and nut so that it overlaps the bore.
5. With the assembly held upside-down, hold the piston and check the time taken for the suction chamber to fall the full

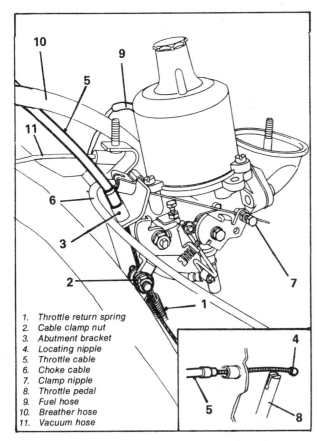

1. Throttle return spring
2. Cable clamp nut
3. Abutment bracket
4. Locating nipple
5. Throttle cable
6. Choke cable
7. Clamp nipple
8. Throttle pedal
9. Fuel hose
10. Breather hose
11. Vacuum hose

Fig. F:9 Throttle & choke cable attachments

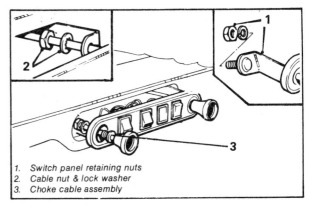

1. Switch panel retaining nuts
2. Cable nut & lock washer
3. Choke cable assembly

Fig. F:10 Choke cable removal — interior

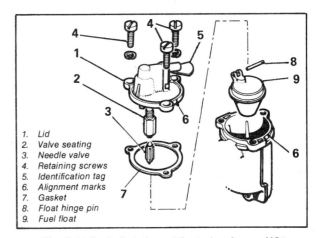

1. Lid
2. Valve seating
3. Needle valve
4. Retaining screws
5. Identification tag
6. Alignment marks
7. Gasket
8. Float hinge pin
9. Fuel float

Fig. F:11 Exploded view of float chamber — HS4

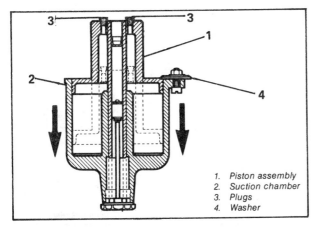

1. Gauge rod or drill
2. Machined lip
3. Adjustment point
4. Needle housing
5. Lever hinge pin

Fig. F:12 Setting float level — early type

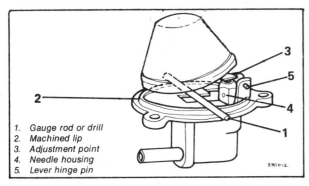

1. Piston assembly
2. Suction chamber
3. Plugs
4. Washer

Fig. F:13 Checking suction chamber & piston

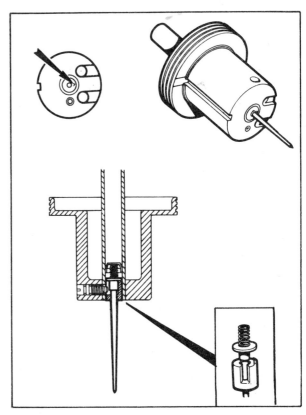

Fig. F:14 Details of spring loaded needle

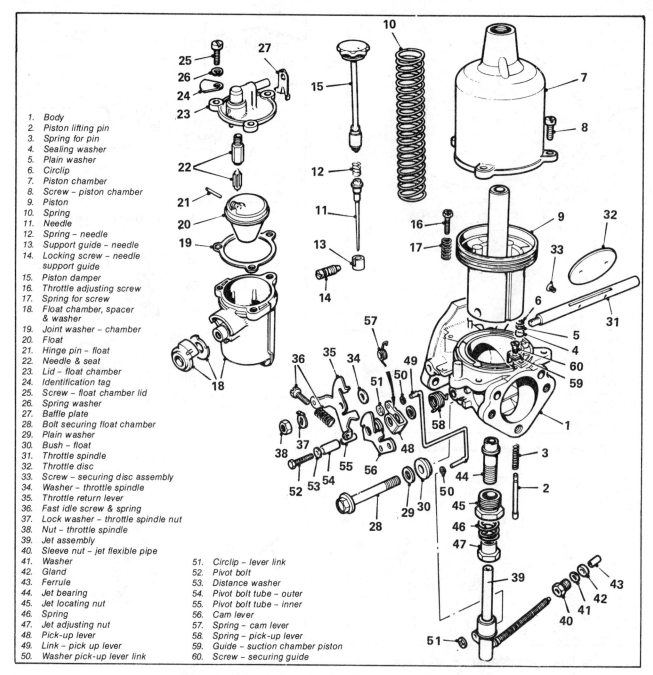

1. Body
2. Piston lifting pin
3. Spring for pin
4. Sealing washer
5. Plain washer
6. Circlip
7. Piston chamber
8. Screw – piston chamber
9. Piston
10. Spring
11. Needle
12. Spring – needle
13. Support guide – needle
14. Locking screw – needle support guide
15. Piston damper
16. Throttle adjusting screw
17. Spring for screw
18. Float chamber, spacer & washer
19. Joint washer – chamber
20. Float
21. Hinge pin – float
22. Needle & seat
23. Lid – float chamber
24. Identification tag
25. Screw – float chamber lid
26. Spring washer
27. Baffle plate
28. Bolt securing float chamber
29. Plain washer
30. Bush – float
31. Throttle spindle
32. Throttle disc
33. Screw – securing disc assembly
34. Washer – throttle spindle
35. Throttle return lever
36. Fast idle screw & spring
37. Lock washer – throttle spindle nut
38. Nut – throttle spindle
39. Jet assembly
40. Sleeve nut – jet flexible pipe
41. Washer
42. Gland
43. Ferrule
44. Jet bearing
45. Jet locating nut
46. Spring
47. Jet adjusting nut
48. Pick-up lever
49. Link – pick up lever
50. Washer pick-up lever link

51. Circlip – lever link
52. Pivot bolt
53. Distance washer
54. Pivot bolt tube – outer
55. Pivot bolt tube – inner
56. Cam lever
57. Spring – cam lever
58. Spring – pick-up lever
59. Guide – suction chamber piston
60. Screw – securing guide

Fig. F:15 Exploded view of carburettor components — HS4

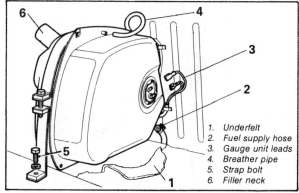

1. Underfelt
2. Fuel supply hose
3. Gauge unit leads
4. Breather pipe
5. Strap bolt
6. Filler neck

Fig. F:16 Fuel tank removal — Saloon

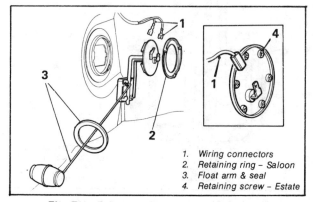

1. Wiring connectors
2. Retaining ring – Saloon
3. Float arm & seal
4. Retaining screw – Estate

Fig. F:17 Removing fuel gauge sender unit

extent of its travel. This should take five to seven seconds. If this time is exceeded, check both the piston and the suction chamber for cleanliness and mechanical damage. If the suction chamber has been dropped at any time this may have damaged the bore. Renew the piston and suction chamber assembly if the time taken cannot be brought within these specified limits.

6. Lubricate the piston rod lightly with a drop of light oil – one of the 'dry' lubricants such as WD 40 may be used for this purpose. Reassemble the components in the reverse order of dismantling, not forgetting the piston spring. Ensure that the assembly marks made previously are correctly aligned, then tighten the securing screws evenly.

7. Finally, fill the piston damper with fresh engine oil until the level is approximately 13 mm (½in) above the top of the hollow piston rod, then refit the piston damper.

Centring the Jet

If the piston does not fall freely on the carburettor bridge with a distinct metallic 'click' when the jet adjusting nut is screwed to its uppermost position, the carburettor jet must be centralised as follows:

If should be noted that this procedure applies only to early type carburettors, as later carburettors have a spring-loaded swing needle which is self-centring (Fig.F:14).

1. Remove the air cleaner assembly to allow access. Support the plastic moulded base of the jet, then remove the screw retaining the jet pick-up link and link bracket to the jet head. Unscrew the sleeve nut from the base of the float chamber and disconnect the jet flexible feed tube. Withdraw the jet assembly from the bottom of the carburettor. Unscrew the jet adjusting nut, remove the locking spring and refit the nut without the spring. Screw the nut up as far as possible. Now slacken the jet bearing locking nut until the jet bearing can be turned with the fingers. Refit the jet assembly in the jet bearing and hold it in the uppermost position with a finger.

2. Remove the damper piston from the top of the suction chamber and using a pencil or similar instrument, apply gentle pressure to the top of the piston rod to push the piston down onto the bridge. Tighten the jet locking nut while holding the jet against the jet bearing. Ensure that the jet is in its correct angular position during this operation.

3. With the jet still in the fully raised position, lift the piston with the lifting pin then release it and check that it falls freely onto the carburettor bridge with a distinct metallic 'click'. Lower the jet with the adjusting nut and repeat the check. An identical sound should be heard with the jet raised or lowered. If a sharper 'click' is heard with the jet in the lowered position, repeat the centring procedure.

4. If difficulty is encountered in correctly centring the jet, this can often be achieved by raising the piston and allowing it to fall onto the jet bridge. The slight impact should locate the jet in its central position in relation to the piston needle.

5. When the centring procedure is successfully completed, remove the jet assembly and refit the adjusting nut with its locking spring. Screw the nut up as far as possible, then turn it down two complete turns (12 flats) to provide the initial setting.

6. Refit the jet in the bearing and reconnect the flexible feed tube to the float chamber. Ensure that the end of the tube projects a minimum of 5 mm (³⁄₁₆in) beyond the sealing gland before fitting the tube. Tighten the sleeve nut only until the gland is compressed as over-tightening can cause leakage.

7. Support the jet head and reconnect the pick-up link and link bracket with the securing screw.

8. Top up the piston damper with engine oil, as necessary, to bring the oil level approximately 13 mm (½in) above the top of the hollow piston rod. Refit the air cleaner assembly.

9. Finally, check the idle and mixture settings and adjust if necessary as described in TUNE-UP.

FUEL TANK . . . . [8]
Replacement — Saloon (Fig.F:16)

1. As a safety precaution, first disconnect the battery earth lead. Empty all possible fuel from the tank. This is best done either by syphoning or pumping it out.

2. Remove the floor covering from the luggage compartment and lift out the spare wheel. Where underfelt is fitted in the luggage compartment, fold it back from around the fuel tank.

3. Disconnect the fuel supply hose from the bottom of tank. Disconnect the leads from the tank gauge unit, also the breather pipe from its connection at the top of the tank (where fitted).

4. Remove the bolt securing the tank retaining straps and withdraw the tank, releasing the filler neck from the grommet in the rear wing panel. Remove the tank from the luggage compartment.

5. If a new tank is being fitted, the tank gauge unit should be transferred to the new tank as detailed in the following section.

6. Install the tank in the reverse order of removal and check for leaks.

Replacement — Estate

1. Raise and support the rear of the car – see BASIC PROCEDURES.

2. Disconnect the battery earth lead. Remove the drain plug from the fuel tank and drain out the fuel into a suitable container. Unscrew and disconnect the fuel supply pipe from the tank. Release the pipe from the retaining clips. Remove the filler cap. Disconnect the leads from the tank gauge unit.

3. Remove the tank securing screws, noting the plastic spacers, and lower the fuel tank out of its location.

4. If a new tank is being fitted, the tank gauge unit should be transferred to the new tank as detailed in the following section.

5. Install the tank in the reverse order of removal and check for leaks.

FUEL GAUGE SENDER UNIT . . . . [9]
Replacement — Saloon (Fig.F:17)

1. Open the boot and disconnect the battery earth lead.

2. Ensure that the fuel level in the petrol tank is below the fuel gauge sender unit. This can be done using a dipstick made from a length of thin flexible wood or plastic inserted through the filler neck to the bottom of the tank.

3. Disconnect the earth wire and the feed wire from the sender unit.

4. Using a blunt punch and a small hammer, tap the retaining ring round anti-clockwise until it can be removed.

5. Lift out the sender unit and manoeuvre the float through the aperture in the tank.

6. Install the sender unit in the reverse order of removal, using a new sealing ring, and check for leaks and correct operation of the gauge.

Replacement — Estate, Van & Pick-Up (Fig.F:17)

1. Disconnect the battery earth lead.

2. Raise and support the rear of the car – see BASIC PROCEDURES.

3. Remove the fuel tank as described previously.

4. Undo the six cross-head screws and remove the sender unit from the tank aperture.

5. Install the sender unit in the reverse order of removal, using a new gasket, tightening the screws progressively to avoid distorting the flange.

6. Install the fuel tank in the reverse order of removal, check for fuel leaks and correct gauge operation.

Fuel System Problems

FAULT	CAUSE	ACTION
Flooding	☐ Improper seating or damaged float needle valve or seat. ☐ Incorrect float level.	■ Check and replace parts as necessary. ■ Adjust float level.
Excessive fuel consumption	☐ Engine out of tune. ☐ Float level too high. ☐ Loose carburettor plug or jet. ☐ Defective gasket. ☐ Fuel leaks at pipes or connections. ☐ Obstructed air bleed. ☐ Choke malfunction.	■ Tune engine. ■ Adjust float level. ■ Tighten plug or jet. ■ Replace gaskets. ■ Trace leak and rectify. ■ Check and clear. ■ Check choke mechanism.
Stalling	☐ Jet obstructed. ☐ Incorrect throttle opening. ☐ Idle mixture adjustment incorrect. ☐ Incorrect float level.	■ Clean jet assembly. ■ Adjust throttle. ■ Adjust idle mixture. ■ Adjust float level.
Poor acceleration	☐ Float level incorrect. ☐ Inadequate throttle opening. ☐ Accelerator pump faulty.	■ Adjust float level. ■ Adjust throttle linkage. ■ Repair/replace pump.
Spitting (backfire through carburettor)	☐ Weak mixture. ☐ Incorrect ignition timing. ☐ Clogged fuel pipes. ☐ Inlet manifold leak.	■ Clean and adjust carburettor. ■ Tune engine. ■ Clean or replace pipes. ■ Check manifold/replace gasket.
Insufficient fuel supply	☐ Clogged carburettor. ☐ Clogged fuel pipe. ☐ Dirty fuel. ☐ Air in fuel system. ☐ Defective fuel pump. ☐ Clogged fuel filter.	■ Dismantle and clean carburettor. ■ Clean fuel pipe. ■ Clean fuel tank. ■ Check connections and tighten. ■ Repair or replace fuel pump. ■ Clean or replace filter.
Loss of fuel delivery	☐ Pump faulty. ☐ Blocked fuel filter. ☐ Loose fuel pipe connections. ☐ Cracked fuel pipes.	■ Replace pump. ■ Clean/replace fuel filter. ■ Tighten fuel pipe connections. ■ Replace fuel pipes.
Noisy fuel pump	☐ Loose pump mounting. ☐ Worn pump	■ Tighten mounting bolts. ■ Replace pump.

Clutch & Gearbox

INTRODUCTION . . . . [1]

Three different types of clutch have been used on the Mini range since its introduction. The original Borg & Beck type on early Minis has a coil spring type cover to engage the clutch driven plate which is sandwiched between the rear of the flywheel and the pressure plate, and which requires removal of the flywheel to replace the clutch components.

The second type of clutch, introduced in September 1964 is of the same make and is similar to the original clutch, but has a diaphragm spring cover instead of the previous coil springs.

During 1982, the current clutch, manufactured by Verto was fitted, again of the diaphragm spring type but has all the clutch components mounted on the outside of the flywheel. This type of clutch also requires the removal of the flywheel to replace the clutch components. The Verto clutch can be identified from the outside by the shorter operating lever and the slave cylinder mounted on a bracket attached to the clutch cover.

Although the clutch hydraulics need no adjustment, the position of the operating lever return stop on pre Verto clutches can be adjusted to compensate for wear as detailed in ROUTINE MAINTENANCE.

Overhaul of the clutch hydraulic components, when required, is straightforward and overhaul kits containing all the parts necessary are available from Austin/Rover and Unipart dealers, and most auto factors.

There is sufficient room in the Mini engine compartment to replace the clutch on all models, without removing the engine/gearbox unit, but any further repairs to the primary drive gears or the gearbox will require removal of the power unit assembly.

Three main changes have been made to the Mini gearbox over the years, and these are summarised as follows: introduction of baulk ring type synchromesh in late 1962, the addition of 4-speed synchromesh in late 1968, and a revised 'rod change' type gearbox from 1973 onwards.

Overhauling the gearbox is reasonably straightforward for the more experienced DIY mechanic, although some special tools will make the job easier. However, if a number of components are worn then it may well be more economical in the long run to fit a reconditioned or exchange gearbox with a guarantee.

TOOLS & EQUIPMENT . . . . [2]

In addition to those tools listed under Basic Tools & Equipment in BASIC PROCEDURES, the following tools are necessary to carry out all of the operations covered in this chapter. All numbered tools are Austin/Rover special tools.

- Circlip pliers – for removing circlips when dismantling drive gear assembly.
- 18G 587 or 1½in AF socket or ring spanner – for removing the flywheel retaining bolt (Borg & Beck type clutch).

- 18G 304 & 304N – for removing the (Borg & Beck) flywheel/clutch assembly. An alternative is available from most motor accessory shops.
- 18G 1303 – for removing flywheel retaining bolt (Verto type clutch).
- 18G 1381 – for removing the Verto flywheel/clutch assembly. An alternative is available from most motor accessory shops.
- 18G 684 – for centralising the clutch disc on the Verto type clutch.
- 18G 304M – for compressing clutch springs (coil spring type clutch).
- 18G 571 – to centralise clutch disc (coil spring type clutch).
- Sykes-Pickavant kit No.085108 – for carrying out flywheel housing oil seal replacement with housing in-situ.
- 18G 1383 – for checking idler gear endfloat when engine and gearbox are still connected.

The following are all tools used for gearbox overhaul:
- 18G 2
- 18G 186
- 18G 569
- 18G 572
- 18G 613
- 18G 1127

CLUTCH MASTER CYLINDER . . . . [3]
Removal & Installation
1. Drain the clutch hydraulic system as described for clutch slave cylinder removal in the following section.
2. Where applicable, disconnect the heater air intake trunking from the bulkhead and from the front panel.
3. From inside the car, remove the split pin and withdraw the clevis pin securing the master cylinder push rod to the clutch pedal (Fig.G:2).
4. Disconnect the hydraulic pipe union from the master cylinder. Remove the two nuts and spring washers securing the master cylinder to the bulkhead and lift off the master cylinder.
5. Installation is a simple reversal of the removal procedure. When installation is completed, bleed the clutch hydraulic system as detailed later in this section.

Seal Replacement
As with the slave cylinder, a cylinder overhaul kit should be obtained before starting work on the unit.
1. Remove the filler cap from the fluid reservoir and drain out any remaining fluid. Detach the rubber boot from the end of the cylinder and slide it down the push rod.
2. Extract the retaining circlip from the cylinder bore and remove the internal components, as shown in Fig.G:1, from the cylinder. Remove the secondary cup from the piston.
3. Clean all the internal components with methylated spirits

and inspect carefully. Check the master cylinder bore for any signs of scoring, ridging or corrosion pits. If the bore is damaged in any way, the complete unit must be replaced. Also check that the inlet and outlet ports are free from obstruction.

4. Lubricate all the internal components with clean hydraulic fluid. Carefully assemble the secondary cup to the piston. The flat face of the seal must abut the end flange of the piston.

5. Fit the spring retainer into the small diameter end of the piston (or the bottom end, in the case of a non-tapered spring) and insert the spring into the bore, large diameter first (if tapered). Fit the main cup seal and the cup washer over the spring retainer. The main cup must be fitted carefully, lip edge first. Insert the piston assembly, then refit the push rod assembly and secure with the circlip. Refit the rubber boot on the end of the cylinder.

CLUTCH SLAVE CYLINDER . . . . [4]
Removal
1. Attach a length of plastic tube to the slave cylinder bleed screw (Fig.G:3) then open the screw and drain or pump the brake fluid out of the system. Close the bleed screw and disconnect the hydraulic pipe from the cylinder.

2. Undo the two bolts and detach the slave cylinder from the flywheel housing on early models (Fig.G:4) or the mounting plate on later models with Verto clutch (Fig.G:5).

Installation
Insert the pushrod into the slave cylinder and secure the cylinder to the flywheel housing or mounting plate depending on the type. Reconnect the hydraulic pipe and bleed the system as detailed in the next section.

Slave Cylinder Overhaul (Figs. G:6 & G:7)
A cylinder overhaul kit containing all the necessary seals, etc., should be obtained before starting work on the cylinder.

1. Detach the dust cover from the end of the cylinder and remove the piston and coil spring from the cylinder bore. Remove the seal from the piston.

2. Clean all the components with methylated spirits and inspect carefully. Check the cylinder bore for any signs of scores, ridges or corrosion pits. If the bore is in good condition, a new seal can be fitted, otherwise the complete unit must be replaced.

3. Lubricate all the internal components with clean brake fluid and fit the new seal to the piston. The seal should be fitted with the hollow side towards the bottom of the cylinder bore when installed. Insert the return spring, small end outermost, into the bore, then fit the piston. Secure the components in position with the dust cover.

BLEEDING THE CLUTCH . . . . [5]

If any components of the clutch hydraulic system have been disconnected, or if any air is present in the system – indicated by a 'soft' pedal – the system should be bled as follows:

1. Fill or top up the master cylinder reservoir as necessary. Clean the area around the bleed screw on the slave cylinder. Fit one end of a bleed tube to the bleed screw and submerge the other end in a small quantity of brake fluid in a clean jar (Fig.G:3).

2. Open the bleed screw three-quarters of a turn and slowly depress the clutch pedal. Close the bleed screw just before the pedal reaches the bottom position and allow the pedal to return unassisted. Repeat the procedure until the fluid emerging from the bleed tube is completely free from air bubbles. Do not allow the reservoir to become less than half full during this operation.

4. When bleeding has been successfully completed, remove the bleed tube. Check that the bleed screw is properly closed but do not over-tighten it.

5. Finally, top-up the master cylinder reservoir with fresh brake fluid as necessary and refit the reservoir cap.

CLUTCH ASSEMBLY . . . . [6]
Removal — Borg & Beck Type (Figs.G:8 & G:13)
1. Disconnect the earth strap from the battery.
2. Remove the bonnet, after first marking the fitted position of the hinges to facilitate alignment when refitting.
3. Where fitted, detach the ignition shield from the front of the engine.
4. On models where the ignition coil mounting bracket is attached to one of the cylinder head studs, remove the cylinder head nut retaining the coil bracket and move the coil and bracket to one side out of the way.
5. On later models which have a plastic air intake assembly at the right-hand front wing valance, withdraw the intake assembly into the engine compartment after pulling off the flexible pipe from beneath the wing.
6. Where the horn is mounted on the bonnet locking platform, disconnect and remove the horn, where necessary.
7. Disconnect the starter cable(s) from the starter motor and remove the starter motor from the flywheel housing – see ENGINE ELECTRICS.
8. Where the ignition or starter solenoid is mounted on the flywheel housing, disconnect the wiring and remove the coil or solenoid. On models with the starter solenoid mounted on right-hand wing valance, disconnect the wiring and remove the solenoid – see ENGINE ELECTRICS.
9. Undo the bolts and detach the engine steady rod from the side of the cylinder block.
10. Disconnect the return spring between the clutch operating lever and the slave cylinder.
11. Remove the nuts securing the radiator upper support bracket to the thermostat housing, and the bolts securing it to the radiator cowl, and remove the bracket.
12. Raise and support the front of the car – see BASIC PROCEDURES.
13. Remove the air cleaner assembly and disconnect the exhaust down-pipe at the manifold flange. From underneath the car, also detach the exhaust pipe clip from the transmission casing, also the engine steady rod (if fitted).
14. Support the power unit with a hydraulic jack positioned under the transmission casing using a wood block to spread the load.
15. Remove the two bolts and nuts securing the right-hand engine mounting to the subframe side-member.
16. Now raise the power unit sufficiently with the jack to allow the clutch cover retaining bolts and the clutch cover to be removed, but take great care not to let the cooling fan blades damage the radiator core.
17. Remove the cover retaining bolts and detach the clutch cover. Note that the engine earth strap is normally secured by one of the cover front retaining bolts.
18. On very early models (pre September 1964), with the coil spring type clutch, remove the three nuts securing the clutch thrust plate to the pressure spring housing and detach the thrust plate (Fig.G:8).
19. On models with the diaphragm spring clutch, slacken the three dowel bolts (driving pins) retaining the diaphragm spring cover. Slacken the bolts evenly to release the spring pressure, then remove the bolts and detach the diaphragm cover (Fig.G:9).
20. Turn the crankshaft until the slot in the crankshaft and flywheel is horizontal. It is essential that the crankshaft be correctly positioned before attempting to remove the flywheel as the 'C' shaped washer which locates the crankshaft primary gear will then be positioned with its open side facing sideways and thus be unable to drop out. If this precaution is not observed, the 'C' washer may fall out of position and cause severe damage and/or possibly make it impossible to remove the flywheel.
21. Knock back the lock washer tab securing the flywheel retaining bolt. Lock the flywheel to prevent it turning by

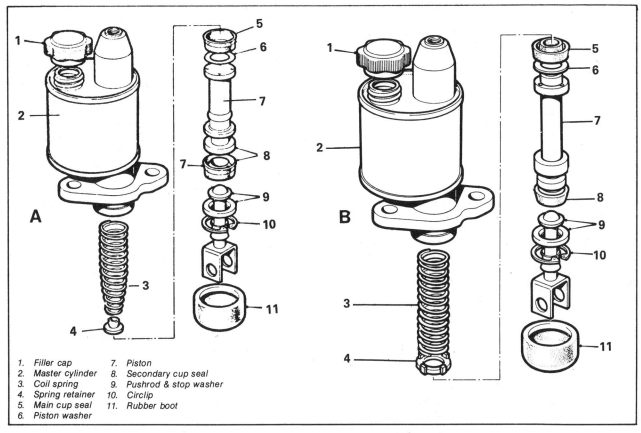

1. Filler cap
2. Master cylinder
3. Coil spring
4. Spring retainer
5. Main cup seal
6. Piston washer
7. Piston
8. Secondary cup seal
9. Pushrod & stop washer
10. Circlip
11. Rubber boot

Fig. G:1 Details of master cylinder; early (A) later (B)

1. Clevis pin at clutch pedal
2. Hydraulic pipe union
3. Securing nuts & washers
4. Master cylinder

Fig. G:2 Clutch master cylinder installation

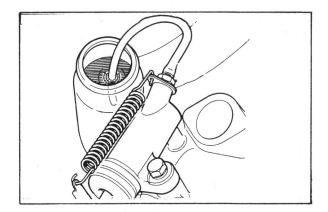

Fig. G:3 Bleeding fluid from the slave cylinder

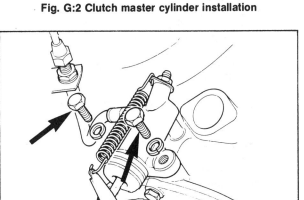

Fig. G:4 Slave cylinder mounting — Borg & Beck clutches

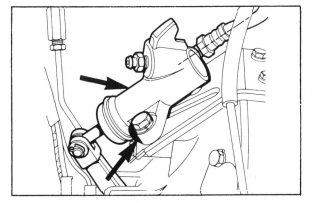

Fig. G:5 Slave cylinder mounting — Verto clutch

engaging a screwdriver into the ring gear teeth through the starter motor aperture, then undo the flywheel bolt. Remove the keyed washer locating the flywheel to the crankshaft.

22. Withdraw the flywheel off the crankshaft taper using a suitable puller (Fig.G:10).

NOTE:As the flywheel may part from the crankshaft taper with some force, it is advisable to bolt a strap across the face of the flywheel housing to prevent the flywheel causing damage when released.

First locate the thrust button of the puller set into the end of the crankshaft to protect the internal threads (Fig.G:10). Screw the three adaptor screws into the threaded holes provided in the flywheel. Fit the plate of the puller tool over the screws and secure with the three nuts. Tighten the nuts evenly so that the plate remains parallel with the flywheel. Screw in the tool centre-bolt until it contacts the thrust button then tighten further while holding the flywheel to prevent it turning. Once the flywheel is freed, the puller can be removed.

NOTE:The adaptor screws for use on the diaphragm clutch are different from those for the coil spring clutch and must not be interchanged.

23. On models with the diaphragm spring clutch, remove the flywheel, clutch plate and pressure plate as indiviual items from the flywheel housing (Fig.G:13).

24. On early models with the coil spring type clutch, the clutch and flywheel are removed as an assembly. If required, they can be separated as described under the appropriate heading later.

Installation — Borg & Beck Type

Installation is a simple reversal of the removal procedure, with special attention to the following points:

1. Ensure that the crankshaft taper and flywheel hub bore are perfectly clean and free from grease. They must be assembled dry. This is most important.

2. Lightly smear the splines of the crankshaft primary gear with molybdenum disulphide grease.

3. Ensure that the crankshaft is correctly positioned, with the end slot in the horizontal position.

4. On the diaphragm spring clutch, the clutch pressure plate is marked with a notch or a letter 'A' in its edge and the diaphragm cover is also marked with the letter 'A'. These marks must align with the 1/4 mark on the flywheel (Fig.G:11).

5. To assemble the diaphragm spring clutch, first fit the pressure plate into the flywheel housing with the 'A' mark to the top, then fit the clutch plate with the hub facing inwards. Centralise the pressure plate onto the clutch disc then fit the flywheel onto the crankshaft taper so that the 1/4 timing mark aligns with the 'A' mark on the pressure plate (Fig.G:11). Temporarily fit the three dowel bolts (driving pins) lightly into the pressure plate to align the assembly and pull it together. Once the flywheel retaining bolt has been fitted and tightened, the dowel bolts can be removed and the diaphragm cover installed with its balance mark 'A' aligned with the 1/4 timing mark (Fig.G:11).

6. Fit and progressively tighten the three dowel bolts ensuring that they pass squarely through each pair of driving straps. Incorrect assembly can cause clutch judder. Tighten the dowel bolts to their specified torque – see TECHNICAL DATA.

7. When fitting the flywheel retaining bolt, first align the offset slot in the end of the crankshaft and flywheel, then refit the keyed washer. Fit a new lock washer under the flywheel bolt, and tighten the bolt to the specified torque – see TECHNICAL DATA, while holding the flywheel to prevent it turning. Secure the bolt with the lock washer tab.

8. When assembly is complete, check the clutch throw-out stop setting as described later in this section and the return stop clearance – see ROUTINE MAINTENANCE.

Dismantling & Reassembly — Coil Spring Type Clutch (Fig.G:8)

Once the flywheel and clutch assembly have been removed from the engine, it can be dismantled as follows:

1. Three screws (tool No.18G 304 M) will be required to hold the pressure springs compressed while removing the driving pins (Fig.G:12).

2. Mark the driving pins so that they can be refitted in their original positions. Also note the balance mark 'A' on the clutch spring cover (Fig.G:11).

3. Insert the three special screws through the holes in the spring cover and screw them into the threaded holes provided in the flywheel. Screw the nuts down against the cover with the fingers, then tighten them one turn at a time until the load is released from the driving pins. Unscrew and remove the three driving pins. Unscrew the three nuts gradually to release the spring cover, then lift off the cover and the springs. The pressure plate will then be released from the flywheel and the individual items can be separated.

4. When reassembling the components, the balance mark 'A' on the pressure plate and spring cover must be aligned with the 1/4 mark on the flywheel (Fig.G:11). Place the clutch plate on the pressure plate with its longer boss towards the plate. Tool No.18G 571 will be required to centralise the clutch disc with the flywheel hub. Locate the coil springs, spring housing on the flywheel, then fit the special screws and tighten the nuts evenly to compress the pressure springs. Fit the driving pins in their original locations, ensuring that they pass squarely through each pair of driving straps, and tighten them to their specified torque – see TECHNICAL DATA. Release the nuts and remove the special screws.

Replacement — Verto Clutch (Fig.G:14)

1. Carry out procedures 1-16 under Removal – Borg & Beck Clutches previously.

2. Release the clutch slave cylinder mounting plate from the flywheel housing, collect the spacer and position the clutch slave cylinder and mounting plate aside.

3. Remove the cover retaining bolts, noting that the engine earth strap is secured to one bolt, also note the position of the carburettor drain tube before removing the clutch cover.

4. Remove the thrust bearing sleeve from the clutch hub. Prise the lockwasher from the clutch hub slots. Position the crankshaft and clutch hub slots horizontally and prevent the flywheel from turning by engaging a large screwdriver between the starter ring gear teeth. Remove the flywheel retaining bolt, using tool No.18G 1303. Remove the key plate from the crankshaft.

5. Release the flywheel from the crankshaft using tool No.18G 1381. Remove the tool and withdraw the flywheel and clutch as an assembly.

NOTE:If the crankshaft is not positioned correctly, the primary drive gear 'C' washer may become displaced and make it impossible to remove the flywheel.

6. Remove the pressure plate bolts, lift off the pressure plate assembly and remove the driven plate from the flywheel.

7. Inspect the clutch components and flywheel as detailed later in this section. Replace any parts as necessary.

8. Check the crankshaft primary gear endfloat as detailed under Primary Drive Gears.

9. Fit the driven plate with the hub boss offset facing the flywheel, fit the pressure plate assembly and lightly tighten the bolts.

10. Using tool No.18G 684, centralise the driven plate then tighten the pressure plate bolts to the torque specified in TECHNICAL DATA.

11. Fit the flywheel and clutch assembly onto the crankshaft and locate the key plate.

12. Tighten the flywheel retaining bolt using tool No.18G 1303 and observe the tightening torque given in TECHNICAL DATA.

13. Lock the flywheel retaining bolt by drifting the lockwasher into the slots in the clutch hub, then fit the thrust bearing sleeve.

14. Fit the clutch cover, ensuring that the carburettor drain

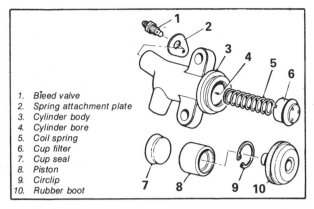

1. Bleed valve
2. Spring attachment plate
3. Cylinder body
4. Cylinder bore
5. Coil spring
6. Cup filter
7. Cup seal
8. Piston
9. Circlip
10. Rubber boot

Fig. G:6 Details of slave cylinder — Borg & Beck clutches

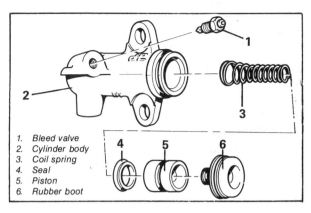

1. Bleed valve
2. Cylinder body
3. Coil spring
4. Seal
5. Piston
6. Rubber boot

Fig. G:7 Details of slave cylinder — Verto clutch

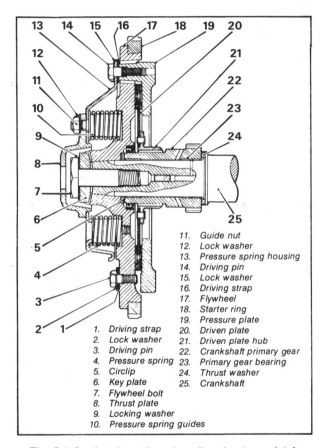

11. Guide nut
12. Lock washer
13. Pressure spring housing
14. Driving pin
15. Lock washer
16. Driving strap
17. Flywheel
18. Starter ring
19. Pressure plate
20. Driven plate
21. Driven plate hub
22. Crankshaft primary gear
23. Primary gear bearing
24. Thrust washer
25. Crankshaft

1. Driving strap
2. Lock washer
3. Driving pin
4. Pressure spring
5. Circlip
6. Key plate
7. Flywheel bolt
8. Thrust plate
9. Locking washer
10. Pressure spring guides

Fig. G:8 Section through early coil spring type clutch

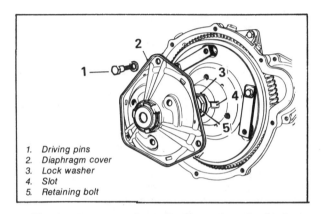

1. Driving pins
2. Diaphragm cover
3. Lock washer
4. Slot
5. Retaining bolt

Fig. G:9 Removing clutch diaphragm from flywheel

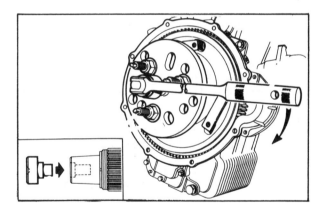

Fig. G:10 Using puller to remove flywheel (tool shown)

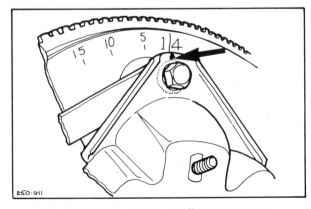

Fig. G:11 Balance mark on diaphragm cover aligned with TDC

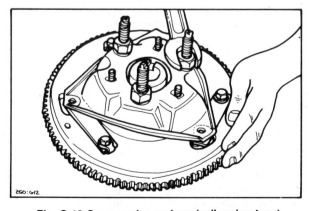

Fig. G:12 Compressing springs (coil spring type)

tube is secured. Continue installation in the reverse order of removal.

15. When assembly is complete, check the clutch throw-out stop setting as described later in this section.

Release Bearing (Borg & Beck) — Replacement (Fig.G:15)

1. Remove the clutch cover from the flywheel housing as detailed previously for clutch removal but do not remove the starter motor.
2. Unscrew and remove the plunger stop and locknut.
3. Remove the split pin and washer and withdraw the clevis pin.
4. Pull the release lever out of the release bearing plunger.
5. Remove the release bearing and plunger assembly from the cover.
6. Drift or press the plunger through the release bearing (Fig.G:18).
7. Installation of the release bearing assembly is carried out in the reverse order of removal, noting the following points:
a) Lubricate the operating surfaces of the plunger and the lever ball-end with a graphite based grease.
b) When a self-aligning type bearing is fitted (Fig.G:17), assemble as follows: Adjust the return stop (A) to bring the shoulder of the plunger 5 mm ($^3/_{16}$ in) 'X' above the face of the lever. Fit the bearing (B) over the lever and fit a NEW lock-ring (C) over the plunger using a suitable size of socket to apply steady hand pressure. Ensure that the lock-ring has clamped the bearing sufficiently to require a force of 3.6-5.4 kg m (8-12 lb ft) to move the bearing radially. Do not disturb the return stop setting until the push-rod is inserted in the slave cylinder. This will ensure that any pressure applied to the release lever does not displace the lock-ring. Adjust the throw-out stop as detailed later in this section and the return stop as detailed in ROUTINE MAINTENANCE.

Clutch Release Bearing — Verto Clutch (Fig.G:16)

1. Remove the clutch cover as detailed previously for clutch removal.
2. Pull the release bearing assembly from the plunger and collect the 'O' ring seal. Prise the legs of the spring clip from the bearing retainer plate and remove the release bearing from the retainer plate and plunger.
3. Position the bearing on its retainer plate with the seal facing away from the plate. Secure it with the spring clip.
4. Locate the bearing assembly on the plunger and refit the 'O' ring seal.
5. Continue reassembly in the reverse order of removal.
6. Adjust the clutch throw-out stop as detailed later in this section.

Clutch Throw-out Stop — Borg & Beck (Fig.G:19)

1. Screw the plunger stop and locknut away from the clutch housing to the limit of the plunger thread. With an assistant in the car, fully depress the clutch pedal and screw the plunger stop up against the housing.
2. Release the clutch pedal, screw the stop in a further one flat and secure the stop in this position with the locknut.
3. After carrying out this operation adjust the return stop clearance as detailed in ROUTINE MAINTENANCE.

Clutch Throw-out Stop — Verto (Fig.G:20)

1. Screw the plunger stop and locknut from the clutch cover to the limit of the plunger thread.
2. Pull the release lever from the clutch cover until the release bearing makes light contact with the thrust sleeve.
3. Screw the plunger stop in until a gap of 6,5 mm (0.26 in) exists between the plunger and the face of the cover (A,Fig.G:20). Tighten the locknut.

Clutch Plate — Inspection

Inspect the friction linings on the plate for wear, burning or contamination by oil or grease. If the linings are worn down to or near the rivet heads or if any other of the above conditions are apparent, the plate must be renewed.

If oil or grease contamination is found on the friction faces of the plate, the source must be determined and the fault rectified before fitting a new plate, otherwise the trouble may recur. This may be due to a defective primary drive gear oil seal.

Release Bearing — Inspection

Inspect the bearing for wear, damage or looseness. Hold the bearing inner race and rotate the outer race whilst applying pressure to it. If the bearing rotation is rough or noisy, the bearing should be replaced. If it is obviously dry through lack of lubricant, it must be replaced as it is a sealed unit. Do not wash the bearing in solvent as this will remove the lubricant contained within it.

Flywheel Housing Oil Seal — Replacement In-Situ

1. Remove the clutch assembly and the flywheel as detailed previously.
2. Using Sykes-Pickavant oil seal replacing kit No. 085108 (Fig.G:21), position the protective sleeve (085113) over the splines of the primary drive.
3. Locate the puller (085121) over the crankshaft nose and the protective sleeve so that the ridge in the end of the puller locates with the groove at the rear of the primary drive splines.
4. Screw the bolt at the end of the puller inwards so that it pulls the primary drive gear forward, bringing the oil seal with it.
5. Remove the gear, oil seal and puller. Refit the primary gear and its protective sleeve then drift the new seal into place in the flywheel housing using the drift provided in the kit (085114). Remove the protective sleeve (085113).
6. Install the flywheel and clutch assembly as detailed previously.

GEAR LEVER & REMOTE CONTROL .... [7]

Three types of gearchange assembly have been fitted to the Mini since the beginning of production. The original gearchange has a long gear lever which passes through the floorpan direct from the back of the gearbox. The second type has a remote casting which bolts to the differential housing at one end and is mounted under the car floor between the front seats at the lever end. The current type of gearchange has a remotely located lever and an open locating rod and selecting rod under the car; this type is identified by having a 'lift for reverse' function and is known as the 'rod change' type.

Gear Lever — Removal & Installation (Original Type, Fig.G:22)

1. Pull back the covering from the bulkhead and undo the self-tapping screws which retain the gear lever gaiter surround plate to the floor.
2. Remove the plate and slide the gaiter up the lever.
3. Through the opening in the floor, undo the two bolts securing the gear lever retaining plate to the differential casing.
4. Lift out the lever complete with retaining plate and bolts.
5. Apply a little multipurpose grease to the gearchange lever socket then refit the lever in the reverse order of removal, making sure that the lever ball is clean and properly located with the socket.

Gearchange Remote Casting — Removal & Installation (Fig.G:23)

1. From inside the car, unscrew the gear lever knob. Lift the front floor covering and remove the rubber gaiter and retaining plate.
2. Raise and support the front of the car – see BASIC

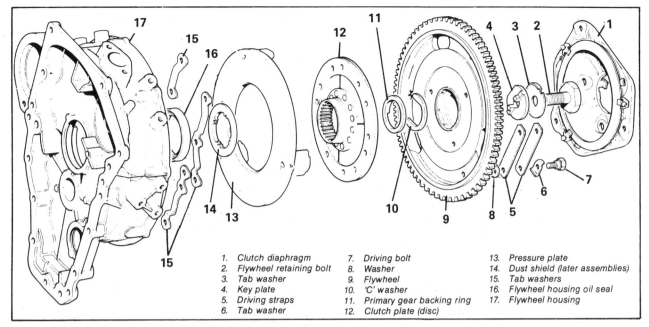

1. Clutch diaphragm	7. Driving bolt	13. Pressure plate
2. Flywheel retaining bolt	8. Washer	14. Dust shield (later assemblies)
3. Tab washer	9. Flywheel	15. Tab washers
4. Key plate	10. 'C' washer	16. Flywheel housing oil seal
5. Driving straps	11. Primary gear backing ring	17. Flywheel housing
6. Tab washer	12. Clutch plate (disc)	

Fig. G:13 Exploded view of Borg & Beck diaphragm clutch

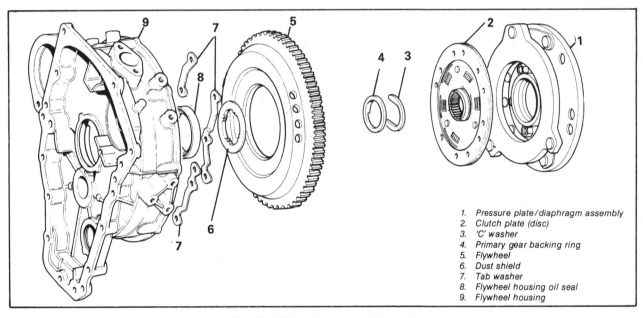

1. Pressure plate/diaphragm assembly
2. Clutch plate (disc)
3. 'C' washer
4. Primary gear backing ring
5. Flywheel
6. Dust shield
7. Tab washer
8. Flywheel housing oil seal
9. Flywheel housing

Fig. G:14 Exploded view of Verto clutch

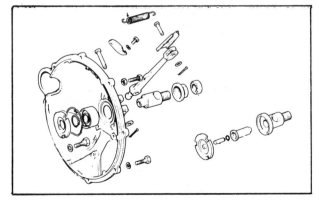

Fig. G:15 Clutch cover assembly — Borg & Beck

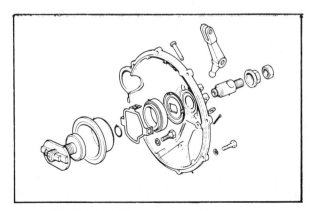

Fig. G:16 Clutch cover assembly — Verto

PROCEDURES. From underneath the car remove the three bolts securing the extension rear support bracket to the floor pan.

3. Remove the four bolts securing the gearchange extension to the gearbox casing and detach the extension housing. Take care not to lose the rubber half-moon plug fitted between the extension and the gearbox casing.

4. Installation is carried out in the reverse order of removal noting the following points: ensure that the half-moon rubber plug is correctly located between the extension and the final drive housing prior to refitting, and apply a bead of silicone sealant to the mating face of the extension prior to tightening the bolts.

Rod Change Gear Lever — Removal & Installation (Fig.G:24)

1. If a console is fitted, remove the console retaining screws to enable the console to be moved as necessary.

2. Unscrew the knob from the gear lever.

3. Remove the front floor covering, then undo the gaiter retaining ring screws and pull the gaiter up the lever.

4. Press down and turn the bayonet cap fixing to release the lever from the gearchange box. Lift out the lever.

5. Carry out installation in the reverse order of removal but smear the operating surfaces with multipurpose grease first.

Rod Change Assembly — Removal & Installation (Figs. G:25 & G:26)

1. Raise and support the front of the car – see BASIC PROCEDURES.

2. From underneath the car, drift out the roll pin retaining the extension rod to the selector rod at the final drive housing (Fig.G:25).

3. Remove the nut and bolt securing the gearchange to steady rod to the final drive housing on the gearbox (Fig.G:25).

4. Fold back the rear of the front floor covering, then undo and remove the two nuts which secure the gearchange box mounting rubbers to the floor (Fig.G:26).

5. Release the gear lever from the gearchange box from underneath the car.

6. Remove the nut and bolt which secures the gearchange box to the mounting bracket and remove the bracket.

7. Remove the nuts to release the mounting rubbers from the mounting bracket, then remove the gearchange assembly from the car.

8. Installation is carried out in the reverse order of removal.

PRIMARY DRIVE GEARS .... [8]

The primary drive gear train (Fig.G:29) comprises the primary drive gear on the end of the crankshaft, the first motion shaft pinion (gearbox input gear) and an idler gear between them. These gears are situated between the engine/gearbox end-face and the inside of the flywheel housing, and the power unit must be removed from the car in order to gain access to them; see ENGINE for details.

Removal

1. Remove the clutch and flywheel assembly as detailed previously under Clutch.

2. Drain the engine/gearbox oil and refit the drain plug.

3. Bend back the locktabs and undo the flywheel housing bolts.

4. Carefully remove the flywheel housing from the engine/gearbox assembly.

5. Remove the 'C' shaped thrust washer and backing ring from the crankshaft, then withdraw the crankshaft primary gear and front thrust washer (see Figs.G:13 or G:14).

6. Using circlip pliers, remove the circlip from the first motion shaft and lever off the roller bearing, either by using a universal bearing puller or by careful use of two screwdrivers. Note that the bearing cage is VERY easily damaged.

7. Remove the idler gear with its thrust washers.

8. Prevent the first motion shaft from turning; there are two possible ways of doing this: either refit the idler gear and wedge a piece of wood between it and the first motion shaft pinion, or use an oil filter strap wrench pulled tightly around the pinion, (idler gear removed).

9. Undo the first motion shaft pinion nut and pull the pinion off its splines.

Gear Train Overhaul

Check the condition of all the gear teeth, looking for signs of a wear ridge, and cracked or chipped teeth. If the gears show any signs of wear or damage they should be replaced as a set. If the primary gear oil seal is damaged or has been leaking, drift out the old seal and fit a new one.

Check the idler gear shaft and bearings for damage and for signs of blueing indicating hot running through lack of oil. Inspect the first motion shaft roller bearing and its outer track in the flywheel housing; if it requires replacement, then the track can be levered out and a new one drifted in using a suitable size of socket. If removal of the track proves difficult, then the flywheel housing should be heated up by immersion in hot water. Examine the internal bushes of the primary drive gear for heavy scoring or 'tearing' of the surface. If the bushes are damaged they can be replaced, but this work will have to be entrusted to an auto engineering works.

If either of the idler gear needle roller bearings is worn or damaged then it will have to be replaced. Replacement of the bearing on the gearbox casing side is straightforward as the bearing can be drifted out and a new one drifted in after the retaining circlips on either side of it have been removed. Replacement of the idler gear bearing on the flywheel housing side, however, requires the use of extractor No.18G 581 as shown in Fig.G:27.

Installation

1. Fit the first motion shaft gear, lock the gear and tighten the retaining nut to the correct torque – see TECHNICAL DATA.

2. Fit the primary drive rear thrust washer with its chamfered side facing towards the engine. Fit the primary gear and the front thrust washer, followed by the 'C' shaped washer.

3. Using a feeler gauge placed between the front of the primary drive gear and its front thrust washer (Fig.G:28), check the gear endfloat against the figure given in TECHNICAL DATA. If it is outside the specified limits, fit an alternative thickness thrust washer at the rear to give the correct endfloat. Remove the primary drive gear after checking or adjustment.

4. If there is any reason to suspect the idler gear endfloat of being excessive then check it as follows:

a) Fit the idler gear to the flywheel housing with a nominal sized thrust washer (see TECHNICAL DATA) fitted to each side.

b) Position tool No.18G 1383 on the flywheel housing with its recessed face downwards over the idler gear thrust washer as shown in Fig.G:30. Measure the gap between the recessed face of the tool and the front thrust washer using a feeler gauge blade. Compare this measurement with the endfloat specification given in TECHNICAL DATA.

c) Maintain the original front thrust washer if the same gears are to be refitted. Select thrust washers to bring the endfloat within the limits given in TECHNICAL DATA, and recheck the endfloat.

d) Oil the thrust washers and fit the idler gear and thrust washers as an assembly to the gearbox casing.

5. Drift the roller bearing into place on the first motion shaft spigot, and locate it with a new circlip.

6. Fit the primary drive rear thrust washer, gear, front thrust washer and 'C' washer.

7. Wrap the primary drive gear teeth with adhesive tape and

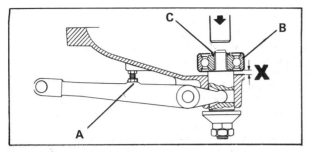

Fig. G:17 Positioning of self-aligning type release bearing

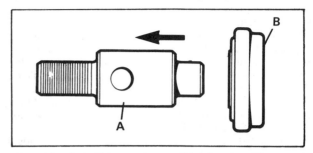

Fig. G:18 Release plunger (A) & bearing (B)

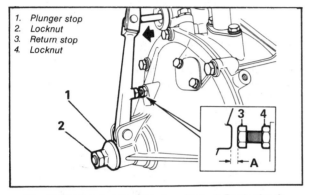

1. Plunger stop
2. Locknut
3. Return stop
4. Locknut

Fig. G:19 Clutch adjustment — Borg & Beck clutch

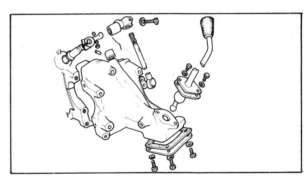

1. Release lever
2. Plunger stop & locknut
A. Stop to cover clearance

Fig. G:20 Clutch adjustment — Verto clutch

1. Protective sleeve
2. Puller
3. Refitting drift

Fig. G:21 Flywheel housing oil seal replacement kit

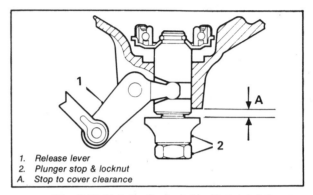

Fig. G:22 Details of original type gearchange

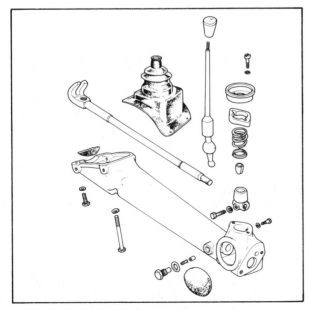

Fig. G:23 Details of remote casting type gearchange

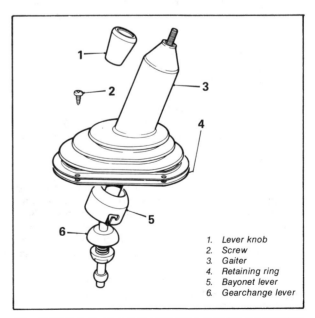

1. Lever knob
2. Screw
3. Gaiter
4. Retaining ring
5. Bayonet lever
6. Gearchange lever

Fig. G:24 Details of rod change type gear lever assembly

smear the outside of the tape with grease. This will prevent damage to the primary drive housing oil seal as the flywheel housing is refitted.

8. Make sure that the engine/gearbox and flywheel housing mating faces are clean, then fit a new oil feed 'O' ring and joint gasket before refitting the flywheel housing. Tighten the housing nuts evenly and to the correct torque (see TECHNICAL DATA) then bend over the NEW locking tabs.

9. Remove the tape from the primary drive gear and refit the flywheel and clutch, observing the correct tightening torques for both – see TECHNICAL DATA.

10. Continue the reassembly in the reverse order of removal and do not forget to refill the engine/gearbox assembly with oil.

GEARBOX OVERHAUL .... [9]

The engine/gearbox unit must be removed from the car and the gearbox separated from the engine before the gearbox can be overhauled. Details of these operations can be found in ENGINE.

If work is to be carried out on the final drive unit, then the gearbox housing need not be separated from the engine unless it is necessary to remove the final drive pinion, or if final drive unit components have suffered damage with the result that swarf has contaminated the gearbox.

Final Drive Unit — Removal

1. On early type gearboxes with no remote gearchange and a direct-acting gear lever, remove the gear lever bottom cover from the final drive housing.

2. Unscrew the clamp bolt from the control shaft lever (Fig.G:22), remove the lever from the top of the control shaft and withdraw the shaft downwards out of the gearchange extension.

3. On models which have driveshafts with rubber couplings at the inner end, extract the split pin from the castellated nut at each driving flange then unscrew each nut while holding the driving flange with a suitable lever or bar. Remove the nut and washer and draw each drive flange off its splines.

4. Remove the five retaining bolts and washers from each side cover on the final drive housing, then detach the covers with gaskets. Note that rod-change type gearboxes have a gearchange detent ball, spring and plunger located by the right-hand cover; take care not to lose these. Differential bearing preload shims are fitted between the left-hand side cover and the drive gear bearing; these should be removed and retained for reassembly.

5. Undo the final drive housing stud nuts and withdraw the final drive assembly from the gearbox.

6. Remove the final drive unit from its housing.

7. If it is necessary to remove the final drive pinion, then remove the speedometer drive pinion, housing and gear first. Lock the gear train by selecting 1st and 4th gears at once. On non rod-change type gearboxes, this is achieved by removing the interlock plate from the speedometer drive side of the casing, and gently drifting the selector forks into 1st and 4th gears respectively. Access to the forks is gained via the final drive opening in the casing. On rod-change type gearboxes, rotate the selector shaft anti-clockwise to disengage the operating stud and the interlock spool from the bellcrank levers, then lever the 1st/2nd speed selector fork towards the centre web of the gearbox casing to engage 1st gear. Using a screwdriver, carefully drift the centre bellcrank lever inwards to select 4th gear; the gear train is now locked in two gears simultaneously.

8. Knock back the tab washer and undo the third motion shaft nut using a deep socket or box spanner. Slide the final drive pinion off the splines.

Final Drive Unit — Dismantling (Fig.G:32)

1. Withdraw the differential bearings from the spigots on the crown wheel and differential case, using tool No.18G 2 or another suitable puller.

2. Release the lockplate tabs and remove the six bolts securing the crown wheel to the differential case. Mark the relative positions of gear wheel and case before separating to ensure correct reassembly.

3. Extract the left-hand differential gear from the bore of the crown wheel and remove the thrust washer from the gear shaft.

4. Drive the taper locking pin out of the differential case and remove the pinion centre pin, thrust block and differential pinion, and their thrust washers.

5. Extract the right-hand differential side gear from the differential case, and remove the thrust washer from the gear shaft.

6. Identify all parts to ensure that they are refitted in their original positions.

Final Drive Unit — Reassembly (Fig.G:32)

Reassemble the final drive unit in the reverse order of dismantling. Ensure that the differential gear thrust washers are fitted on the gear shafts with their chamfered bore against the machined face of the gear.

On later differential assemblies, increased thrust capacity differential bearings are used and these must be fitted with the 'THRUST' mark facing outwards.

Final Drive Unit — Installation (Fig.G:32)

1. Fit the final drive pinion to the third motion shaft, then fit the tabwasher and tighten the securing nut to the torque recommended in TECHNICAL DATA. Bend up the tabwasher to secure the nut.

2. On rod-change type gearboxes, move the selector bellcrank levers into the neutral position and rotate the interlock spool and selector shaft stub into engagement with bellcrank levers.

3. On non rod-change types, tap the selector forks back into their neutral positions and refit the interlock plate to the speedometer drive end of the gearbox casing.

4. Fit the speedometer drive housing, gear and pinion.

5. Fit the final drive unit (without its housing) into place in the gearbox housing with a slight bias towards the clutch end of the gearbox.

6. Position two new final drive gasket halves on the gearbox mating face, then fit the final drive housing in position.

7. Finger-tighten the four nuts on the long retaining studs so that the bearings are held, but the assembly can still be moved sideways.

8. Tap a new oil seal into place in the right-hand end cover, making sure that it is fully home and seated squarely. Apply a smear of oil or grease to the lip of the seal to prevent damage when the driving flange (or driveshaft joint, later models) is fitted.

9. Fit the end cover, together with its gasket onto the final drive housing. On rod-change type gearboxes make sure that the detent ball spring, plunger and 'O' ring are located first.

10. Fit the cover retaining bolts and tighten them carefully and evenly so as to displace the final drive unit away from the clutch end of the gearbox. Ensure that full contact is obtained between the register on the inner face of the cover and the differential case bearing. Tighten the bolts to the torque specified in TECHNICAL DATA.

11. Fit the left-hand end cover, WITHOUT gasket and without the bearing preload shims. Tighten the cover retaining bolts only sufficiently for the cover register to nip the bearing outer race. Do NOT overtighten the bolts otherwise the cover flange will be distorted.

12. Using feeler gauges, measure the gap between the cover flange and the final drive housing (Fig.G:31). Repeat the measurement at several points around the cover. Any variation will indicate that the cover bolts have not been tightened evenly. Adjust the cover bolts accordingly until identical measurements are obtained.

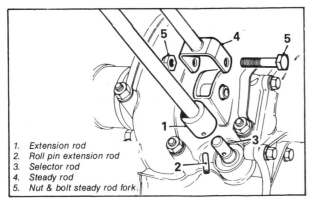

1. Extension rod
2. Roll pin extension rod
3. Selector rod
4. Steady rod
5. Nut & bolt steady rod fork

Fig. G:25 Details of rod change attachment at gearbox

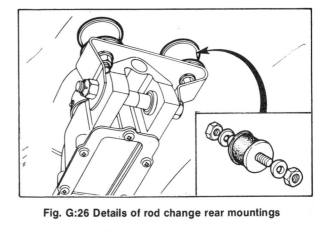

Fig. G:26 Details of rod change rear mountings

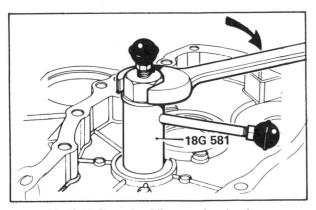

18G 581

Fig. G:27 Removing idler gear bearing from flywheel housing

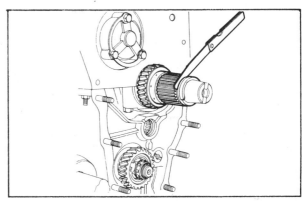

Fig. G:28 Checking primary gear endfloat

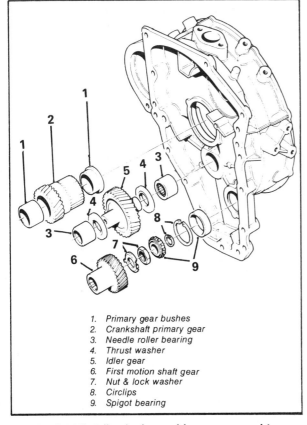

1. Primary gear bushes
2. Crankshaft primary gear
3. Needle roller bearing
4. Thrust washer
5. Idler gear
6. First motion shaft gear
7. Nut & lock washer
8. Circlips
9. Spigot bearing

Fig. G:29 Details of primary drive gear assembly

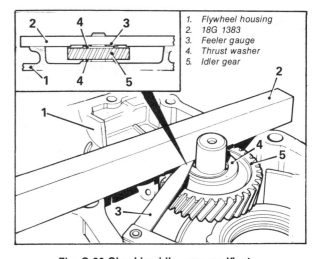

1. Flywheel housing
2. 18G 1383
3. Feeler gauge
4. Thrust washer
5. Idler gear

Fig. G:30 Checking idler gear endfloat

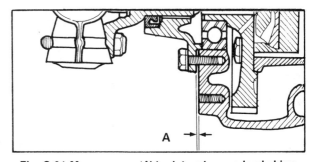

Fig. G:31 Measure gap 'A' to determine pre-load shims

13. The compressed thickness of the cover gasket is 0,18 mm (0.007 in). Subtract the measured gap from this figure to obtain the actual clearance which exists between the cover register and the differential bearing outer race. Add the specified bearing preload to this result to determine the thickness of the bearing shims required. See TECHNICAL DATA for the preload specification and note that later bearings marked 'THRUST' have a different preload.

14. Remove the side cover and fit the oil seal as detailed previously for the other side cover.

15. Place the selected shims against the outer race of the differential bearing, using a light smear of grease to hold them in position. Refit the side cover together with its gasket. Tighten the cover retaining bolts evenly to the torque specified in TECHNICAL DATA.

16. On those models with rubber coupling type driveshafts, apply a smear of oil or grease to the oil sealing surface on the driving flanges, then fit both flanges on their respective differential side gear shafts. Fit the washer and castellated nut to each shaft and tighten the nut to the torque specified in TECHNICAL DATA while preventing the driving flange from turning by the same method used to undo the nut. Secure the nuts with new split pins.

17. Check that both drive flanges (or output stubs, models with offset sphere joints on the driveshafts) are equally free to rotate, otherwise the steering may pull to one side.

18. Insert the remote control shaft into the gearchange extension, position the control shaft lever on the ball end of the change shaft lever and engage the control shaft lever on the splines of the control shaft. Ensure that the clamp bolt hole in the lever is aligned with the recess in the shaft, then fit and tighten the clamp bolt.

19. On early gearboxes without a remote control gearchange, refit the gearchange extension bottom cover with gasket to the final drive housing.

20. Assemble the gearbox assembly to the engine, if separated, then install the engine/gearbox unit in the car as detailed in ENGINE. Do not forget to refill with the recommended grade of oil.

Gearbox Dismantling (Figs.G:33 & G:34)

1. Remove the final drive unit as detailed previously.

2. Withdraw the idler gear with its thrust washers from the flywheel end of the transmission casing.

3. Remove the retaining bolts and nuts and withdraw the front cover together with the gaskets from the transmission casing. Remove the cover gasket. If required, the speedometer drive pinion bush retainer can be removed and the bush and drive pinion withdrawn from the front cover. Similarly, the speedometer drive gear and spindle can be withdrawn after removing the end plate from the cover.

4. Unscrew the reverse stop plug at the front of the transmission casing, and withdraw the check plunger and spring. If a reverse light switch is fitted, this replaces the plug and spring.

5. On non rod-change type gearboxes, unscrew the clamp bolts from the gearchange operating lever and remove the key from the gearchange operating shaft. Withdraw the shaft, complete with the top lever, from the transmission casing.

6. Again on non rod-change types, remove the gearchange gate from the transmission casing.

7. Release the locking plate tabs and remove the bolts securing the oil pick-up pipe to the strainer mounting bracket and the transmission casing, then withdraw the pipe from the strainer.

8. Remove the circlip retaining the roller bearing on the transmission input shaft, and withdraw the bearing using a suitable bearing puller.

9. On non rod-change type gearboxes, lock the transmission by moving the selector shafts to engage both 1st and 4th gears.

NOTE:Do not lock the transmission by engaging 2nd and 3rd gears as this can cause damage.

10. On rod-change type gearboxes, rotate the selector shaft anti-clockwise to disengage the operating stub and the interlock spool from the bellcrank levers. Engage 1st and 4th gears simultaneously to lock the gear train.

11. Release the lock washer tab and unscrew the drive gear retaining nut from the input shaft.

12. Remove the final drive pinion retaining nut from the end of the mainshaft using a deep socket or box spanner and extension bar, and withdraw the final drive pinion from the shaft.

13. On rod-change type gearboxes, move 1st and 4th gears to the neutral position.

14. Release the lock washer tabs and remove the four bolts securing the mainshaft bearing retainer to the gearbox casing centre web. Withdraw the retainer and the adjustment shims behind it.

15. Remove the reverse and layshaft locating plate from the centre web and push the layshaft from the clutch end of the casing. Remove the laygear cluster and its thrust washers.

NOTE:On the 4 speed synchromesh gearbox, the layshaft is stepped and can only be removed from the clutch end of the casing. After removal of the layshaft, the laygear cluster will drop out of mesh with the mainshaft but it cannot be removed from the casing until the mainshaft assembly has been removed.

16. On non rod-change type gearboxes, unscrew the two selector detent plugs from the rear right-hand corner of the transmission casing and withdraw the interlocking plungers and springs.

17. Extract the input shaft bearing circlip from the groove in the casing using a pair of internal circlip pliers. Tap the input shaft towards the clutch end of the casing, taking care not to disengage the 3rd/4th gear synchro sleeve from its hub as this might release its balls and springs. Insert a suitable spacer between the 1st gear pinion and the bearing (Fig.G:36); the correct spacer to use is 18G 613 for 3-synchro units or 18G 1127 for 4-synchro. Ensure that the correct tool is used for respective gearboxes as otherwise damage may occur. Now tap the mainshaft assembly in the reverse direction in order to push the bearing from the centre web.

18. On the all-synchro gearbox, the laygear cluster can now be removed.

19. Lift out the mainshaft assembly.

20. Remove the strainer assembly.

21. Withdraw the reverse idler shaft and lift out the idler gear and selector fork.

22. If required, the selector shafts and forks can now be removed. On non rod-change gearboxes, this is achieved by unscrewing the taper locking bolts from the forks on 1st/2nd and 3rd/4th forks and removing the retaining circlip from the arm pivot pin in order to release the reverse gear shifter arm. Remove the reverse detent plunger and spring from the same bore as the 3rd/4th gear detent plunger.

On rod-change type gearboxes, drift out the roll pin securing the 3rd/4th speed selector fork to its shaft and remove the shaft and forks. Remove the bellcrank lever pivot post nut and washer then lift out the bellcrank levers, washers and pivot sleeve. Note the location and markings on the levers for reassembly. Withdraw the interlock spool and selector shaft from inside the casing and drift the bellcrank lever pivot post out of the gearbox casing if the 'O' ring oil seal is to be removed.

23. If required, the idler gear needle roller bearing can be removed from the transmission casing after extracting the outer circlip (when fitted) from the casing bore. Refer to the Primary Drive Gears section for details.

Mainshaft Dismantling — 3-Synchro Bronze Bush Type (Fig.G:33)

1. Slide the 1st gear assembly (which also includes the 2nd gear synchroniser assembly and reverse mainshaft gear) and

2nd gear baulk ring off the end of the mainshaft. Take care not to lose the locking plunger located in the gear hub.

2. Similarly, slide the 3rd / 4th gear synchroniser assembly and 3rd and 4th gear baulk rings off the rear end of the mainshaft.

3. Place the mainshaft in a vice with 3rd gear upwards. Using a sharp pointed instrument, press in the spring-loaded locking peg located just above 3rd gear in the mainshaft, hold it there and rotate the 3rd gear locking collar until the splines line up with those on the shaft. Slide the collar up off the mainshaft and remove the locking peg and spring from the shaft. Withdraw the 3rd gear.

4. Withdraw the 3rd gear bush and interlocking ring from the shaft, then remove the 2nd gear, 2nd gear bush and thrust washer.

NOTE: Interference fit of existing bushes will have been lost when they were removed, therefore new ones MUST be used on reassembly.

5. If it is necessary to separate the 2nd or 3rd / 4th synchro sleeve from its hub, use tool No.18G 572 to retain the three synchroniser balls and springs which are located in the hub. Alternatively, use a piston ring clamp around the hub to catch the springs and balls.

Mainshaft Dismantling 3-Synchro Needle Roller Type (Fig.G:35)

1. Remove the 1st gear assembly and the 3rd / 4th synchroniser assembly as described above for the bronze bush type mainshaft gears.

2. Also remove the 3rd locking collar as described above, but lift the 3rd gear carefully up off the mainshaft as 26 needle rollers will then be displaced from the gear bore. Remove and retain the rollers.

3. Reverse the mainshaft in the vice so that the 2nd gear is upwards. There are two locking pegs at the 2nd gear locking collar and these must be depressed together to allow the collar to be rotated into alignment with the shaft splines. Slide the collar up off the mainshaft, then remove the two locking pegs and spring from the shaft. Remove the two halves of the split thrust washer from the end of 2nd gear. As for 3rd gear, lift the 2nd gear carefully up off the mainshaft and remove the 26 needle rollers.

Mainshaft Dismantling — 4-Synchro Type (Fig.G:34)

1. Slide the 1st gear, 1st gear baulk ring and caged needle roller bearing off the front end of the mainshaft.

2. Carefully lever the 1st gear bearing the sleeve forwards sufficiently to allow tool No.18G 2, or a similar suitable puller to be fitted, then draw the sleeve off the mainshaft.

3. Slide the 1st / 2nd synchroniser assembly (which also includes the reverse mainshaft gear) and the 2nd gear baulk ring off the mainshaft.

4. Slide the 3rd / 4th synchroniser assembly and 3rd and 4th gear baulk rings off the rear end of the mainshaft.

5. Place the mainshaft in a vice with 3rd gear upwards. Using a sharp pointed instrument, press in the spring-loaded locking peg located just above 3rd gear in the mainshaft, hold it there and rotate the 3rd gear locking collar until the splines line up with those on the shaft. Slide the collar up off the mainshaft and remove the locking peg and spring from the shaft. Withdraw the 3rd gear with its caged needle roller bearing.

6. Reverse the mainshaft in the vice so that the 2nd gear is upwards. There are two locking pegs at the 2nd gear locking collar and these must be depressed together to allow the collar to be rotated into alignment with the shaft splines. Slide the collar up off the mainshaft, then remove the two locking pegs and spring from the shaft. Withdraw the 2nd gear and its split caged needle-roller bearing.

Gearbox Components Check — General

Examine all gear teeth for wear or chipping and any bearing surfaces (including thrust washer faces) for scoring or roughness. Mainshaft and layshaft surfaces should be inspected for ridging or deterioration of the case hardening. The dog-teeth on the gear pinions must be examined for chipping or breakage and the synchroniser cone projection on each gear must not in any way be rough or pitted. It is advisable to determine synchroniser cone or baulk ring wear by fitting each ring onto its corresponding cone and attempting to rotate it while pressing it fully home. If the baulk ring can turn easily, this is indicative of wear, either of the cone or of the baulk ring itself and the faulty component can be isolated by repeating the test with a new baulk ring. Also check that the clearance between the side of the gear pinion dogteeth and the face of the baulk ring (when the ring is pressed fully on) is no less than 0,76 mm (0.030 in); if it is then this is also indicative of wear.

Ball bearings should be spun and felt for roughness while needler roller bearings should be visually inspected for pitting of the roller surfaces. Check the synchroniser hub internal splines for burring or obstruction and also check that they are not a sloppy fit on the mainshaft.

Mainshaft Reassembly — 3-Synchro Bronze Bush Type (Fig.G:33)

1. When fitting new bronze bushes, heat the bushes to a temperature of 180°-200°C (356°-392°F) to allow them to be fitted without force and to obtain a permanent 'shrink fit' on cooling. Smear the bushes with a molybdenum disulphide grease and apply engine oil to the grooves in the gear bores prior to assembly. Do NOT pack the gear grooves with grease.

2. Place the mainshaft in a vice with the speedometer drive slot end downwards.

3. Slide the 2nd gear thrust washer onto the shaft, then fit the 2nd gear bush (plain bore) with its flat end against the thrust washer. Install the 2nd gear on the bush with synchroniser cone facing downwards towards the thrust washer.

4. Position the interlocking ring on the end of the 2nd gear bush, then fit the 3rd gear bush (splined bore) so that the dogs of the bush engage the slots in the ring.

5. Fit the locking peg and spring in the bore in the shaft, depress the peg and fit the 3rd gear, plain side towards, 2nd gear. With the peg still depressed, fit the 3rd gear thrust washer, then rotate the washer until the plunger engages the spline and lock the washer.

6. Check the endfloat of both 2nd and 3rd gears on the mainshaft. This must be 0,09-0,13 mm (0.0035-0.0055 in) and is achieved by selective assembly of the gears and shaft.

7. Place the baulk ring on the cone of the 3rd gear, then fit the 3rd / 4th synchroniser assembly with the plain side of the hub towards the 3rd gear. Ensure the three lugs on the baulk ring correctly engage corresponding slots in the hub.

8. Remove the mainshaft assembly from the vice.

9. If the 1st gear and 2nd gear synchroniser assembly has been dismantled, ensure that the gear is correctly positioned on the hub when reassembling, otherwise the selection of 2nd gear will be impossible. The plunger in the hub must be aligned with the cut-away tooth in the gear assembly (Fig.G:39). Also check that the cone end of hub and tapered side of the gear teeth are on opposite sides of the assembly.

10. Place the baulk ring on the cone of the 2nd gear. Ensure that the locking plunger is correctly located in the drilling of the 2nd gear synchroniser hub, then fit 1st gear and 2nd gear synchroniser assembly with the cone end of the hub towards the 2nd gear. Again ensure that the baulk ring lugs locate correctly in the synchroniser hub.

Mainshaft Reassembly — 3-Synchro Needle Roller Type (Fig.G:35)

1. Place the mainshaft in a vice with the speedometer drive slot end uppermost.

2. Using a liberal quantity of light grease to hold them in position, assemble the 26 needle rollers on the 2nd gear bearing surface of the mainshaft. Fit the spring and two locking pegs in the shaft, then depress the pegs and slide the 2nd gear into

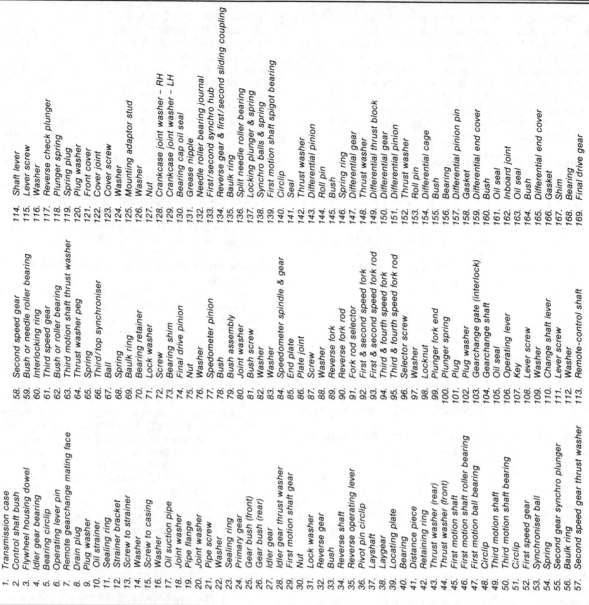

Fig. G:32 Final drive assembly (rubber coupling driveshafts)

Key for Figs. G:33 and G:34

Fig. G:33 Details of 3-synchro transmission (bronze bush type)

position over the needle rollers with the plain side downwards towards the shaft flange. Fit the two halves of the split thrust washer to the face of the gear with the lugs slightly to the clockwise side of the locking pegs. Slide the 2nd gear locking collar onto the shaft. Ensure that the recesses on the underside of the collar will engage the two lugs on the split thrust washer, then depress the two locking pegs. Push the collar home and rotate it until the pegs are heard to engage in the collar splines.

3. Reverse the mainshaft in the vice so that the speedometer slot end is downwards.

4. Again using light grease, assemble the 26 needle rollers on the 3rd gear bearing surface of the shaft. Fit the spring and locking peg in shaft, depress the peg and slide the 3rd gear over the roller with the plain side downwards. With the peg still depressed, fit the 3rd gear locking collar, ensuring that the grooved thrust side faces the gear and that the machined flute on the periphery of the collar is home and rotate it so that the peg locates and locks in the collar splines.

5. Check the endfloat of both the 2nd and 3rd gears on the mainshaft. This must be 0,09-0,13 mm (0.0035-0.0055 in) and is achieved by selective assembly of the gears and shaft.

6. Assemble the remainder of the mainshaft components as described in operations 7-10 previously for the bronze bush type shaft.

Mainshaft Reassembly — 4-Synchro Type (Fig.G:34)

1. Place the mainshaft in a vice with the speedometer drive slot end uppermost.

2. Lubricate the two halves of the split caged needle roller bearing and position the bearing on the 2nd gear bearing surface of the mainshaft. Fit the spring and the two locking pegs in the shaft, then depress the pegs and slide the 2nd gear into position over the bearing with the plain side of the bearing down towards the shaft flange. With the pegs still depressed, fit the 2nd gear locking collar, push the collar home and rotate it until the pegs locate and lock in the collar and splines.

3. Reverse the mainshaft in the vice so that the speedometer slot end is downwards.

4. Lubricate the 3rd gear caged needle roller bearing and slide the bearing onto the mainshaft. Fit the locking peg and spring in the bore in the shaft, depress the peg and fit the 3rd gear over the roller bearing with the plain side of the bearing towards the shaft flange. With the peg still depressed, fit the 3rd gear locking collar, press the collar home and turn it until the plunger engages the spline and the lock collar.

5. Remove the mainshaft from the vice.

6. If the synchroniser assemblies have been dismantled, ensure that the long boss on both the sleeve and hubs are on the same side when reassembling.

7. Place the baulk ring on the cone of the 2nd gear, then the fit 1st/2nd synchroniser assembly with the long boss towards the adjacent end of the shaft. If the synchroniser position is reversed, the 2nd gear synchro action will be lost.

Ensure the three lugs on the baulk ring correctly engage the corresponding slots in the hubs.

8. Install 1st gear bearing sleeve on the front end of the shaft with the collar facing the synchro assembly. The sleeve should be a push fit on the shaft, but if necessary tool No.18G 186 can be used to drift it into position.

9. Lubricate the 1st gear caged roller bearing and slide it onto the bearing sleeve. Place the baulk ring on the cone of the 1st gear and fit the 1st gear over the roller bearing with the synchroniser cone towards the synchro assembly. Again ensure the baulk ring lugs locate correctly in the synchroniser hub.

10. Place the baulk ring on the cone of the 3rd gear, then fit the 3rd/4th synchroniser assembly with the long boss towards the adjacent end of the shaft. Ensure the baulk ring engages correctly with the synchroniser.

Reassembly — Selectors & Oil Strainer

NOTE:Jointing compound must be used on all gaskets when reassembling the transmission case.

1. On non rod-change type gearboxes, refit the reverse gear shifter arm onto its pivot pin and secure it with the circlip. Insert the reverse gear detent spring followed by its plunger into the bottom of the two holes in the rear right-hand corner of the transmission casing. Slide the reverse selector rod part way into the casing and position the reverse selector and push the rod through it. Push the reverse detent plunger right home in its bore with a screwdriver, then push the selector shaft fully home in the casing. Tighten the selector taper bolt, ensuring that it locates correctly in the indent in the rod, otherwise the selector will slip on the shaft and reverse gear will not be obtainable. Secure the bolt with its locknut.

2. On rod-change type gearboxes, lubricate and fit a new 'O' ring oil seal into the bellcrank lever pivot post and drift it into the gearbox casing. Insert the selector shaft into the interlock spool and refit the assembly into the gearbox casing. Insert the selector shaft into the interlock spool and refit the assembly into the gearbox with the operating stub facing away from the pivot post. Refit the sleeve, bellcrank levers (in their correct order) onto the pivot post and tighten the self locking nut (Fig.G:38).
NOTE:Do not turn the selector shaft and interlock spool into engagement with the bellcrank levers until the first and third motion shaft gear retaining nuts have been tightened to their correct torques.

3. On non rod-change type gearboxes, install the 1st/2nd and 3rd/4th selector rods and forks and secure as detailed under procedure 1. The selector forks can only be fitted one way round because of the position of the bolt indents. Fit the reverse selector shaft into reverse position against the detent plunger. Fit the reverse selector fork into the hole in the shifter arm and place the reverse idler gear in the fork. Slide the idler shaft through the centre web of the casing and into place through the gear. The shaft must be fitted with the locating plate slot adjacent to the centre web.

4. On rod-change type gearboxes, refit the 3rd/4th speed selector fork then refit the 1st speed selector fork and drift the selector rod through the casing and forks. Align the hole in the shaft with the hole in the 3rd/4th speed fork. Drift in the roll pin until it is flush with the fork. Refit the reverse idler gear into engagement with the reverse bellcrank lever pivot and refit the shaft.

5. Fit a new sealing ring to the oil pick-up strainer. Apply a smear of oil or grease to the ring to facilitate fitting the old pick-up pipe, then position the strainer in the bottom of the transmission casing.
NOTE:Take great care to avoid damaging the strainer during assembly as, if the gauze is distorted it may allow a small metal disc at its base to move up against the pick-up pipe and subsequently restrict the oil flow.

Mainshaft & Speedo Drive Installation

6. On the 4-synchro gearbox (non rod-change type), assemble the caged needle roller bearings (two at 4th gear end) in the bore of the laygear and place the gear assembly in the bottom of the casing.

7. Fit the mainshaft assembly in place in the transmission casing, with the speedometer drive slot passing through the centre web in the casing. Ensure that the synchro sleeve engages correctly with the selector forks.

Input Shaft Installation

8. Fit the needle roller bearing into the end of the input shaft. Place the 4th gear baulk ring on the cone of the input shaft gear, then feed the input shaft through the bearing opening in the casing and into position on the end of the mainshaft. Ensure that the lugs on the baulk ring correctly engage the three slots in the 3rd/4th synchromniser hub.

9. Drift the input shaft bearing squarely into place in the casing, then secure the bearing in the casing with the circlip.
NOTE:The circlip is available in two thicknesses and should be

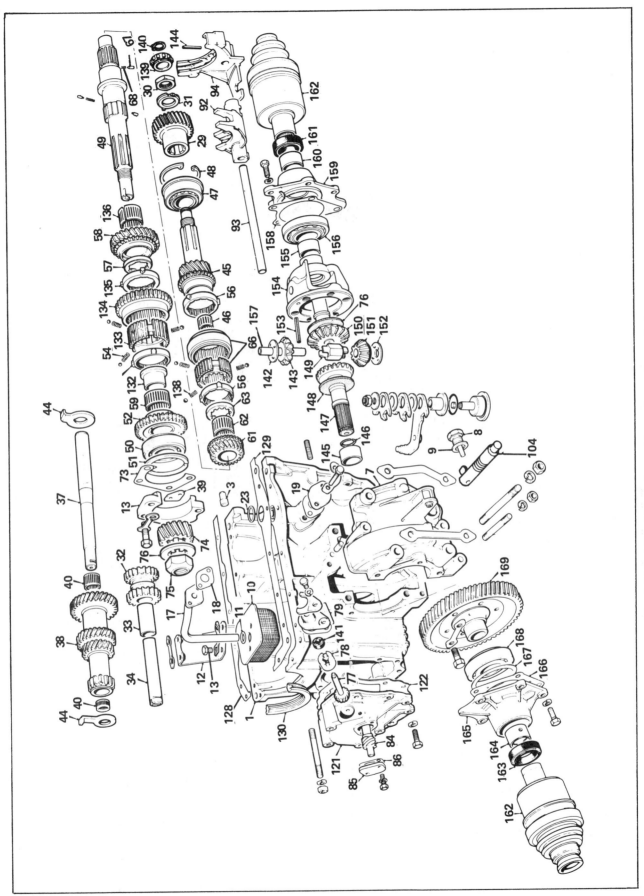

Fig. G:34 Details of 4-synchro rod type-change transmission

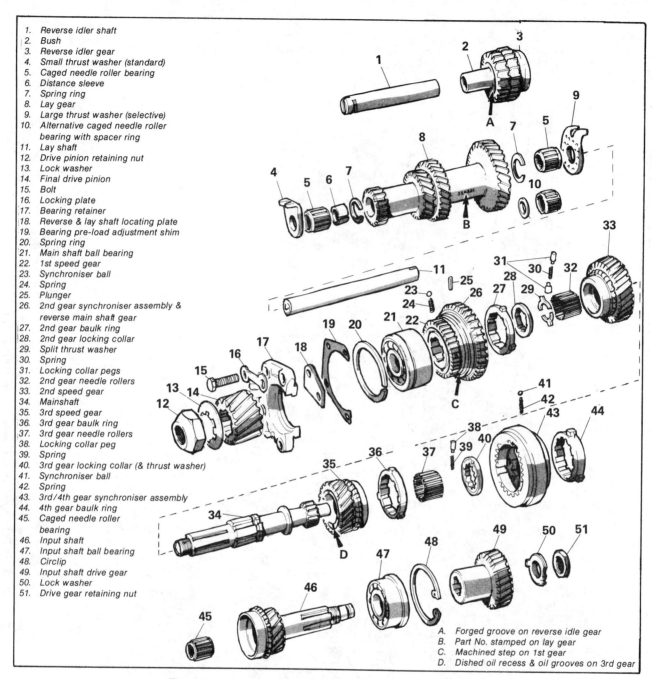

1. Reverse idler shaft
2. Bush
3. Reverse idler gear
4. Small thrust washer (standard)
5. Caged needle roller bearing
6. Distance sleeve
7. Spring ring
8. Lay gear
9. Large thrust washer (selective)
10. Alternative caged needle roller bearing with spacer ring
11. Lay shaft
12. Drive pinion retaining nut
13. Lock washer
14. Final drive pinion
15. Bolt
16. Locking plate
17. Bearing retainer
18. Reverse & lay shaft locating plate
19. Bearing pre-load adjustment shim
20. Spring ring
21. Main shaft ball bearing
22. 1st speed gear
23. Synchroniser ball
24. Spring
25. Plunger
26. 2nd gear synchroniser assembly & reverse main shaft gear
27. 2nd gear baulk ring
28. 2nd gear locking collar
29. Split thrust washer
30. Spring
31. Locking collar pegs
32. 2nd gear needle rollers
33. 2nd speed gear
34. Mainshaft
35. 3rd speed gear
36. 3rd gear baulk ring
37. 3rd gear needle rollers
38. Locking collar peg
39. Spring
40. 3rd gear locking collar (& thrust washer)
41. Synchroniser ball
42. Spring
43. 3rd/4th gear synchroniser assembly
44. 4th gear baulk ring
45. Caged needle roller bearing
46. Input shaft
47. Input shaft ball bearing
48. Circlip
49. Input shaft drive gear
50. Lock washer
51. Drive gear retaining nut

A. Forged groove on reverse idle gear
B. Part No. stamped on lay gear
C. Machined step on 1st gear
D. Dished oil recess & oil grooves on 3rd gear

Fig. G:35 Gear assembly — 3-synchro (needle roller type)

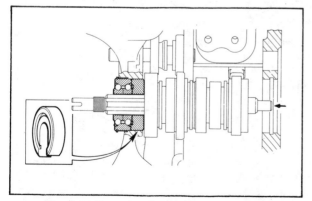

Fig. G:36 Removing 3rd motion shaft bearing

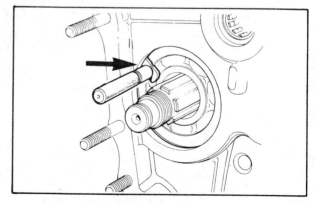

Fig. G:37 Measuring bearing circlip groove

112   Clutch & Gearbox

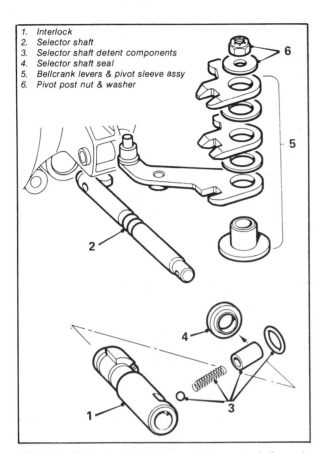

1. Interlock
2. Selector shaft
3. Selector shaft detent components
4. Selector shaft seal
5. Bellcrank levers & pivot sleeve assy
6. Pivot post nut & washer

Fig. G:38 Selector shaft & bellcrank levers (rod change)

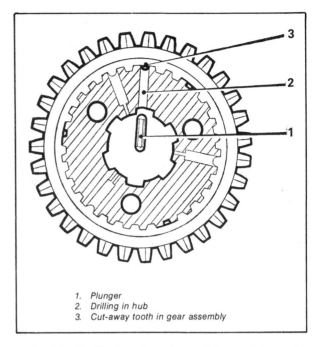

1. Plunger
2. Drilling in hub
3. Cut-away tooth in gear assembly

Fig. G:39 Positioning of synchro unit (3-synchro trans)

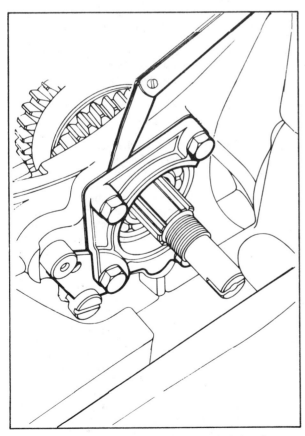

Fig. G:41 Measuring 3rd motion shaft bearing retainer gap

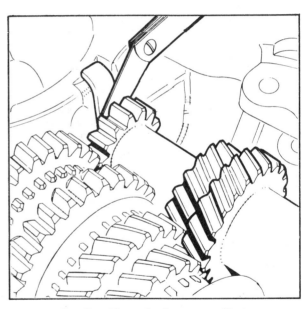

Fig. G:40 Measuring laygear endfloat

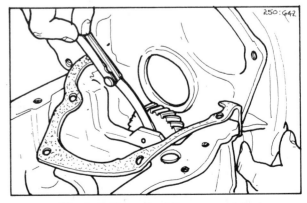

Fig. G:42 Measuring idler gear end float

selected according to the gap between the bearing outer race and the register on the transmission casing (Fig.G:37). Always use the larger circlip if this will fit into the groove, tool No.18G 569 can be used to gauge the correct thickness of the circlip required, and the thicker side of the gauge should be tried first.

When Measured Gap is	Use circlip Part No
2,43-2,48 mm (0.096-0.098 in)	2A 3710
2,48-2,54 mm (0.098-0.100 in)	2A 3711

Mainshaft Bearing Installation

10. Fit the circlip to the groove in the outer race of the mainshaft ball bearing, then slide the bearing onto the mainshaft with the circlip furthest from the casing centre web. Tap the bearing squarely into place in the centre web with a drift.

NOTE:If the later improved-type bearing is being used as a replacement on the 3-speed baulk ring type gearbox, a modified 2nd gear synchroniser assembly must also be fitted in conjunction with it.

Laygear Installation

11. On 3-synchro gearboxes, assemble the needle roller bearings, spacers and circlips in the bore of the laygear.

NOTE:Early gearboxes were fitted with uncaged needle roller bearings and grease should be used to retain the rollers in position. Later caged-type bearings are interchangeable with the early types.

12. On 3-synchro gearboxes, start the layshaft into the bore in the centre web of the casing with the slotted end of the shaft leading. The slot across the end of the shaft is to allow turning with a screwdriver when locating the locking plate in the shaft. Position the laygear assembly in the gearbox, slide the small thrust washer (standard) into place between the end of the gear and the centre web and push the layshaft through the thrust washer and gear. If the layshaft and casing are new, the shaft may require gentle tapping.

13. On 3-synchro gearboxes, measure the gap between the outer end of the laygear and the casing (Fig.G:40) and select a thrust washer from the range given in TECHNICAL DATA to give the specified endfloat of 0,05-0,15 mm (0.002-0.006 in). If possible, a figure of 0,13-0,15 mm (0.005-0.006 in) is preferable.

14. On 3-synchro gearboxes, fit the large thrust washer into place at the outer end of the gear and push home the layshaft. Ensure that the locking plate groove at the inner end of the shaft is correctly positioned to engage the locking plate.

15. On rod-change type gearboxes, insert the caged needle roller bearings into the ends of the laygear and position the laygear in the gearbox casing.

16. On all-synchro type gearboxes, start the smaller diameter end of the layshaft into the transmission casing from the clutch side. Lift the laygear assembly into position from the bottom of the casing, slide the large thrust washer (standard) into place between the end of the gear and the transmission casing and push the layshaft through the thrust washer and the gear. Measure the gap between the inner end of the laygear and the centre web (Fig.G:40) and select a thrust washer from the range given in TECHNICAL DATA to give the specified endfloat of 0,05-0,15 mm (0.002-0.006 in). If possible, a figure of 0,13-0,15 mm (0.005-0.006 in) is preferable.

17. On 4-synchro gearboxes, slide the selected small thrust washer into place at the inner end of the gear and push home the layshaft. Ensure that the locking plate groove at the inner end of the shaft is correctly positioned to engage the locking plate.

Mainshaft Bearing Pre-load

18. Fit the mainshaft bearing retainer onto the centre web, WITHOUT any shims and lightly tighten the retaining bolts. Using feeler gauges, measure the gap between the mating faces of the retainer and the centre web (Fig.G:41) and select a shim pack from the range given in TECHNICAL DATA.

19. Remove the bearing retainer and fit the selected shim pack onto the centre web. Fit the reverse idler and layshaft locating plate. Ensure that the plate engages correctly inside the slots in both shafts and that the shim pack is fitted under the locating plate. Fit the retainer bolts with new locking plates and tighten them to the torque specified in TECHNICAL DATA. Bend over the locking plates.

Final Drive Pinion & Input Shaft

20. On non rod-change type gearboxes, insert the oil pick-up pipe into the oil strainer assembly, taking care not to displace the sealing ring from the strainer. Fit and tighten the external flange securing bolts, then the bracket retaining bolts.

21. Fit the final drive pinion, the lockwasher and the securing nut on the end of the mainshaft. If the original pinion is being refitted, ensure it is installed the same way round as before. Fit the drive gear, the lockwasher and the securing nut on the input shaft. Lock the transmission; on non rod-change type gearboxes simply move both selector shafts to engage 1st and 4th gears simultaneously. On rodchange types refer to operation No.10 under Gearbox Dismantling. Tighten both the final drive pinion nut and the first motion shaft nut to the torques given in TECHNICAL DATA and bend over the lock washer tabs.

22. Tap the roller bearing onto the end of the input shaft and secure it in position with a new circlip.

23. On rod-change type gearboxes move 1st and 4th gears to the neutral position. Rotate the selector shaft and interlock spool into engagement with the bellcrank levers.

24. On rod-change type gearboxes, insert the oil suction pipe into the strainer. Fit a new joint washer and locking plates, tighten the external flange securing screws first, then the pipe bracket screws. Tap over the locking plate tabs.

Gearchange Levers & Interlock (Non Rod-change)

25. On non rod-change type gearboxes, install the gearchange plate with the tongues engaged in the notches of the selector forks. If removed, refit the top lever on the gearchange operating shaft. Ensure that the notch in the shaft is correctly aligned with the clamp bolt hole in the lever, then fit and tighten the clamp bolt. Fit a new operating shaft oil seal in the transmission casing. Apply a smear of oil or grease to the shaft to avoid damaging the seal, then slide the shaft through the bore in the casing. Install the key in the lower end of the shaft then fit the operating lever to the shaft. Fit and tighten the lever clamp bolt.

26. If removed, reassemble the speedometer drive assembly to the front cover, using new gaskets. Place a new cover gasket on the transmission casing and fit the front cover assembly, ensuring that the speedometer drive spindle engages with the slot in the end of the mainshaft. Fit the cover retaining bolts and nuts and tighten them to the torque given in TECHNICAL DATA.

27. On non rod-change type gearboxes, insert the 3rd/4th gear detent spring and plunger into the bottom of the two holes in the rear right-hand corner of the transmission casing (same hole as for reverse detent plunger) and screw in the plugs. Insert the reverse check plunger, the spring and the plug (or reverse light switch) in the bore at the front of the transmission casing.

Idler Gear

28. Assemble the idler gear with its thrust washers to the transmission casing; each washer must be fitted with the chamfered side against the gear. If a new idler gear or transmission casing has been fitted, temporarily assemble the flywheel housing to the side of the transmission casing with a new gasket and tighten the retaining bolts to the torque given in TECHNICAL DATA. Measure the idler gear endfloat by using a feeler gauge passed down between the idler gear and the transmission casing (Fig.G:42); this should be between 0.08-0.2 mm (0.003-0.008 in). Adjust, if necessary, by using a different thickness of thrust washer on the idler gear; the range of washer thicknesses is given in TECHNICAL DATA.

29. Refit the final drive unit as detailed under Final Drive Unit - Installation.

Clutch & Gearbox Problems

FAULT	CAUSE	ACTION
Clutch slips	☐ Driven plate lining worn. ☐ Driven plate lining contaminated with oil. ☐ Clutch incorrectly adjusted.	■ Replace clutch assembly. ■ Check cause and replace driven plate or clutch assy. ■ Adjust clutch.
Clutch drags – i.e. gear fails to engage: smoothly	☐ Faulty clutch release mechanism. ☐ Clutch incorrectly adjusted. ☐ Driven plate sticking on hub shaft splines. ☐ Broken clutch pressure plate fingers. ☐ Broken release bearing or release arm.	■ Check/overhaul release mechanism. ■ Adjust clutch (if adjustable). ■ Remove clutch, clean and lubricate splines with graphite. ■ Check and replace pressure plate assembly. ■ Check and replace components.
Clutch grabs	☐ Oil on driven plate lining. ☐ Driven plate cushion springs broken. ☐ Warped or damaged pressure plate. ☐ Weak or broken engine mountings.	■ Replace driven plate ■ Replace driven plate. ■ Check pressure plate and replace if necessary. ■ Check/replace mounting rubbers.
Scream from clutch – pedal fully depressed	☐ Worn release bearing or broken pressure plate/driven plate springs.	■ Remove gearbox and check/replace spigot or release bearing.
Constant noise/chatter from clutch – pedal released, disappearing when pedal depressed	☐ Worn spigot bearing in flywheel or worn release bearing.	■ Remove gearbox and check/replace clutch components.
Gearchange difficult when cold	☐ Incorrect grade of oil in gearbox. ☐ Clutch driven plate not clearing. ☐ Normal condition on some models. ☐ Worn or incorrect adjustment on gearchange linkage.	■ Check/replace gearbox oil with known correct grade. ■ See Clutch drag. ■ Check possible causes 1 and 2. ■ Check for play in linkage joints. Replace and/or adjust.
Gearchange difficult when hot – gears grate	☐ Worn synchromesh unit. ☐ Incorrect clutch adjustment.	■ Overhaul or replace gearbox. ■ Check clutch adjustment.
Constant moan or grating noise from gearbox	☐ Insufficient oil in gearbox. ☐ Worn shaft bearings.	■ Check/top up gearbox oil. ■ Overhaul or replace gearbox.
Oil leakage from final drive output shaft seals	☐ Output shaft oil seal worn.	■ Remove driveshaft and replace output shaft seal.

Automatic Transmission

INTRODUCTION .... [1]

An automatic transmission is probably the most complicated part of any car, and specialised tools as well as a certain amount of practical mechanical knowledge are necessary to carry out repairs satisfactorily.

Because the Mini uses a common oil supply with the engine, it is most important that the engine oil and filter are changed at the intervals as specified in SERVICE SCHEDULE.

Scrupulous cleanliness is essential when working on the automatic transmission as the slightest dirt or other foreign matter can prevent the transmission from operating correctly.

If there is any malfunction of the automatic transmission, the first step must always be to check the oil level, and then carry out a thorough fault diagnosis check to ascertain the cause of the trouble. As pressure testing equipment will be needed, this job should be done by an Austin/Rover dealer or automatic transmission specialist.

It is possible to get an indication of the problem by carrying out a stall speed test – see Adjustments.

It is pointless to remove the transmission and dismantle it in the hope that the fault will be visible, for invariably it will not.

However, there are certain straightforward service adjustments that can be carried out by the DIY owner without removing the transmission, and these are covered in this chapter.

NOTE:Many drivers fail to realise how much the engine performance affects the operation of an automatic transmission. If the engine is in a bad state of tune or in need of an overhaul, this may appear to be a transmission fault when, in fact, the cause is the engine. In all cases of apparent automatic gearbox troubles, always check the oil level and the engine tune first.

TOOLS & EQUIPMENT .... [2]

Other than those tools itemised under Basic Tools & Equipment in BASIC PROCEDURES, the following tools are required to carry out the operations detailed in this chapter.
- A multi-meter or test lamp – for testing the inhibitor switch operation.
- 6 mm (0.25 in) drill bit or rod – for setting the kickdown rod adjustment.
- 18G 587 – for removing the torque converter retaining bolt.
- 18G 1086 – for removing the torque converter from the crankshaft taper.
- 18G 1088 torque converter output gear holder – necessary when removing convertor housing.
- 18G 1089A & 1089/1 – for adjusting transfer gears.
- External micrometer – for measuring the thickness of idler gear washers.
- A dial gauge, mounting block and surface plate – for checking component height.

Some bolts require locking in position with tab locking washers. New washers should always be fitted.

ADJUSTMENTS .... [3]
Stall Speed Test

Although testing of the transmission calls for pressure test equipment, a test of the engine speed when the transmission is locked will give some indication of the cause of any problem.

Warm the engine. Connect an accurate rev counter to the car, see TUNE-UP.

With the wheels chocked and the hand and foot brakes applied start the engine. Select R and hold the throttle fully down for 10 seconds, no more. Note the highest engine speed indicated. Then repeat the test with the transmission in D.

If the transmission is in good condition, the highest speed should be in the range of 1,400 to 1,500 rpm. If not, then an approximate diagnosis can be made.

Below 1,000 rpm – the torque converter stator may be slipping.

Below 1,300 rpm – the engine is down on power and in need of tuning.

Over 1,500 rpm – the transmission is slipping. Try adjusting the brake bands.

Selector Cable

To check if the selector cable requires adjustment, ensure that the handbrake is applied and that the transmission is in N, then start the engine. Move the lever to R and check that the reverse gear is engaged. Moving the lever back to N, check that the reverse gear is disengaged at the same point as the lever reaches the N position. Repeat this procedure with the N and 1 position. If the gears do not engage and disengage correctly, reset the cable adjustment.

1. Raise and support the front of the car – see BASIC PROCEDURES. On early cars, adjust the transverse rod as detailed below.

2. Pull back the rubber sleeve or remove the metal guard from the bellcrank lever on the transmission unit (Figs.H:1 & H:2). On models with the original forged type bellcrank lever, extract the split pin and remove the clevis pin securing the selector cable fork to the bellcrank lever. On units fitted with the later pressed-type bellcrank lever, the cable fork is secured to the lever by a bolt and nut instead of a clevis pin.

3. On early cars with 7 selector positions on the change quadrant, select N in the transmission by pulling the transverse rod fully out then pushing back in two detents.

4. On cars with 6 selector positions on the change quadrant select N in the transmission by pulling the transverse rod fully out then pushing back in one detent.

5. With the selector lever in N, slacken the adjusting nuts holding the outer cable to the casing.

6. Adjust the position of the inner cable fork until the pin or bolt

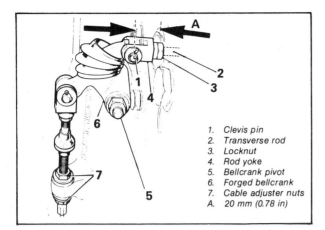

1. Clevis pin
2. Transverse rod
3. Locknut
4. Rod yoke
5. Bellcrank pivot
6. Forged bellcrank
7. Cable adjuster nuts
A. 20 mm (0.78 in)

Fig. H:1 Early type gearchange bellcrank

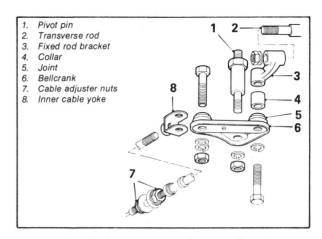

1. Pivot pin
2. Transverse rod
3. Fixed rod bracket
4. Collar
5. Joint
6. Bellcrank
7. Cable adjuster nuts
8. Inner cable yoke

Fig. H:2 Later type gearchange bellcrank

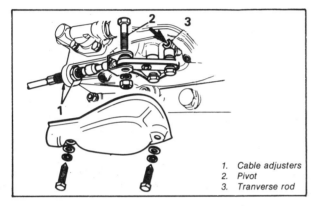

1. Cable adjusters
2. Pivot
3. Tranverse rod

Fig. H:3 Refit pivot with lever & rod in N

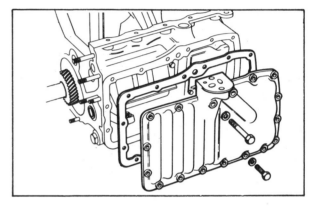

Fig. H:4 Transmission front cover removal

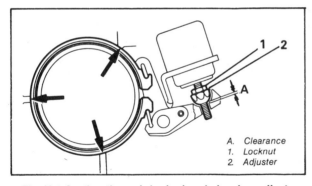

A. Clearance
1. Locknut
2. Adjuster

Fig. H:5 Section through brake band showing adjuster

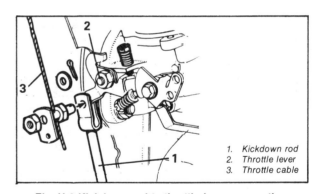

1. Kickdown rod
2. Throttle lever
3. Throttle cable

Fig. H:6 Kickdown rod to throttle lever connection

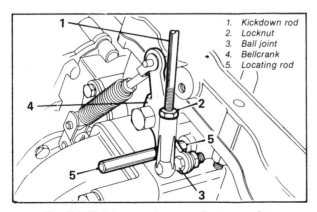

1. Kickdown rod
2. Locknut
3. Ball joint
4. Bellcrank
5. Locating rod

Fig. H:7 Kickdown rod connection to gearbox

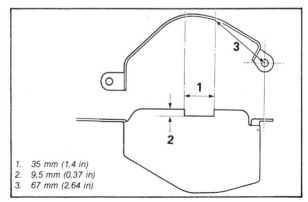

1. 35 mm (1.4 in)
2. 9,5 mm (0.37 in)
3. 67 mm (2.64 in)

Fig. H:8 Modify housing when fitting later bellcrank

is a sliding fit through fork and bellcrank (Fig.H:3).

7. Tighten the clamp bolts and recheck the setting. Then check the starter inhibitor switch setting.

8. Where a rubber boot is fitted, it should be packed with rubber grease before refitting. Refit the metal guard over the bellcrank lever, where applicable. The operation of the transmission in each selector position should be finally checked by carrying out a road test.

Selector Linkage Transverse Rod

The transverse rod adjustment should be checked before setting the selector cable.

NOTE:This adjustment applied only to early models fitted with the original forged-type bellcrank lever (Fig.H:1). Later transmissions with the pressed-type bellcrank have a fixed transverse rod bracket and the rod length cannot be adjusted (Fig.H:2).

1. Raise and support the front of the car – see BASIC PROCEDURES.

2. At the bellcrank lever on the transmission unit, pull back the rubber boot, extract the split pin and remove the clevis pin from the transverse rod fork.

3. Do NOT start the engine while the transverse rod is disconnected. Check that the clevis fork is screwed tightly onto the transverse rod. Also ensure that the rod is pushed fully into the transmission case. Swivel the bellcrank lever clear of the clevis fork and refit the clevis pin. Check the dimension between the clevis pin centre line and the flat machined face of the transmission case, not the oil seal retainer. This should be 20 mm (0.78 in) (A,Fig.H:1).

4. If necessary, slacken the locknut and turn the clevis fork until the correct setting is obtained. Retighten the locknut, ensuring that the clevis fork is correctly aligned with the bellcrank lever. Reconnect the fork to the bellcrank lever and secure the clevis pin with a new split pin. Pull the rubber boot back into position over the fork.

Brake Bands

1. Remove the front grille. Drain the engine/automatic gearbox oil, see ROUTINE MAINTENANCE. Raise and support the front of the car – see BASIC PROCEDURES.

2. Remove the transmission front cover securing bolts and lift off the cover complete with the oil filter assembly (Fig.H:4).

3. Check the brake band adjustment. The free movement (A,Fig.H:5) between the servo lever and the spherical nut should be as specified, see TECHNICAL DATA.

4. Slacken the locknut and turn the spherical adjusting nut until the brake band is in contact with the transmission casing stops, and all slack is eliminated.

5. Turn the spherical adjusting nut downwards nine flats to obtain the clearance (A,Fig.H:5), this should give the minimum clearance.

6. Recheck that the clearance is correct. Hold the spherical nut and tighten the locknut. Repeat the procedure to adjust the other two brake bands.

7. Fit a new joint washer coated with Hylomar jointing compound or equivalent.

Kickdown Control Rod

1. Before attempting to adjust the kickdown control rod, check that the throttle cable operates freely without sticking and is correctly adjusted. When the accelerator is fully depressed, it should open the throttle completely.

2. Disconnect the control rod from the carburettor throttle lever (Fig.H:6). Insert a 6 mm (0.25 in) diameter drill or gauge rod through the hole in the intermediate bellcrank lever and locate it in the corresponding hole in the transmission casing (Fig.H:7).

3. Check that the hole in the control rod fork aligns with the bore in the throttle lever, and that the fulcrum pin is an easy sliding fit through both. If not, slacken the locknut on the lower

end of the control rod and turn the rod until the correct length is obtained. Ensure that the rod fork is correctly aligned with the throttle lever after tightening the locknut.

4. Reconnect the control rod and return spring at the carburettor, then remove the checking rod. Check that full throttle opening has not been restricted.

5. Road test the car and check the transmission kickdown shift speeds against those given in TECHNICAL DATA.

SELECTOR CABLE .... [4]

Cable Replacement

1. Pull back the carpet and slacken the nuts holding the mounting plate to the floor. Raise and support the front of the car – see BASIC PROCEDURES.

2. Pull back the rubber sleeve (early models) or remove the cover plate (later models) from the bellcrank lever on the transmission unit. On models with the original forged-type bellcrank lever, extract the split pin and remove the clevis pin securing the selector cable fork to the bellcrank arm (Fig.H:1). On units fitted with later pressed-type bellcrank lever, the cable fork is secured to the lever by a nut and bolt instead of a clevis pin (Fig.H:2).

3. Slacken the locknut at the selector cable fork and remove the fork, locknut, both rubber ferrules and the sleeve (where fitted) from the cable. Remove the cable front adjusting nut from the outer cable and pull the cable clear of the bracket or abutment on the transmission (Fig.H:3).

4. Release the clip holding the cable to the floor. Disconnect the leads to the inhibitor switch, making a note of the terminals and lead colours.

5. Remove the nuts holding the selector mechanism to the floor and withdraw from the car with the cable. Take care not to damage the joint washer or it will require replacement.

6. Remove the rubber grommet from the selector mechanism. Holding the housing in a vice slacken the large nut holding the cable to the housing. Release the return spring from below the housing. Remove the four bolts holding the lever housing to the base plate and the lower housing.

7. Remove the lever housing disengaging the lever from the plunger. Note the rubber dust excluder between the lower housing and base plate. Unscrew the cable outer from the lower housing and pull the plunger from its bore. Unscrew the plunger from the inner cable.

8. Lubricate all parts with graphite grease. Screw the new inner cable to the plunger and fit into the bore. The chamfered side of the slot should face upwards for the selector lever.

9. Refit in reverse order ensuring that the selector lever engages with the plunger slot. Adjust the cable as detailed under Adjustments. Check the operation of the inhibitor switch and adjust as necessary.

SELECTOR MECHANISM .... [5]

Removal and refitting of the selector mechanism is detailed under Cable Replacement previously. The following information applied to early cars with a forged bellcrank lever.

If seizure of the bellcrank lever has occurred on models fitted with original forged-type bellcrank lever, due to over-tightening of pivot pin nut, replace the pivot pin and distance tube with a modified pivot pin having a shoulder.

If backlash is excessive on the original forged-type bellcrank lever, replace with later pressed-type minimum backlash bellcrank lever assembly. Remove bellcrank lever and its pivot pin, then front cover and transverse rod. Fit a modified type of pivot pin and clevis, non-adjustable transverse rod and pressed-type bellcrank lever. Refit the front cover the bellcrank lever guard must be modified as shown (Fig.H:8).

If a pressed-type bellcrank lever assembly has been fitted in place of the original forged-type lever, the reverse position of selector lever indicator gate should be modified to ensure that

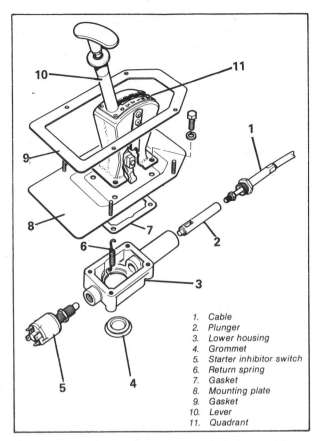

1. Cable
2. Plunger
3. Lower housing
4. Grommet
5. Starter inhibitor switch
6. Return spring
7. Gasket
8. Mounting plate
9. Gasket
10. Lever
11. Quadrant

Fig. H:9 Selector change lever exploded assembly

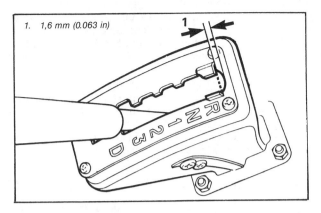

1. 1,6 mm (0.063 in)

Fig. H:10 Modify selector lever gate with later bellcrank

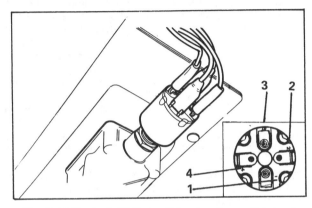

Fig. H:11 Starter inhibitor switch, showing switch back

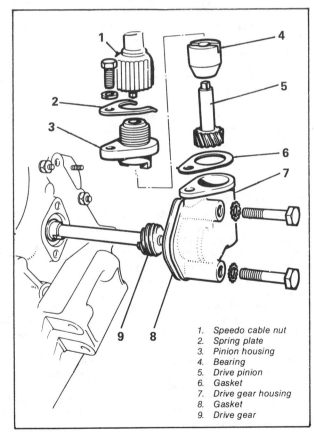

1. Speedo cable nut
2. Spring plate
3. Pinion housing
4. Bearing
5. Drive pinion
6. Gasket
7. Drive gear housing
8. Gasket
9. Drive gear

Fig. H:12 Speedo drive gear & pinion assembly

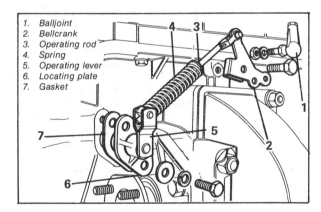

1. Balljoint
2. Bellcrank
3. Operating rod
4. Spring
5. Operating lever
6. Locating plate
7. Gasket

Fig. H:13 Kickdown control linkage on casing

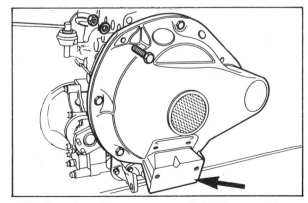

Fig. H:14 Converter cover removal showing mounting

the selector valve detent is fully engaged when selector lever is moved into reverse position. Unscrew the handle from the gear selector lever, then remove the four screws securing the indicator gate to the quadrant. File a radius 1,6 mm (0.063 in) deep in the end of the gate (Fig.H:10). Refit the gate and lever handle.

If slip or loss of drive occurs in reverse gear after a replacement transmission with a pressed-type minimum backlash bellcrank lever has been fitted, check whether the indicator gate has been modified. If not, and adjusting the selector cable as described under Adjustments fails to remedy the fault, then gate modifications should be carried out.

STARTER INHIBITOR SWITCH .... [6]

1. The starter inhibitor switch is located at the rear of the selector lever housing. Early type switches also incorporate the reverse light switch and these have four terminals (Fig.H:11), two for the ignition/starter circuit and two for the reverse light. Later switches have only two terminals and the reverse light switch in this case is a separate unit which is screwed into the reverse check plunger bore in the front of the transmission casing.
2. When the starter inhibitor switch is functioning correctly, the starter will operate only when the selector lever is in the 'N' position. If the starter will not operate in the N position, or if it operates in any other selector positions, then the switch requires adjustment. The reverse light switch (where incorporated) should operate only when the selector lever is in R.
3. Before attempting to adjust the switch, check the adjustment of the selector cable and the transverse rod as previously described.
4. To adjust the switch, place the selector lever in N and disconnect the electrical connection from the switch. Slacken the switch locknut. Connect a continuity meter or small battery and test lamp across number 2 and 4 terminals on the switch. Unscrew the switch almost out of the housing, then screw it in again until the test lamp illuminates and mark the position of the switch. Continue screwing in the switch noting the number of turns required, until the lamp just goes out. Remove the test lamp and battery and unscrew the switch from the housing half the number of turns counted. Tighten the switch locknut and reconnect the electrical leads to their respective terminals. The ignition/starter circuit leads can be fitted either way round to number 2 and 4 terminals, and the reverse light leads (where fitted) to number 1 and 3 terminals.
5. Check that the switch functions as described above. If the switch still does not operate correctly, check the switch wiring and connections before renewing the switch.

SPEEDOMETER DRIVE GEAR & PINION ..... [7]

The speedometer drive gear and pinion are mounted in a housing on the side of the differential (Fig.H:12). The drive pinion can be replaced with the engine in place. Replacement of the drive gear will require removal of the engine and transmission assembly – see ENGINE.

Drive Pinion

Disconnect the speedometer cable from the pinion housing. Remove the screw and withdraw the spring plate, bearing housing and pinion.

Examine the fit of the pinion shaft in the bearing housing. Examine the pinion teeth. If damaged or worn check the drive gear teeth in the housing. If necessary, new parts should be fitted.

Refit in the reverse order using a new gasket below the bearing housing.

Drive Gear

Remove the engine and transmission unit, see ENGINE. Remove the radiator from the adaptor brackets. Then remove the nuts holding the adaptor bracket to the governor housing.

Remove the drive pinion as detailed above. Remove the two housing bolts and detach the housing. Withdraw the drive gear.

Refit the drive gear. If the gear does not easily engage with the governor, disconnect the kickdown linkage and remove the kickdown control assembly (Fig.H:13). Raise the governor into position by lifting with a finger. Push the gear spindle through the governor.

Refit the kickdown control with a new gasket. Refit the pinion assembly. Reassemble and refit in the reverse order of removal.

TORQUE CONVERTER .... [8]

The torque converter can be removed with the engine and transmission in place in the car.

Raise and support the front of the car – see BASIC PROCEDURES. Support the engine from above using lifting tackle. Remove the tie rod from the rear of the block then disconnect the exhaust system. Remove the oil filter and mounting flange assembly. Disconnect the right-hand engine mounting from the subframe, see ENGINE.

Raise the rear of the engine until the nuts and bolts securing the starter motor and converter cover are revealed. Remove the starter motor, see ENGINE ELECTRICS. Remove the cover retaining bolts and withdraw (Fig.H:14).

Release the locktab on the converter centre bolt. Hold the ring gear with a screwdriver and remove the bolt using tool No.18G 587. Then remove the tab washer and key plate (Fig.H:15).

Remove three equally spaced bolts from the hub. Turn the crankshaft until the crankshaft slot is horizontal (Fig.H:16). Special tool No.18G.1086 is needed to pull the converter from the converter output gear splines. Fit the tool over the hub and fit the three bolts. Screw in the centre bolt until the converter is released (Fig.H:17). The converter can then be withdrawn.
NOTE:At no time attempt to remove all six hub bolts.

Remove each pair of bolts in turn to fit new locking washers. Tighten to the specified torque then turn the tabs over.

Fit the converter to the output gear hub, sliding it onto the splines. Align the offset slots in the converter and crankshaft. Fit the key plate and a new tab washer. Tighten the bolt to the specified torque – see TECHNICAL DATA, jamming the ring gear with a suitable lever. Tap over the washer.

Refit the converter cover and other components in the reverse order of removal.

Converter Oil Seal

Remove the converter as detailed above. The oil seal fits in the converter housing face concentric with the crankshaft. Using a broad bladed screwdriver or a hooked end tool, carefully lever out the converter housing oil seal. Note that a special extractor tool is available. Take care not to scratch the housing.

Examine the converter hub for grooving caused by the seal edge.

The new seal must be fitted to the correct depth. The outer face of the seal must be 9,5 mm (0.375 in) from the undercut face of the housing (Fig.H:18). If the housing depth is less than this figure, fit the seal proud.

Fit a new oil seal, liberally lubricating with clean engine oil. Protect the inner lip by wrapping Sellotape around the splines. Alternatively a protecting sleeve is available.

Use a socket or length of tubing of suitable diameter to drive the seal into position. Note that a special tool is available to press the seal into place.
NOTE:If difficulty is encountered replacing the oil seal with the housing in place, remove the housing as detailed below.

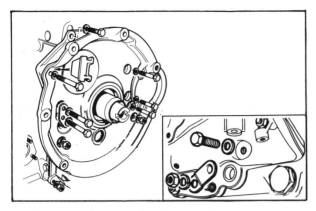

Fig. H:22 Converter housing retaining nuts & bolts

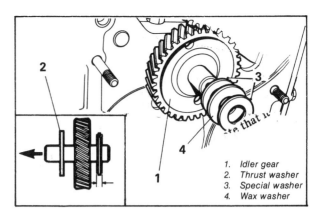

1. Idler gear
2. Thrust washer
3. Special washer
4. Wax washer

Fig. H:23 Idler gear endfloat check

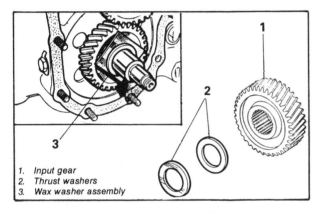

1. Input gear
2. Thrust washers
3. Wax washer assembly

Fig. H:24 Early input gear endfloat check

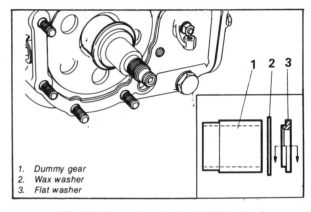

1. Dummy gear
2. Wax washer
3. Flat washer

Fig. H:25 Later input gear endfloat check

Fig. H:26 Measure later input gear height & zero gauge

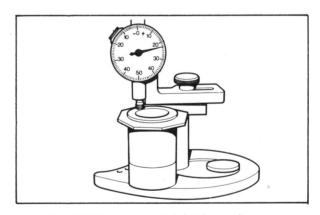

Fig. H:27 Dummy gear height shows clearance

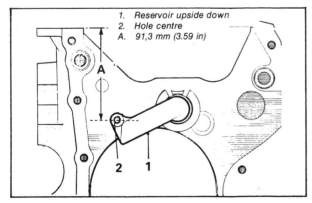

1. Reservoir upside down
2. Hole centre
A. 91,3 mm (3.59 in)

Fig. H:28 Idler bearing reservoir mounting hole

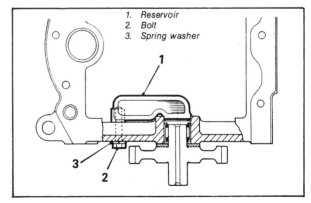

1. Reservoir
2. Bolt
3. Spring washer

Fig. H:29 Idler gear reservoir in position

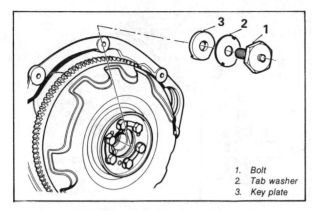

1. Bolt
2. Tab washer
3. Key plate

Fig. H:15 Converter drive key assembly

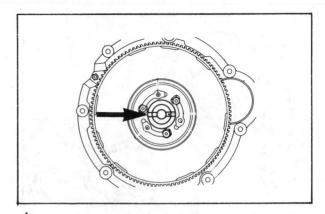

Fig. H:16 Before removing converter turn key horizontal

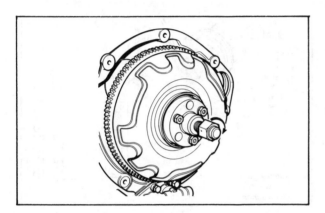

Fig. H:17 Use special puller to extract converter

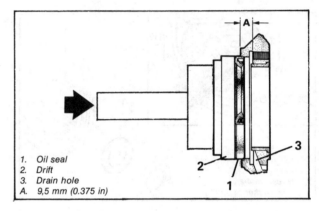

1. Oil seal
2. Drift
3. Drain hole
A. 9,5 mm (0.375 in)

Fig. H:18 Fit converter oil seal to specified height

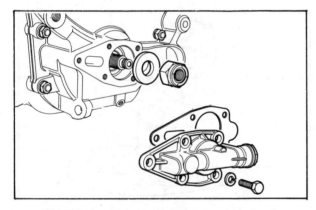

Fig. H:19 Low pressure valve & input shaft nut

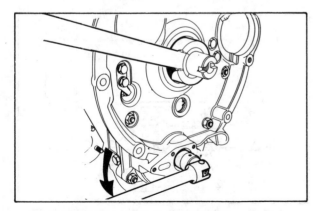

Fig. H:20 Slacken input shaft nut holding output gear

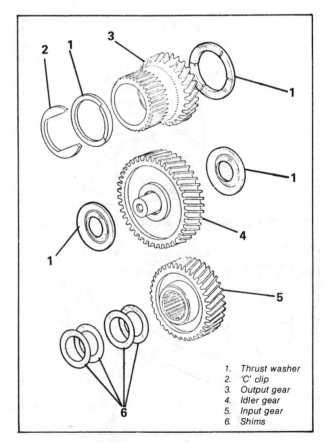

1. Thrust washer
2. 'C' clip
3. Output gear
4. Idler gear
5. Input gear
6. Shims

Fig. H:21 Transfer gear assembly

CONVERTER HOUSING & GEARS .... [9]
Converter Housing Removal & Refitting
The transmission can be separated from the engine after the complete engine and gearbox assembly has been removed. See ENGINE for removal/refitting details.

Remove the torque converter as detailed above. Undo the bolts holding the low pressure valve and withdraw with the gasket (Fig.H:19).

Hold the crankshaft using a strap wrench, or special tool 18G 1088 which fits over the splines. Undo and remove the input shaft nut (Fig.H:20). Remove the bolts holding the bellcrank to the housing.

Remove the nuts and bolts holding the housing to the engine and transmission. Pull the housing away, disconnecting the converter oil feed pipe. The housing and gasket can then be withdrawn (Fig.H:22).

Clean the mating faces and fit a new gasket. A new oil seal should be fitted to the housing as a matter of course. Protect the oil seal lip, see above. Refit the converter housing, connecting the converter feed pipe. Align the pipes for the low pressure valve.

When refitting the nuts and bolts, note that the UNC (coarse thread) bolts fit in the gearbox casing, UNF (fine thread) bolts fit in the engine block.

Reassemble the converter housing in the reverse order of removal. Fit the low pressure valve with a new gasket.

Transfer Gears (Fig.H:21)
After removing the converter housing, access is gained to the transfer gears. These gears should be checked and replaced as necessary. The converter output gear or primary drive gear endfloat is set as detailed in CLUTCH & GEARBOX.
1. After determining the output gear endfloat, remove the gear. Fit the idler gear with a thrust washer on the gearbox side. Fit a dental wax washer between the halves of tool 18G 1089 and fit to the idler gear (Fig.H:23).
2. Note that on early cars the input gear uses similar thrust washers to the idler gear (Fig.H:24). The pre-load can be checked as detailed for the idler gear endfloat. On subsequent cars with shims fit a wax washer between the halves of tool 18G 1089 A and 18G 1089/1. This assembly replaces the input gear (Fig.H:25).
3. Fit the housing with a new gasket. Ensure the mating surfaces are clean and dry. Fit the nuts and bolts, tightening to the specified torque. Do not fit the output shaft nut.
4. Remove the housing without damaging the gasket.
5. Check the idler gear clearance. Remove the washers and wax assembly with care. Measure the thickness of the thrust washer and wax washer assembly with a micrometer. This will given the total clearance.
6. Subtract the clearance specified in TECHNICAL DATA. Choose thrust washers to give a clearance between the two limits. When calculating the required thrust washer thickness, note that two shims of equal thickness should be used. Place one washer on either side of the gear. The thrust washer thicknesses available are given in TECHNICAL DATA.
7. Check the input gear pre-load. On early cars add the washer assembly clearance to the specified pre-load and choose thrust washers to suit. Note that the thrust washers are similar to those used on the idle gear.
8. On later cars remove the special tool and washer from the gear shaft, keeping the assembly in one piece.
9. Determine the height of the input gear. If possible, a dial gauge and surface plate should be used. Set the gauge at zero (Fig.H:26). Remove the input gear and substitute the special tool assembly. The reading on the gauge will give the exact clearance (Fig.H:27).
NOTE:When using a dial gauge in this way, check around the full circumference of the gear and tool. Some small variation may be found, therefore take the mean reading or average zero position.
10. To the dial gauge reading add the pre-load setting, see TECHNICAL DATA. Select shims to give the specified setting.
11. Reassemble in the reverse order of removal. Fit the converter housing with a new gasket.

Idler Gear Bearing Oil Reservoir
Later type automatic transmission units have a cast-in oil reservoir in the transmission casing to provide additional lubrication to the idle gear bearings. This was introduced at engine nos. 8AH-A-H11338, 99H-143-H5983 and 99H-147-H834. If the transmission is of the early type, it is advisable to modify the unit by fitting a separate reservoir as follows:
1. Remove the engine and transmission unit from the car and separate the transmission from the engine, see ENGINE.
2. Mark a horizontal line across the outside of transmission case, 91,3 mm (3.59 in) from the top face (Fig.H:28).
3. Fit the reservoir upside-down on the outside of the casing with the spigot located in the roller gear bearing bore and the hole in the securing lug positioned centrally on the horizontal line.
4. Centre-punch the position of the lug hole on the marked line, then remove the reservoir.
5. Place a piece of plasticine on the inside of the casing where the hole will break through to trap any swarf, then drill through the casing at the marked point using a 9/32 in drill. Remove the plasticine with any swarf.
6. Ensure that the reservoir fits snugly against the transmission casing, if not, relieve the reservoir casting as necessary with a file.
7. Smear the reservoir spigot with Hylomar jointing compound and fit the reservoir to the transmission casing.
NOTE:It may be necessary to fit a flat washer between the reservoir securing lug and the transmission casing to ensure that the spigot is square in the idler gear bearing bore. Later reservoirs have a built-up boss around the securing lug.
8. Leave the idler gear bearing circlip in position and tighten the securing bolt (Fig.H:29).
9. Assemble the transmission to engine and install the engine/transmission unit in the car as described in ENGINE.

Automatic Transmission Problems

FAULT	CAUSE	ACTION
Car will not move with selector in any forward range	☐ Insufficient fluid. ☐ Incorrect operation of manual selector lever. ☐ Transmission locked by parking pawl. ☐ Internal transmission fault.	■ Check/top up fluid. ■ Check selector linkage for wear or adjust. ■ Check/adjust selector linkage. ■ Consult dealer.
Car will not move with selector in 'R' position	☐ Incorrect operation of manual selector lever. ☐ Internal transmission fault.	■ Check/adjust selector linkage. ■ Consult dealer.
Slow acceleration	☐ Maladjusted or worn engine. ☐ Incorrect carburettor throttle opening or kick-down adjustment. ☐ Internal transmission fault	■ Check engine tune and cylinder compression. ■ Check carburettor throttle opening and kick-down adjustment. ■ Carry out Stall Test, consult dealer.
Car will start with selector in any position	☐ Faulty/maladjusted inhibitor switch operation.	■ Adjust/replace unit.
Fluid leak from converter housing	☐ Leaking oil seal either from engine or torque converter.	■ Check colour of oil, reddish for automatic, black for engine. Replace oil seal.
Fluid leak from sump pan	☐ Leaking gasket	■ Replace gasket

Steering

INTRODUCTION . . . . [1]

The steering system is of the rack and pinion type, with a solid type steering column.

With the introduction of Mk 2 cars, the steering rack and hub steering arms were modified. Individual components on the later type are not interchangeable with earlier models. Note that with the later type assembly it is very important to keep the alignment correct to give adequate clearance between wheels and suspension tie bars.

Both the steering rack and the steering column can be fully overhauled. Normally, the only parts to wear are the bushes in the steering column and rack. Early cars use felt column bushes but later cars have a plastic upper bush. The rack end bush (nearside) is a common wear point on all Mini models. Note that the steering rack damper may be preloaded by a disc-type spring washer, or a coil spring depending on the year of manufacture. Before actually replacing any parts of the rack, first check the cost of replacement parts against that of an exchange unit. The latter may prove to be more economical.

Kits of parts are available for overhauling the steering rack. There are kits for rack gaiters and clips, track rods and balljoints, also for rack internal components. The internal kit contains rack and pinion bushes and a rack damper, although the rack and the pinion are not available as separate replacement parts. If these components are worn, an exchange steering rack should be obtained.

After replacing or adjusting any part of the steering system, the front wheel alignment should be checked by an Austin/Rover dealer or local tyre centre using optical measuring equipment.

However, after any repairs or adjustments the wheel alignment can be set approximately as detailed under Front Wheel Alignment, before driving the car to a specialist.

When dealing with any steering or suspension components it is most important that any bolts or nuts are tightened to the specified tightening torques, see TECHNICAL DATA for details.

TOOLS & EQUIPMENT . . . . [2]

In addition to the conventional tool kit, as described in BASIC PROCEDURES, a certain number of specialised function tools will be required when working on the steering. These are:

- Offset lever or wedge type ball joint taper breaker – for separating the track rod end joint from the steering arm.
- A mechanical tracking bar – for checking the front wheel alignment.
- An electric drill and screw extractors – for removing the shear bolts from the steering column bracket.
- Tool No.18G 1278 – for removing the steering rack ball housing.

FRONT WHEEL ALIGNMENT . . . . [3]
Toe Setting

The toe setting of the front wheels affects the stability and controllability of the car, also the wear characteristics of the front tyres.

In practice, the toe setting is the amount by which the wheels point inwards or outwards at the front, in relation to each other (Fig.I:1). This is measured from the wheel rims at hub height, and may be given either as a total dimension for both wheels, or as angular measurement for each wheel in degrees. When the wheels both point inwards they are said to have toe-in, and toe-out when they point outwards.

Ideally, the front wheel toe setting should be checked after any repair or overhaul operation in which a steering or suspension component has been removed, or its location altered. It should also be checked if the front wheels have been subjected to heavy impact, such as hitting the kerb – even at low speeds (when parking, for example).

A reasonably accurate indication of whether or not the front wheels are correctly aligned can be gained by examining the wear pattern of the tyre treads. The presence of 'fins' or 'feathers' on the tread surface are an indication of incorrect alignment. This condition takes the form of a sharp 'fin' on the edge of each pattern rib, and the position of this indicates the direction of misalignment. Fins on the outboard edges of the pattern ribs indicate excessive toe-out.

Preliminary Conditions

Before attempting to check or adjust the front wheel alignment, the following items should first be carried out:
1. Check that there is no excessive wear or looseness in any of the steering or front suspension balljoints, bushes or mountings, or in the front wheel bearings.
2. Check that all tyres are inflated to their correct pressures.
3. Ensure that the car is in its normal unladen condition (i.e. spare wheel in place, luggage compartment empty, etc.).
4. Position the car on a level patch of ground, bounce the car a few times at each corner, then roll back and forth to settle the suspension. Once this has been done, the ride height must not be disturbed either by jacking up the car or by someone sitting in it.
5. Ensure that the front wheels are in the straight-ahead position. On cars from October 1967 onwards, the steering rack can be locked in the central (straight-ahead) position by lifting the carpet and removing the grommet from the floor on the driver's side to give access to the rack centralising hole, covered by a plastic plug. Remove the plug and insert a 6 mm (0.25 in) dia. bolt or drill bit fully into the hole to accurately centre the rack (Fig.I:2).
6. Roll the car forwards a few feet and stop it without using the brakes. It must not be moved backwards after this.

Checking & Adjusting

As stated previously, the front wheel toe setting can be checked and roughly set using a mechanical tracking bar. This should normally be treated only as a temporary measure, but if great

care is taken a fairly accurate setting can be obtained.
1. Position the tracking bar in front of the front wheel axis and adjust it so that the bar ends are just contacting the wheel rims at hub height (Fig.I:3). Note the reading on the bar scale.
2. Similarly, take a second reading of the distance between the wheel rims, this time behind the wheel axis.
3. The difference by which the first (front) reading differs from the second (rear) reading will give the existing toe setting figure. The correct toe setting figure is given in TECHNICAL DATA.
4. If necessary, to minimise the possibility of inaccuracy due to wheel rim run-out, the car can be moved forwards sufficiently to rotate the front wheels through 180°, and the measuring procedure repeated. An average of the two readings can then be taken.
5. If adjustment is necessary, the track rod on each side should be adjusted by an equal amount. Note that both track rods must be of equal overall length.
6. Slacken the clip on the outer end of the rack bellows. This is to prevent damage to the bellows as the rod is turned.
7. To adjust the toe setting, slacken the locknut adjacent to the track rod end joint. Use one spanner to hold the flats on the balljoint and another spanner to loosen the nut. Do not use only one spanner as this will tend to force the joint ball pin from its socket. Rotate the track rod, using a pair of self-locking grips on the rod until the correct setting is obtained (Fig.I:4). Note that both track rods have a right-hand thread.
8. The two track rods must be turned by the same amount to equalise any adjustment. Roll the car back and forth, then check the setting and readjust as necessary. When adjustment is completed, tighten the locknut at the track rod end. Both track rods must be the same length after adjustment.
9. Tighten the clips on the steering rack bellows. Remove the centralising pin from the rack and refit the plugs, this is important.

TRACK ROD JOINTS & RACK BELLOWS .... [4]
Track Rod End Joint Replacement
Wear in the track rod end ball joint cannot be compensated for by adjustment. Replacement of the complete ball joint is necessary when it is worn (Fig.I:5). If the joint boot is damaged, but the joint is in good condition, the boot can be replaced separately, and fresh grease applied to the joint before fitting the new boot.
1. Apply the handbrake and slacken the front road wheel nuts.
2. Raise and support the front of the car – see BASIC PROCEDURES and remove the road wheel.
3. Slacken the track rod end joint locknut first then undo the ball pin retaining nut and separate the ball pin from the steering arm using a balljoint taper breaking tool (Fig.I:6).
4. Unscrew and remove the joint from the track rod end. Screw the new balljoint on as far as the locknut and nip up the locknut.
5. Clean the ball pin taper to remove all trace of grease before connecting it to the steering arm and tightening the ball pin nut to the specified torque – see TECHNICAL DATA.
6. Refit the road wheel and lower the car to the ground. Tighten the road wheel nuts.
7. Check, and if necessary, adjust the front wheel alignment as detailed previously.

Rack Bellows Replacement
1. Remove the ball joint from the track rod end as detailed previously. Count the number of threads exposed between the locknut face and the track rod end before unscrewing the locknut. This will enable the balljoint to be refitted in approximately the correct position on reassembly. Remove the retaining clips at both ends of the bellows and pull the bellows off the rack and over the track rod.
2. Allow any oil to drain from the rack, wipe any dirt or water from inside the rack if the bellows was damaged for some time before removal.
3. Smear the inside of the new bellows with the recommended

grease, see TECHNICAL DATA, before sliding it into position over the track rod.
4. Centralise the rack and fill the rack gaiter with the specified quantity of oil, see TECHNICAL DATA. Slip the bellows into position over the race and secure at the inner end with the retaining clip. Ensure that the gaiter is correctly located on the rack housing and track rod grooves.
5. Turn the rack from side to side to distribute the oil. This should be done slowly to prevent the rack bellows from being ruptured or displaced by hydraulic pressure.
6. Screw the locknut onto the track rod end, leaving the original number of threads exposed.
7. Refit the track rod joint as detailed previously, and check the wheel alignment. Refit the outer clip to the bellows.

STEERING WHEEL .... [5]
Removal & Installation
1. Disconnect the battery earth lead. Remove the wheel centre cover. On early cars the cover is secured by a grub screw in the wheel hub. On later cars the cover may be held by clips or by screws.
2. Hold the steering wheel in place and slacken the retaining nut using a suitable socket and extension bar. Leave the nut engaged on the column by at least two threads, Mark the relationship of the steering wheel to the shaft splines with a dab of paint or punch mark. Gently thump the steering wheel from behind with the hands until it is free of the column shaft splines. Rocking the wheel can help free it. Remove the nut washer and steering wheel.
3. If the wheel cannot be released, use puller tool No.18G 2 and 18G 2E as illustrated (Fig.I:7). Undo the screw at the bottom of the steering column cowl and remove the screws holding the halves together. Withdraw the cowl. The puller can then fit around the back of the wheel. Remove the nut and the wheel.
4. Installation is a reversal of the removal procedure. The triangle on the indicator switch bush should point toward the horn push (Fig.I:8). Ensure that the paint or punch marks between steering wheel and column shaft made before removal, are aligned. Fit the washer and nut then tighten to the specified torque.
5. Position the cowl upper edge 3 mm (0,125 in) from the back of the wheel. Check that the wheel does not rub on the cowling, and that the horn operates correctly.

STEERING COLUMN ASSEMBLY .... [6]
Removal & Installation
If necessary, remove the steering wheel and cowl as detailed above. Ensure that the relationship between shaft and wheel hub is marked beforehand. This will not be needed if the column is not being dismantled.
1. Disconnect the electrical connectors for the column switches. These are located below the parcel shelf.
2. Remove the locknut and pinchbolt holding the shaft to the rack pinion. This is accessible from inside the car at the bottom of the column (Fig.I:10). Mark the alignment of the column and shaft clamp with paint, also mark the pinion spline engaged with the shaft clamp split.
3. Remove the bolt holding the outer column to the upper bracket at the parcel shelf. On later cars, a shearhead bolt is used. A saw cut can be made across the top of the bolt head and a screwdriver used to unscrew it. Alternatively, drill a hole in the bolt and use an Easiout stud extractor. Pull the steering column shaft to disconnect it from the rack pinion, and withdraw the assembly from inside the car.
4. Pull back the front carpet and slacken the rack mounting 'U' bolt retaining nuts, also the column upper bracket bolts. This is to allow the rack housing and bracket to move during refitting.
5. Install the steering column in the reverse order of removal.
6. Place the front wheels in the straight-ahead position as detailed under Front Wheel Alignment. If the steering wheel has been removed, refit it to the column with the alignment marks

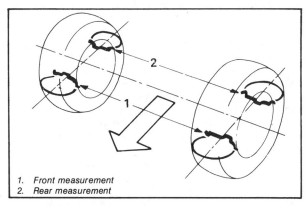

1. Front measurement
2. Rear measurement

Fig. I:1 Measurements to determine toe setting

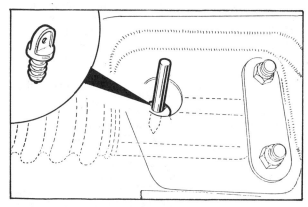

Fig. I:2 Centralise steering rack with bolt or drill bit

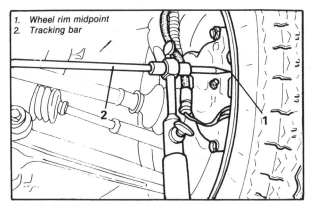

1. Wheel rim midpoint
2. Tracking bar

Fig. I:3 Measure wheel alignment with a track bar

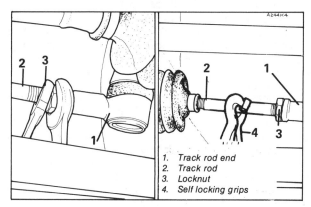

1. Track rod end
2. Track rod
3. Locknut
4. Self locking grips

Fig. I:4 Adjusting wheel alignment

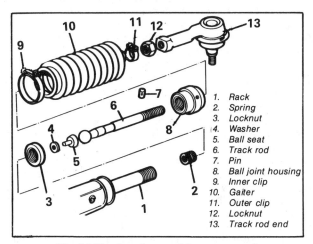

1. Rack
2. Spring
3. Locknut
4. Washer
5. Ball seat
6. Track rod
7. Pin
8. Ball joint housing
9. Inner clip
10. Gaiter
11. Outer clip
12. Locknut
13. Track rod end

Fig. I:5 Track rod assembly components

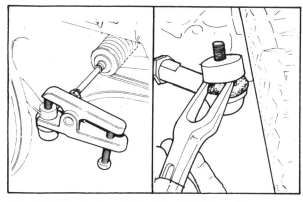

Fig. I:6 Method of separating track rod from steering arm

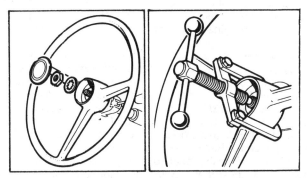

Fig. I:7 Steering wheel nut & wheel removed with puller

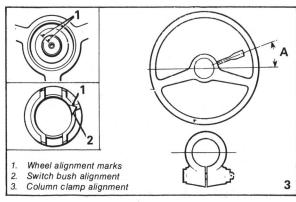

1. Wheel alignment marks
2. Switch bush alignment
3. Column clamp alignment

Fig. I:8 Steering wheel hub & switch alignment

made before removal, aligned (Fig.I:8). Support the column with the steering wheel in the straight-ahead position and fit the column clamp to the rack pinion shaft. Make sure the marked pinion shaft spline is aligned with the split section of the clamp.

7. Push the clamp onto the pinion shaft until the clamp pinchbolt can be fitted. Tighten the bolt and locknut to the specified torque.

8. The column should engage with the upper bracket without any sideways strain. If the column will not fit cleanly, slacken the bolts holding the clamp plate to the parcel shelf and align the column with the clamp plate. Fit the retaining bolt. A used shear-head bolt should not be refitted. Replace with a new bolt. Tighten the clamp plate mounting bolts first, then tighten the column retaining bolt until the shear-head breaks off.

9. Tighten the rack 'U' mounting bolt nuts progressively a half turn at a time to the specified torque. The thread of each bolt should protrude equally through each nut. Finally check the front wheel alignment as detailed previously.

Column Support Bush Replacement

Early cars use felt bushes at the top and bottom of the column. Later cars use a plastic bush at the top of the column. Note that the plastic bush can be replaced with the shaft in place, although a special puller is essential to make this operation possible in-situ.

1. Remove the steering column assembly and detach the steering wheel as detailed previously. Remove the switch from the steering column as detailed in GENERAL ELECTRICS. On early cars undo the locknut and remove the indicator stud from the shaft. On models with a steering wheel centre horn push fitted, remove the slip ring assembly.

2. Withdraw the steering shaft from the lower end of the outer column. The bushes can then be removed from the column.

3. Soak the new felt bushes in clean oil. A plastic bush must be lubricated with graphite based grease.

4. Fit a new plastic bush to the top of the outer column. The bush cut-out should engage with the locating stud in the column (Fig.I:11). If a felt bush is to be used, fit in position on the column inner wall.

5. Insert the shaft into the outer column, and roll the lower felt bush around the shaft so that the edges meet. Push the shaft fully into the column to fit the bush. Check that the shaft can turn freely after the lower bush is fitted.

6. Refit the indicator switch cancelling stud and locknut. Screw the stud into the shaft until the stud head is 29,87-30,35 mm (1.176-1.195 in) from the opposite side of the shaft. The edge of the stud should be in line with the shaft.

7. Refit the remainder of the components to the column, then refit the column to the car as detailed previously.

Steering Column Lock — Replacement

Access to the steering column lock/ignition switch is gained by removing the two halves of the shroud from around the steering column.

The lock assembly is secured to the steering by a clamp plate and two shear bolts which must be removed by dot punching and drilling out. It may be possible to remove the bolts by tapping them round with a centre punch then unscrewing them (Fig.I:12).

The switch wiring is connected to the wiring loom by means of a push-fit multi-connector under the parcel shelf.

Position the new lock housing on the steering column and centralise it over the slot in the outer column. Fit the clamp plate and secure with the two shear bolts, but tighten them only finger-tight at this stage. Connect the multi-plug connector and check that the steering lock and ignition switch operate correctly. If satisfactory, tighten the shear bolts until their heads break off.

STEERING RACK ASSEMBLY . . . . [7]
Wear Check

If wear is apparent in the steering system after a relatively high mileage and it can be attributed to the rack and pinion unit itself (i.e. all suspension and steering joints are found to be sound) then it is possible to ascertain further which components are at fault.

If a heavy 'clonk' noise is evident whenever the steering wheel is moved from one direction to another then it is likely that the rack end bush is worn. Check this as follows:

With an assistant rocking the steering wheel back and forth, grip the rack shaft through the bellows at the end opposite to the pinion. If the knocking can be felt distinctly at this point and there is up and down movement of the rack shaft in its housing, then the bush is clearly worn. The rack end bush can easily be replaced with the rack in-situ.

Track rod end joints should be checked for wear by separating them from the steering arms, holding the joint housing and moving the ballpin around. If no resistance to movement is felt, i.e. the pin moves around very freely, then it is best to replace both joints.

Check the rack end balljoints as follows:

1. Depending on which side is being checked, turn the steering wheel so that the rack shaft protrudes as far out of its housing as is possible.

2. Disconnect the track rod end from the steering arm.

3. Grasp the rack shaft firmly through the bellows with one hand and hold the track rod with the other. Move the track rod backwards and forwards along the axis of the rack, ensuring that the rack shaft does not move. If play can be detected between the two then the joint should be replaced as detailed in the appropriate section.

Wear of the pinion bearings or rack damper can only be accurately ascertained with the rack unit removed from the car. With the rack housing and the rack shaft each held firmly (preferably in a vice) turn the pinion backwards and forwards by small amounts and feel for any 'clonking' between the pinion and the rack. If the pinion bearings are worn, then the pinion shaft will be seen to rise and fall slightly as it is turned. If excess play is apparent at this point then you can either overhaul the complete rack yourself as detailed later, or leave the job to an Austin/Rover dealer or specialist who will have the necessary equipment to carry out the operation satisfactorily. Alternatively exchange the rack for a reconditioned unit.

Steering Rack Removal & Refitting

1. Remove the carpet from the front of the car to expose the steering rack 'U' bolt nuts on the floor.

2. Remove the bolt securing the steering column upper support bracket at the parcel shelf, see Steering Column section previously.

3. Remove the pinch bolt securing the lower end of the steering column to the steering rack pinion shaft, then pull the column assembly upwards to disengage it from the pinion shaft.

4. Still inside the car, remove the four self-locking nuts securing the rack 'U' bolts to the floor (Fig.I:13).

5. Inside the engine compartment, remove the air cleaner assembly from the carburettor. Also disconnect the exhaust pipe from the exhaust manifold.

6. Disconnect the engine steady rod from the cylinder block and move the rod out of the way, see ENGINE. On later models, note that the engine earth strap is also secured by the steady rod bolt.

7. Remove the bolts securing the sub-frame towers to the body crossmember at the engine compartment bulkhead.
NOTE:Early cars are fitted with a sub-frame mounted directly to the body. Later cars have a rubber mounted sub-frame. See FRONT SUSPENSION for details of the mountings.

8. Raise and support the front of the car – see BASIC PROCEDURES. Use wooden blocks between the stands and the floor panel. Remove both front wheels.

9. On models with rubber cone ('dry') suspension, disconnect the shock absorbers from the mounting studs on the suspension upper arms.

10. Disconnect both track rod end joints from their respective

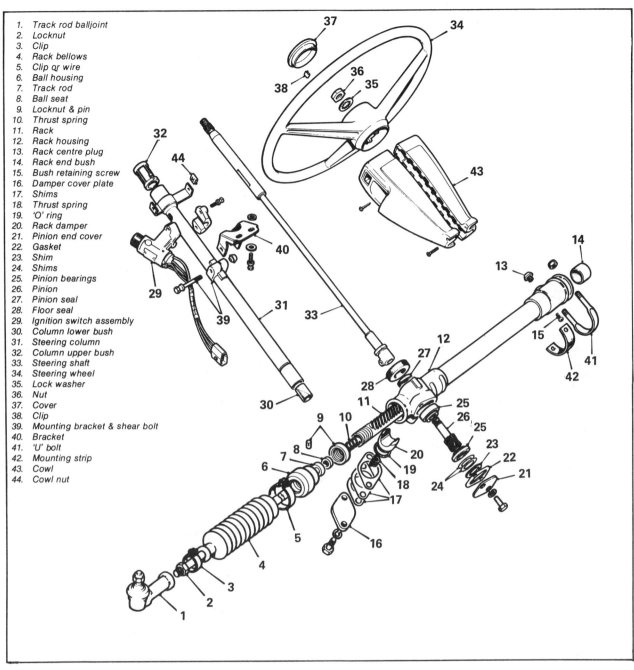

1. Track rod balljoint
2. Locknut
3. Clip
4. Rack bellows
5. Clip or wire
6. Ball housing
7. Track rod
8. Ball seat
9. Locknut & pin
10. Thrust spring
11. Rack
12. Rack housing
13. Rack centre plug
14. Rack end bush
15. Bush retaining screw
16. Damper cover plate
17. Shims
18. Thrust spring
19. 'O' ring
20. Rack damper
21. Pinion end cover
22. Gasket
23. Shim
24. Shims
25. Pinion bearings
26. Pinion
27. Pinion seal
28. Floor seal
29. Ignition switch assembly
30. Column lower bush
31. Steering column
32. Column upper bush
33. Steering shaft
34. Steering wheel
35. Lock washer
36. Nut
37. Cover
38. Clip
39. Mounting bracket & shear bolt
40. Bracket
41. 'U' bolt
42. Mounting strip
43. Cowl
44. Cowl nut

Fig. I:9 Exploded view of steering rack assembly

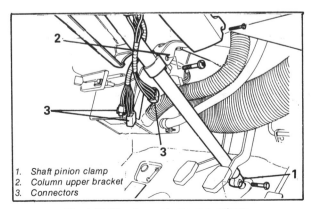

1. Shaft pinion clamp
2. Column upper bracket
3. Connectors

Fig. I:10 Steering column mountings

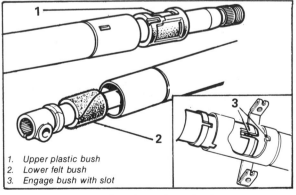

1. Upper plastic bush
2. Lower felt bush
3. Engage bush with slot

Fig. I:11 Steering column bushes

Fig. I:12 Steering column lock assembly

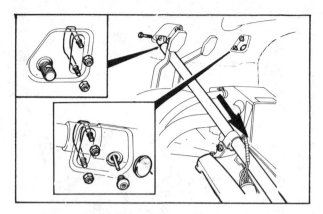

Fig. I:13 Steering rack mountings inside car

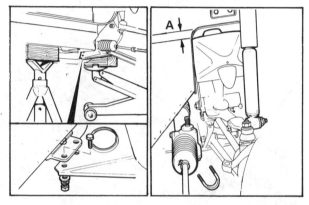

Fig. I:14 Lower sub-frame to remove steering rack

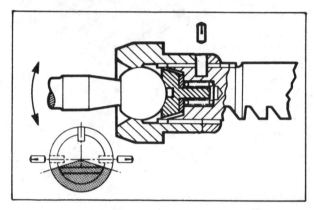

Fig. I:15 Section through later rack balljoint
showing lockpin

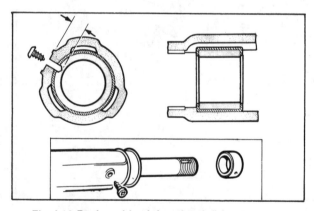

Fig. I:16 Rack end bush location & fixing screw

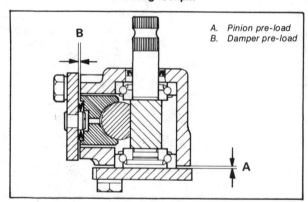

A. Pinion pre-load
B. Damper pre-load

Fig. I:17 Early rack pinion with flat spring

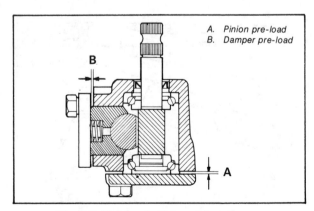

A. Pinion pre-load
B. Damper pre-load

Fig. I:18 Early rack pinion with coil spring

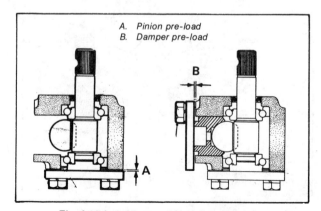

A. Pinion pre-load
B. Damper pre-load

Fig. I:19 Later type rack pinion setting

steering arms, using a ball joint separator tool (Fig.I:6).

11.   Disconnect the exhaust pipe from the support bracket on the final drive unit housing.

12.   On models with remote-control gearchange, detach the gearchange extension housing rear mounting from the floor panel. On later models with the single-rod type remote change, remove the bolt securing the gear-change housing to its mounting bracket and free the housing from the bracket. It may be necessary to lever the housing over to enable the bolt to be removed.

13.   Support the sub-frame with a jack and wooden batten positioned across the car so that it locates on the underside of the sub-frame at the lower suspension arm pivot points.

14.   Slacken, but do not remove, the centre bolts securing the sub-frame front mountings to the body. These are accessible through the apertures in the front panel below the bumper.

15.   Remove the four bolts and nuts securing the sub-frame rear mountings.

16.   Lower the jack under the sub-frame and allow the rear of the sub-frame to drop until a gap of about 20 mm (¾in) is present between the top of the sub-frame turrets and the valance aperture (A,Fig.I:14). If necessary, use a lever to force the sub-frame downwards to obtain sufficient clearance.

17.   Extract the 'U' bolts and plastic anti-friction strips (when fitted) from between the steering rack housing and the sub-frame.

18.   Move the steering rack downwards and turn it to bring the pinion vertical to clear the aperture. Carefully manoeuvre the rack unit out from between the sub-frame and the body on the driver's side. Note the sealing ring fitted at the pinion housing on the rack.

Install the steering rack in the reverse order of removal but pay special attention to the following points.

1.   Ensure that the sealing ring is in position at the pinion housing before installing the steering unit.

2.   Where fitted, use new plastic anti-friction strips at the 'U' bolts.

3.   When installing the rack, initially tighten the rack 'U' bolts only lightly so that the pinion can be aligned with the column assembly.

4.   Align and fit the column as detailed previously. When in place, tighten the rack 'U' mounting bolt nuts progressively a half turn at a time to the specified torque. The thread of each bolt should protrude equally through each nut.

5.   Check the front wheel alignment as detailed previously.

Steering Rack Overhaul (Fig.I:9)

NOTE:During dismantling all parts should be labelled for position. If any parts are to be reused, they should be fitted to their original sides or locations.

1.   Holding the rack housing in a soft-jawed vice, first remove the track rod end ball-joints. Slacken the locknuts while holding the joint with a spanner. Undo the clips and remove the bellows from each end of the rack. Drain all the lubricant from the rack housing.

2.   Separate the track rod assemblies from the rack. Early cars have either a locknut peened to the housing or a lockwasher. Release the peening or bend back the tab washer. On later cars, the housing is retained by a pin through the housing and rack (Fig.I:15). If the rack has been overhauled before, and the end of the rack has been drilled three times, the assembly should be replaced. Using a 4 mm (⁵⁄₃₂in) dia. drill bit, drill out the pins retaining the ball housings. Use a stop on the drill bit to prevent drilling any deeper than 6,3 mm (0.248 in). Unscrew the locknuts and ball-joints, turning the joint using a peg spanner or tool 18G 1278. Remove the ball seat and locknut from each assembly.

3.   Remove the rack damper cover plate, 'O' ring or gasket, shims, thrust spring and damper from the housing.

4.   Remove the pinion end cover, gasket and shims, then push out the pinion and lower bearing.

5.   Withdraw the rack from the pinion end of the rack housing, not the rack bush end.

6.   Withdraw the pinion upper bearing and oil seal from the rack housing.

7.   The rack end bush may be held by a rivet or screw (Fig.I:16). Remove the screw or drill out the rivet. Extract the bush from the housing. Early models may have a steel backed felt bush. If replacement is necessary, extract the steel sleeve.

8.   Wash the internal components with paraffin and dry with air. Inspect all the rack and pinion unit components. Inspect the rack and pinion teeth for wear, scoring or damage. Examine the bearings for signs of seizing or damage. The gaskets and oil seal should be replaced as a matter of course.

9.   Fit the new rack end bush. If a felt bush is to be fitted, it should be soaked in E.P. 140 oil.

If a plastic bush and spacer are to be fitted as a replacement for a felt bush, fit the spacer with the plain end first, followed by the plastic bush, plain end first, into the sleeve. The flats on the bush should be offset from the hole in the rack housing. Drill through the existing housing hole with a 7/64 in dia. drill bit. Remove any swarf and coat the retaining screw with gasket sealing compound. The screw must not protrude above the bush bearing surface when fitted.

If a plastic bush is to be replaced, engage the bush projections with the housing slots. Retain the bush by drilling a hole as detailed previously to a depth of 10,5 mm (0.142 in). After fitting the screw, check that the bore is not distorted.

10.   Smear all the components with the appropriate lubricant, see TECHNICAL DATA, prior to reassembly. Using the pinion as a locating tool, fit the upper bearing to the housing. Remove the pinion and fit the rack from the pinion end. Set the pinion adjustment as detailed in the next section.

11.   Fit a new pinion oil seal using a suitable drift. The flat face should be flush with the housing with the open side facing inward.

12.   Check the rack damper adjustment as detailed in the next section.

13.   Screw a new locking ring onto each end of the rack as far as it will go, then a new lockwasher if fitted. Lubricate the components. Fit the thrust spring and ball seat to the rack. Fit the housing to the track rod and lubricate with the specified grease. Tighten the housing until the ball is pinched.

14.   Attach a spring balance to the end of the track rod and measure the force required to articulate the joint 25° from the rack centre line. See TECHNICAL DATA for the setting figure. Note that the measurement obtained from the spring balance is dependent upon distance from the joint. An alternative way is to support the rod horizontally and tighten the housing until the clamping force will just hold the rod in place without support.

15.   Lock the housing in place. Punch the lockwasher into the slots on the housing and ring. If no lock washer is used, peen the locking ring into the rack and housing slots. On later cars, drill a ⁵⁄₃₂in. diameter hole, ⁵⁄₁₆in. deep. If previously drilled, the new hole should be separated by 90° (Fig.I:15). Do not drill into the rack in the arc of the teeth. Drive in a new pin and peen at 4 points around the edge using a sharp chisel.

16.   Fit one of the rack bellows, then hold the rack up by the open end and pour in the specified quantity of oil see TECHNICAL DATA. Fit the other bellows followed by the track rod end balljoints.

17.   Each track rod end balljoint should be screwed the same number of threads on the track rod. On early cars this is 8 threads. On Mk 2 and later cars it is 11 threads, or 1056 mm (41,64 in) between balljoints centre.

Pinion Adjustment (Figs.I:17, I:18 & I:19)

On Mk I cars, refit the pinion cover plate without any shims, but do not overtighten the screws. Measure the gap between cover and housing using feeler gauges. Make up a shim pack to this measurement, minus the distance given in TECHNICAL DATA.

On Mk 2 cars, refit the pinion and bearings, then centralise the rack using a 6 mm (0.25 in) bolt in the housing hole. Make up a shim pack with the spacer washer to give a clearance of approximately 0,25 mm (0.010 in) between the housing and cover plate. Refit the cover plate and lightly tighten the bolts. Measure the gap between the housing and the cover plate, then remove the shim pack and reduce the shims by the measurement taken. Now add shims to give the correct pre-load as specified in TECHNICAL DATA.

Adjustment of subsequent models is similar, noting the change in pre-load specification.

Rack Damper Adjustment

On Mk I cars with a disc type spring washer, the damper adjustment is measured by the force necessary to turn the pinion. Fit the damper yoke with disc spring, but without packing shims. With the rack centred, tighten the retaining screws until the force necessary to turn the pinion is 0,17 kg m

(15 lb in). An accurate gauge or torque wrench will be needed for this although it can be done with a spring balance hooked over the end of a large self-locking wrench. Measure the gap between the housing flange and the casing. Remove the flange and make up a shim pack to the clearance measured, then take away shims to give the correct pre-load as detailed in TECHNICAL DATA.

On cars with a coil spring, refit the damper yoke and cover without the spring, then check the clearance as detailed for earlier cars. Make up a shim pack to the distance measured, then add shims to the thickness specified in TECHNICAL DATA. Then refit the damper, with a new 'O' ring, and the shims.

Turn the pinion a half turn in each direction, checking for tightness or binding.

Steering Problems

FAULT	CAUSE	ACTION
Steering feels heavy	☐ Low/uneven tyre pressures. ☐ Incorrect wheel alignment. ☐ Stiff track rod end joints. ☐ Steering rack needs adjustment. ☐ No lubricant in rack. ☐ Stiff hub swivel joints.	■ Adjust pressures. ■ Adjust alignment. ■ Replace joints. ■ Adjust rack. ■ Check condition & add lubricant. ■ Replace joints.
Steering wheel shake	☐ Wheel nuts loose. ☐ Wheels and tyres need balancing. ☐ Tyre pressures incorrect. ☐ Incorrect wheel alignment. ☐ Wheel hub nut loose. ☐ Wheel bearings worn. ☐ Front suspension distorted. ☐ Steering rack needs adjustment. ☐ Shock absorber(s) faulty.	■ Tighten nuts. ■ Balance as necessary. ■ Adjust pressures. ■ Adjust alignment. ■ Adjust wheel bearings. ■ Replace wheel bearings. ■ Check and repair suspension. ■ Adjust rack. ■ Replace in pairs.
Steering pulls to one side	☐ Uneven tyre pressure. ☐ Wheel alignment incorrect. ☐ Wheel bearings worn ☐ Brakes improperly adjusted/ seizing on. ☐ Shock absorbers faulty. ☐ Suspension distorted. ☐ Steering rack worn.	■ Adjust pressures. ■ Adjust alignment. ■ Replace bearings. ■ Adjust/repair brakes. ■ Replace in pairs. ■ Check and rectify suspension. ■ Adjust or replace rack.
Wheel tramp (front end shake at speed)	☐ Over-inflated tyres. ☐ Unbalanced tyre and wheel ☐ Defective shock absorber(s). ☐ Defective tyre(s).	■ Adjust pressures. ■ Balance tyre & wheel. ■ Replace in pairs. ■ Repair or Replace tyre(s).
Abnormal tyre wear	☐ Incorrect tyre pressures. ☐ Incorrect wheel alignment. ☐ Excessive wheel bearing play. ☐ Improper driving.	■ Adjust pressures. ■ Adjust alignment. ■ Renew wheel bearings. ■ Avoid sharp turning at high speeds, rapid pull-away and hard braking.
Tyre noises	☐ Incorrect tyre pressures. ☐ Incorrect wheel alignment.	■ Adjust pressures. ■ Adjust alignment.

Front Suspension

INTRODUCTION . . . . [1]

The front suspension layout on the Mini is basically very simple, comprising upper and lower arms pivoted on the sub-frame and connected to swivel joints at the hub assembly. The lower arm is located by a diagonal tie-rod mounted by rubber bushes to the front of the sub-frame (Fig.J:26).

Originally all models were fitted with a 'dry' rubber cone springing system which was changed to the 'wet' Hydrolastic system for the 1965 model year (Saloon models only). Mark 3 cars from 1970 model year onwards reverted to the 'dry' rubber cone system once more. Estate, Van and Pick-up models have retained the 'dry' system throughout their production.

The Hydrolastic system is filled with a mixture of water and alcohol, under high pressure, to link the suspension units (displacers) front and rear on each side of the car. This system is self damping, due to the design of units and the arrangement of valves in the displacers, but models fitted with the 'dry' suspension system have conventional telescopic shock absorbers.

Three different types of inboard drive shaft coupling have been used since the introduction on the Mini and the procedures for replacing or overhauling these are all dealt with separately in this chapter.

The front sub-frame, unlike the rear, does not suffer to the same extent from corrosion, due probably to the presence of a certain amount of oil which usually finds its way onto the assembly. Therefore the sub-frame will very often only be replaced as the result of accident damage.

TOOLS & EQUIPMENT . . . . [2]

The basic tool kit as described in BASIC PROCEDURES, will be required for the overhaul of the front suspension and in addition the following items will be needed for specific operations:

■ Ball joint taper breaking tool – for separating the track rod end and ball joint tapers.
■ A selection of tubing and sockets – to use as drifts when replacing oil seals and bearings.
■ Universal puller – for pulling off the front hubs.
■ 18G 587 – for removing the top and bottom ball joints.
■ 18G 1251 – for replacing the boot to the inner joint.
■ 18G 1240 – for separating the inner joint from the final drive housing.
■ 18G 1243 – for separating the driveshaft from the inner joint.
■ 18G 574B or Sykes Pickavant tool No.660330 – for compressing the suspension rubber cone when overhauling or removing the suspension arm on cars with 'dry' type suspension.

The central spindle of these tools screws into a threaded boss in the rubber cone and this thread is ½ in UNF on early models up to 1976 and 14 mm Metric on later models.

Different spindles are available for the two different threads. Great care must be taken, when using the cone compressor, that the thread is in good condition and is screwed fully into the boss, otherwise the considerable force required to compress the cone may strip the thread with the result that the suspension arm may snap back trapping anything in its path.

Models fitted with Hydrolastic ('wet') suspension require the use of a special pump unit – see REAR SUSPENSION, under Tools & Equipment.

SWIVEL HUB ASSEMBLY . . . . [3]
Removal (Drum Brake Models)

1. With the car still on its wheels and the brakes firmly applied, remove the split pin and slacken the hub nut on the end of the drive shaft. Also slacken the road wheel nuts.
2. Raise and support the front of the car – see BASIC PROCEDURES, then remove the road wheel.
3. If the driving flange is required to be removed from the drive shaft, release the brake shoe adjustment and withdraw the brake drum. Remove the hub nut together with its thrust washer, then pull the driving flange off the drive shaft splines, using a suitable hub puller. Note the distance ring fitted between the driving flange and the hub bearing – this ring must be fitted with the chamfered side towards the driving flange (Fig.J:3).
4. If required, the brake shoes can also be removed from the backing plate at this time.
5. Slacken the flexible brake hose at the brake backplate. The hose will be detached later. Ideally the brake hose should be sealed by clamping it with a proper brake hose clamp, otherwise the hose end must be plugged to minimise fluid loss.
6. Remove the ball pin nut and disconnect the track rod end from the steering arm, using a suitable joint separator tool.
7. Similarly, separate the upper and lower swivel joints from their respective suspension arms.
8. Press or lever down on the lower suspension arm and tie rod to disengage the lower swivel joint from the arm, then pull the swivel hub down to disengage the upper swivel joint.
NOTE:It will aid removal if the rebound rubber under the upper suspension arm is removed and a solid wedge of roughly the same thickness fitted in its place (Fig.J:5). However, this must be done at the outset, while the car is still standing on its wheels.
9. If the driving flange was removed previously, pull the swivel hub outwards to release it from the drive shaft.
10. If the driving flange is still in place in the hub, remove the hub nut and thrust washer and tap the end of the drive shaft to drive it inwards out of the flange and hub. This should be done

with a soft-headed mallet to avoid damaging the drive shaft threads.

11. Disconnect the brake hose by rotating the backplate assembly to release the hose connection threads from the wheel cylinder. Plug or cap the hose end to prevent loss of fluid. The hose is reconnected in the same manner on reassembly.

Installation

The swivel hub is refitted in the reverse order of removing, with special attention to the following points:

1. Ensure that the plastic water shield on the drive shaft is positioned 6 mm (¼ in) from the shouldered edge of the shaft (Fig.J:3).
2. Reconnect the brake hose to the backplate before fitting the hub assembly over the drive shaft. Rotate the backplate to screw the hose connection into the wheel cylinder union. Do not forget to fully tighten the hose connection once the swivel hub assembly has been fitted.
3. If the driving flange was removed, ensure that it locates correctly in the spacer ring between the hub bearings before tapping it fully into position on the drive shaft splines.
4. Tighten the swivel joint ball pin nuts and the track rod ball pin nut to their specified torque – see TECHNICAL DATA.
5. Adjust the brake shoes and bleed the hydraulic system as detailed in BRAKES.
6. Once the car is lowered back onto its wheels, tighten the drive shaft nut to its specified torque – see TECHNICAL DATA and secure with a new split pin. Align the nut to the next split-pin hole, if necessary.

SWIVEL HUB BALL JOINTS .... [4]

The swivel hub upper and lower ball joints are incorporated in the swivel hub assembly and each comprises mainly a hardened steel ball pin, seat and pin retainer. Wear in these joints is normally due to lack of regular lubrication and it is very important that these joints be greased frequently to keep them adequately lubricated and prevent the ingress of dirt and water. A grease nipple for this purpose is provided at each joint.

Only dismantling will show the extent of wear of the components. If the main components mentioned above are in good condition, it may be possible to re-shim the joint, but if wear is present, all the components of the joint should be renewed. These are normally available either as a complete joint assembly, or as a kit of four. All the new components in the kit should be used when reassembling.

The swivel joints can be overhauled without completely removing the swivel hub assembly from the car, but this operation is made easier if the assembly is removed and the work carried out under the more ideal conditions of a workshop. In the former case, the joint ball pins must be separated from the suspension arms and the track rod disconnected from the steering arm.

Overhaul (Fig.J:4)

1. Remove the swivel hub assembly from the car, as detailed previously.
2. Secure the swivel hub assembly in a vice with the appropriate ball joint uppermost.
3. Remove the rubber dust cover from the ball pin. Knock back the lockwasher tabs and unscrew the ball pin retainer from the joint using tool No.18G 587. Alternative sockets are available from most motor accessory shops.
4. Remove the retainer, together with the ball pin, then extract the ball pin seat from the recess in the housing. In the case of the lower swivel joint, a small spring is fitted below the ball seat and this should also be removed.
5. Unscrew the grease nipple and lift off the retainer lockwasher, together with the adjustment shims.
6. Thoroughly clean all the components of the joint assembly,

then examine them carefully. If the contact surfaces on either the ball pin, seat or retainer show any signs of wear, ridging, scoring or corrosion, all the components of the joint assembly should be renewed.

7. To determine the thickness of shim pack required, assemble the ball pin without the shims or lockwashers. In the case of the lower joint, also leave out the coil spring. Tighten the retainer until there is no free movement between the ball pin and its seating, but the pin is still free to swivel. Now measure the gap, 'A' in illustration, between the lower edge of the retainer and the hub with feeler gauges. The thickness of a new lockwasher is 0,90 mm (0.035 in) and this figure should be deducted from the gap measured to obtain the thickness of shim pack required. When correctly adjusted, the ball pin must have no nip to 0,08 mm (0.003 in) endfloat. Add a further 0,05 mm (0.002) in shim, if necessary. Shims available are as follows, and these are normally supplied in the ball joint kit: 0,05/08/13/51 mm (0.002/003/005/010/020 in).
8. Great care should be taken during the adjustment procedure, as it is imperative that the ball joint should be able to rotate freely in all planes after adjustment has taken place.
9. When the shim pack has been selected, assemble a new lockwasher on the housing and secure lightly in position with the grease nipple. Position the shim pack on top of the lockwasher.
10. Pack the joint with grease then assemble the ball seat, ball pin and retainer to the housing. In the case of the lower joint, remember to fit the coil spring under the ball seat. Press down lightly on the ball pin to hold the seat correctly in position on its recess while tightening the retainer.
11. Tighten the retainer to its specified torque – see TECHNICAL DATA, then secure by tapping the lock washer against three flats of the retainer – one adjacent to the brake backplate/disc. Fully tighten the grease nipple.
12. Finally, refit the swivel hub assembly on the car. Do not forget to fit the rubber dust cover at each of the joint ball pins before connecting them to the suspension arms.

Swivel Hub Assembly — Removal (Disc Brake Models)

1. With the car still on its wheels, remove the split pin and slacken the hub nut on the end of the drive shaft. Also slacken the road wheel nuts.
2. Raise and support the front of the car – see BASIC PROCEDURES, and then remove the road wheel.
3. Remove the two securing bolts and detach the brake caliper from the swivel hub. Support the caliper from a suitable point on the suspension to avoid straining the brake hose.
4. Remove the hub nut together with its split tapered collar, then withdraw the driving flange and brake disc assembly from the drive shaft, using a suitable hub puller.
5. Remove the ball pin nut and disconnect the track rod end from the steering arm, using a suitable joint separator tool.
6. Similarly, separate the upper and lower swivel joints from their respective suspension arms.
7. Press or lever down on the lower suspension arm and tie rod to disengage the lower swivel joint from the arm, then pull the swivel hub down to disengage the upper swivel joint. It will facilitate removal if the rebound rubber under the upper suspension arm is removed and a solid wedge of roughly the same thickness fitted in its place (Fig.J:5). However, this must be done at the outset, while the car is still standing on its wheels.
8. Pull the swivel hub assembly outwards to release it from the drive shaft.

Installation

Installation is basically a reversal of the removal procedure, but special attention should be paid to the following points:
1. Ensure that the plastic water shield on the drive shaft is located 6 mm (¼ in) from the shouldered edge of the shaft (Fig.J:7).

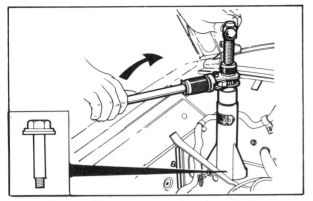

Fig. J:1 Rubber cone compressor 18G 574B

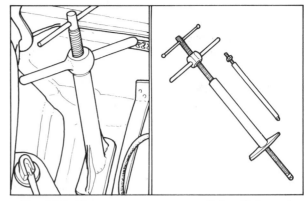

Fig. J:2 Rubber cone compressor — Sykes Pickavant

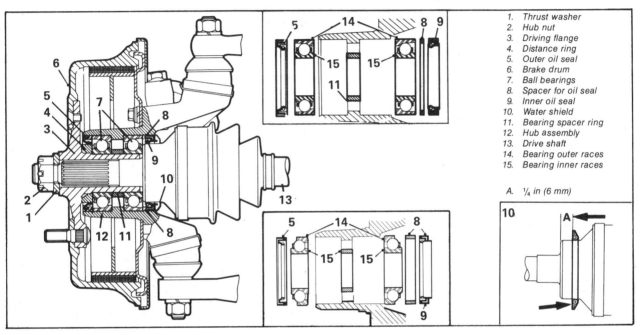

1. Thrust washer
2. Hub nut
3. Driving flange
4. Distance ring
5. Outer oil seal
6. Brake drum
7. Ball bearings
8. Spacer for oil seal
9. Inner oil seal
10. Water shield
11. Bearing spacer ring
12. Hub assembly
13. Drive shaft
14. Bearing outer races
15. Bearing inner races

A. ¼ in (6 mm)

Fig. J:3 Sectional view of front hub assembly — drum brake models

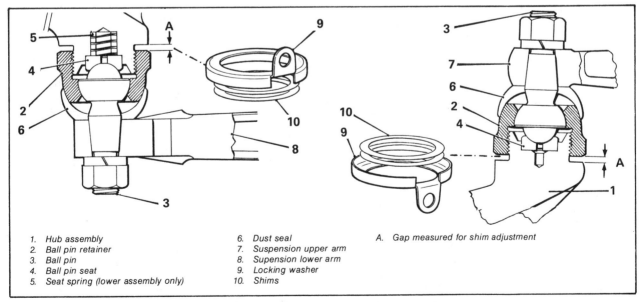

1. Hub assembly
2. Ball pin retainer
3. Ball pin
4. Ball pin seat
5. Seat spring (lower assembly only)
6. Dust seal
7. Suspension upper arm
8. Suspension lower arm
9. Locking washer
10. Shims

A. Gap measured for shim adjustment

Fig. J:4 Sectional view through swivel hub ball joints

2. Tighten the swivel hub ball pin nuts and the track rod ball pin nut to their specified torque – see TECHNICAL DATA.
3. Once the car is lowered back onto its wheels, tighten the drive shaft nut to its specified torque – see TECHNICAL DATA and secure with a new split pin. Align the nut to the next split pin hole, if necessary.

FRONT HUB BEARINGS .... [5]
Replacement (Drum Brake Models) (Fig.J:3)
1. Remove the swivel hub assembly from the car as previously detailed.
2. If the driving flange is still in position in the hub, the brake drum should be removed and the flange tapped out of the hub assembly from the inboard side, using a suitable mandrel.
NOTE:The distance ring fitted between the driving flange and the outer bearing must be fitted with the chamfered side towards the driving flange.

The brake shoes should also be removed to avoid the possibility of contamination by grease during the subsequent operations.
3. Extract the outer oil seal from the outboard end of the hub bore. Similarly, remove the inner oil seal together with its spacer ring from the opposite end of the bore. Discard the oil seals. Also remove the plastic water shield from the drive shaft.
4. Drift out the inner race of each bearing and remove the spacer ring, if fitted between the bearings. Drive out the bearing outer races from the hub bore, but take great care to avoid damaging the bore.
5. Clean all old grease, etc., from the hub bore.
6. Pack the new bearings with suitable high-melting point grease, then install them in the hub. On bearings with a separate spacer ring between them, the bearings must be fitted with the sides marked 'THRUST' facing inwards towards each other. Tap the bearings squarely into position, bearing only on the outer race. On bearings which do not require a spacer, this is because of the lengthened inner races which butt up together, these bearings must be fitted in pairs and the markings fitted outwards.
7. Lubricate the new oil seals before fitting them. The seals must be installed with the sealing lips facing inwards. Note that the inner seal also has a lip on its outer face. The seals can normally be installed by pressing them into position by hand, or by tapping gently on their outer edge.
8. Fit the water shield on the drive shaft so that it is positioned 6 mm (1/4 in) from the shouldered edge (10,Fig.J:3). Fill the sealing face of the water shield with grease.
9. Assemble the swivel hub on the car as detailed previously. When refitting the driving flange, ensure that it locates correctly in the bearing spacer before tapping it fully into position. The distance ring must be positioned on the driving flange, with its chamfered side towards the flange, before installing. It should be noted that the brake backplate must be fitted before the driving flange is installed.
10. Once the car is lowered back onto its wheels, tighten the drive shaft nut to its specified torque – see TECHNICAL DATA and secure with a new split pin. Align the nut to the next split pin hole, if necessary.

Front Hub Bearings — Replacement (Disc Brake Models) Fig.J:7
1. Remove the swivel hub assembly from the car as detailed previously. This should include withdrawing the driving flange and brake disc assembly.
2. Extract the outer oil seal from the outboard end of the hub bore. Similarly, remove the inner oil seal, together with its spacer ring from the opposite end of the bore. Discard the oil seals. Also remove the plastic water shield from the drive shaft.
3. Remove the bearing inner races, together with the bearing spacer ring, from the hub bore. The inner bearing race may be left on the drive shaft when the swivel hub assembly is removed.

Drive out the bearing outer races from the hub bore, but take great care to avoid damaging the bore.
4. Clean all old grease, etc., from the hub bore.
5. Tap the outer races of the new bearings into position in the hub bore, bearing only on their outer edge. Ensure that the races are correctly seated. Pack the inner race and roller assemblies with high-melting point grease then install them in the hub with the spacer ring between them.
6. Lubricate the new oil seals before fitting them. The seals must be installed with the sealing lips facing inwards. Note that the inner seal also has a lip on its outer face. The seals can normally be installed by pressing them into position by hand, or by tapping gently on their outer edge. Pack the space between each seal and its adjacent bearing with grease, but do not fill the space between the bearings.
7. Fit the water shield on the drive shaft so that it is positioned 6 mm (1/4 in) from the shouldered edge (10,Fig.J:3). Fill the sealing face of the water shield with grease.
8. Assemble the swivel hub on the car as detailed previously. When fitting the driving flange and brake disc assembly, ensure that the split tapered collar is correctly fitted under the drive shaft nut.
9. Once the car is lowered back onto its wheels, tighten the drive shaft nut to the specified torque – see TECHNICAL DATA and secure with a new split pin. Align the nut to the next split-pin hole, if necessary.

SHOCK ABSORBERS .... [6]

Telescopic shock absorbers are fitted only to models with 'dry' suspension. The front shock absorber installation is shown in Fig.J:6 and is mainly self-explanatory.

Ensure that a large washer is fitted on each side of the mounting bush, and the spacer is fitted adjacent to the suspension arm at the lower mounting. Use new self-locking nuts if the existing ones are worn.

LOWER SUSPENSION ARMS .... [7]
Removal & Installation (Fig.J:8)
Before jacking up the car, fit a packing piece between the upper suspension arm and the rebound rubber; this will take the strain off the swivel hub lower joint and make it easier to disconnect the lower arm.
1. Raise and support the front of the car – see BASIC PROCEDURES and remove the road wheel.
2. Remove the retaining nut and separate the swivel hub ball joint from the lower suspension arm, using a suitable joint separator tool. Remove the through-bolt and nut securing the tie-rod to the lower arm.
3. At the lower arm pivot shaft, remove the nut and washer from the rear end of the shaft, then tap the shaft forwards to release the arm. Remove the arm mounting bushes.
4. Installation is a simple reversal of the above procedure. Ensure that the flat on the head on the pivot shaft locates correctly with the tab at the mounting hole.
5. The pivot shaft nut should not be fully tightened until the suspension is supporting the weight of the car, to prevent pre-tensioning of the rubber bushes. Tighten the pivot shaft nut to the specified torque – see TECHNICAL DATA.

UPPER SUSPENSION ARMS .... [8]

Removal of the upper suspension arm is only normally required to allow replacement of the suspension spring unit. It is unusual that removal be occasioned by the need to renew the arm pivot bearings, which are of the needle roller type.

On models with Hydrolastic suspension, the Hydrolastic system on the appropriate side of the car must be depressurised and then repressurised once the arm has been refitted. Full details of these operations are included in REAR SUSPENSION.

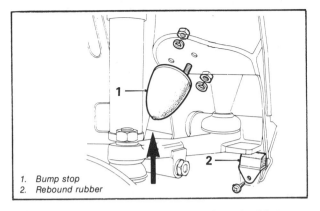

1. Bump stop
2. Rebound rubber

Fig. J:5 Removal of bump stop & rebound rubbers

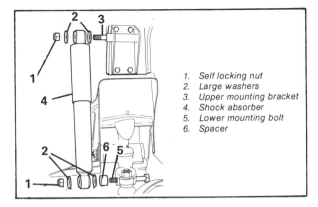

1. Self locking nut
2. Large washers
3. Upper mounting bracket
4. Shock absorber
5. Lower mounting bolt
6. Spacer

Fig. J:6 Removal of shock absorber

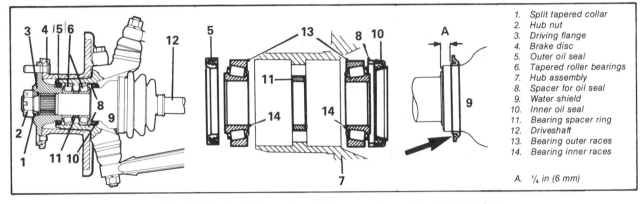

1. Split tapered collar
2. Hub nut
3. Driving flange
4. Brake disc
5. Outer oil seal
6. Tapered roller bearings
7. Hub assembly
8. Spacer for oil seal
9. Water shield
10. Inner oil seal
11. Bearing spacer ring
12. Driveshaft
13. Bearing outer races
14. Bearing inner races

A. ¼ in (6 mm)

Fig. J:7 Sectional view of front hub assembly — disc brake models

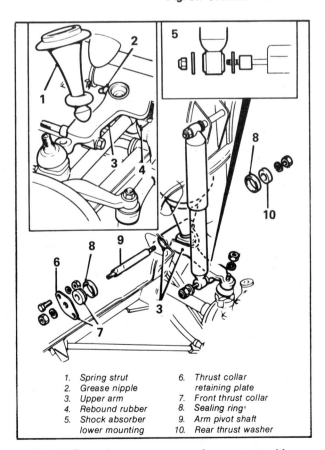

1. Spring strut	6. Thrust collar
2. Grease nipple	retaining plate
3. Upper arm	7. Front thrust collar
4. Rebound rubber	8. Sealing ring
5. Shock absorber	9. Arm pivot shaft
lower mounting	10. Rear thrust washer

Fig. J:9 Removing upper suspension arm assembly

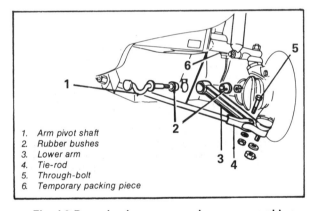

1. Arm pivot shaft
2. Rubber bushes
3. Lower arm
4. Tie-rod
5. Through-bolt
6. Temporary packing piece

Fig. J:8 Removing lower suspension arm assembly

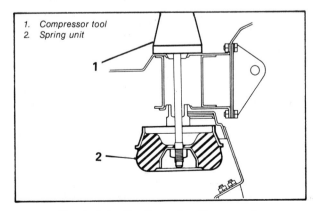

1. Compressor tool
2. Spring unit

Fig. J:10 Section through rubber cone in compressed state

On models with 'dry' suspension, a special compressor tool will be required to compress the rubber cone spring until before the arm can be removed. This tool is shown in Figs.J:1 & J:2, and is generally available for hire from most good accessory and tool hire shops.

Note:Hydrolastic upper arms are not interchangeable with the rubber cone type.

Removal (Fig.J:9)

1. Raise and support the front of the car – see TECHNICAL DATA, and then remove the road wheel.
2. On models with Hydrolastic suspension, depressurise the Hydrolastic system.
3. On models with 'dry' suspension, compress the rubber cone spring unit. Early models have a rubber grommet covering the access hole in the bulkhead crossmember and this must be removed to allow the compressing tool to be fitted. Later models have the sub-frame turrets attached by the large bolt each side and this must be removed to enable the compressor spindle to be fitted.
4. Insert the threaded spindle of the compressor tool through the access hole and locate the body of the tool against the bulkhead crossmember. Screw the spindle nine complete turns into the spring unit ensuring that the adaptor thread is the correct type to suit the rubber cone (UNF or Metric). Tighten the centre nut until it makes contact with the body of the tool and then turn the handle clockwise to compress the spring sufficiently to allow the spring strut to be extracted from between the upper suspension arm and the spring unit (Fig.J:10). Do not over-compress the spring.
5. Disconnect the hydraulic shock absorber from the upper suspension arm, where applicable. Compress the shock absorber to clear it from the arm. Remove the ball pin retaining nut and disconnect the swivel hub ball joint from the upper suspension arm, using a suitable joint separator tool. Support the swivel hub to prevent straining the brake hose.
6. Lever the spring strut ball end from its seat in the upper suspension arm and extract the strut assembly. It may be necessary to remove the rebound rubber located under the suspension arm to enable the arm to drop sufficiently for the strut to be withdrawn.
7. Remove the nut and spring washer from the rear end of the arm pivot shaft. Remove the two screws securing the thrust collar retaining plate to the sub-frame at the front end of the shaft. Lever the pivot shaft forward, twist the suspension arm outwards and pull it from the pivot shaft. Remove the rear thrust washer and seals from the suspension arm. Remove the arm assembly from the front of the sub-frame. Remove the front thrust collar from the pivot shaft.

Installation

Installation is basically a reversal of the removal procedure, but special attention should be paid to the following points.
1. When fitting the shaft thrust washers, they must be located with their lubrication grooves towards the suspension arm.
2. Grease the arm pivot shaft before installing it.
3. Apply suitable grease, such as Dextragrease Super G.P., to the strut cup in the suspension arm.
4. Once the spring strut has been installed, ensure that the dust cover at the ball end locates correctly around the nylon cup.
5. Tighten the upper arm pivot shaft nuts and the swivel hub ball pin nut to their specified torque – see TECHNICAL DATA.
6. After releasing the compression on the rubber cone spring, check that the strut is correctly located at the suspension arm and spring unit. Refit the two subframe mounting bolts and the rubber grommet or the sub-frame mounting bolt depending on the type.
7. On Hydrolastic models, repressurise the Hydrolastic system as detailed in REAR SUSPENSION.

RUBBER CONE SPRING UNITS .... [9]
Removal & Installation

A rubber cone spring unit is used on models with 'dry' suspension, and is located in the sub-frame tower. The upper suspension arm must first be removed as previously detailed, before the spring unit can be removed.

Turn the handle on the spring compressor tool anti-clockwise, while holding the centre screw, to release the spring compression. Unscrew the tool centre spindle from inside the sub-frame tower.

The spring unit is installed in the reverse order of removing. Ensure that the spring unit locates correctly in the sub-frame tower.

HYDROLASTIC DISPLACER UNITS .... [10]
Removal & Installation

On models with Hydrolastic suspension, a Hydrolastic displacer unit is used in place of the rubber cone spring unit and this must be depressurised before removal is attempted. As with the spring unit above, the suspension arm must be removed before the displacer unit can be withdrawn.

Disconnect the displacer hose from the union on the engine compartment bulkhead (Fig.J:11).

Push the displacer unit upwards and remove the two screws to release the displacer bracket from inside the subframe tower. Turn the displacer unit anti-clockwise and withdraw it from the sub-frame tower.

When refitting the displacer unit, rotate it clockwise to lock it into the registers on the locating plate. The Hydrolastic system must now be repressurised ensuring that the knuckle joint is correctly located in the upper arm.

DRIVE SHAFTS .... [11]

Three different types of drive shaft are used, and the removal technique varies dependent on the type fitted. Early manual models have drive shafts which have a rubber coupling with 'U' bolts at the inboard end and a sliding joint connecting the inner flange to the main member of the shaft. Later models have an offset sphere type joint at the inboard end and the drive shaft is splined into the inner member of the joint. The joint assembly itself is a splined fit in the final drive unit stub shaft.

On models with automatic transmission, the drive shaft is similar to the early manual one, but a Hardy Spicer flanged universal joint is fitted at the inboard end.
NOTE:In each case the drive shaft can be removed as an assembly with the swivel hub if required. In this case the procedure given for swivel hub removal should be followed, then the drive shaft disconnected at its inboard end.

Removal

1. With the car still on its wheels, remove the split pin and slacken the hub nut on the end of the drive shaft. Also slacken the wheel nuts.
2. It will facilitate disconnection of the swivel hub upper ball joint later if the rebound rubber at the upper suspension arm is removed and a solid wedge of roughly the same thickness fitted in its place. This should be done before the car is jacked up.
3. Raise and support the front of the car – see BASIC PROCEDURES, then remove the road wheel.
4. Remove the retaining nut and disconnect the track rod from the steering arm, using a suitable joint separator tool.
5. Similarly, disconnect the upper swivel joint from the upper suspension arm. Refit the ball pin retaining nut loosely.
6. On early manual models, disconnect the inner end of the drive shaft by removing the 'U' bolts securing the rubber coupling.
7. On automatic models, remove the four bolts securing the universal joint flange to the final drive unit.
8. On later manual models with the offset sphere type inboard

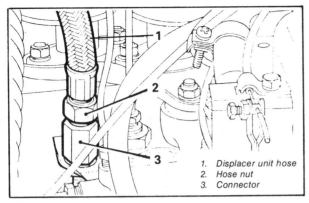

1. Displacer unit hose
2. Hose nut
3. Connector

Fig. J:11 Hydrolastic hose connection — R/H front

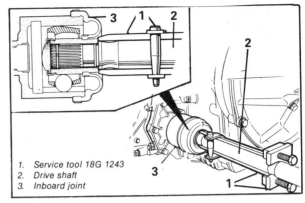

1. Service tool 18G 1243
2. Drive shaft
3. Inboard joint

Fig. J:12 Releasing offset sphere drive shaft joint

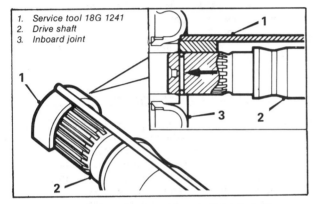

1. Service tool 18G 1241
2. Drive shaft
3. Inboard joint

Fig. J:13 Compressing drive shaft joint circlip

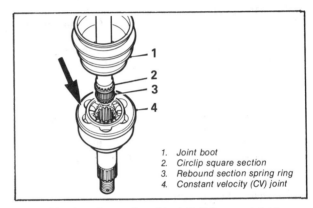

1. Joint boot
2. Circlip square section
3. Rebound section spring ring
4. Constant velocity (CV) joint

Fig. J:14 Separating drive shaft from constant velocity joint

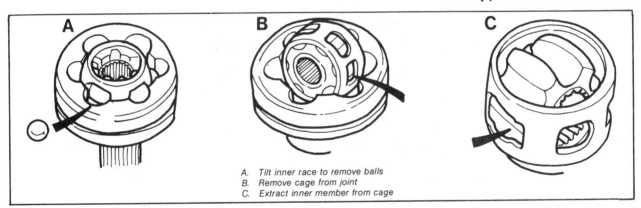

A. Tilt inner race to remove balls
B. Remove cage from joint
C. Extract inner member from cage

Fig. J:15 Sequence of operations for dismantling constant velocity joint

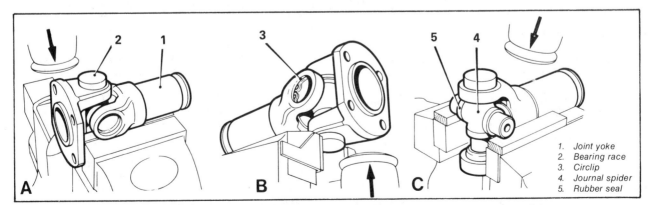

1. Joint yoke
2. Bearing race
3. Circlip
4. Journal spider
5. Rubber seal

Fig. J:16 Sequence of operations for dismantling universal joint — automatic models

joint, a special tool 18G 1243, as shown in Fig.J:12, will be required to release the inner end of the drive shaft from the joint. Assemble the tool to the drive shaft, press it hard against the inboard joint and fit the tapered pin, as shown in Fig.J:12. Insert the 'U' shaped part of the tool into the groove on the shaft, then tighten the two bolts evenly until the drive shaft is released from the inboard joint. Remove the tool.

9. Remove the nut from the swivel hub upper joint and separate the joint from the suspension arm. Support the swivel hub to avoid straining the brake hose.

10. On models with the offset sphere type inboard joint, hold the inboard joint boot in position and at the same time withdraw the drive shaft from the joint. Push the shaft inwards and over the top of the final drive unit.

11. On the other models, prise off the large retaining clip at the sliding joint rubber seal, turn back the seal and slide the joint flange off the drive shaft splines.

12. Remove the hub nut from the outer end of the drive shaft and carefully tap the drive shaft out of the driving flange. This should be done with a soft-headed mallet to avoid damaging the drive shaft threads.

13. Withdraw the drive shaft out of the swivel hub assembly, and then outwards away from under the car.

Installation

Install the drive shaft assembly in the reverse order of removing, with special attention to the following points.

1. Ensure that the plastic water shield on the drive shaft is positioned 6 mm ($\frac{1}{4}$ in) from the shouldered edge of the shaft (Figs.J:3 & J:7).

2. On models with disc front brakes, when inserting the drive shaft into the swivel hub, ensure that the shaft locates correctly in the spacer ring between the hub bearings as it is pushed through.

3. On drive shafts with the sliding type joints, secure the joint seal with a new retaining clip or soft iron wire after assembling the joint flange to the drive shaft.

4. On models with the offset sphere type inboard joint, push the drive shaft smartly into the inboard joint to lock the shaft into the joint. It may be necessary to compress the circlip in the end of the shaft to enable it to enter the joint. The special tool for compressing the circlip is shown in Fig.J:13, but this can also be done using two small screwdrivers.

5. With the rubber coupling type inboard joint, new-locking nuts should be used on the 'U' bolts. Tighten the nuts equally until approximately 1,6 mm ($\frac{1}{16}$in) of thread protrudes beyond the nuts.

6. Tighten the swivel hub ball pin nut and the track rod ball pin nut to their specified torque – see TECHNICAL DATA.

7. Once the car is lowered back onto its wheels, tighten the drive shaft nut and secure with a new split pin. The nut should be tightened to its specified torque – see TECHNICAL DATA. Align the nut to the next split pin hole, if necessary.

DRIVESHAFT RUBBER COUPLINGS .... [12]

Early manual models have a rubber coupling with 'U' bolts at the inboard end of the driveshafts. Couplings are prone to deterioration through age and contamination by oil and should be renewed if they show any signs of movement between the two 'X' members. If left too long, excessive movement in the coupling will eventually allow it to contact the transmission casing, causing damage to both the casing and the joint 'U' bolts.

Replacement

1. Raise and support the front of the car – see BASIC PROCEDURES, remove the road wheel.

2. Disconnect the upper and lower swivel joints from their respective suspension arms, using a suitable joint separator tool.

3. Remove the 'U' bolts and nuts securing the rubber coupling to the drive shaft and final drive unit flanges.

4. Press or lever down on the lower suspension arm and tie rod to disengage the lower swivel joint from the arm, then pull the swivel hub down to disengage the upper swivel joint.

5. Pull the swivel hub assembly outwards sufficiently to allow the rubber coupling to be removed.

6. Support the swivel hub assembly until it is refitted, to avoid straining the brake hose.

7. Before fitting the new coupling, check that the 'U' bolts will fit easily in their respective locations in the drive flanges. It may be necessary to squeeze the threaded ends together in the jaws of a vice to close them up slightly until they are in alignment. Use new self-locking nuts at the 'U' bolts.

8. Fit the coupling to the final drive flange first, then refit the swivel hub assembly to the suspension arms, at the same time engaging the drive shaft flange with the coupling. Tighten the 'U' bolt nuts equally until approximately 1,6 mm ($\frac{1}{16}$ in) of thread protrudes beyond the nuts.

9. Tighten the swivel hub joint nuts to their specified torque – see TECHNICAL DATA.

CONSTANT VELOCITY JOINTS .... [13]

A constant velocity joint is incorporated at the hub end of the drive shaft and is enclosed by a rubber boot. Most cases of wear or damage to the C/V joint are caused by damage to the boot, thus allowing dirt and water into the joint. The boot should be examined periodically for any signs of tears or grease leakage, indicating damage, and renew if necessary.

Wear in the C/V joint is normally indicated by 'knock-on-lock'. That is, a clicking sound from the front wheel in question when the steering is on lock.

Joint Replacement

The C/V joint is easily replaced once the drive shaft has been removed from the car. The new joint is supplied as a complete assembly with the stub shaft.

Prise off the clips securing the joint boot and pull the boot back from the joint. It is recommended that only a new boot be used on reassembly.

If the old boot is to be re-used, it should be examined very carefully for any signs of tears or other damage.

The drive shaft is retained in position in the C/V joint by a round section spring ring, located in the end of the shaft, which expands into the chamfered end of the joint inner race bore. To remove the drive shaft, this ring must be contracted into the groove. This is done by holding the shaft vertically, as shown in Fig.J:14 and giving the outer edge of the joint a sharp tap with a soft-faced mallet. This should contract the spring ring so that the joint can be drawn off the shaft. It should not be necessary to use heavy blows for this operation.

If not pre-lubricated, pack the new C/V joint with 30 cc (1 oz) of Duckhams Bentone Grease Q5795. A sachet of grease is normally supplied with a new boot kit.

Remove the spring ring from the end of the drive shaft, and fit a new spring ring in the groove. Start the drive shaft splines into the bore of the joint inner member. Compress the spring ring using one or two small screwdrivers, then tap the end of the shaft to drive it fully into place. Make sure that the shaft is fully engaged in the joint, with the outer circlip against the inner race.

Fit the rubber boot and secure with new retaining clips. Ensure that the ends of the boot engage correctly in the locating grooves in the joint housing and drive shaft. The retaining clips must be fitted with the tab folded back away from the direction of forward rotation of the shaft.

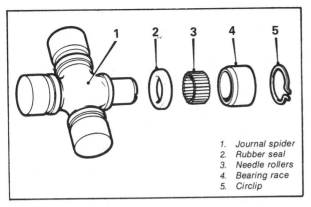

Fig. J:17 Exploded view of universal joint components

1. Journal spider
2. Rubber seal
3. Needle rollers
4. Bearing race
5. Circlip

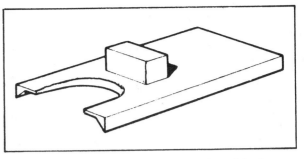

Fig. J:18 Tool for separating offset sphere joint from final drive

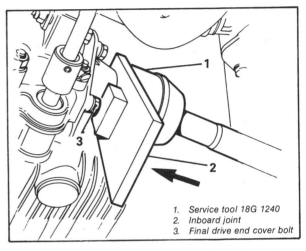

1. Service tool 18G 1240
2. Inboard joint
3. Final drive end cover bolt

Fig. J:19 Separating offset sphere joint from final drive

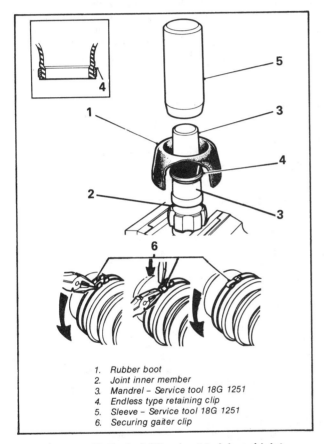

1. Rubber boot
2. Joint inner member
3. Mandrel – Service tool 18G 1251
4. Endless type retaining clip
5. Sleeve – Service tool 18G 1251
6. Securing gaiter clip

Fig. J:20 Method of fitting boot to inboard joint

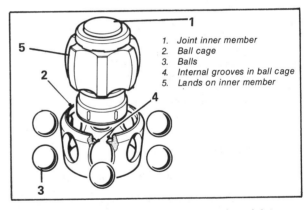

1. Joint inner member
2. Ball cage
3. Balls
4. Internal grooves in ball cage
5. Lands on inner member

Fig. J:21 Exploded view of offset sphere joint

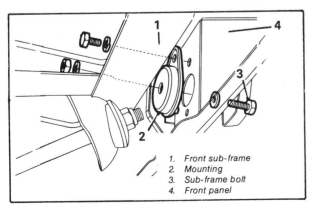

1. Front sub-frame
2. Mounting
3. Sub-frame bolt
4. Front panel

Fig. J:22 Front sub-frame mounting — front

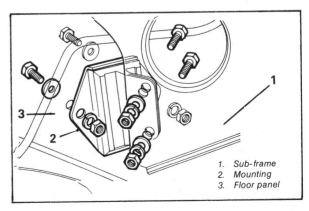

1. Sub-frame
2. Mounting
3. Floor panel

Fig. J:23 Front sub-frame mounting — rear

Boot Replacement

The joint rubber boot should be replaced if perished, worn or otherwise damaged. Before fitting the new boot, the C/V joint should be removed from the drive shaft for inspection. If there is any sign of water, road dirt or corrosion in the joint, it is recommended that a new joint assembly be fitted. The joint should be dismantled only if there is reason to believe that it is still serviceable.

1.   Remove the old boot and C/V joint from the drive shaft as detailed above.
2.   If the joint is to be dismantled, wash it thoroughly first with petrol and dry it off.
3.   Mark the relative positions of the joint inner and outer members and the ball cage with paint to ensure correct alignment on reassembly. This is most important if the joint is to be re-used.
4.   Tilt the joint inner race, as shown in A,Fig.J:15, until one ball is released. It may be necessary to ease each ball out with a pointed tool.
5.   Swivel the cage upwards, as shown in 'B', and turn it until two opposite elongated windows coincide with two lands of the joint housing. One land will drop into a window, allowing the cage and inner race assembly to be lifted out.
6.   Swivel the inner race at right-angles to the cage and turn it until two of the lands between the inner race tracks are opposite elongated windows in the cage (C,Fig.J:15). One land will drop into a window, allowing the inner race to be extracted from the cage.
7.   Clean all the components and examine carefully for any sings of wear, damage or corrosion pits. Discard the joint if any of these conditions are present.
8.   If the joint is in serviceable condition, reassemble it in the reverse order of dismantling. It is important that the components be assembled in their original relative positions as marked prior to dismantling. The components should go together easily and no force should be required.
9.   After assembling, check that the inner race articulates freely with the cage in the joint housing, but take care not to release the balls.
10.   Pack the joint with 30 cc (1 oz) of Duckhams Bentone Grease Q5795. A satchet of grease is normally supplied with a new boot kit.
11.   Assemble the C/V joint and new boot to the drive shaft as detailed previously under Joint Replacement.

INNER UNIVERSAL JOINTS . . . . [14]

A universal joint is fitted at the inner end of the drive shaft on models with automatic transmission. The joint is similar to the type normally used on propshafts, and the overhaul procedure is also similar.

If wear has taken place in the joint bearings, a service kit containing a new journal spider, bearings, etc., is available.

Overhaul

1.   Remove the retaining circlip from each of the joint bearings with a pair of long nosed pliers and prise them out with a screwdriver. If a circlip cannot be removed easily, tap the end of the bearing race to relieve the pressure on the clip.
2.   Hold the joint in one hand and support the underside of the yoke on the top of a vice. Tap the radius of the yoke lightly with a copper mallet until the bearing race emerges from the yoke (A,Fig.J:16).
3.   Turn the joint over and grip the bearing race in the vice. Tap the underside of the yoke until the bearing race is extracted (Fig.J:16).
4.   Repeat this operation on the opposite bearing.
5.   Support the two exposed bearing trunnions on the top of the

vice, with wood or soft metal packings between the vice and the bearing trunnions. Tap the top lug of the flange yoke, as in Item 2 above, to extract the two remaining bearing races.
6.   Withdraw the journal spider from the drive shaft yoke (Fig.J:17).
7.   Check that the bearing apertures in the yoke journals are clean and undamaged.
8.   Smear the inside of the new bearing races to hold the needle rollers in position. Also fill the bottom of each race to a depth of 3 mm ($\frac{1}{8}$ in) with grease.
9.   Tap one of the new bearing races into position in the yoke journal. Insert the spider into the yoke and engage it into the bearing race. Repeat this operation on the opposite side of the yoke, holding the spider into the race as it is drifted into position to retain the needle rollers in position.
10.   Engage the other joint journal over the spider and repeat the operation above.
11.   Fit the bearing circlips, ensuring that they are firmly located in their grooves.
12.   Finally, tap each of the yoke journals lightly with a wooden mallet to relieve the pressure of the bearing races on the ends of the journals, then check that the joint articulates freely without binding.

DRIVESHAFT INBOARD JOINTS . . . . [15]

The offset sphere type joint is used on later manual models and is a splined fit onto the final drive unit stub shaft. The joint is retained by a circlip on the splined shaft which expands to lock the shaft in the joint.

Joint Replacement

The drive shaft must first be withdrawn out of the inboard joint, as detailed for Driveshaft – Removal previously.

A special service tool 18G 1240 (Fig.J:18) is required to lever the joint assembly out of the final drive unit, but it should be possible to use a lever, with a suitably cranked end, to prise the joint away from the final drive. On no account must leverage be applied direct to the casing, but only to the bolt head adjacent to the joint.

Insert the tool between the joint and the final drive unit end cover, with its relieved side against the joint. Drift it into position until the block is adjacent to the end cover bolt (Fig.J:19). Give the tool a sharp blow on its outside face to release the joint.

Withdraw the joint assembly from the final drive unit and remove the oil flinger from the joint.

Check the condition of the nylon oil flinger and fit a replacement if it has been damaged in any way.

Insert the new inboard joint into the final drive unit and push it in until the joint is securely engaged over the retaining circlip on the splined shaft.

Refit the driveshaft, following the relevant steps given under the appropriate heading previously.

Boot Replacement

The joint rubber boot should be replaced if perished, worn or otherwise damaged. Before fitting the new boot, the inboard joint should be inspected for any signs of wear, road dirt or corrosion in the joint. If any of these conditions are present, it is recommended that a new joint assembly be fitted. The joint should be dismantled only if there is reason to believe that it is still serviceable.

To replace the boot, the drive shaft must first be withdrawn out of the inboard joint, as detailed for Driveshaft – Removal previously.

1.   Remove the outer retaining ring securing the boot to the joint housing. Turn back the boot and remove the inner retaining

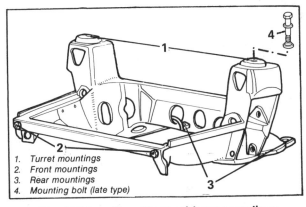

1. Turret mountings
2. Front mountings
3. Rear mountings
4. Mounting bolt (late type)

Fig. J:24 Location of front subframe mountings

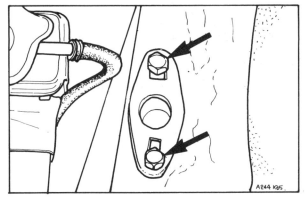

Fig. J:25 Sub-frame turret mounting bolts (early type)

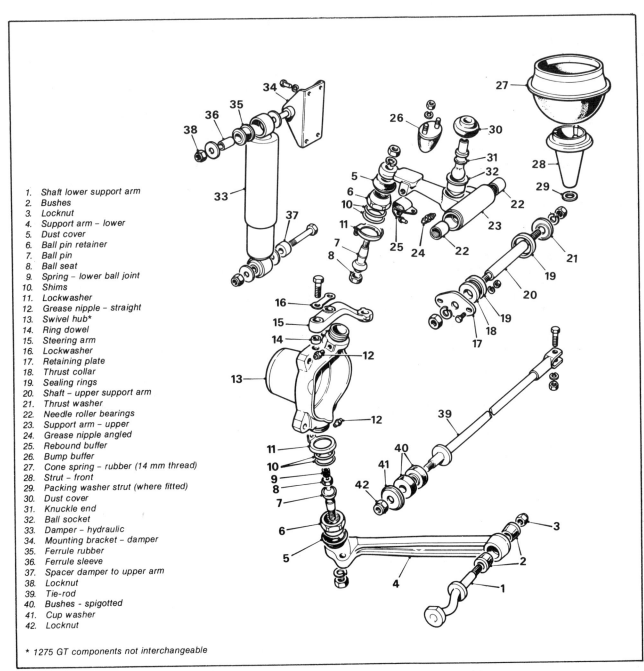

1. Shaft lower support arm
2. Bushes
3. Locknut
4. Support arm – lower
5. Dust cover
6. Ball pin retainer
7. Ball pin
8. Ball seat
9. Spring – lower ball joint
10. Shims
11. Lockwasher
12. Grease nipple – straight
13. Swivel hub*
14. Ring dowel
15. Steering arm
16. Lockwasher
17. Retaining plate
18. Thrust collar
19. Sealing rings
20. Shaft – upper support arm
21. Thrust washer
22. Needle roller bearings
23. Support arm – upper
24. Grease nipple angled
25. Rebound buffer
26. Bump buffer
27. Cone spring – rubber (14 mm thread)
28. Strut – front
29. Packing washer strut (where fitted)
30. Dust cover
31. Knuckle end
32. Ball socket
33. Damper – hydraulic
34. Mounting bracket – damper
35. Ferrule rubber
36. Ferrule sleeve
37. Spacer damper to upper arm
38. Locknut
39. Tie-rod
40. Bushes - spigotted
41. Cup washer
42. Locknut

* 1275 GT components not interchangeable

Fig. J:26 Exploded view of front suspension components — rubber cone

ring securing the small diameter of the boot to the joint inner member. Remove the rubber boot from the inboard joint.

2. Inspect the internal components of the joint assembly. If necessary, the joint can be dismantled for cleaning and further inspection as detailed below.

3. Fit a new 'endless' type retaining clip to the inner neck of the rubber boot, with the chamfered end of the ring towards the inner end of the boot (see inset, Fig.J:20). Fold back the boot and fit the smaller diameter over the inner member of the inboard joint. The use of a special mandrel and sleeve (18G 1251) is recommended for this operation to facilitate fitment of the boot (inset,Fig.J:20). In this case, the mandrel must be lubricated with a liquid detergent or rubber lubricant to ease fitting.

4. If necessary, pack the joint with 50 cc of Shell S7274 Tivella 'A' grease. This is normally supplied in a sachet with the new boot kit.

5. Turn the boot back and locate it on the outside of the joint housing. Secure the boot with a new retaining clip as shown in Fig.J:20. This clip must be fitted with the tab folded back away from the direction of forward rotation of the joint.

6. Finally, refit the drive shaft following the relevant steps given under the appropriate heading previously.

Joint Overhaul

1. Remove the inboard joint from the final drive unit housing as detailed previously for Joint Replacement.

2. Remove the rubber boot from the joint.

3. Withdraw the joint inner member and ball cage assembly from the joint housing.

4. Push the balls out of the ball cage by inserting a screwdriver between the joint inner member and each ball in turn.

5. Rotate the ball cage until the grooves inside the cage coincide with the lands on the joint inner member, then withdraw the cage from the inner member.

6. Clean all the components of the joint and examine carefully for any signs of wear, damage or corrosion pits. Discard the joint if any of these conditions are present.

7. If the joint is in serviceable condition, reassemble the inner member, ball cage and balls in the reverse order of dismantling. Ensure that the long tapered end of the ball cage faces towards the drive shaft end of the inner member.

8. Fit the inner member assembly into the joint housing.

9. Pack the joint with 50 cc of Shell S7274 Tivella 'A' grease. A sachet of grease is normally supplied with a new boot kit.

10. Fit the rubber boot to the joint as detailed above (Fig.J:20).

11. Finally, refit the inboard joint to the final drive housing and refit the drive shaft as detailed previously.

SUB-FRAME . . . . [16]
Removal (Fig.J:24)

1. Disconnect the battery earth lead.

2. Remove the bonnet, disconnect all the cables and connections to the engine and gearbox and remove the unit as described in ENGINE.

3. Raise and support the front of the car – see BASIC PROCEDURES. Ensure that the sub-frame is clear of the supports.

4. Remove the cap from the brake fluid reservoir, cover it with a sheet of polythene and then refit the cap. This will minimise fluid loss.

5. Disconnect the brake fluid lines to both front brakes.

6. On cars fitted with Hydrolastic suspension, depressurise the system – see REAR SUSPENSION.

7. Disconnect the Hydrolastic fluid hoses from the unions on the bulkhead.

8. Disconnect the two steering track rod end joints using a ball joint taper breaking tool – see STEERING.

9. Support the sub-frame on a jack and remove the upper sub-frame retaining bolts which are situated at each side of the engine compartment bulkhead, near the inner wing panel. Early models have the sub-frame bolted directly to the bodyshell by two nuts with tab washers (Fig.J:25) on each side. Later cars have rubber insulating mountings between the sub-frame and the body and these have a single large bolt (4,Fig.J:24) each side retaining the upper mounting.

10. Undo the front mounting bolts which are accessible through holes in the front valance below the bumper (Fig.J:22).

11. Disconnect the lower end of the damper from the upper suspension arm each side (where applicable).

12. Undo and remove the two nuts and bolts from each side at the rear of the sub-frame. These are accessible once the front carpet has been lifted up and are situated at the front of the floor pan on each side.

Early models have the sub-frame bolted directly to the floor, but later models have rubber mountings (Fig.J:23).

13. Carefully lower the sub-frame, ensuring that it remains level until the towers are clear of the bodyshell.

14. Remove the suspension components as described earlier in this chapter.

Installation

Install the sub-frame in the reverse order of removal, ensuring that any packing pieces between the sub-frame and body shell are refitted in their original positions.

Bleed the braking system as described in BRAKES and evacuate and repressurise the Hydrolastic suspension system (where applicable).

Rear Suspension

INTRODUCTION . . . . [1]

The rear suspension system on the Mini can be one of two distinct types. Originally all models were fitted with a 'dry' rubber cone system which was changed to the 'wet' Hydrolastic system for the 1965 model year (Saloon versions only). Mark 3 cars from 1970 model year onwards reverted to the 'dry' rubber cone system once more.

Whichever system is being used, the layout of the main components is very similar. A pressed steel subframe is used to mount all the suspension components, these consisting of trailing arm units pivoted on short shafts bolted to the subframe brackets and operating the suspension units through ball jointed, cone shaped struts (Fig.K:1).

The subframe is attached to the body shell by four rubber bushed mountings, one at each corner.

The Hydrolastic system is filled with a mixture of water and alcohol, under high pressure, to link the suspension units (displacers) front and rear on each side of the car.

Although some of the components of the two types of suspension are similar they are not interchangeable and therefore, when buying spares for instance, care must be taken to ensure that the correct items are obtained.

TOOLS & EQUIPMENT . . . . [2]

Other than those tools itemised under Basic Tools & Equipment in BASIC PROCEDURES, the following tools are needed to carry out the operations detailed within this chapter.
- Universal puller – for removing the rear hub flanges.
- A selection of tubing and sockets – to use as drifts when replacing oil seals and bearings.
- A Hydrolastic suspension service unit – for depressurising and repressurising the suspension units on models with Hydrolastic suspension.

After repairs have been carried out, the car can be driven to an Austin/Rover dealer with the suspension resting on the bump stops. This should only be done on smooth roads at speeds below 30 mph (50 kph).

The outer bush in the trailing arm has to be reamed to size after fitting and this is a task best left to your local Austin/Rover dealer who will have the special tool required to do this accurately.

REAR HUB BEARINGS . . . . [3]

It should be noted that some models, including the 1275 GT, have a slightly different rear hub assembly in that they are fitted with taper roller bearings instead of the usual ball bearings. The replacement procedure for both types, however, is very similar.

Replacement (Figs.K:2 & K:3)

1. Raise and support the rear of the car – see BASIC PROCEDURES, remove the road wheel.
2. Release the handbrake, slacken off the brake shoe adjustment; then remove the two retaining screws and withdraw the brake drum.
3. Prise the dust cap from the centre of the rear hub. Extract the split pin, unscrew the hub nut and remove the special thrust washer from the stub axle. Note that the nut at the left-hand hub assembly has a left-hand thread, as opposed to the normal right-hand thread at the right-hand hub.
4. On taper-roller type bearings, withdraw the hub assembly from the stub axle. The bearings will normally come away with the hub. Remove the bearing inner race and roller assembly from the outer end of the hub bore. Also remove the spacer ring fitted between the bearings. Extract the oil seal from the inboard end of the hub bore and withdraw the inner bearing inner race and roller assembly. Drive out the bearing assembly. Drive out the bearing outer races from the hub bore.
5. On other models, a hub puller will probably be required to withdraw the hub assembly from the stub axle. Drift out the inner race of each of two bearings and remove the spacer ring fitted between the bearings. The oil seal at the inboard end of the hub will be driven out with the inner bearing. Drive out the bearing inner races from the hub bore.
6. Clean all old grease, etc., from the hub bore.
7. Pack the new bearings with suitable high-melting point grease.
8. On taper-roller type bearings, tap the outer races of the new bearings into position in the hub bore, bearing only on their outer edge. Ensure that the races are correctly seated. Install the bearing inner race and roller assemblies in the hub with the spacer ring between them. Lubricate the new oil seal and install it at the inner end of the hub bore with the sealing lip away from the bearing.
9. On other models, install the new bearings in the hub with the spacer ring between them. Tap the bearings squarely into position, bearing only on the outer race. Lubricate the new oil seal and install it at the inner end of the hub bore with the sealing lip facing towards the inner bearing.
10. The oil seal can normally be installed by pressing it into position by hand, or by tapping gently on its outer edge.
11. Assemble the hub on the stub axle and fit the thrust washer and hub nut. The thrust washer must be fitted with its chamfered bore towards the bearing.
12. Tighten the hub nut to the specified torque – see TECHNICAL DATA, not forgetting that a left-hand thread is used at the left-hand hub. Align the nut to the next split pin hole, if necessary, then secure the nut with a new split pin.
13. Refit the dust cap to the hub, but do not fill the cap with grease.

14. Refit the brake drum and adjust the brake shoes, then fit the road wheel and lower the car onto its wheels.

SHOCK ABSORBERS .... [4]

Telescopic hydraulic shock absorbers are fitted only to models with 'dry' suspension (Fig.K:7).

Replacement

1. On Saloon models, the petrol tank must be removed to gain access to the top mounting of the near-side (left-hand) shock absorber. Details of the tank removal are included in FUEL SYSTEM.
2. Raise and support the rear of the car – see BASIC PROCEDURES. Remove the road wheel.
3. Working from inside the luggage compartment, remove the buffer from the damper top mounting stud, when fitted. Hold the damper mounting stud and unscrew the self-locking nut securing the top mounting. Remove the upper cupped washer and the spigotted rubber mounting bush.
4. At the radius arm, remove the self-locking nut and large washer securing the damper lower mounting to the arm. Compress the damper, then rotate it rearwards to the horizontal and remove it from the mounting stud on the radius arm.
5. Remove the rubber bush and lower cupped washer (where fitted) from the top of the damper.
6. Install the damper in the reverse order of removing. Ensure that the rubber bushes and cupped washers are correctly located at the top mounting, and that a large washer is fitted at either side of the lower mounting bush. When raising the radius arm to reconnect the shock absorber top mounting, ensure that the spring unit strut is correctly engaged at both the spring unit and the radius arm.

RUBBER CONE SPRING UNITS .... [5]
Removal & Installation (Fig.K:4)

A rubber cone spring unit is used on models with 'dry' suspension, and is located in the sidemember of the rear subframe.
1. Remove the shock absorber as detailed above. Lower the radius arm and pull or lever the trumpet-shaped connecting strut from the spring unit and the ball seat in the radius arm.
2. Release the rubber cone spring unit from its location on the subframe.
3. If required, the knuckle joint end can be removed from the strut to fit a replacement. The knuckle joint is merely a push fit in the end of the strut. The nylon seat in the radius arm can also be replaced after levering it out of its location.
4. Refit the spring unit in the reverse order of removing. Apply suitable grease, such as Dextragrease Super G.P., to the knuckle joint and nylon cup before installing the strut. Ensure that the dust cover at the ball end locates correctly around the nylon cup.
5. As the radius arm is raised to refit the shock absorber, ensure that the strut is correctly engaged at both the spring unit and the radius arm.

HYDROLASTIC SUSPENSION .... [6]

NOTE:On models with Hydrolastic suspension, a coil helper spring is located between the rear end of each of the rear radius arms and the body to maintain the rear trim height when the car is unladen.

Depressurising & Repressuring the System

Before any major work can be carried out on the suspension or its components, the Hydrolastic system must be depressurised. For this operation an Hydrolastic Suspension Service unit (Fig.K:5) is required and it would normally be necessary to take the car to an Austin Rover dealer for the suspension to be depressurised and/or repressurised.

If a unit is available, in most cases, instructions for operating the unit are supplied with it and are normally printed on the top of the unit. These instructions should be read through carefully before attempting to use the unit, and followed accurately throughout the operation.

The unit consists basically of a vacuum pump, a pressure pump and a fluid reservoir. Before using the unit, check the fluid level in the pressure/vacuum tank and top up with fluid if necessary. The vacuum and pressure valves are normally identified by colour; YELLOW for vacuum, and BLACK for pressure (Fig.K:6).

The Hydrolastic system pressure valves are located at the rear of the car on the subframe crossmember.

Remember that the ride height of the car will drop as the Hydrolastic system is depressurised, so be careful when working at the rear of the car.

It should be noted that, with the Hydrolastic system in the depressurised state, the suspension arms will contact the bump rubbers at both front and rear, but the car can still be driven with complete safety at speeds up to 30 mph (50 kph) over smooth roads.

When any part of the Hydrolastic system has been disconnected, or after fitting new displacer units or interconnecting pipes, it is essential that the air is evacuated from the system and a partial vacuum created before the system is pressurised. Once evacuated, the system should be pressurised with the car resting on all four wheels in an unladen condition and with a maximum of 4 galls (18,2 litres) of petrol in the tank.

If a new displacer unit has been fitted, pressurise the system initially to 28 kg/cm² (400 lb/in²) or 24,5 kg/cm² (350 lb/in²) on early models – see TECHNICAL DATA for details of specific models application. The system should be left in this over-pressurised condition for about 30 minutes to allow the vehicle to settle, then the pressure reduced to its normal specified setting.

Checking/Adjusting System Pressure

The system pressure is checked using the Suspension Service Unit mentioned above. The car must be resting on all four wheels with a load as described above for pressurising.

The pressure tank on the unit should be pumped up to the system specified working pressure before opening the connector valve, which will already have been connected to the system pressure valve. If a different pressure reading is now indicated, the system pressure should be adjusted by operating the pressure pump to raise the pressure, or opening the pressure valve on the unit to lower the pressure, until the specified figure is obtained.

Checking Vehicle Ride Height

The car ride height is governed by the Hydrolastic system pressure and should be checked with the car resting on level ground and a load condition as described above for pressurising the system.

Measure the height from the axle centre-line to the underside of the wing opening at both the front and rear of the car (Fig.K:8) and compare with the specified trim heights given in TECHNICAL DATA. If the dimensions are outside the specified

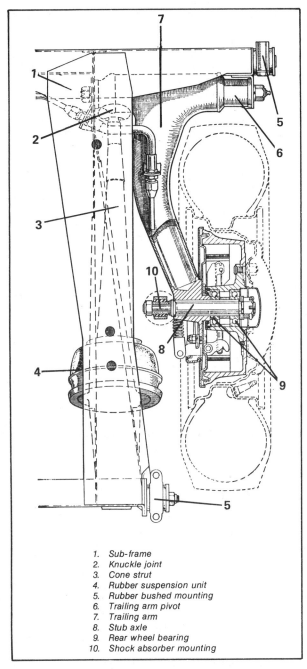

1. Sub-frame
2. Knuckle joint
3. Cone strut
4. Rubber suspension unit
5. Rubber bushed mounting
6. Trailing arm pivot
7. Trailing arm
8. Stub axle
9. Rear wheel bearing
10. Shock absorber mounting

Fig. K:1 Rear suspension components — dry type

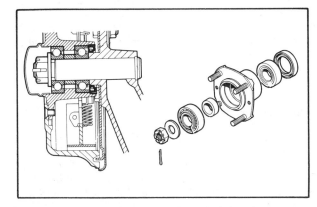

**Fig. K:2 Exploded view of rear hub bearings
— ball race type**

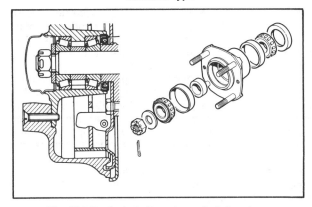

**Fig. K:3 Exploded view of rear hub bearings
— taper roller type**

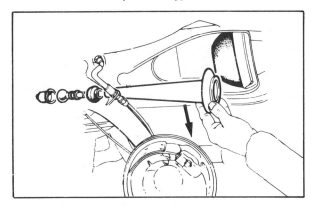

Fig. K:4 Removing suspension cone & strut — dry type

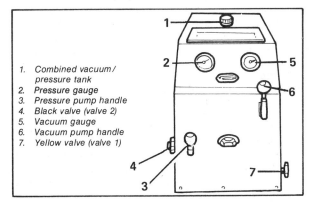

1. Combined vacuum/
   pressure tank
2. Pressure gauge
3. Pressure pump handle
4. Black valve (valve 2)
5. Vacuum gauge
6. Vacuum pump handle
7. Yellow valve (valve 1)

Fig. K:5 Hydrolastic suspension service unit

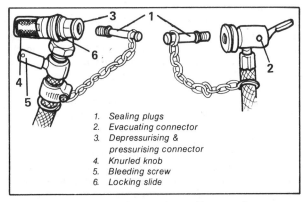

1. Sealing plugs
2. Evacuating connector
3. Depressurising &
   pressurising connector
4. Knurled knob
5. Bleeding screw
6. Locking slide

Fig. K:6 Suspension service unit connectors

limits, the system pressures should be checked and adjusted if necessary to obtain the correct ride height.

The system pressures can be adjusted slightly from the specified figures to obtain the specified trim heights, but large variations will indicate wear or damage to the suspension components or body shell.

HYDROLASTIC PIPES .... [7]

The Hydrolastic system interconnecting pipes are made from Bundy tubing, and therefore, like the brake pipes, are susceptible to corrosion damage after a period of time. The worst areas for corrosion appear to be the points at which the pipes pass between the subframes and the vehicle floor pan, and particular attention should be paid here for any signs of fluid leakage. This is usually easily spotted as the suspension fluid is bright green in colour.

The pipes may also suffer physical damage from the impact of stones, etc., due to their open location on the underside of the car. Damage may also be caused to the pipes when attempting to disconnect them, particularly at the rear, as the pipe unions are especially susceptible to corrosion.

Replacement of the interconnecting pipes is reasonably straightforward but is time consuming in that it involves dropping the rear edge of the front subframe and the front edge of the rear subframe to allow the old pipe to be removed and the new pipe to be installed. The procedure for dropping the front subframe is similar to that described for removing the steering unit.

Needless to say, the Hydrolastic system must be depressurised and repressurised, as described previously, in the course of the work.

Ensure that the pipe unions are tightened securely, as even a slight leakage will prevent the system from retaining its correct pressure.

HYDROLASTIC DISPLACER UNITS .... [8]
Removal and Installation
On models with Hydrolastic suspension, a Hydrolastic displacer unit is used in place of the rubber cone spring unit mentioned above.

Raise and support the rear of the car – see BASIC PROCEDURES, then remove the road wheel. Remove the retaining clip and disconnect the lower end of the suspension helper spring from the spigot on the radius arm. It may be necessary to raise the radius arm to allow the spring to be detached.

Depressurise the Hydrolastic system as detailed in the Hydrolastic System section of this chapter. Disconnect the displacer hose from the valve assembly on the rear member of the subframe (Fig.K:10).

Depress the radius arm sufficiently to allow the displacer unit strut to be extracted from the displacer unit, then pull the tube-shaped strut rearwards to disengage the knuckle joint from the seat in the radius arm. Turn the displacer unit anti-clockwise to release it from its locating plate on the subframe, then withdraw the displacer unit (Fig.K:9).

The knuckle joint is a simple push-fit in the end of the connecting strut and can be removed to fit a replacement. The nylon seat in the radius arm can also be levered out if a replacement is to be fitted.

When refitting the displacer unit, turn it clockwise to lock it in position on the locating plate lugs. Lubricate the knuckle joint and the nylon cup in the radius arm with a suitable grease, such as Dextragrease Super G.P., before installing the strut. Ensure the rubber dust cover at the knuckle joint locates correctly around the lip of the nylon cup.

When installation is completed, evacuate and repressurise the Hydrolastic system as detailed previously. Ensure that the strut remains correctly engaged at both the displacer unit and the radius arm.

The radius arms pivot on a bronze bush at the outer end of the pivot shaft and a needle roller bearing at the inner end. These are one of the main points of wear at the rear suspension, and this is invariably due to lack of regular lubrication. A grease nipple is provided at the outer end of each pivot shaft and it is very important that these be greased frequently to keep the bearings adequately lubricated and prevent the ingress of dirt and water.

The bearings can be checked for wear once the wheel is jacked up clear of the ground. Grasp the wheel at the front and rear edge and rock the whole suspension assembly in and out. Wear will be indicated by movement of the arm casting in relation to the subframe at its outer pivot point. The bronze bush at the outer pivot point is more susceptible to wear than the needle bearing at the inner end.

RADIUS ARMS .... [9]

It should be noted that different radius arms are used on 'wet' and 'dry' suspension models. The Hydrolastic arm is most easily identified by the bump stop platform on the top side of the arm and the unthreaded spigot opposite the stub axle for the helper spring attachment. The 'dry' arm has a threaded spigot for mounting the lower end of the shock absorber and no bump stop is fitted. The brake pipe attachment bracket is on the top of the 'dry' arm, and on the bottom on hydrolastic models. The knuckle joint housing is also in a different position, being set further forward on the arm on Hydrolastic models, but this will be less obvious.

Removal (Fig.K:11)

1. Raise and support the rear of the car – see BASIC PROCEDURES. Remove the road wheel.
2. On 'dry' suspension models, support the radius arm and remove the shock absorber as detailed previously.
3. On Hydrolastic models, depressurise the Hydrolastic system as detailed under the appropriate heading in this section. Support the radius arm and detach the helper spring from its mounting spigot on the radius arm.
4. Remove the clevis pin and disconnect the handbrake cable from the lever at the brake backplate. Also detach the cable from the abutment bracket at the backplate.
5. At the handbrake cable sector on the underside of the radius arm, lever back the flange at the sector corners where it retains the cable and release the cable from the sector.
6. Disconnect the brake pipe from the brake hose, then release the brake hose from the abutment bracket on the radius arm. Plug the hose and pipe ends to prevent loss of fluid and the ingress of dirt. Ideally, the brake hose should be sealed using a brake hose clamp.
7. Remove the support from under the radius arm and depress the arm sufficiently to allow the connecting strut to be extracted from the spring unit or displacer. Pull the strut rearwards to disengage the knuckle joint from the seat in the radius arm.
8. Remove the nut and spring washer securing the inner end of the arm pivot shaft to the subframe.
9. Remove the end finisher panel from the sill panel, where fitted. Remove the nut and spring washer securing the outer end of the pivot shaft to the support bracket. Remove the four bolts securing the support bracket to the subframe and detach the bracket.
10. Withdraw the radius arm assembly from the subframe.

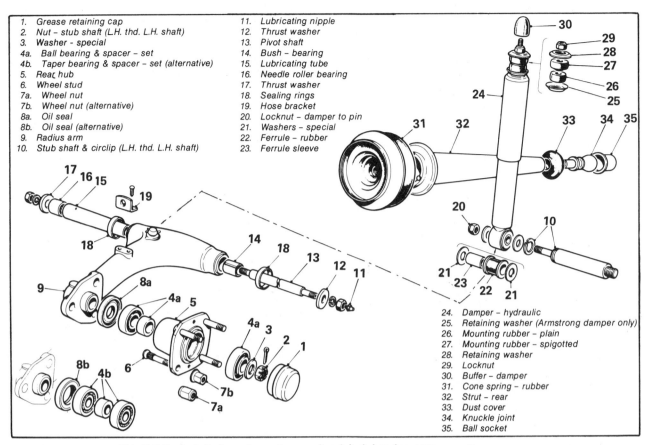

1. Grease retaining cap
2. Nut – stub shaft (L.H. thd. L.H. shaft)
3. Washer - special
4a. Ball bearing & spacer – set
4b. Taper bearing & spacer – set (alternative)
5. Rear hub
6. Wheel stud
7a. Wheel nut
7b. Wheel nut (alternative)
8a. Oil seal
8b. Oil seal (alternative)
9. Radius arm
10. Stub shaft & circlip (L.H. thd. L.H. shaft)

11. Lubricating nipple
12. Thrust washer
13. Pivot shaft
14. Bush – bearing
15. Lubricating tube
16. Needle roller bearing
17. Thrust washer
18. Sealing rings
19. Hose bracket
20. Locknut – damper to pin
21. Washers – special
22. Ferrule – rubber
23. Ferrule sleeve

24. Damper – hydraulic
25. Retaining washer (Armstrong damper only)
26. Mounting rubber – plain
27. Mounting rubber – spigotted
28. Retaining washer
29. Locknut
30. Buffer – damper
31. Cone spring – rubber
32. Strut – rear
33. Dust cover
34. Knuckle joint
35. Ball socket

Fig. K:7 Exploded view of rear suspension & hub bearing components

Fig. K:8 Checking suspension trim heights

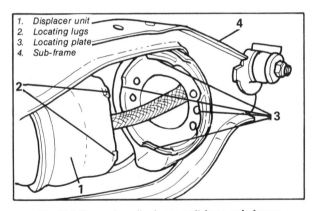

1. Displacer unit
2. Locating lugs
3. Locating plate
4. Sub-frame

Fig. K:9 Removing displacer unit from sub-frame

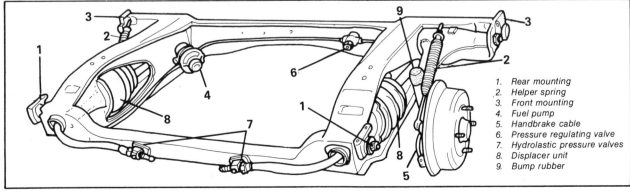

1. Rear mounting
2. Helper spring
3. Front mounting
4. Fuel pump
5. Handbrake cable
6. Pressure regulating valve
7. Hydrolastic pressure valves
8. Displacer unit
9. Bump rubber

Fig. K:10 Rear sub-frame components — Hydrolastic suspension

Retain the thrust washers and rubber seals fitted at either end of the arm pivot shaft.

Installation

Installation is basically a reversal of the removal procedure, but special attention should be paid to the following points:
1. Invariably, the reason for removing the radius arm is to renew the pivot shaft and bearings and in this case ensure that both the pivot shaft and bearings are liberally lubricated with grease before installing the shaft in the arm.
2. Assemble the thrust washers on the ends of the pivot shaft with the lubrication grooves towards the radius arm. The large washer is fitted at the inner end of the shaft, and the small washer at the outer end. Fit the rubber sealing ring over the thrust washer and the spigot at each end of the arm. Ensure that neither the thrust washer or sealing rings are displaced during installation of the arm.
3. Tighten the pivot shaft nuts to the specified torque – see TECHNICAL DATA.
4. Lubricate the knuckle joint and the nylon cup in the radius arm with a suitable grease, such as Dextragrease Super G.P., before installing the strut. Ensure that the rubber dust cover at the ball end is located correctly around the lip of the nylon cup.
5. When raising the radius arm to reconnect the shock absorber or helper spring, ensure that the strut is correctly engaged at both the spring or displacer unit and the radius arm seat.
6. Bleed the brake hydraulic system as detailed in BRAKES.
7. On Hydrolastic models, repressurise the Hydrolastic system as detailed under Hydrolastic Suspension.

Pivot Shaft Bearings

As mentioned previously, the radius arm pivot shaft runs in a bronze bush at its outer end and a needle roller bearing at its inner end. These bearings are a press fit in the radius arm and require special tools to remove and install them. The bronze bush must be fitted first and line-reamed to size before installing the needle bearing. A lubrication tube is fitted between the two bearings and must be installed with its small diameter towards the bush.

Because of the work involved and the need for special tools, it is recommended that this job be left to an Austin/Rover dealer who will have the necessary equipment and knowledge to carry out the work successfully.

The pivot shaft and bearings are normally supplied as a complete kit containing all the parts necessary for overhaul.

SUBFRAME & MOUNTINGS .... [10]
Front Mounting Replacement
Replacement of the subframe front mounting involves removal of the radius arm to gain access to the support pin nut at the subframe front member (Fig.K:12). Once the radius arm is removed, remove the locknut and washer from the inner end of the support pin. This will normally be hidden under caked mud and dirt which will have to be scraped away. Remove the two bolts securing the mounting trunnion assembly. Withdraw the support pin from the trunnion and remove the bushes.

Assemble the trunnion with new bushes and refit it in the reverse order of removal. Note that the step in the trunnion block and the short bolt are at the top.

Rear Mounting Replacement
Replacement of the rear mounting is quite straightforward after jacking up the car and removing the road wheel. The mounting trunnion block is secured to the mounting pin on the subframe by a self-locking nut and washer and to the body by two bolts and nuts, or merely two bolts on Estate, Van and Pick-up models (Fig.K:13). Lever the subframe away from the body and detach the trunnion assembly. Extract the bushes and fit new ones.

Assemble the trunnion to the subframe and body in the reverse order of removal. Note that the step on the trunnion and the short screw are at the front.

Subframe

Replacement of the rear subframe is usually necessary due to corrosion damage as it is exposed to all the water, salt and other corrosive agents thrown up from the road.

Repair, in terms of welding plates over affected areas, should only be regarded as a temporary measure and replacement of the subframe is the only satisfactory long term answer.

Removal (Figs.K:10 & K:14)

1. Disconnect the battery leads and remove the battery. The non-earth lead (positive or negative, dependent on the age of the car) to the front of the car will have to be released from the luggage compartment to allow it to clear the subframe when it is removed. This is best accomplished either by cutting the terminal off the end of the battery lead and fitting a new screw-clamp type one on reassembly, or by making the hole in the luggage compartment floor big enough to allow the existing terminal to be pushed through. If the floor panel is pulled back carefully to minimise the amount of tearing, it can be easily pushed back on reassembly and the tear sealed with a suitable body sealer.
2. On Hydrolastic models, the Hydrolastic suspension system on both sides of the car should be depressurised before the car is jacked up. However, remember that the ride height of the car will drop as the system pressure is released and it may then be difficult to get a jack underneath the rear.
3. Jack up the rear of the car to a suitable working height, bearing in mind that sufficient clearance should be left to lower the subframe. Support the rear end of the car securely on stands at the jacking points at the rear ends of the sill panels. Remove both road wheels.
4. Detach the complete exhaust system and remove it from under the car – see ENGINE.
5. At each rear brake assembly, remove the clevis pin and disconnect the handbrake cable from the lever at the backplate. Also detach the cable from the abutment bracket at the backplate. At the handbrake cable sector on the underside of the radius arm, lever back the flange at the sector corners where it retains the cable and release the cable from the sector. Pull the cable through the subframe towards the centre of the car and detach it from the guide plate at the centre of the subframe.
6. Disconnect the main brake pipe from the brake pressure regulating valve on the subframe. Fit a suitable plug in the valve and cap the pipe end to prevent loss of fluid and the ingress of dirt.
7. Support each radius arm in turn and remove the shock absorber ('dry' suspension) or disconnect the helper spring from the radius arm (Hydrolastic suspension). On 'dry' suspension models, leave the fuel tank in its removed position as access to the subframe rear near-side mounting bolts will be required later on.
8. On models with the fuel pump mounted on the rear subframe, disconnect the fuel pipes and detach the pump, together with its mounting bracket from the subframe. Plug the fuel pipe from the tank to prevent loss of fuel.
9. On Hydrolastic models, disconnect the Hydrolastic pipes from the valve assemblies at the subframe rear crossmember. Take great care when releasing the pipe unions as these pipes

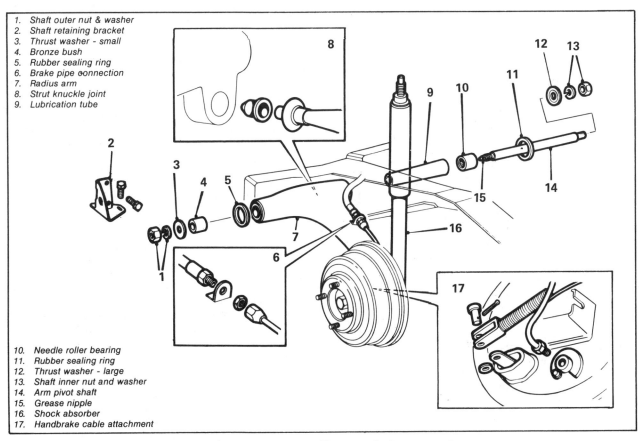

1. Shaft outer nut & washer
2. Shaft retaining bracket
3. Thrust washer - small
4. Bronze bush
5. Rubber sealing ring
6. Brake pipe connection
7. Radius arm
8. Strut knuckle joint
9. Lubrication tube

10. Needle roller bearing
11. Rubber sealing ring
12. Thrust washer - large
13. Shaft inner nut and washer
14. Arm pivot shaft
15. Grease nipple
16. Shock absorber
17. Handbrake cable attachment

Fig. K:11 Exploded view of trailing arm pivot components

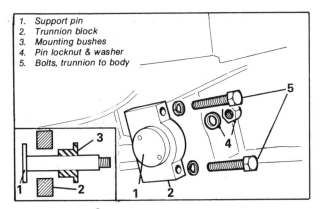

1. Support pin
2. Trunnion block
3. Mounting bushes
4. Pin locknut & washer
5. Bolts, trunnion to body

Fig. K:12 Rear sub-frame mounting — front

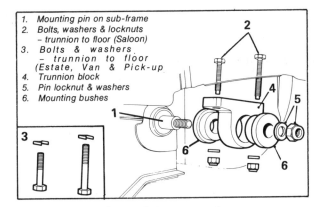

1. Mounting pin on sub-frame
2. Bolts, washers & locknuts
   – trunnion to floor (Saloon)
3. Bolts & washers
   – trunnion to floor
   (Estate, Van & Pick-up)
4. Trunnion block
5. Pin locknut & washers
6. Mounting bushes

Fig. K:13 Rear sub-frame mounting — rear

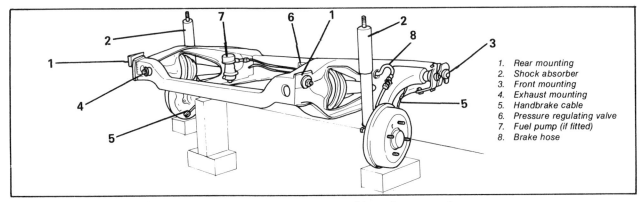

1. Rear mounting
2. Shock absorber
3. Front mounting
4. Exhaust mounting
5. Handbrake cable
6. Pressure regulating valve
7. Fuel pump (if fitted)
8. Brake hose

Fig. K:14 Removing rear sub-frame assembly — dry suspension

are easily crushed if excessive force is used. If the pipes are corroded, the unions may break off and new pipes will have to be fitted on reassembly.

10. Support the subframe on wooden blocks, or something similar, at the brake drums and the subframe front crossmember. A wooden plank about 36 inches long, bearing on the subframe sidemembers will also do.

11. Where fitted, remove the end finishers from the rear ends of the sill panels. The finisher is merely a piece of trim and is secured in position by screws – these will probably shear off when unscrewed. On reassembly the finishers can be left off as on the later models.

12. The four subframe mounting blocks can now be unbolted from the body. The mountings are located at each corner of the subframe and a fair bit of poking with a screwdriver may be required to uncover the securing bolts from the accumulated road dirt. The two bolts at the front mountings go forward into tapped holes in the crosspanel on the body, whereas the rear mountings are secured by bolts and nuts through the floor panel on Saloon models, or merely bolts into tapped holes on Estate, Van and Pick-up models (Figs.K:12 and K:13). On Saloon models the rear mounting bolts are accessible from inside the luggage compartment, but the fuel tank will have to be displaced to gain access to the near-side bolts. These rear mounting bolts can be sheared off if seized, or at worst drilled out from inside the boot, but if the front ones shear they must be drilled out and the hole retapped to size.

13. Carefully lower the subframe assembly out of position, or lift the rear of the car up to clear the subframe. It may be necessary to lever the mountings clear of their body locations to release the subframe.

Installation

Installation is mainly a reversal of the removal procedure, noting the various points mentioned during removal.

If either of the Hydrolastic pipes is corroded or was damaged during subframe removal, it should be replaced as detailed later in this chapter, before the subframe is installed.

When installation is completed, bleed the braking system as detailed in BRAKES.

On Hydrolastic models, evacuate and repressurise the Hydrolastic suspension system as detailed earlier in this chapter.

Replacement

If a new subframe is being fitted, all the components should be transferred from the old unit. This should be done systematically, and it is recommended that the sequence of removing the parts from the existing subframe be noted down to facilitate their reassembly to the new unit. A few points of note when building up the new subframe assembly are given below:

1. Renew any brake pipes or hoses which appear in any way defective. When fitting a new brake pipe, use the old pipe as a template for bending the new pipe.

2. Mark the locations of all clips, brackets, etc., on the new subframe with paint, using the old subframe for reference.

3. Check that the hole for the radius arm pivot shaft in the new subframe has sufficient clearance for the shaft to fit in easily. It may be necessary to relieve the hole with a round file.

4. Check that the threads in the bolt holes for the pivot shaft support bracket are clear and not clogged with paint by screwing in the bolts prior to assembling them properly.

5. Change over the parts of one radius arm assembly first so that the position and location of the components can be compared.

6. If the radius arm pivot shaft bearings are worn, they should be renewed before assembling the radius arm assembly to the new subframe.

7. On models with Hydrolastic suspension, do not forget to change over the radius arm bump stops from the subframe front crossmember. Each is secured by a nut and bolt.

8. On models with Hydrolastic suspension, it may be necessary to saw up the old subframe in order to release the Hydrolastic valve connector assemblies from the subframe rear crossmember, if the retaining nuts are seized. It should then be possible to slacken off the nuts with the assemblies secure in a vice. A spark plug socket spanner fits these nuts.

9. When changing over the Hydrolastic displacer unit, ensure that the plastic sleeves at the hose apertures are also changed over. These are secured by three crosshead screws.

Brakes

INTRODUCTION . . . . [1]

Several different braking systems have been used on the Mini range including drum brakes on all four wheels, disc front/drum rear, single circuit, dual-circuit, with or without servo assistance, also pressure differential and inertia valves to limit the braking effort at the rear wheels. The dual-circuit systems also take differing forms, some being split front/rear and others being split diagonally.

Models fitted with a dual-circuit braking system have an additional Pressure Differential Warning Actuator (PDWA) in the hydraulic circuit. This may be either a separate unit or it may be incorporated in the master cylinder, but whichever type is fitted,it operates a warning light whenever there is a loss of pressure in one of the dual systems.

All these systems are described in this chapter, and it is essential that you are familiar with the system fitted to your particular car, especially when bleeding the braking system.

Early drum type front brakes are the leading and trailing shoe type but later models (from 1964) have twin leading shoes operated by two brake cylinders per wheel. Disc front brakes have self-adjusting twin piston calipers, and the rear brakes on all models are leading and trailing shoe drum type.

Early front drum brakes have one adjuster but later models have two adjusters per wheel, and the rear drum brakes have one adjuster per wheel – see ROUTINE MAINTENANCE, under Brakes. All models have a rear brake pressure limiting valve or inertia valve which restricts the pressure to the rear brakes under conditions of heavy braking, to limit the tendency of the rear wheels to lock.

The handbrake is cable operated on the rear brakes only and can be adjusted to compensate for wear and cable stretch.

Apart from the inertia valve and the vacuum servo, all the components described in this chapter can be overhauled by the experienced DIY mechanic.

NOTE:Great care should be taken to avoid brake fluid coming into contact with the paintwork as it is a very efficient paint stripper. If brake fluid is accidentally spilt on the paintwork it should be washed off as quickly as possible with copious amounts of soapy water.

Brake pad and lining materials contain asbestos and care should be taken to avoid any brake dust becoming airborne where it will be inhaled and could cause illness. Any asbestos dust on the skin should be washed off as soon as possible.

TOOLS & EQUIPMENT . . . . [2]

Other than those tools itemised under Basic Tools & Equipment in BASIC PROCEDURES, the following equipment will be required in order to carry out some of the operations detailed in this chapter:
- Universal brake spanner – necessary for adjusting the front and rear brakes and sometimes required when removing the brake drums.
- Brake hose clamp – for preventing fluid loss whenever opening the brake fluid system.
- Approximatey 18 inches of narrow section plastic or rubber tubing – for bleeding the brake hydraulic system.
- Clean jar – into which the old brake fluid can be drained.
- Dial test indicator gauge (DTI) – for the accurately checking the 'run-out' on front brake discs.

FRONT BRAKE SHOE REPLACEMENT . . . . . . [3]

The procedure detailed below refers to the two leading shoe type brake but with the exception of the handbrake mechanism, refer to the section dealing with Rear Brake Shoe Replacement when changing early type shoes (Fig.L:1).
1. Slacken the wheel nuts, raise and support the front of the car – see BASIC PROCEDURES, and remove the front wheels.
2. Slacken off the brake shoe adjusters – see ROUTINE MAINTENANCE. Remove the two brake drum securing screws (Fig.L:2) and withdraw the brake drum.
3. Where shoe steady springs are fitted at the wheel cylinder end of the brake shoes, release the springs from the wheel cylinder pistons. These may be omitted on some models.
4. Lever the leading edges of the brake shoes away from the wheel cylinders, and the trailing edges away from the brake shoe adjusters, and remove both brake shoes as an assembly together with their return springs (Fig.L:3).
5. Fit an elastic band or suitable clamp over the wheel cylinders to retain their pistons in position.
6. Clean out all dirt and lining dust from the brake drum and backplate, using a soft brush and methylated spirit. Check for any signs of oil, grease or brake fluid contamination. If any of these are present, the cause must be established and dealt with before fitting new brake shoes. Grease or oil can be cleaned off with petrol or paraffin; brake fluid should be removed using

methylated spirits.

7. Check that the brake shoe adjusters turn freely in the backplate. Apply a small amount of high melting point grease to the adjuster spindles, also, sparingly to the raised brake shoe support pads on the backplate.

8. Remove the elastic band or clamp from each wheel cylinder. Assemble the return springs to the new brake shoes, ensuring that they are engaged in the correct holes in the shoe webs (Fig.L:3). Also ensure that the shoes are correctly positioned.

9. Lever the shoes into position over the adjuster pegs and the wheel cylinder slots, then fit the shoe steady springs, where applicable.

10. When correctly located, the shoes should be positioned with the toe (end at which the greatest portion of web platform is exposed) engaged in the wheel cylinder piston.

11. Check that both shoes are correctly seated, and that the brake adjusters are in the fully released position, then install the brake drum.

12. Finally, adjust the brake shoes as detailed in ROUTINE MAINTENANCE.

FRONT BRAKE PAD REPLACEMENT . . . . [4]

On models with disc front brakes, the brake pads are replaced as follows:

1. Slacken the wheel nuts, raise and support the front of the car – see BASIC PROCEDURES and remove both front wheels.

2. Straighten the legs of the pad retaining pins, depress the pad anti-rattle springs and withdraw the two pins from the caliper (Fig.L:5). Remove the anti-rattle springs.

3. Withdraw the brake pads and anti-squeal shims from the caliper, using long-nosed pliers, if necessary.

4. Clean all dust, dirt, etc., from the caliper recess and inspect the piston dust covers for any signs of damage. Also examine the brake disc for any signs of damage or excessive wear. Wear on one side may indicate that one of the caliper pistons is seized, in which case, the caliper should be overhauled.

5. Rotate the brake disc by hand and remove all rust from around the edge of the disc with a scraper. Also scrape any dirt or deposits from the pad locating surfaces in the caliper.

6. Press each of the caliper pistons back into their cylinder using a tyre lever or other flat piece of metal. Lever against the hub of the brake disc during this operation, not the outside edge of the disc. The fluid level in the master cylinder reservoir will rise when the pistons are pressed back, and it may be necessary to syphon off excess fluid to prevent it overflowing. Alternatively, fluid can be drained off by opening the caliper bleed nipple while the piston is being pressed back, and closing it afterwards.

7. Check that the cut-away portion on each piston is positioned upwards, then fit the new brake pads and shims in the caliper. Ensure that both the pads and shims are correctly positioned, and that the pads are free to move easily in the caliper recess.

8. Fit the pad anti-rattle springs, press them down and insert the new retaining pins from the outboard side of the caliper. Splay the legs of the pins to secure them in position.

9. Depress the brake pedal several times to bring the pads into their correct working clearance with the disc – this is important.

10. Finally, when the operation has been completed at both front brakes, lower the car back onto its wheels and check the fluid level in the master cylinder reservoir.

REAR BRAKE SHOE REPLACEMENT . . . . [5]

1. Slacken the wheel nuts raise and support the rear of the car – see BASIC PROCEDURES and remove both rear road wheels.

2. Release the handbrake and slacken off the rear shoe adjuster – see ROUTINE MAINTENANCE. Remove the two brake drum securing screws and withdraw the brake drum.

3. Release the brake shoes from the adjuster wedges and then from the wheel cylinder (Fig.L:6). Disengage the handbrake operating lever from the shoes and remove the brake shoes together with their return springs.

4. Fit an elastic band or suitable clamp over the wheel cylinder to retain the pistons in position.

5. Clean out all dirt and lining dust from the brake drum and backplate using a soft brush and methylated spirit. Check for any signs of oil, grease or brake fluid contamination. If any of these are present, the cause must be established and dealt with before fitting new brake shoes. Grease or oil can be cleaned off with petrol or paraffin; brake fluid should be removed using methylated spirits.

6. Check that the brake shoe adjuster spindle turns freely in the backplate, and that the adjuster wedges are free to slide in the adjuster body. Apply a small amount of high melting point grease to the adjuster spindle threads, the adjuster wedges, the support points on the tips of the new brake shoes, and sparingly to the raised brake shoe support pads on the backplate.

7. Before fitting the brake shoes, check that the handbrake operating lever is free to pivot on its link, and apply a small amount of grease around the pivot point.

8. If required, the link and lever can be removed from the backplate after disconnecting the handbrake cable from the lever. Disengage the rubber dust boot from the backplate and from the lever, and remove the lever and link assembly. The assembly should not be dismantled further.

9. Remove the elastic band or clamp from the wheel cylinder. Position the new brake shoes on the backplate as shown in Fig.L:6, and fit the lower return spring. Ensure that the connecting wire between the spring coils is positioned downwards otherwise it will rub on the rear hub in use. Locate the handbrake lever in the shoes, and fit the shoes onto the wheel cylinder.

10. Fit the upper return spring between the appropriate holes in the shoe webs, and lift the shoes into position on the adjuster wedges.

11. Check that the handbrake link and lever are correctly engaged in the shoe webs, and that the mechanism operates the shoes in the correct manner, then install the brake drum.

12. Finally, adjust the brake shoes as detailed in ROUTINE MAINTENANCE.

HYDRAULIC SYSTEM OVERHAUL . . . . [6]

Overhaul of the components of the hydraulic system should always be carried out under conditions of scrupulous cleanliness. Clean all dirt and grease from the exterior of components before removal and dismantling.

After dismantling, wash all parts in commercial alcohol, methylated spirits or clean brake fluid. Do NOT use mineral based oils such as petrol, paraffin or carbon tetrachloride. Blow out all internal passages with compressed air.

Inspect pistons and cylinder bores of the master cylinder, looking for scores, ridges or corrosion pits. The unit MUST be discarded if any of these conditions are present. Calipers and wheel cylinders should also be inspected for leaks and signs of wear after dismantling. If any signs of wear are present, the unit must be replaced.

It is essential that only new seals are used when reassembling. These are normally available in the form of a repair kit containing all the necessary parts required for the overhaul of a particular unit.

All seals should be inspected carefully before fitting, even when new. Check that the sealing lips are perfectly formed, concentric with the bore of the seal, and free from 'knife edge'

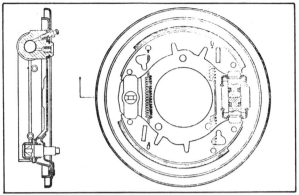

Fig. L:1 Leading & trailing shoe front brake — right-hand shown

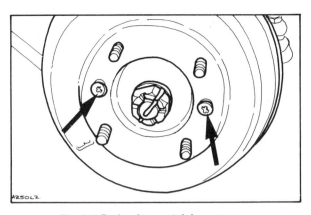

Fig. L:2 Brake drum retaining screws

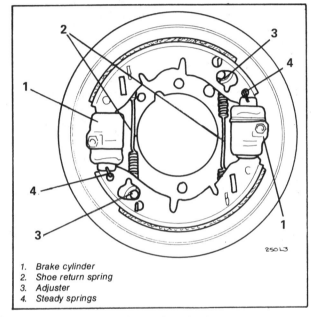

1. Brake cylinder
2. Shoe return spring
3. Adjuster
4. Steady springs

Fig. L:3 Layout of front drum brake components

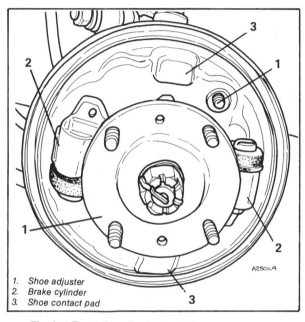

1. Shoe adjuster
2. Brake cylinder
3. Shoe contact pad

Fig. L:4 Front drum brake backplate components

1. Pad retaining pins
2. Anti-rattle springs
3. Brake pads & shims

Fig. L:5 Removing front disc brake pads

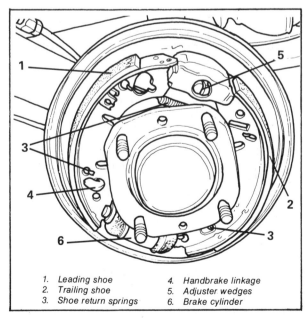

1. Leading shoe
2. Trailing shoe
3. Shoe return springs
4. Handbrake linkage
5. Adjuster wedges
6. Brake cylinder

Fig. L:6 Layout of rear brake components

cuts, surface blemishes or marks. Any seal which does not appear perfect, no matter how minute the blemish may appear to be, should be discarded.

Blocking the Hydraulic System

Whenever components are disconnected from the brake hydraulic circuit, the system will rapidly empty unless measures are taken to prevent it. An effective way of doing this is to block the top of the brake fluid reservoir by wrapping a piece of plastic sheet around the reservoir cap and refitting it. This will form an effective seal which will stop the fluid from escaping from any disconnected union.

Alternatively, a special brake pipe clamp can be used to pinch a flexible hydraulic hose to prevent fluid loss (Fig.L:10).

Such clamps are available under the Girling name from car accessory shops. Any brake pipe unions that have been disconnected should be temporarily plugged to prevent seepage, as well as to stop the ingress of dirt.

Note that whatever method is used to stop the system draining, it is essential that the reservoir is unblocked and pipes unclamped after the operation has been completed.

BLEEDING THE HYDRAULIC SYSTEM .... [7]

The fluid level in the brake master cylinder must be maintained at a reasonable level throughout the bleeding operation as, if allowed to drop excessively, air may be drawn into the system. Use only fresh hydraulic fluid of the correct specification – see TECHNICAL DATA.

Never re-use fluid which has already been passed through the system. Take care when topping up the master cylinder with fluid since it is an effective paint stripper, and any spilt on the bodywork should be washed off with soapy water immediately.

Note that an assistant will be needed to operate the brake pedal during the bleeding operation.
1.   The vehicle should be on level ground when bleeding the brakes, not up at one side or end.
2.   On models fitted with drum brakes all round, all four brakes should be correctly adjusted, and the handbrake should be 'off'. Cars with disc front brakes should have the rear drum brakes adjusted and the handbrake 'off' – see ROUTINE MAINTENANCE.
3.   Remove the cap and top up the master cylinder reservoir, making sure both chambers on tandem cylinders, are topped up with the recommended fluid. Note that the fluid level should be topped up regularly during the bleeding operations.
4.   Clean all the brake bleed nipples and attach a bleed tube to the first nipple to be bled – see Fig.L:8. Each of the alternative systems has a different sequence of bleeding which must be followed carefully (Fig.L:9).
5.   Immerse the other end of the tube in a clean jar containing a small quantity of clean brake fluid.

Throughout the bleeding operation, the end of the tube must remain immersed in this fluid.
6.   Slacken the bleed nipple approximately half a turn and then depress the brake pedal fully, allowing it to return to the fully released position. Brake fluid and/or air should have been pumped into the jar. If not, slacken the bleed nipple further until fluid and/or air can be pumped into the jar.
7.   Continue depressing the brake pedal, pausing briefly (about three seconds) after each stroke, until the fluid coming from the bleed tube is completely free of air bubbles and is perfectly clean.
8.   Finally with the brake pedal in the fully depressed position, close the bleed nipple. Take care not to over-tighten the nipple; tighten it only enough to seal it.
9.   Remove the bleed tube and transfer it to the next nipple to be bled, see Figs. L:8 & L:9.
10.   Repeat the bleeding operation as previously described on

each of the remaining nipples.
NOTE:If only one part of a split system has been disturbed, it will only be necessary to bleed that half of the system.
11.   Top up the master cylinder reservoir with the correct brake fluid and replace the cap, after first checking that the vent hole in it is clear. Do not fill the reservoir above the MAX mark on the side.
12.   Check the operation of the brakes. If, after bleeding, the brake pedal is still 'spongy', or goes right down to the floor, this indicates that air is still present in the system, and the bleeding operation must be repeated.

If subsequent attempts at bleeding still fail to produce a satisfactory result, the system should be checked for leaks, as air is obviously being drawn into the system.

BRAKE PIPES & HOSES .... [8]

Brake pipes and hoses should be inspected for corrosion and leakage , and should be replaced if at all suspect. Consideration should be given to replacing all the flexible hoses as a matter of course every 3 years or 36,000 miles. If the pipes come loose from their clips they may vibrate and fatigue fracturing may result. Brake pipes rust especially between the car body and the pipe, and should have any mud washed off to aid inspection. When fitting a new pipe or replacing an old fitting, the union nuts should be tightened to a torque of approximately 1,1 kg m (8 lb ft). Take care not to overtighten the nut or the fitting will distort and leak. Use only short spanners to avoid the risk of damage.

Before reconnecting a pipe or hose union, ensure that both sides of the connection are clean, and free from grit, which will prevent the joint from seating.

Whenever a hydraulic fitting is disturbed, the brake system should be bled as described previously.

FRONT BRAKE CYLINDER .... [9]
Removal (Fig.L:11)

1.   Slacken the wheel nuts raise and support the front of the car – see BASIC PROCEDURES and remove the front wheel(s).
2.   Clean all road dirt from the brake back plate and bridging pipe unions at the rear of the brake cylinders, using a wire brush.
3.   Block the hydraulic system, either at the reservoir, or with a clamp on the flexible pipe as detailed previously.
4.   Remove the brake shoes as detailed previously.
5.   Disconnect the bridging pipe from the appropriate hydraulic cylinder and plug the pipe end to prevent loss of fluid and the ingress of dirt.
6.   If removing the front cylinder, slacken the brake hose at the back of the cylinder. If removing the rear cylinder, unscrew the bleed valve from the back of the cylinder.
7.   Remove the two bolts securing the cylinder to the backplate, and detach the cylinder together with its gasket. In the case of the front cylinder, pull it through the backplate and unscrew the cylinder from the brake hose. Plug the hose end to prevent loss of fluid.

Installation
Installation is a straight reversal of the removal procedure but the following points should be noted:
1.   Always use a new gasket between the brake cylinder and the backplate, taking care to remove all traces of the old gasket from the backplate and brake cylinder flanges beforehand.
2.   After reassembly, remove the brake pipe clamp from the flexible hose. Adjust and then bleed the brakes and check brake operation.
NOTE:When reconnecting the bridging pipe to the cylinders,

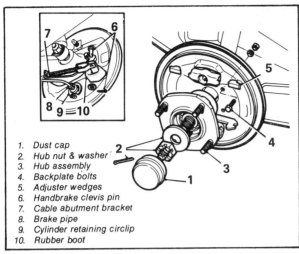

1. Dust cap
2. Hub nut & washer
3. Hub assembly
4. Backplate bolts
5. Adjuster wedges
6. Handbrake clevis pin
7. Cable abutment bracket
8. Brake pipe
9. Cylinder retaining circlip
10. Rubber boot

Fig. L:7 Exploded view of rear brake components

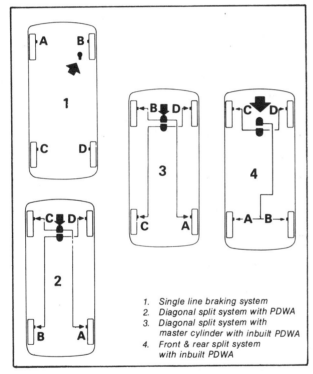

1. Single line braking system
2. Diagonal split system with PDWA
3. Diagonal split system with master cylinder with inbuilt PDWA
4. Front & rear split system with inbuilt PDWA

Fig. L:9 Sequence for bleeding hydraulic system

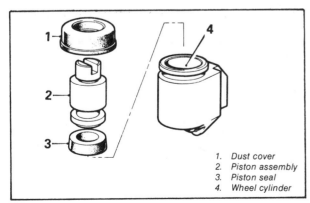

1. Dust cover
2. Piston assembly
3. Piston seal
4. Wheel cylinder

Fig. L:12 Exploded view of brake cylinder components

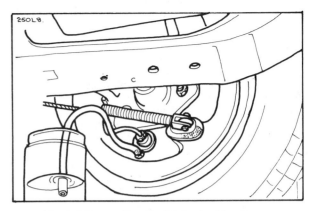

Fig. L:8 Connecting jar & tube for bleeding

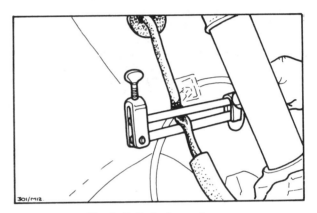

Fig. L:10 Brake hose clamp

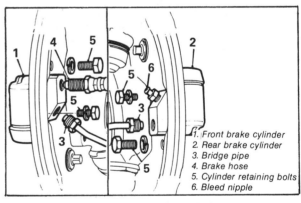

1. Front brake cylinder
2. Rear brake cylinder
3. Bridge pipe
4. Brake hose
5. Cylinder retaining bolts
6. Bleed nipple

Fig. L:11 Exploded view of brake cylinder attachments

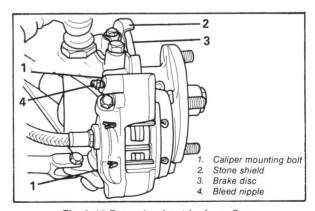

1. Caliper mounting bolt
2. Stone shield
3. Brake disc
4. Bleed nipple

Fig. L:13 Removing front brake caliper

connect the pipe unions first, then bolt the cylinder in position. This will avoid the chances of cross threading the unions.

Seal Replacement (Fig.L:12)

The brake cylinders need not be removed from the backplate to inspect or overhaul them. Removal is only necessary when the cylinder must be replaced due to wear or damage.

To overhaul a brake cylinder, first remove the brake drum and brake shoes as detailed earlier. Clean all dirt and brake dust from the exterior of the cylinder and the surrounding area using a brush and methylated spirit.

Detach the rubber cover from the end of the wheel cylinder and withdraw the piston, complete with seal, from the cylinder bore. Remove the rubber seal from the piston.

Clean and inspect the components of the wheel cylinder.

If the pistons and cylinders are in good condition, reassemble the cylinder as follows:

Lubricate the pistons, piston seals and the cylinder bores with clean brake fluid and then fit the new seal to the piston with its flat face towards the slotted outer end of the piston.

Place the piston into the cylinder bore, taking great care to avoid damaging the seal lip in the process. Fit the rubber cover over the end of the piston, making sure that the outer part is properly located in the groove around the cylinder edge.

Refit the brake shoes and brake drum, then reconnect the brake pipes to the wheel cylinders if disconnected. Remove the brake pipe clamp from the flexible hose and bleed the hydraulic circuit.

FRONT BRAKE CALIPER .... [10]
Removal (Fig.L:13)

1.   Slacken the wheel nuts, raise and support the front of the car – see BASIC PROCEDURES and remove the front wheels.
2.   If the caliper is being removed for overhaul, remove the brake pads as detailed previously, then depress the brake pedal to move the caliper pistons outwards from their wheel cylinders and thus facilitating removal of the pistons later.
3.   Remove the two bolts securing the brake caliper to the swivel hub and slide the caliper assembly off the brake disc.
4.   Unscrew the caliper from the brake hose and cap the hose end to prevent loss of fluid. If the caliper is being removed only for access to an adjacent component, do not disconnect the flexible hose but suspend the caliper from a suitable point on the suspension to avoid straining the hose.

Installation

Installation is a reversal of the removal procedure, with special attention to the following points:
a)   If the caliper was completely removed from the car, screw it onto the brake hose before attaching it to the swivel hub.
b)   Ensure that the brake hose is positioned so that it is not twisted and will not foul the body or suspension components during steering and suspension movement.
c)   Tighten the caliper mounting bolts to their specified torque – see TECHNICAL DATA.
d)   If disconnected, finally tighten the brake hose at the caliper connection once the caliper is bolted in position.
e)   If the brake pads were removed, refit them in the caliper as detailed previously.
f)   If the hydraulic system has been disconnected, bleed the hydraulic circuit.

Caliper Overhaul (Fig.L:14)

The caliper must be removed from the car to allow overhaul.
1.   Thoroughly clean the outside of the caliper, especially around the pad recess and the cylinder bores, using a brush

and methylated spirit.
2.   Remove the pistons, one at a time, from their respective cylinder bores. Extract the dust seal and retainer from the top of the cylinder bore, and the piston seal from its groove in the cylinder bore.
NOTE:If the pistons cannot be withdrawn from the caliper by hand, either eject the pistons using compressed air from a tyre foot pump at the hose connection on the caliper, or temporarily reconnect the caliper to the hydraulic circuit and then bleed off any air before pumping the pedal to remove the pistons.

If both these methods fail, then the piston is probably corroded in the caliper and the caliper should be replaced.
3.   Clean and inspect the components of the caliper. If the cylinder bore is scored, corroded or showing signs of wear, the caliper should be replaced. If only the pistons are damaged, new pistons can be fitted.
4.   Lubricate the cylinder bores with clean brake fluid and fit a new piston seal to the groove in one of the cylinder bores. Lubricate the piston and insert it, crown first, into the bore with the cut-away at the top. Press the piston into the bore until approximately 8 mm (0.32 in) remains protruding.
5.   Fit a new dust seal into the retainer ring and lubricate the lips with clean brake fluid. Fit the seal and retainer over the piston and press them into position at the top of the cylinder bore. Press the piston fully into the bore.
6.   Assemble the other piston to the caliper in a similar manner.

FRONT BRAKE DISC .... [11]
Run-out Check

1.   Slacken the wheel nuts, raise and support the front of the car – see BASIC PROCEDURES and remove the road wheels.
2.   Mount a dial gauge so that its pointer rests on the disc face (Fig.L:15) and rotate the disc one complete revolution.
3.   The disc run-out should not exceed 0,5 mm (0.002 in).

If the run-out exceeds this figure it may be possible to minimise the effects by turning the disc round to a different position on the hub, however the only real solution is to fit a new disc.

Disc Removal

1.   Slacken the wheel nuts, raise and support the front of the car – see BASIC PROCEDURES and remove the road wheel.
2.   Undo the caliper retaining bolts, remove the caliper from the disc without disconnecting the flexible hose, and suspend it from the body or suspension, to avoid the weight straining the flexible brake hose.
3.   Remove the split pin from the hub nut, place a long bar between the wheel studs to prevent the hub from turning, then undo the hub nut and pull out the split collar (Fig.L:16).
4.   Pull the hub flange and disc assembly from the driveshaft.
NOTE:If the hub assembly cannot be pulled from the driveshaft splines it will be necessary to use a universal two legged puller – see FRONT SUSPENSION under Tools & Equipment.
5.   Clamp the disc in a vice fitted with soft jaws and undo the four disc retaining bolts.
6.   The disc can now be separated from the hub flange.

Inspection

Inspect the disc friction surface carefully. Moderate scoring is permissible, but heavy scoring or grooving, cracking or pitting of the surface, or excessive corrosion build up necessitates replacement of the disc.

Ensure that all the disc/hub mating surfaces are free from dirt, corrosion and oil or brake fluid.

Installation

1.   Make sure that the mating surfaces of the hub flange and disc are spotlessly clean, then refit the disc and tighten the four

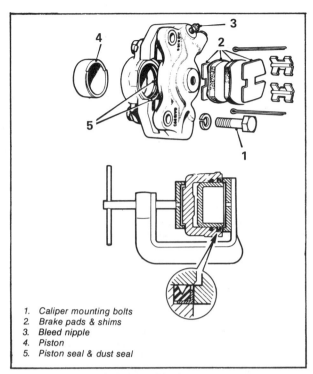

1. Caliper mounting bolts
2. Brake pads & shims
3. Bleed nipple
4. Piston
5. Piston seal & dust seal

Fig. L:14 Exploded view of brake caliper components

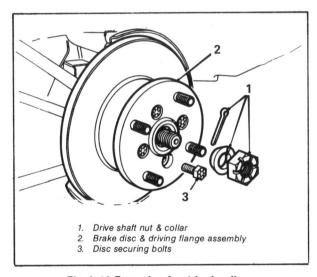

1. Drive shaft nut & collar
2. Brake disc & driving flange assembly
3. Disc securing bolts

Fig. L:16 Removing front brake disc

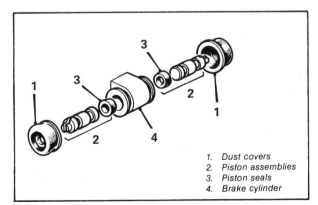

1. Dust covers
2. Piston assemblies
3. Piston seals
4. Brake cylinder

Fig. L:18 Exploded view of rear brake cylinder

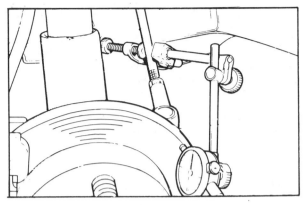

Fig. L:15 Checking brake disc run-out

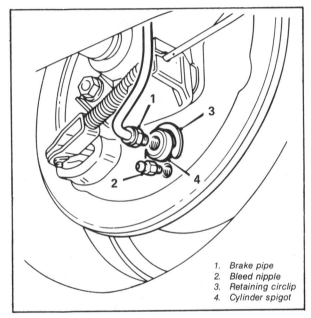

1. Brake pipe
2. Bleed nipple
3. Retaining circlip
4. Cylinder spigot

Fig. L:17 Removing rear wheel cylinder

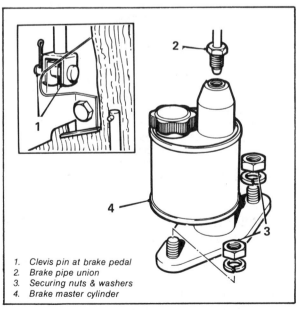

1. Clevis pin at brake pedal
2. Brake pipe union
3. Securing nuts & washers
4. Brake master cylinder

Fig. L:19 Removing brake master cylinder

retaining bolts to the specified torque – see TECHNICAL DATA.
2. Fit the hub/disc assembly to the driveshaft, refit the split collar and the hub nut.
3. Tighten the hub nut to the specified torque by the method used to undo it, – see TECHNICAL DATA – and then tighten until the split pin hole is aligned. Fit a new split pin.
4. Position the brake caliper over the disc and bolt it in position. Tighten the retaining bolts to the specified torque – see TECHNICAL DATA.
5. Refit the road wheel and lower the car to the ground. Pump the brake pedal several times to bring the pads into contact with the disc – this is important.

REAR BRAKE CYLINDER .... [12]
Replacement (Fig.L:17)

1. Remove the brake shoes from the backplate as described previously.
2. Clean all dirt from the rear of the brake backplate and brake pipe using a wire bush.
3. Unscrew the brake pipe union from the rear of the brake cylinder and pull the pipe outwards slightly so that it clears the cylinder spigot. Plug the pipe end to prevent loss of brake fluid. Ideally the system should be sealed off by clamping the flexible brake hose with a brake hose clamp (Fig.L:10).
4. Unscrew the bleed valve from the wheel cylinder. Extract the retaining circlip from the cylinder spigot protruding through the backplate and withdraw the wheel cylinder together with its gasket.
5. Install the new brake cylinder in the reverse order of removal. It will facilitate reconnecting the brake pipe, if the threads are started into the cylinder connection before the cylinder circlip is fitted. Use a new circlip to secure the cylinder, and position the circlip as shown in Fig.L:17.
6. Refit the brake shoes, then bleed the hydraulic circuit.

Overhaul
As with the front drum brakes, the cylinder piston seals can be replaced without removing the cylinder from the backplate, but again great care must be taken to ensure that all dirt, etc., is cleaned away from the exterior of the cylinder before dismantling.

With the brake shoes removed, remove the rubber dust covers from the ends of the cylinder and withdraw the piston assemblies (Fig.L:18). Remove the rubber seal from each piston.

Clean and inspect the wheel cylinder components and check that the inlet port is free from obstruction.

If the pistons and cylinder bore are in good condition, lubricate the pistons with clean brake fluid and fit a new seal to each piston. The flat face of the seal must face towards the slotted outer end of the piston. Fit a new rubber dust cover at the slotted end of the pistons. Lubricate the cylinder bore with brake fluid and insert the pistons, seal end first, into the bore. Take care to avoid damaging the seal lips as they are installed. Fit the dust covers to the ends of the cylinders, ensuring that they engage correctly in their respective grooves.

Refit the brake shoes, then bleed the hydraulic circuit.

BRAKE MASTER CYLINDER .... [13]
Removal & Installation (Single Piston Type)

First drain the brake fluid out of the master cylinder reservoir. To do this, attach a bleed tube to the bleed valve on the nearest front brake, open the bleed valve and operate the brake pedal until the master cylinder reservoir is empty. Retighten the bleed valve.

Where applicable, disconnect the heater air intake flexible tube from the heater and from the wheel arch in the engine compartment.

From inside the car, remove the split pin and withdraw the clevis pin securing the master cylinder push rod to the brake pedal (Fig.L:19).

Disconnect the hydraulic pipe union from the master cylinder. Remove the two nuts and spring washers securing the master cylinder to the bulkhead and remove the master cylinder, taking care not to spill any brake fluid on the paintwork.

Installation is a reversal of the removal procedure. When installation is complete, bleed the hydraulic circuit.

Overhaul
Remove the filler cap and drain out any remaining fluid from the reservoir. Detach the rubber boot from the end of the cylinder and slide it down the push rod. Extract the retaining circlip from the cylinder bore and remove the internal components, as shown in Fig.L:20, from the cylinder. Remove the secondary cup from the piston.

Clean and inspect the components of the master cylinder.

If the piston and bore are in good condition, lubricate the piston with clean brake fluid and assemble the secondary cup to the piston. The flat face of the seal must abut the end flange of the piston.

Fit the spring retainer into the small diameter end of the piston spring and insert the spring into the bore, large diameter first. Fit the main cup seal and the cup washer over the spring retainer. The main cup must be fitted carefully, lip edge first. Insert the piston assembly, then refit the push rod assembly and secure with the circlip. Refit the rubber boot on the end of the cylinder.

TANDEM BRAKE MASTER CYLINDER ...... [14]

Three types of tandem master cylinder are used, one with an inbuilt pressure differential warning actuator (P.D.W.A.) and two without. The three types can be identified from Figs.L:23 & L:24.

The master cylinder with the actuator, has a wiring connector to the nylon brake failure switch in the side of the cylinder.

Removal & Installation
The removal and installation procedure is similar to that already described for the single piston master cylinder. However, the fluid must be drained out of both sides of the master cylinder reservoir and this will entail repeating the draining procedure at the other front brake, or rear brake, depending on the system.

On the master cylinder shown in Fig.L:23, it is unnecessary to disconnect the cylinder push rod from the brake pedal as the cylinder can be lifted off without the push rod.

In the case of the other types of cylinder, the wiring connector is a simple push fit at the failure warning switch or at the reservoir cap.

Installation is a simple reversal of the removal procedure. When installation is completed, bleed both circuits of the split braking system as detailed previously.

Overhaul — Tandem Cylinder — Without PDWA (Fig.L:23)
1. Remove the master cylinder as described previously.
2. Blank off the pipe ends to prevent fluid loss and the ingress of dirt. Clean the exterior of the master cylinder thoroughly and mount it in a soft jawed vice with the open end of the bore uppermost.
3. Compress the piston return spring cup and hook out the 'Spirolex' ring from its groove in the primary piston, taking care not to score the walls of the piston bore (19,Fig.L:23).
4. Extract the circlip from the piston bore using circlip pliers.
5. Insert the blade of a screwdriver into the cylinder bore and

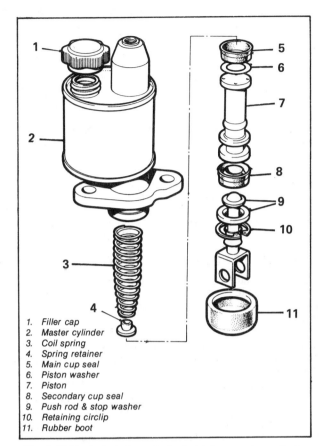

1. Filler cap
2. Master cylinder
3. Coil spring
4. Spring retainer
5. Main cup seal
6. Piston washer
7. Piston
8. Secondary cup seal
9. Push rod & stop washer
10. Retaining circlip
11. Rubber boot

Fig. L:20 Exploded view of single piston master cylinder

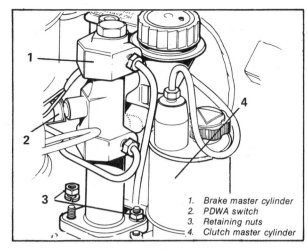

1. Brake master cylinder
2. PDWA switch
3. Retaining nuts
4. Clutch master cylinder

Fig. L:21 Tandem master cylinder with inbuilt PDWA

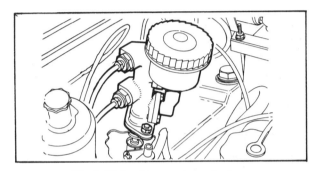

Fig. L:22 Tandem master cylinder

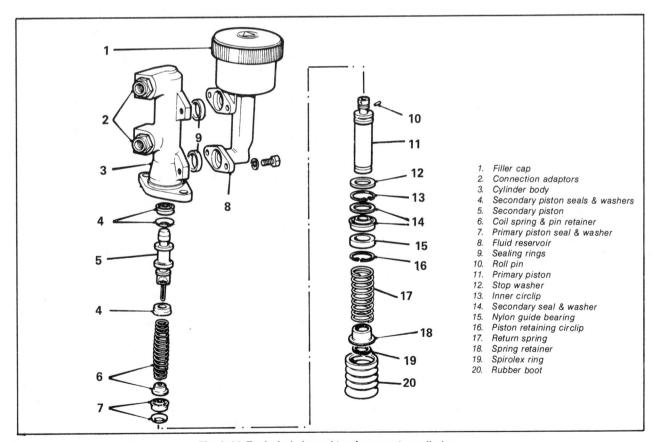

1. Filler cap
2. Connection adaptors
3. Cylinder body
4. Secondary piston seals & washers
5. Secondary piston
6. Coil spring & pin retainer
7. Primary piston seal & washer
8. Fluid reservoir
9. Sealing rings
10. Roll pin
11. Primary piston
12. Stop washer
13. Inner circlip
14. Secondary seal & washer
15. Nylon guide bearing
16. Piston retaining circlip
17. Return spring
18. Spring retainer
19. Spirolex ring
20. Rubber boot

Fig. L:23 Exploded view of tandem master cylinder

push the piston down, then allow it to return by spring pressure. Repeat this several times until the stop washer and the secondary seal can be withdrawn from the cylinder bore.

6. Extract the inner circlip from the piston bore using circlip pliers.

7. Remove the master cylinder body from the vice and tap the open end of the bore against a piece of wood to jerk the piston assembly into a position where it can be withdrawn from the bore.

8. Slide the stop washer from the piston assembly and compress the spring positioned between the two piston assemblies until the roll pin (10,Fig.L:23) can be extracted using a small punch.

9. Note the positions of all the piston seals and washers to aid reassembly, and then remove and discard them.

10. Undo the reservoir retaining bolts and separate it from the master cylinder body. Remove the two sealing rings (9,Fig.L:23).

11. Undo the pipe adaptors and discard the copper sealing washers.

12. Examine the master cylinder components, especially the bore, check that the inlet and outlet ports are free from obstruction.

13. Clean all the parts in methylated spirit or clean brake fluid and reassemble in the reverse order of dismantling, using new seals throughout.

14. All the seals should be lubricated with clean brake fluid before fitting and the primary piston seal should be fitted, convex surface first, over the piston, and with the flat surface seated against the stop washer.

15. Fit new copper sealing washers to the pipe adaptors, reconnect the pipes and fit new sealing rings to the reservoir ports.

16. Install the master cylinder as previously described and bleed the hydraulic system in the order shown in 2,Fig.L:9.

Overhaul — Tandem Cylinder (PDWA & Later Non-PDWA Types) — Fig.L:24)

Two types of cylinder with integral PDWA switch have been fitted to the Mini, but the overhaul procedures are very similar and the different internal components are illustrated in Fig.L:24, as are the non-PDWA components.

1. Remove the master cylinder as described previously.

2. Blank off the pipe ends to prevent fluid loss and the ingress of dirt. Clean the exterior of the master cylinder thoroughly and mount it in a soft jawed vice with the push rod end of the bore uppermost.

3. Undo the two cross-head screws securing the fluid reservoir and separate it from the master cylinder body. On the non-PDWA type, tap out the roll pin.

Hook out the two sealing grommets from the master cylinder ports.

4. Peel off the rubber dust cover from the push rod end of the master cylinder body and extract the circlip using circlip pliers. Withdraw the push rod from the cylinder.

5. Insert a screwdriver in the end of the cylinder and push down the piston against the return spring. Extract the stop pin (4,Fig.L:23) with long nosed pliers.

6. Remove the cylinder from the vice and tap the end against a piece of wood until the primary and secondary pistons can be extracted. Alternatively compressed air can be used, applied through the stop pin hole, but care must be taken to cover the open end of the cylinder bore with a piece of cloth to prevent fluid being ejected.

7. On cylinder (A) only, unscrew the PDWA switch and the end plug; withdraw the spacer and the PDWA piston assembly (6,Fig.L:24).

8. Note the positions of all the seals and washers, to aid reassembly and then remove and discard them.

9. Carefully examine all the master cylinder components,

especially the piston bore. Check that the inlet and outlet ports are free from obstruction.

10. Clean all the parts in methylated spirit or clean brake fluid and reassemble in the reverse order of dismantling, using new seals throughout.

11. All the seals should be lubricated with clean brake fluid before fitting, and care must be taken to avoid turning back the lips of the piston seals as they are inserted into the bore.

12. On cylinder type (A), fit new 'O' rings to the PDWA piston assembly and new seals to the reservoir ports. Fit the end plug, using a new washer and tighten to the specified torque – see TECHNICAL DATA.

13. Position the reservoir on the cylinder body and tighten the securing screws to the specified torque – see TECHNICAL DATA, or refit the reservoir roll pin (depending on type).

14. Install the master cylinder as previously described and bleed the hydraulic system in the order shown in 3 or 4,Fig.L:9, depending on which system is fitted to your car.

PRESSURE REGULATING VALVE .... [15]

A pressure regulating valve is incorporated in the hydraulic pipe to the rear brakes to limit the pressure applied to them, and thus prevent the rear wheels locking under conditions when heavy brake applications are made.

The valve is mounted on the front crossmember of the rear sub-frame on cars with the single system (Fig.L:25) and on the engine bulkhead on later cars with the split braking system (Fig.L:27). Disconnect the three or four hydraulic pipes (depending on type) and remove the nut or bolt securing the valve to the mounting bracket on the sub-frame or bulkhead.

The valve body on the early type contains a piston and spring which can be removed once the end cap is unscrewed (Fig.L:26). If the piston and valve bore are in good condition, the valve can be reassembled after fitting new seals to the piston. Also use a new sealing washer at the end cap. The later type (Fig.L:27) is a sealed unit and cannot be overhauled.

INERTIA VALVE .... [16]

On models with a dual-circuit braking system, an inertia valve is fitted in the fluid pipe to the rear brakes in place of the pressure regulating valve described previously. The inertia valve is similarly located on the rear sub-frame and is secured in position by two bolts. The angle at which the assembly is mounted is important as this allows the steel ball inside the unit to hold the valve in the open position under normal conditions so that fluid may pass to the rear brakes. Under heavy braking however, the ball moves away from the valve which is then closed by a light spring and further pressure to the rear brakes is cut off.

When refitting the valve on the sub-frame, ensure that the 'FRONT' marking on the valve body is correctly positioned (Fig.L:28).

The valve assembly is incorporated in the unit end cap which can be unscrewed to allow the steel ball to be removed. If the unit body is in good condition, a new valve and end plug assembly can be fitted, using a new copper washer. Tighten the end plug to the specified torque – see TECHNICAL DATA.

Apart from this, the valve unit cannot be overhauled, and if faulty, a new unit should be fitted.

PDWA UNIT .... [17]

On models with a dual-circuit braking system, a Pressure Differential Warning Actuator is incorporated in the system to warn of brake failure in either of the braking circuits. On some models, the PDWA is incorporated in the master cylinder, but where a separate unit is used this replaces the three-way brake pipe connector at the right-hand side of the engine compartment.

The unit incorporates a shuttle valve piston assembly which,

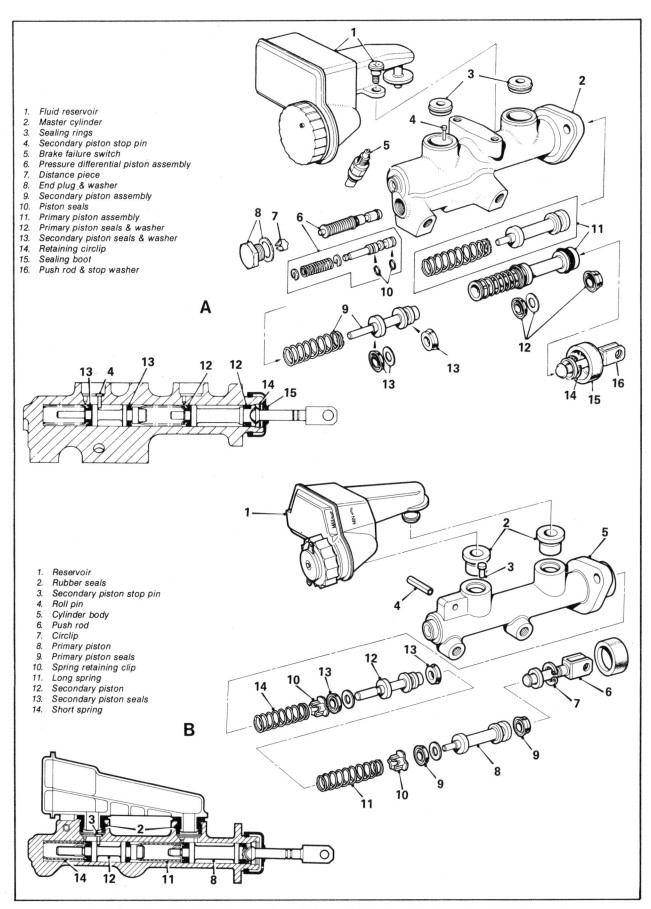

1. Fluid reservoir
2. Master cylinder
3. Sealing rings
4. Secondary piston stop pin
5. Brake failure switch
6. Pressure differential piston assembly
7. Distance piece
8. End plug & washer
9. Secondary piston assembly
10. Piston seals
11. Primary piston assembly
12. Primary piston seals & washer
13. Secondary piston seals & washer
14. Retaining circlip
15. Sealing boot
16. Push rod & stop washer

A

1. Reservoir
2. Rubber seals
3. Secondary piston stop pin
4. Roll pin
5. Cylinder body
6. Push rod
7. Circlip
8. Primary piston
9. Primary piston seals
10. Spring retaining clip
11. Long spring
12. Secondary piston
13. Secondary piston seals
14. Short spring

B

Fig. L:24 Exploded view of tandem master cylinder — PDWA type (A) & later (non-PDWA) type (B)

when moved from the central position by a pressure differential in the two braking circuits, presses upwards on the warning switch plunger and thus activates the brake failure warning light (Fig.L:29).

Resetting

The brake failure warning light on the instrument panel should be checked periodically by pressing the test-push, when the light should come on. If not, this indicates that the warning light bulb is blown.

When the brake pedal is pressed hard, the light should go out and stay out when the pedal is released. If the light does not go out, the pressure in the system in unbalanced or the PDWA unit or its electrical switch are faulty. The switch can be checked by unscrewing it from the PDWA unit and depressing the switch plunger; the warning light should then illuminate.

If, after bleeding the brake system, the warning light stays on, it may be necessary to centralise the shuttle valve piston assembly in the PDWA unit by opening one of the bleed valves and gently depressing the brake pedal unit the warning light goes out. If this does not work at the first bleed valve, repeat this procedure for one of the bleed valves in the other braking circuit.

Overhaul

If required, the PDWA unit can be dismantled for inspection after removing, by unscrewing the end plug from the unit body (Fig.L:29). Also unscrew the nylon switch, then withdraw the piston assembly.

If the piston and cylinder bore are in good condition, fit two new seals to the piston and reassemble the unit. Use a new copper washer when fitting the end plug.

BRAKE SERVO .... [18]

A vacuum servo unit is incorporated in the braking system as standard only on early 1275 GT models (prior to 1974). The servo unit is a Lockheed Type 6 and is mounted on the right-hand side of the engine compartment.

The only routine maintenance necessary is periodic cleaning of the filter element at the servo air intake – see ROUTINE MAINTENANCE.

Servo Testing

With the engine stopped, depress the brake pedal several times to evacuate the vacuum in the system. Depress the pedal, hold it in this position and start the engine. If the servo is operating correctly, the pedal will tend to fall away under foot pressure, and less pressure will be required to hold the pedal in the applied position. If no difference is felt, the system is not functioning.

Check the vacuum hose and connections for leaks or blockage before replacing the servo unit.

Removal & Installation

From beneath the right-hand front wing, pull the heater air hose off the intake unit, and then withdraw the intake unit from inside the engine compartment.

Disconnect the vacuum hose from the servo unit. Remove the securing bracket from the end of the servo unit.

Disconnect the brake pipes and plug the holes, then remove the nuts securing the servo unit to its mounting bracket and withdraw the unit.

Installation is a reversal of the removal procedure. Finally, bleed the braking system as previously described.

BRAKE PEDAL .... [19]

The brake pedal shares a common shaft with the clutch pedal, and the following procedures apply to both.

Removal

1. Pull off the flexible hose from the heater air intake (1,Fig.L:30).
2. Undo and remove the two screws located below the front edge of the parcel shelf (2,Fig.L:30).
3. Slacken, (if necessary), the heater box securing nut (3,Fig.L:30) and lower the heater for clearance to the pedal shaft.
4. Pull out the split pin (4,Fig.L:30) and remove the clevis pin (5,Fig.L:30).
5. Undo the self-locking nut on the pedal shaft, and slide out the shaft.
6. Unhook the return spring and withdraw the pedal.
7. If the pedal bearings are worn, knock or press out the old bushes and fit new ones. Press or knock in the new bushes until they are just below the end of the pedal tube and check that the pedal does not bind on the shaft.

Installation

Lightly lubricate the pedal shaft and install the brake (or clutch) pedal in the reverse order of removal.

BRAKE LIGHT SWITCH .... [20]

The brake light switch can be either hydraulic or mechanically operated. The hydraulic brake light switch is mounted on the subframe on the drivers-side (off-side), of the engine compartment. The mechanical type is located at the top of the brake pedal.

Hydraulic Type Replacement

1. Slide the rubber boot up the wires and disconnect the terminals from the switch.
2. Unscrew the switch from the brake pipe adaptor, and screw in the new switch as quickly as possible to prevent unnecessary fluid loss.
3. Reconnect the two wires and slide the rubber boot down into position on the switch.
4. Bleed the braking system as previously described.

Mechanical Type Replacement

1. Disconnect the two terminals from the switch above the brake pedal.
2. Unscrew the brake light switch locknut from its mounting bracket and manoeuvre the switch from under the fascia assembly.
3. Refit the switch in the reverse order of removal. Adjust the locknut so that there is approximately 6,5 mm (0.25 in) of brake pedal travel before the brake lights operate.

HANDBRAKE LEVER & CABLE(S) .... [21]

Depending on whether the early twin cable system is fitted, with both cables coming through the floor up to the lever, or the later system with a single cable to the lever, different types of lever will be fitted. However, the removal and installation procedures are almost identical.

Removal — Handbrake Lever

1. Chock the wheels and release the handbrake.
2. Lift up the carpet at the base of the lever.
3. Twin cables – hold the hexagonal ferrule on the end of the each cable with an open ended spanner, and undo the adjusting nuts (1,Fig.L:32).
Single cable – Slacken the locknut (2,Fig.L:33), and undo the front cable from the adjusting nut (1,Fig.L:33).
Withdraw the cable(s) from the lever assembly.
4. Undo the two nuts and bolts retaining the handbrake lever to the floor mounting brackets (4,Figs.L:32 & 33), and remove the lever from the car.

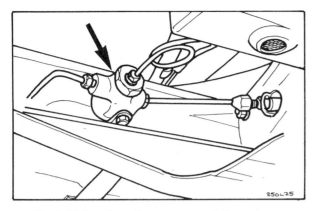

Fig. L:25 Location of pressure regulating valve

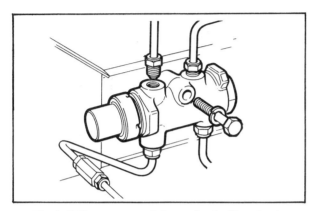

Fig. L:27 Pressure regulating valve (split system)

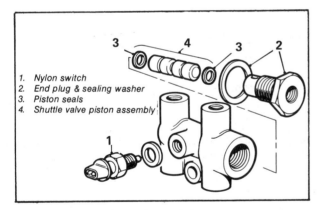

1. Nylon switch
2. End plug & sealing washer
3. Piston seals
4. Shuttle valve piston assembly

Fig. L:29 Exploded view of PDWA components

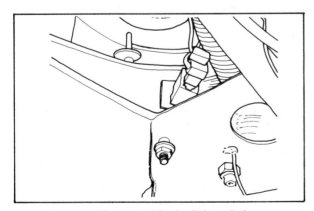

Fig. L:31 Mechanical brake light switch

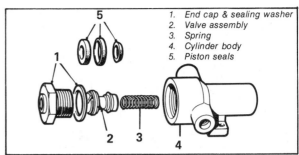

1. End cap & sealing washer
2. Valve assembly
3. Spring
4. Cylinder body
5. Piston seals

Fig. L:26 Exploded view of pressure regulating valve (single system)

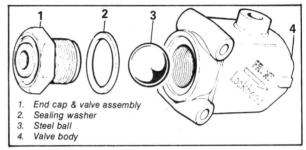

1. End cap & valve assembly
2. Sealing washer
3. Steel ball
4. Valve body

Fig. L:28 Exploded view of inertia valve

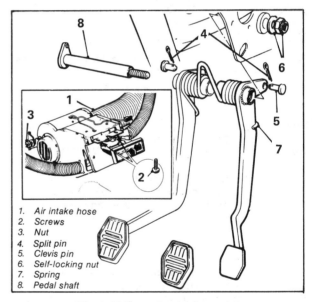

1. Air intake hose
2. Screws
3. Nut
4. Split pin
5. Clevis pin
6. Self-locking nut
7. Spring
8. Pedal shaft

Fig. L:30 Removing brake pedal

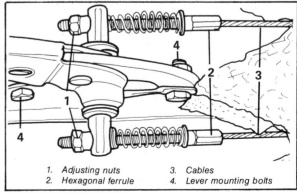

1. Adjusting nuts
2. Hexagonal ferrule
3. Cables
4. Lever mounting bolts

Fig. L:32 Handbrake lever mounting — early type

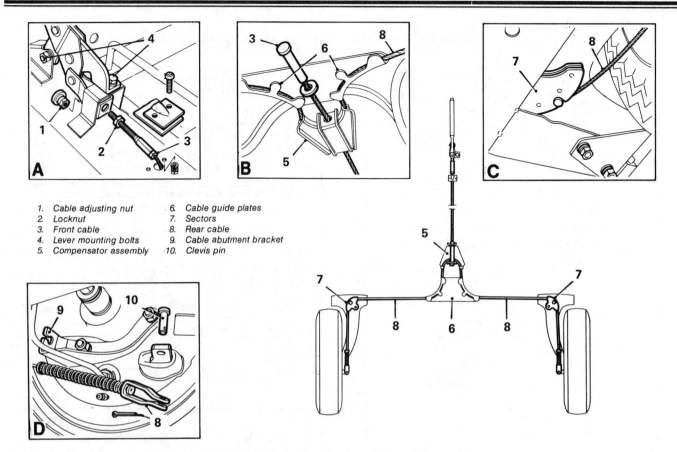

1. Cable adjusting nut
2. Locknut
3. Front cable
4. Lever mounting bolts
5. Compensator assembly
6. Cable guide plates
7. Sectors
8. Rear cable
9. Cable abutment bracket
10. Clevis pin

Fig. L:33 Layout of handbrake cables — later models

Installation

Install the handbrake lever in the reverse order of removal, and adjust the cables as described in ROUTINE MAINTENANCE.

Replacement — Handbrake Cable

Later models have a primary and secondary cable handbrake linkage which incorporates a separate front and rear cable, as opposed to the twin front-to-rear cable system used on early models.

Separate Cables — Early Models

With this system, either of the two cables can be replaced separately without disturbing the other one.

With the handbrake lever fully released, screw the cable adjustment nuts off the front end of the cable at the lever trunnion. Remove the cable guide plate located in the centre of the floor between the front seats.

Raise and support the rear of the car – see BASIC PROCEDURES. Remove the appropriate rear wheel. Draw the cable through the floor pan from underneath the car and release it from the guide channel on the sub-frame front crossmember. Lever back the corners of the flange at the pivotting sector on the rear radius arm and release the cable from the sector.

Draw the cable through the aperture in the sub-frame towards the outside.

Remove the split pin and clevis pin securing the rear end of the cable to the handbrake lever at the brake backplate. Release the cable from the abutment bracket at the backplate and remove it from the car.

Install the new cable in the reverse order of removing the old one. Nip the corners of the sector flange to hold the cable in position. Also ensure that the guide channel, section pivot and operating lever clevis pin are adequately lubricated with high

melting point grease.

Finally, adjust the handbrake cable as detailed in ROUTINE MAINTENANCE.

Primary/Secondary Cables — Later Models

With this system, the front cable must first be removed before the rear cable assembly can be detached.

With the handbrake lever fully released, screw the cable adjustment nut off the front end of the cable and detach the cable from the handbrake lever (A,Fig.L:33). Detach the cable guideplate, together with its sealing pad, from the floor pan between the front seats.

Raise and support the rear of the car - see BASIC PROCEDURES. Remove the appropriate rear wheel. Pull the front cable through the floor pan and disconnect it from the compensator assembly on the rear cable.

At each brake backplate, remove the split pin and clevis pin securing the rear end of the cable to the handbrake operating lever. Also release the cable from the abutment brackets at the backplates.

At the rear radius arms, lever back the flange at the pivotting sector corners where it retains the cable and release the cable from the sectors. Pull the cable through the aperture in the sub-frame towards the centre of the car. Lever back the retaining tags at the sub-frame guide plate and remove the rear cable complete with the compensator assembly.

Install the new cable in the reverse order of removing the old one. Nip the corners of the sector flange to hold the new cable in position. Ensure that the cable run is adequately lubricated with grease at the guide channel, sector pivots and operating lever clevis pins.

Finally, adjust the handbrake cable as detailed in ROUTINE MAINTENANCE.

Braking Problems

FAULT	CAUSE	ACTION
Excessive brake pedal travel	☐ Brakes need adjusting or replacement. ☐ Air in system. ☐ Leaking or contaminated fluid. ☐ Faulty master cylinder.	■ Adjust or renew brake shoes. ■ Bleed hydraulic system. ■ Rectify leaks/renew brake fluid ■ Fit new master cylinder.
Brake fade	☐ Incorrect pad or lining material. ☐ Old or contaminated fluid. ☐ Excessive use of brakes or car overloaded.	■ Fit new pads or shoes. ■ Renew brake fluid. ■ Check vehicle load.
Spongy brake pedal	☐ Air in hydraulic system. ☐ Shoes badly lined or distorted. ☐ Faulty hydraulic cylinder.	■ Bleed system. ■ Fit new pads or shoes. ■ Check hydraulic circuit.
Brake pedal too hard	☐ Seized wheel cylinder or caliper piston. ☐ Glazed friction material. ☐ No clearance on master cylinder operating rod.	■ Replace seized component. ■ Fit new shoes/pads. ■ Adjust push rod if possible.
Brake pedal requires pumping or pedal sinks to floor	☐ Brakes wrongly adjusted. ☐ Air in hydraulic system. ☐ Fluid leak from component or brake pipe. ☐ Loss of fluid from master cylinder. ☐ Seized caliper piston.	■ Adjust brakes. ■ Bleed system. ■ Check hydraulic circuit and replace parts as necessary. ■ Fit new master cylinder ■ Replace caliper.
Brakes grab when applied	☐ Contaminated friction material. ☐ Wrong linings fitted. ☐ Scored drums or discs. ☐ Rusty drums or discs.	■ Replace pads or shoes. ■ Fit correct linings ■ Fit new drum or disc. ■ Clean or replace drums or discs.
Brake squeal	☐ Worn retaining pins (disc). ☐ Faulty or incorrectly fitted damping shims or shoe retaining clips. ☐ Dust in drum. ☐ Loose backplate or caliper. ☐ Linings contaminated with brake fluid or hub grease.	■ Fit new pins. ■ Fit new shims or clips or refit correctly. ■ Remove dust from drums/shoe. ■ Tighten caliper or backplate. ■ Replace leaking cylinder and contaminated shoes or pads.

Brake judder	☐ Distorted discs or drums.	■ Replace discs or drums.
	☐ No clearance at master cylinder operating rod.	■ Adjust rod if possible.
	☐ Shoe tension springs either broken or weak.	■ Replace tension springs.
	☐ Wheel cylinder or caliper piston seizing.	■ Fit new caliper or cylinder.
	☐ Faulty self-adjusting mechanism.	■ Check mechanism.
	☐ Seized handbrake mechanism.	■ Check handbrake operation.

Brake pull to one side	☐ Contaminated friction material on one side (grease, oil or brake fluid).	■ Replace shoes/pads in axle sets.
	☐ Loose backplate.	■ Tighten backplate.
	☐ Seized cylinder.	■ Replace seized cylinder.
	☐ Faulty suspension or steering.	■ Check suspension and steering.

Handbrake ineffective	☐ Worn rear shoes or pads.	■ Fit new pads/shoes.
	☐ Brakes require adjusting.	■ Adjust brakes.
	☐ Faulty handbrake linkage.	■ Check linkage and operating mechanism.
	☐ Cable or rod requires adjustment.	■ Adjust cable or rod.

| **Servo (where fitted) late in operation** | ☐ Blocked filter. | ■ Clean or replace filter. |
| | ☐ Bad vacuum sealing or restricted air inlet. | ■ Tighten vacuum hose connections and check hoses. |

| **Loss of servo action** | ☐ Air leak in servo - vacuum low. | ■ Replace servo |

| **Loss of fluid – general** | ☐ Wheel cylinder or caliper seal failure. | ■ Replace wheel cylinder/caliper. |
| | ☐ Damaged or corroded fluid pipes. | ■ Inspect and fit new pipes. |

General Electrics

INTRODUCTION . . . . [1]

The Mini range has a very simple electrical system with no sophisticated 'gadgets' and is therefore ideally suited to the DIY mechanic with little electrical experience.

Minis built before September 1969 have a Positive (+) earth electrical system, and those built after this date have a Negative (-) earth system.

All the electrical components are of conventional design and fitting and are easily accessible. The fuses are located at the rear of the engine compartment, on the driver's side of the bulkhead, and the battery is mounted in a tray in the boot floor on Saloon models, under the driver's side rear seat on Estate versions and behind the passenger seat on Vans.

When working on any part of the Mini electrical system it is very important to disconnect the battery earth lead first, to avoid the possibility of damaging components or starting a fire due to a short circuit.
NOTE:Some of the circuits are 'live' even when the ignition is switched off.

The battery can be isolated from the electrical system by undoing the screw or clamp bolt holding the earth lead to the battery terminal post, and removing the clamp or terminal.

For details of checking the battery electrolyte level and concentration – see ROUTINE MAINTENANCE.

Instructions for charging the battery and for jump starting are given in BASIC PROCEDURES.

If the headlamps are removed for any reason, the alignment should be checked and adjusted if necessary – see ROUTINE MAINTENANCE.

TOOLS & EQUIPMENT . . . . [2]

In addition to the tools recommended under Tools & Equipment in BASIC PROCEDURES the following items will be required to carry out some of the operations detailed below:
- A pair of wire cutters / strippers – for making wiring repairs.
- A range of small sockets and flat bladed screwdrivers – for removing and refitting components.
- A crimping tool – for securing crimp type connectors (this may be used as an alternative to soldering).
- A soldering iron and multi-core solder – for renewing fusible links.

BULB & LAMP REPLACEMENT . . . . [3]
Headlamps (Figs.M:2 & M:3)

The headlamp may either be of the bulb type, or the sealed beam type depending on fitment. It may also incorporate the side lamp on certain models. The headlamp bulb or sealed beam unit can be easily replaced as follows:

Remove the screw securing the headlamp rim and detach the rim from the headlamp unit. On Clubman and 1275 GT models, the headlamp grille surround must be removed instead (Fig.M:1).

Remove the three headlamp rim retaining screws and detach the rim. The headlamp unit can then be withdrawn. With the sealed beam type unit, merely withdraw the three pin connector from the back of the unit and remove the lamp unit.

With the bulb type unit, withdraw the three pin connector from the rear of the lamp unit. Disengage the spring clip from the reflector lugs and withdraw the bulb from the rear of the reflector. Fit the new bulb, ensuring that the pip on the bulb flange engages the slot in the reflector. Refit the spring clip ensuring that the coils in the clip are resting on the base of the bulb and that the legs of the clip are fully engaged under the reflector lugs.

In either case, reconnect the three-pin connector and refit the lamp unit in the reverse order of removal.

Where the side lamp is incorporated in the headlamp, the bulb holder may be incorporated in the headlamp three-pin connector or may be a separate push-fit holder which locates in an aperture in the headlamp reflector. In either case, replacement of the bulb is a straight forward procedure after removing the headlamp unit as detailed above.

Whenever the headlamp unit has been disturbed the alignment should be checked at the earliest opportunity – see ROUTINE MAINTENANCE.

Headlamps — Alternative Type (Cibie)

1. Pull the bottom edge of the outer rim forwards and lift it away from the retaining lug at the top.
2. Ease the three adjusting screws (1,Fig.M:4) from their locations in the mounting plate.
3. Pull the light unit forward and disconnect the multi-connector from the bulb.
4. Pull the side lamp bulb holder (2,Fig.M:4) from the light unit and remove the unit from the car.
5. Lever the spring clips (3,Fig.M:4) outwards and withdraw the bulb.
6. Push the side lamp bulb into its holder, twist it anti-clockwise and remove it from the holder.
7. Install the bulbs in the reverse order of removal, ensuring that the adjustable bulb locator is positioned correctly (4,Fig.M:4) for use in 'keep left' countries or (5,Fig.M:4) for 'keep right' countries.
8. Check and adjust the headlamp alignment as necessary – see ROUTINE MAINTENANCE.

Direction Indicator Lamp — Front (Fig.M:5)

1. Peel back the rubber sealing flange, using the blade of a small screwdriver, and remove the chrome plated rim.
2. Peel back the inner rubber flange and remove the glass.

3. Push the bulb into the holder, turn it anti-clockwise and remove it.

4. If the bulb holder is being replaced, undo the three cross-head screws securing the bulb holder to the front wing and carefully ease the unit from the rubber moulding until the wires can be disconnected.

5. Install the bulb and holder in the reverse order of removal.

Front Indicator/Side Lamp (Fig.M:6)

1. Undo the two cross-head screws securing the lens.
2. Remove the lens and rubber gasket.
3. To remove the bulbs, push in and turn anti-clockwise.
4. To remove the lamp assembly from the body, disconnect the wiring snap connectors and undo the four nuts accessible from within the wheelarch.
5. Install the bulbs and the lamp assembly in the reverse order of removal.

Rear Lamps — Saloon (Fig.M:7)

1. Undo and remove the three cross-head screws securing the plastic lens moulding.

NOTE:These three screws are different lengths and a note should be made of their respective positions.

2. All 850 models and early 1000 models have only two bulbs in each lamp, but later models have an extra bulb for the reversing lamps.

3. Remove the appropriate bulb by pressing it into the bulb holder and twisting anti-clockwise.

NOTE:The stop/tail lamp bulb has offset retaining pins and is not interchangeable, however, the reversing lamp bulb is identical with the direction indicator bulb and can therefore be substituted in an emergency, until a replacement can be obtained.

4. If the lamp assembly is being removed from the body, open the boot lid and disconnect the wiring snap connectors.

5. Undo the retaining nuts and washers and pull the lamp and rubber gasket away from the body.

NOTE:For access to the passenger-side (near-side) lamp retaining nuts, it will be necessary to release the fuel tank strap and move the tank – see FUEL SYSTEM.

6. Install the lamp assembly and the bulbs in the reverse order of removal.

Rear Lamps — Estate, Van & Pick-Up (Fig.M:8)

Removal and installation of the lens and bulbs follows the same procedure as that described for the Saloon in the previous section.

Number Plate Lamp — Saloon (Fig.M:9)

Undo the two screws securing the lens to the lamp body and pull the lens downwards. Spring the contacts apart and withdraw the festoon bulb.

The lamp assembly is held to the boot lid by two screws (2,Fig.M:9) accessible from inside the boot lid.

Install the new bulb in the reverse order of removal, ensuring that the leads are securely connected.

Number Plate Lamp — Estate, Van & Pick-up (Fig.M:10)

1. Undo the central slotted screw and remove the lamp cover and glass.

2. Push in the bulb, twist anti-clockwise and withdraw.

3. Install the new bulb in the reverse order of removal, ensuring that the bulb makes good contact with the holder and that the rubber gasket is sealing tightly against the glass.

4. To remove the lamp assembly from the number plate mounting, undo the two nuts (2,Fig.M:10) and disconnect the wiring.

Interior Lamp (Fig.M:11)

Grip the lamp lens firmly and squeeze the sides until the securing lugs are free of the base. The bulb contacts can now be sprung apart and the festoon bulb removed.

Install the new bulb in the reverse order of removal.

Rear Fog Lamp(s)

To replace the bulb, undo the two crosshead lens retaining screws and lift off the lens and gasket. Push in the bulb, twist anti-clockwise and withdraw.

The lamp assembly is held to the rear apron of the car by two bolts. Undo these bolts and disconnect the wiring bullet connectors to remove the lamp assembly.

Installation of bulb and lamp are carried out in the reverse order of removal.

SPEEDOMETER & CABLE .... [4]

Speedometer Replacement — Central Mounting (Fig.M:12)

1. Working inside the car, undo the four screws securing the instrument shroud, disconnect the panel light switch wiring and withdraw the shroud from the fascia.

2. Undo the two screws securing the instrument panel brackets and distance pieces.

3. Working under the bonnet, remove the air cleaner assembly – see FUEL SYSTEM – remove the insulating material from the rear of the instrument and unscrew the speedometer cable.

4. Disconnect the fuel gauge wiring.

5. Pull out the warning lamp and instrument illumination bulb holders.

6. Undo the nut securing the earth lead eyelet terminal.

7. Withdraw the speedometer into the engine compartment. On later models the speedometer can be withdrawn into the passenger compartment.

8. Install the speedometer in the reverse order of removal.

Speedometer Replacement — Clubman & 1275 GT (Fig.M:13)

1. Disconnect the battery earth cable.

2. Grip both sides of the nacelle and pull it away from the fascia.

3. Remove the plastic trim strip from the top edge of the instrument assembly and undo the upper securing screw and the two side securing screws.

4. Ease the instrument pack away from the fascia until the speedometer cable can be disconnected by pressing down the release lever.

5. Disconnect the wiring multi-plug and the two wires from the tachometer (if fitted).

6. Withdraw the instrument pack from the fascia, taking care not to damage the printed circuit.

Installation

Install the speedometer in the reverse order of removal and reconnect the battery earth lead.

Speedometer Cable — Replacement

1. Disconnect the upper end of the speedometer cable as described in the appropriate speedometer replacement section above.

2. Unscrew the knurled nut at the gearbox end of the cable and withdraw the inner cable from the drive pinion (Fig.M:14).

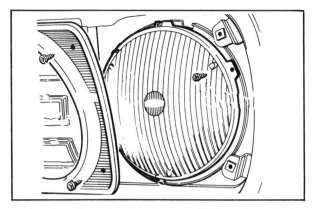

Fig. M:1 Removing headlamp — Clubman/1275 GT

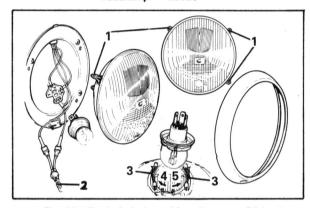

Fig. M:2 Exploded view of sealed beam headlamp — Lucas

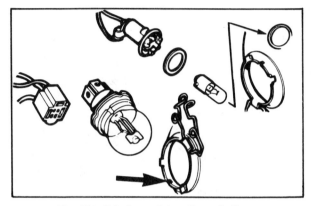

Fig. M:3 Side lamp & headlamp bulbs

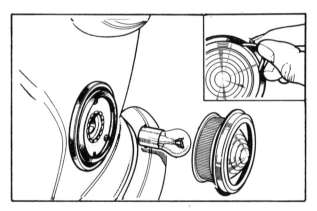

Fig. M:4 Exploded view of headlamp — Cibie

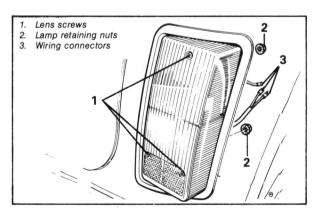

Fig. M:5 Removing direction indicator bulb

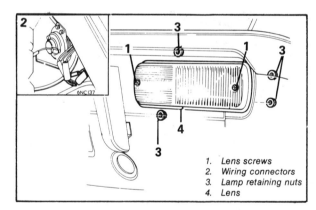

1. Lens screws
2. Wiring connectors
3. Lamp retaining nuts
4. Lens

Fig. M:6 Combined side/direction indicator lamp

1. Lens screws
2. Lamp retaining nuts
3. Wiring connectors

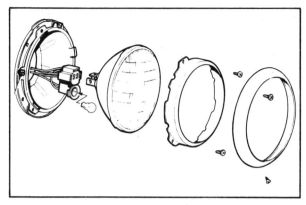

Fig. M:7 Rear lamp assembly — Saloon

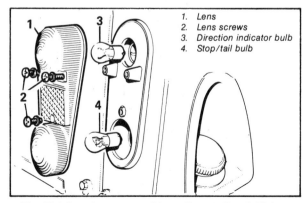

1. Lens
2. Lens screws
3. Direction indicator bulb
4. Stop/tail bulb

Fig. M:8 Rear lamp assembly — Estate, Van & Pick-up

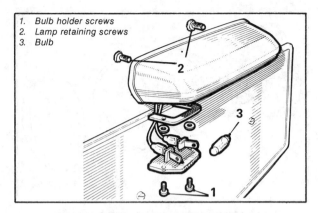

1. Bulb holder screws
2. Lamp retaining screws
3. Bulb

Fig. M:9 Number plate lamp — Saloon

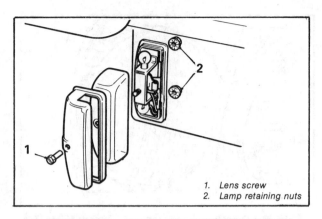

1. Lens screw
2. Lamp retaining nuts

Fig. M:10 Number plate lamp — Estate, Van & Pick-up

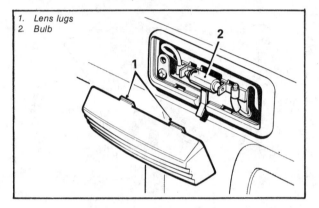

1. Lens lugs
2. Bulb

Fig. M:11 Interior lamp & lens

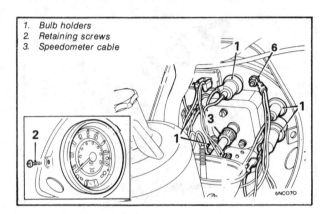

1. Bulb holders
2. Retaining screws
3. Speedometer cable

Fig. M:12 Replacing speedo — central mounting

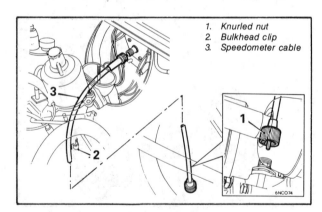

1. Knurled nut
2. Bulkhead clip
3. Speedometer cable

Fig. M:14 Speedometer cable — lower fitting

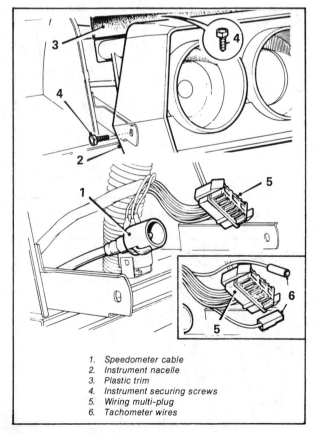

1. Speedometer cable
2. Instrument nacelle
3. Plastic trim
4. Instrument securing screws
5. Wiring multi-plug
6. Tachometer wires

Fig. M:13 Removing speedometer — Clubman/1275 GT

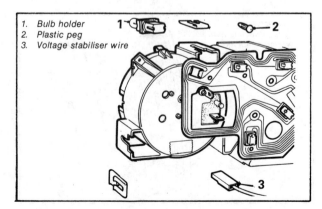

1. Bulb holder
2. Plastic peg
3. Voltage stabiliser wire

Fig. M:15 Removing tachometer — 1275 GT & Special

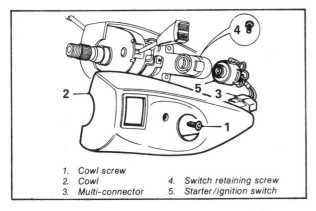

1. Cowl screw
2. Cowl
3. Multi-connector
4. Switch retaining screw
5. Starter/ignition switch

Fig. M:16 Removing starter/ignition switch

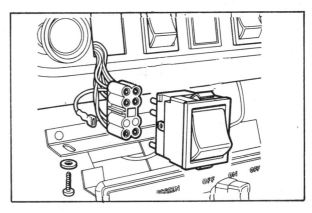

Fig. M:17 Removing rocker type panel switch

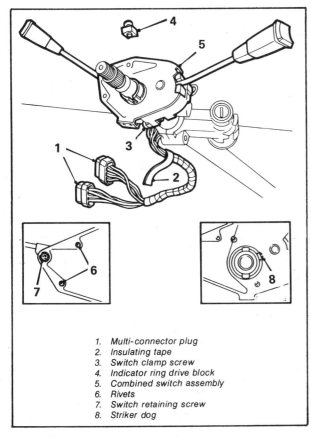

1. Multi-connector plug
2. Insulating tape
3. Switch clamp screw
4. Indicator ring drive block
5. Combined switch assembly
6. Rivets
7. Switch retaining screw
8. Striker dog

Fig. M:18 Removing steering column switches (late type)

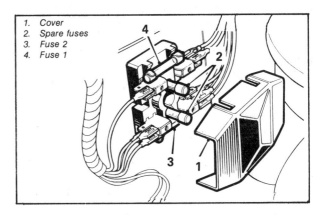

1. Cover
2. Spare fuses
3. Fuse 2
4. Fuse 1

Fig. M:19 Fuse box — Early type

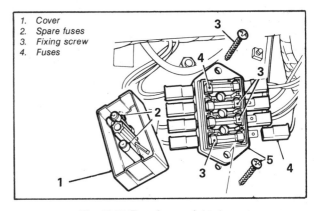

1. Cover
2. Spare fuses
3. Fixing screw
4. Fuses

Fig. M:20 Fuse box — later type

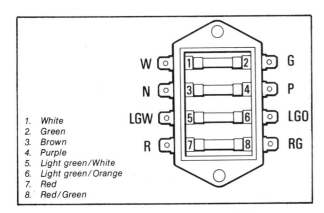

1. White
2. Green
3. Brown
4. Purple
5. Light green/White
6. Light green/Orange
7. Red
8. Red/Green

Fig. M:21 Fuse layout — late models

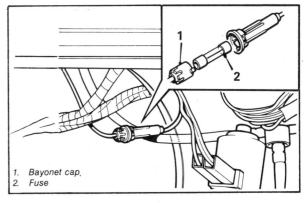

1. Bayonet cap
2. Fuse

Fig. M:22 Auxiliary in — line fuse

3. Detach the cable from the bulkhead clip and pull the upper end through the bulkhead grommet (where applicable).
4. Install the cable in the reverse order of removal.

TACHOMETER . . . . [5]
Replacement — 1275 GT & Special (Fig.M:15)
1. Remove the nacelle and instrument pack as described for the speedometer.
2. Unclip the bulb holder from the rear of the tachometer and prise out the two plastic pegs retaining the printed circuit.
3. Disconnect the voltage stabiliser lead and separate the tachometer from the instrument pack.
4. Installation is a reversal of the removal procedure.

SWITCHES . . . . [6]
Ignition/Starter Switch — Replacement (Fig.M:16)
1. Remove the two screws retaining the right-hand half of the cowl to the steering column and detach the right-hand cowl.
2. Disconnect the ignition/starter switch wiring multi-connector plug.
3. Remove the single screw securing the switch to the rear of the steering column lock and withdraw the switch from the lock.
4. Fit the new switch in the reverse order of removal.

Panel Switches
The switches in the central panel assembly may be of either toggle type, or rocker type on later cars. In either case, the interior heater unit must be lowered to gain access to the rear of the panel and allow the switch to be withdrawn.

Replacement
1. Slacken the nut at the rear of the heater unit.
2. Remove the two screws securing the front of the heater and lower the heater from the fascia.
3. With the toggle type switch, unscrew the switch retaining ring and withdraw the switch from the switch panel. Note the respective positions of the wires and disconnect the connectors from the switch terminals.
4. With the rocker type switch, merely push the switch out of the switch panel and disconnect the multi-connector plug from the switch (Fig.M:17).
5. Install the new switch in the reverse order of removing.

Steering Column Switches
There are three types of steering column switch, the original operating the indicators, was fitted on the right-hand side of the column with a green dome shaped warning lamp on the end. This was superseded by an indicator switch without a warning lamp but incorporating a horn push on the end, and headlamp dip/main beam switch. The third type, with two stalks, combined wipers, washers, horn, headlamp flasher, and dip/main beam switches. On later cars conforming to ISO Standards the headlamp/indicator switch position was reversed and fitted to the left-hand side of the column with the wiper switch on the right.

Replacement — Early Type
1. Remove the screws clamping the two halves of the steering column cowling together and remove the cowling.
2. Disconnect the wiring connectors located near the parcel shelf.
3. Unscrew the 'U' clamp screws from the switch and remove the clamp and switch.
4. Replace the switch in the reverse order of removal.

Replacement — Late Type (Fig.M:18)
1. Remove the screw from the bottom of the steering column cowl. Also remove the two screws securing the two halves of the cowl to the column bracket and detach the cowl.
2. Prise the hub cover from the centre of the steering wheel and remove the wheel retaining nut and lock washer.
3. Mark the steering wheel hub and the inner column to ensure correct alignment on reassembly, then withdraw the steering wheel off the inner column.
4. Disconnect the column switch wiring connectors.
5. Remove the indicator cancelling ring drive block.
6. Slacken the switch clamp screw and withdraw the switch assembly from the steering column.
7. Remove the insulating tape to separate the wiring harness of the two switches.
8. Drill out the two rivets securing the wiper/washer switch to the mounting plate.
9. Remove the screw and detach the wiper/washer switch from the direction indicator switch mounting plate.
10. Assemble and install the new switch in the reverse order of removal.
11. Ensure that the striker dog on the nylon switch centre is in line with and adjacent to the direction indicator stalk see Fig.M:18.
12. When refitting the steering wheel, align the slots in the switch bush with the steering wheel hub, ensuring that the triangle is pointing towards the horn push. Also ensure that the steering spokes are positioned symetrically with the front wheels in the straight-ahead position.
13. Set the column cowl to give a clearance of 3 mm (⅛ in) from the steering wheel hub. If necessary, slacken the steering clamp bolt and reset the position of the outer column to achieve this.

FUSES . . . . [7]
The main fuse box is mounted on the right-hand side of the engine compartment on the wing valance, and may contain either two or four fuses dependent on model year.

Early models were fitted with only two fuses (Fig.M:19). The lower fuse protects the auxiliary units, namely the interior lights and the horn, which operate without the ignition being switched on. The top fuse protects the auxiliary units which operate only when the ignition is switched on. The units connected into this circuit include the direction indicators, wiper motor, interior heater blower motor and the brake lights. In addition to the main fuse block, an in-line fuse adjacent to the wiper motor protects the side/tail lighting circuit. All these fuses are rated at 35 amps.

The later four-fuse block protects the following circuits, reading from the top (Fig.M:20).
Fuse 1-2 (17/35 A) Direction indicators & brake lights.
Fuse 3-4 (12/25 A) Headlamp flasher, brake failure warning lamp.
Fuse 5-6 (12/25 A) Screen wipers & washers.
Fuse 7-8 (8/15 A) Side/tail lamps.
An additional in-line fuse protects the interior lights and the hazard warning flashers, and another the radio when fitted (Fig.M:22).

WINDSCREEN WIPERS & WASHERS . . . . [8]
Wiper Motor Removal (Fig.M:23)
1. Disconnect the battery earth lead as a safety precaution.
2. Disconnect the wiring connector from the wiper motor. This is a simple push-fit. Also release the earth wire from the valance, where applicable.
3. Remove the wiper arms from the drive spindles.
4. Unscrew the sleeve nut securing the rack outer tubing to the motor gearbox.
5. Remove the screws securing the motor retaining strap and release the strap from the mounting bracket.

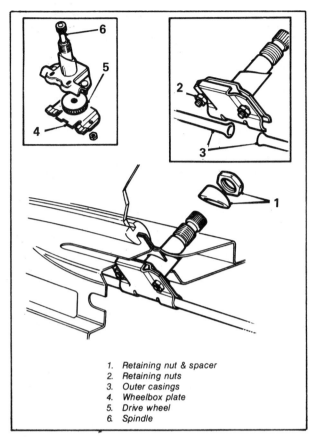

1. Retaining nut & spacer
2. Retaining nuts
3. Outer casings
4. Wheelbox plate
5. Drive wheel
6. Spindle

Fig. M:24 Exploded view of wiper wheelbox

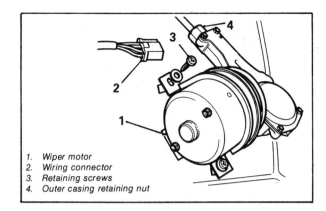

1. Wiper motor
2. Wiring connector
3. Retaining screws
4. Outer casing retaining nut

Fig. M:23 Removing wiper motor

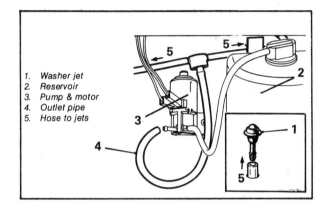

1. Washer jet
2. Reservoir
3. Pump & motor
4. Outlet pipe
5. Hose to jets

Fig. M:25 Windscreen washer pump — electric

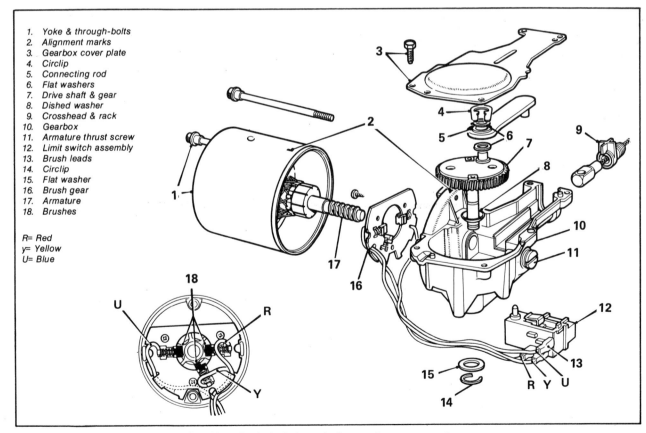

1. Yoke & through-bolts
2. Alignment marks
3. Gearbox cover plate
4. Circlip
5. Connecting rod
6. Flat washers
7. Drive shaft & gear
8. Dished washer
9. Crosshead & rack
10. Gearbox
11. Armature thrust screw
12. Limit switch assembly
13. Brush leads
14. Circlip
15. Flat washer
16. Brush gear
17. Armature
18. Brushes

R= Red
y= Yellow
U= Blue

Fig. M:26 Exploded view of wiper motor components

6. Withdraw the motor assembly, pulling the cable rack from its outer tubing.
7. If required, the wiper wheelboxes can now be removed as follows:
8. Remove the sound insulation material from the bulkhead.
9. Unscrew the retaining nut at each wiper spindle and remove the spacer (Fig.M:24).
10. Slacken the nuts clamping the wheelboxes to the rack outer tubing and release the Bundy tubing from the wheelboxes. The wheelboxes can then be removed.

Installation

Installation is a simple reversal of the removal procedure, but special attention should be paid to the following points:
a) Leave the tubing clamp nuts at the wheelboxes slack until after the cable rack has been inserted and the motor secured.
b) Ensure the cable rack is adequately lubricated before installing it in the outer tubing.
c) Ensure that the cable rack engages correctly with the wheelbox gear teeth.
d) After tightening the wheelbox clamp nuts, check the action of the wheelboxes before refitting the wiper arms.
e) When refitting the wiper arms, switch on the motor and stop it at the end of its stroke. Position the arms to give maximum wipe area and park position at the end of the stroke.

Brush Replacement (Fig.M:26)

1. Note the alignment marks on the motor yoke and gearbox casing for reassembly.
2. Unscrew the two through-bolts and withdraw the yoke and armature from the gearbox. Keep the yoke and armature clear of metallic particles which will be attracted to the pole pieces by their magnetic effect.
3. Note the respective positions of the wiring connectors at the limit switch and disconnect the brush wiring.
4. Remove the screws securing the brush gear assembly to the gearbox casing and detach the brush gear.
5. If required, the brushes can be withdrawn from their insulating plate.
6. If the main brushes (diametrically opposite) are worn down to 5 mm (0.020 in), or if the narrow section of the third brush is worn to the full width of the brush, the brushes must be renewed. If the brush springs are not satisfactory, the complete brush gear assembly should be replaced.
7. Assemble the brushes to the insulating plate and refit the plate on the gearbox casing.
8. Refit the yoke and armature, ensure that the alignment marks are adjacent.
9. Reconnect the brush leads to the limit switch, ensuring that they are refitted in their original positions.
10. Test the motor before refitting it on the car.

Washers (Manual Type) — Replacement

1. Undo the screws securing the front of the heater box to the parcel shelf, slacken the rear mounting and lower the heater for access.
2. Undo the locking ring securing the washer pump to the switch panel and withdraw it from the rear of the panel.
3. Disconnect the pipes from the pump inlet and outlet.
4. Install the washer pump in the reverse order of removal, ensuring that the pipes are connected, to the inlet and outlet, correctly.

Washers (Electric Type) — Replacement (Fig.M:25)

1. Open the bonnet and support with the stay.
2. Remove the air cleaner – see FUEL SYSTEM.
3. Disconnect the inlet and outlet pipes from the pump.
4. Disconnect the two wires from the pump terminals.
5. Undo the two pump mounting screws and remove the pump from the car.
6. Install the pump in the reverse order of removal, ensuring that the inlet and outlet pipes are connected correctly. The pump is marked with arrows indicating the direction of flow.

HORN . . . . [9]

Replacement

1. Open the bonnet and support with the stay.
2. Disconnect the wires from the horn.
3. Undo the two small nuts and spring washers securing the horn to the top edge of the front panel.
4. Remove the horn from the car.
5. Install the horn in the reverse order of removal.

Electrical Problems

FAULT	CAUSE	ACTION
No lights (or very dim)	☐ Flat or faulty battery, bad battery connections.	■ Check battery and connections.
Side and rear lights inoperative although stoplights and flashers work	☐ Fuse blown.	■ Fit correct value fuse.
One lamp fails	☐ Blown bulb. ☐ Poor bulb contact. ☐ Bad earth connection. ☐ Broken feed.	■ Fit new bulb. ■ Clean contacts. ■ Check connections. ■ Check feed.
Flasher warning bulb on or flashes twice as fast	☐ Faulty bulb or connection on front or rear of offending side.	■ Fit new bulb, make good connection.
Lights dim when idling or at low speed	☐ Loose alternator drive belt. ☐ Flat battery. ☐ Faulty charging circuit.	■ Tighten belt. ■ Check charge output and battery.
One dim light	☐ Blackened bulb. ☐ Bad earth. ☐ Tarnished reflector.	■ Fit new bulb or sealed-beam. ■ Check earth connections. ■ Clean or replace reflector.

WINDSCREEN WIPERS

FAULT	CAUSE	ACTION
Wipers do not work	☐ Blown fuse. ☐ Poor connection. ☐ Faulty switch. ☐ Faulty motor.	■ Fit new fuse of correct rating. ■ Check connections. ■ Check switch. ■ Remove and examine motor.
Motor operates slowly	☐ Excessive electrical resistance in wiper circuit. ☐ Wiper drive binding or fouling. ☐ Worn brushes.	■ Check wiper circuit. ■ Free off or reposition wiper drive. ■ Remove motor and check brushes.

HORN

FAULT	CAUSE	ACTION
Horn(s) do not work	☐ Faulty horn push. ☐ Faulty or broken connection. ☐ Faulty horn(s).	■ Replace steering column switch. ■ Check wiring continuity. ■ Replace horn(s).
Horn operates continuously	☐ Horn push shorted or stuck down.	■ Remedy cause of shorting or free-off horn push.

FUEL GAUGE

FAULT	CAUSE	ACTION
Fuel gauge not reading	☐ No fuel in tank. ☐ Sender unit to gauge cable broken or disconnected. ☐ No earth on fuel gauge or tank ☐ Supply to gauge disconnected. ☐ Gauge faulty.	■ Add fuel. ■ Reconnect or repair cable. ■ Reconnect earth or clean connections ■ Check wiring and reconnect or repair. ■ Replace gauge.
Fuel gauge registering full	☐ Sender unit to gauge cable earthed.	■ Trace cause of earthing out and re-insulate.

Wiring Diagrams

How to use the Autodata Wiring Diagram

Autodata Wiring Diagrams are terminal diagrams without the interconnecting wires. Every electrical component is given an identifying code (e.g. **M2** = Wiper motor) which is used only for that component on any wiring diagram for any car.

The component code is shown together with graphic symbols from ISO 2575 (International Standards Organization) and DIN 40 700 (Deutsche Industrie Norm) which identify a component pictorially.

All the electrical components fitted to the car are displayed in component code alphabetical sequence. This makes identification easier and quicker. The terminals on each component are identified, where possible, by their DIN codes which identify the circuit function. The type of connection at each terminal is also shown with a special symbol.

The cable disconnected to each terminal is shown as a short line followed by an Address Code which identifies - **Destination: Terminal/Colour Size** of cable within the electrical circuit.

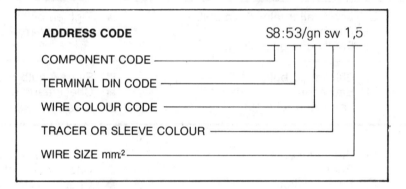

S8 the Component Code, shows the component to which the cable is connected at its other end.

| S8:53/gn sw 1,5 |

53 the Terminal Code shows the markings at the destination terminal.

| S8:**53**/gn sw 1,5 |

gn sw the Colour Code shows the cable colour(s) or alternative colour according to the key. (Note: any colour code underlined is a sleeve colour, see symbols and codes).

| S8:53/**gn sw** 1,5 |
| S8:53/gn **sw** 1,5 |

1,5 the Cable Size mm², the cable size shown relates to the cable at the destination terminal.

| S8:53/gn sw **1,5** |

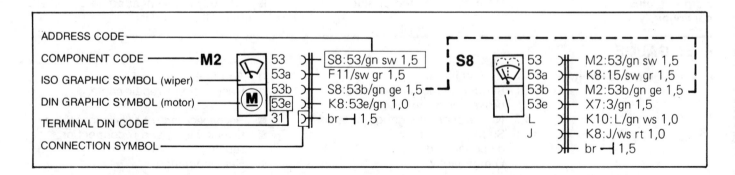

The superimposed dotted line indicates the actual connection made by the gn ge = green and yellow wire. Interconnecting wires are not shown on an Autodata Wiring Diagram as the destination of any wire can be read directly from the address code - without the need to trace the route of the wire through a maze of lines.

SYMBOLS AND CODES

⊃—	Plug and socket (e.g. Lucar)
⊐‖⊏	Multi-plug connector
•—	Fixed (e.g. soldered joint)
○—	Fixed (e.g. disconnectable nut and bolt)
⊃—sw⊣	Earth return cable
•—⊣	Direct earth (no cable) e.g. earthed through component body
⊃- - -	Cable leading to optional or alternative equipment
⊃— / ⊃— / ⊃—	Alternative method of wiring according to model/year etc (marked)
⊃⊣ ⊦br⊣	Capacitor
⊃—M1/x	x = Braided strap
⊃—T1/y	y = High Tension cable
⊃—X28:30/z	z = Non cable connection, e.g. by printed circuit or internal connection.
—K4:87/140	140 = In certain diagrams colour codes are replaced by numbers, which identify a particular cable and not the relevant colour. In this instance, the cables will be numbered at each end.

Two component keys combined to identify a spare cable or approximate component location e.g.

W1[H13]	Spare cable for indicator repeater lamp, left.

X6 [S13]	Connector, near the stoplamp switch.
⊃—K9:3/<u>bl</u> rt	Any colour code underlined is a sleeve colour and not a cable colour (e.g. sleeve colour can be, rubber or plastic ring, painted strip on cable or colour of plastic connector cover).
—•—	Soldered or crimped joint where cable divides for several destinations.
X14 (J) rt	Multi-plug identified by a letter, number and/or colour (e.g. X14 is connector J, multi-plug colour red).
– sw ws (sw ge)	Alternative colour
– sw–⊃–sw ge	Colour change
==========	Single shielded cable
========== ==========	Multi shielded cable
—→ ←—	Spark plug
S3 (R4)	Two components combined as a unit
—⋀⋀⋀—	Resistor
—⊏□⊐—	Resistor cable
—►⊢	Blocking diode
—○•○—	Line fuse

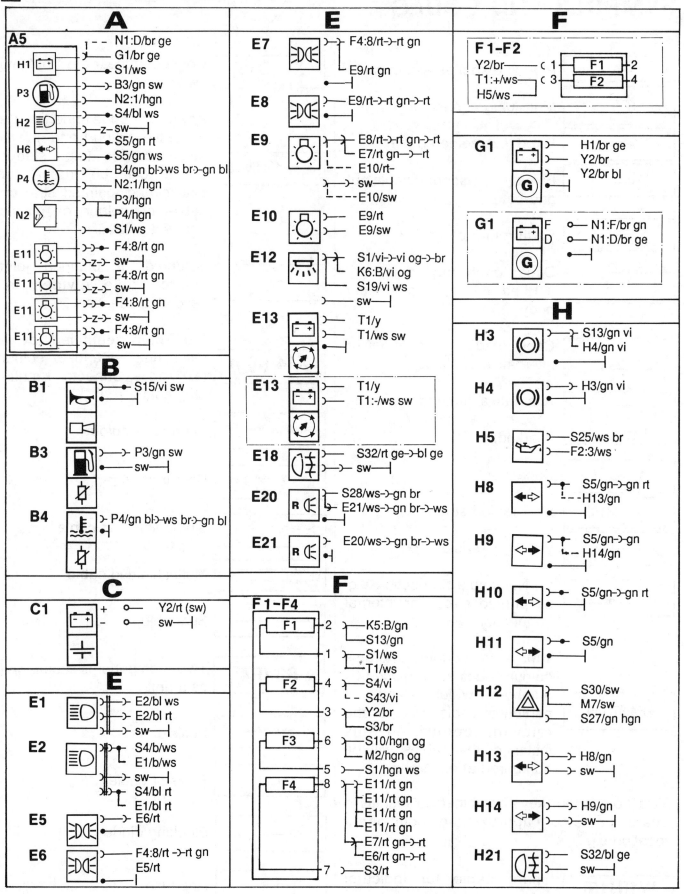

A

A5

H1		N1:D/br ge
		G1/br ge
		S1/ws
P3		B3/gn sw
		N2:1/hgn
H2		S4/bl ws
		z–sw
H6		S5/gn rt
		S5/gn ws
P4		B4/gn bl–ws br–gn bl
		N2:1/hgn
N2		P3/hgn
		P4/hgn
		S1/ws
E11		F4:8/rt gn
		z–sw
E11		F4:8/rt gn
		z–sw
E11		F4:8/rt gn
		z–sw
E11		F4:8/rt gn
		sw

B

B1		S15/vi sw
B3		P3/gn sw
		sw
B4		P4/gn bl–ws br–gn bl

C

C1	+	Y2/rt (sw)
	–	sw

E

E1		E2/bl ws
		E2/bl rt
		sw
E2		S4/b/ws
		E1/b/ws
		sw
		S4/bl rt
		E1/bl rt
E5		E6/rt
E6		F4:8/rt –rt gn
		E5/rt

E

E7		F4:8/rt–rt gn
		E9/rt gn
E8		E9/rt–rt gn–rt
E9		E8/rt–rt gn–rt
		E7/rt gn–rt
		E10/rt–
		sw
		E10/sw
E10		E9/rt
		E9/sw
E12		S1/vi–vi og–br
		K6:B/vi og
		S19/vi ws
		sw
E13		T1/y
		T1/ws sw
E13		T1/y
		T1:-/ws sw
E18		S32/rt ge–bl ge
		sw
E20		S28/ws–gn br
		E21/ws–gn br–ws
E21		E20/ws–gn br–ws

F

F 1–F4

F1	2	K5:B/gn
		S13/gn
	1	S1/ws
		T1/ws
F2	4	S4/vi
		S43/vi
	3	Y2/br
		S3/br
F3	6	S10/hgn og
		M2/hgn og
	5	S1/hgn ws
F4	8	E11/rt gn
		E11/rt gn
		E11/rt gn
		E11/rt gn
		E7/rt gn–rt
		E6/rt gn–rt
	7	S3/rt

F

F 1–F2

Y2/br	1	F1	2
T1:+/ws	3	F2	4
H5/ws			

G1		H1/br ge
		Y2/br
		Y2/br bl

G1	F	N1:F/br gn
	D	N1:D/br ge

H

H3		S13/gn vi
		H4/gn vi
H4		H3/gn vi
H5		S25/ws br
		F2:3/ws
H8		S5/gn–gn rt
		H13/gn
H9		S5/gn–gn
		H14/gn
H10		S5/gn–gn rt
H11		S5/gn
H12		S30/sw
		M7/sw
		S27/gn hgn
H13		H8/gn
		sw
H14		H9/gn
		sw
H21		S32/bl ge
		sw

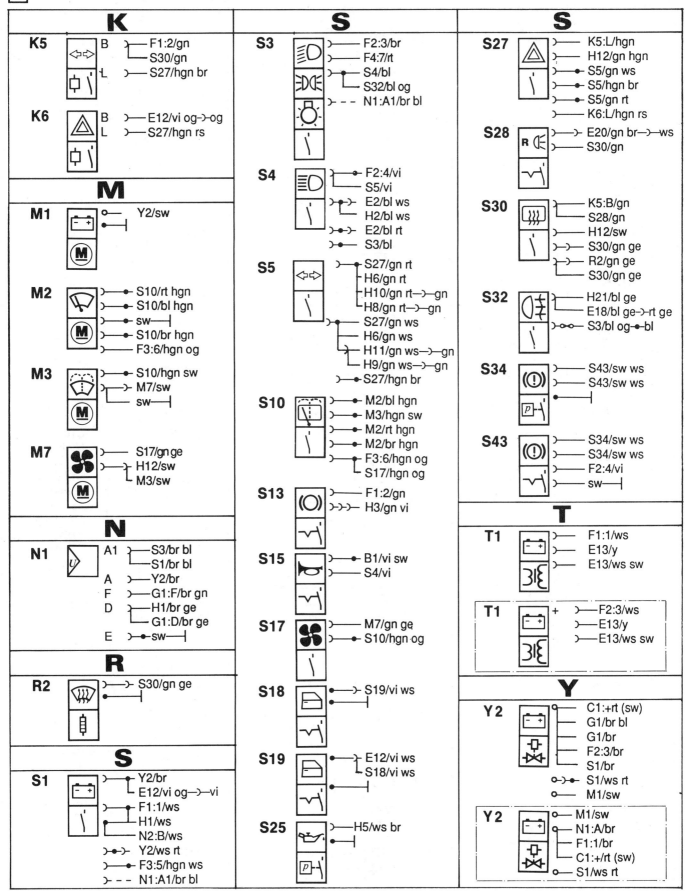

K

K5
B)— F1:2/gn
— S30/gn
L)— S27/hgn br

K6
B)— E12/vi og–)–og
L)— S27/hgn rs

M

M1
o— Y2/sw

M2
)— • S10/rt hgn
)— • S10/bl hgn
)— • sw—|
)— • S10/br hgn
)— F3:6/hgn og

M3
)— • S10/hgn sw
)—)– M7/sw
— sw—|

M7
)— S17/gn ge
)— H12/sw
— M3/sw

N

N1
A1 — S3/br bl
— S1/br bl
A)— Y2/br
F)— G1:F/br gn
D)— H1/br ge
— G1:D/br ge
E)—•—sw—|

R

R2
)—)– S30/gn ge

S

S1
)— Y2/br
— E12/vi og–)–vi
)— F1:1/ws
— H1/ws
— N2:B/ws
)—•–)– Y2/ws rt
)—•– F3:5/hgn ws
)– – – N1:A1/br bl

S

S3
)— F2:3/br
)— F4:7/rt
•— S4/bl
— S32/bl og
)– – – N1:A1/br bl

S4
)—• F2:4/vi
— S5/vi
)—•–)– E2/bl ws
— H2/bl ws
)—•–)– E2/bl rt
)—•– S3/bl

S5
•— S27/gn rt
— H6/gn rt
— H10/gn rt–)–gn
— H8/gn rt–)–gn
)– S27/gn ws
— H6/gn ws
— H11/gn ws–)–gn
— H9/gn ws–)–gn
)—• S27/hgn br

S10
)—• M2/bl hgn
)—• M3/hgn sw
)—• M2/rt hgn
)—• M2/br hgn
)— F3:6/hgn og
— S17/hgn og

S13
)— F1:2/gn
)–)–)– H3/gn vi

S15
)—• B1/vi sw
)—• S4/vi

S17
)— M7/gn ge
)—• S10/hgn og

S18
•—)– S19/vi ws

S19
)— E12/vi ws
— S18/vi ws

S25
)— H5/ws br

S

S27
)— K5:L/hgn
)— H12/gn hgn
)—• S5/gn ws
)—• S5/hgn br
)—• S5/gn rt
)— K6:L/hgn rs

S28
)—)– E20/gn br–)–ws
)— S30/gn

S30
)— K5:B/gn
)— S28/gn
)— H12/sw
)—)– S30/gn ge
)—)– R2/gn ge
— S30/gn ge

S32
)— H21/bl ge
— E18/bl ge–)–rt ge
)—o—o— S3/bl og–•–bl

S34
)— S43/sw ws
— S43/sw ws
•—|

S43
)— S34/sw ws
— S34/sw ws
)— F2:4/vi
)— sw—|

T

T1
)— F1:1/ws
)— E13/y
)— E13/ws sw

T1
+)— F2:3/ws
)— E13/y
)— E13/ws sw

Y

Y2
)— C1:+rt (sw)
— G1/br bl
— G1/br
— F2:3/br
— S1/br
o—)–• S1/ws rt
o—• M1/sw

Y2
o— M1/sw
•— N1:A/br
— F1:1/br
— C1:+rt (sw)
o—• S1/ws rt

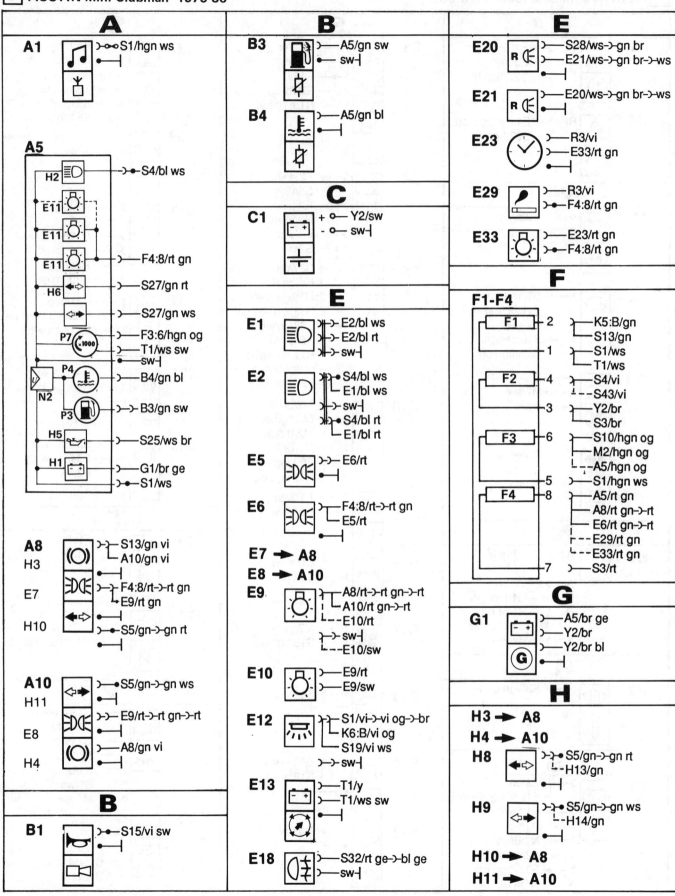

A

A1)─o∞o─ S1/hgn ws
●─┤

A5

H2)─●─ S4/bl ws
E11
E11
E11)─ F4:8/rt gn
H6)─ S27/gn rt
)─ S27/gn ws
P7)─ F3:6/hgn og
)─ T1/ws sw
●─ sw─┤
N2
P4)─ B4/gn bl
P3)─ B3/gn sw
H5)─ S25/ws br
H1)─ G1/br ge
)─ S1/ws

A8
H3)─●─ S13/gn vi
A10/gn vi
●─┤
E7)─ F4:8/rt─)─rt gn
E9/rt gn
H10)─●─ S5/gn─)─gn rt
●─┤

A10
H11)─●─ S5/gn─)─gn ws
●─┤
E8)─ E9/rt─)─rt gn─)─rt
H4)─ A8/gn vi
●─┤

B

B1)─●─ S15/vi sw
)─┤

B

B3)─ A5/gn sw
●─ sw─┤

B4)─ A5/gn bl
●─┤

C

C1 + o─ Y2/sw
- o─ sw─┤

E

E1)╫)─ E2/bl ws
)╫)─ E2/bl rt
)╫)─ sw─┤

E2)╫)─ S4/bl ws
)─ E1/bl ws
)╫)─ sw─┤
)─ S4/bl rt
)─ E1/bl rt

E5)─)─ E6/rt
●─┤

E6)─ F4:8/rt─)─rt gn
)─ E5/rt

E7 → A8
E8 → A10
E9)─ A8/rt─)─rt gn─)─rt
)─ A10/rt gn─)─rt
)─ E10/rt
)─ sw─┤
)─ E10/sw

E10)─ E9/rt
)─ E9/sw

E12)─ S1/vi─)─vi og─)─br
)─ K6:B/vi og
)─ S19/vi ws
)─ sw─┤

E13)─ T1/y
)─ T1/ws sw
●─┤

E18)─ S32/rt ge─)─bl ge
)─ sw─┤

E

E20 R)─ S28/ws─)─gn br
)─ E21/ws─)─gn br─)─ws
●─┤

E21 R)─ E20/ws─)─gn br─)─ws
)─┤

E23)─ R3/vi
)─ E33/rt gn
●─┤

E29)─ R3/vi
)─●─ F4:8/rt gn

E33)─ E23/rt gn
)─●─ F4:8/rt gn

F

F1-F4

F1 ─2)─ K5:B/gn
)─ S13/gn
─1)─ S1/ws
)─ T1/ws
F2 ─4)─ S4/vi
)─ S43/vi
─3)─ Y2/br
)─ S3/br
F3 ─6)─ S10/hgn og
)─ M2/hgn og
)─ A5/hgn og
─5)─ S1/hgn ws
F4 ─8)─ A5/rt gn
)─ A8/rt gn─)─rt
)─ E6/rt gn─)─rt
)─ E29/rt gn
)─ E33/rt gn
─7)─ S3/rt

G

G1)─ A5/br ge
)─ Y2/br
G)─ Y2/br bl

H

H3 → A8
H4 → A10
H8)─)─ S5/gn─)─gn rt
)─ H13/gn
H9)─)─ S5/gn─)─gn ws
)─ H14/gn
●─┤
H10 → A8
H11 → A10

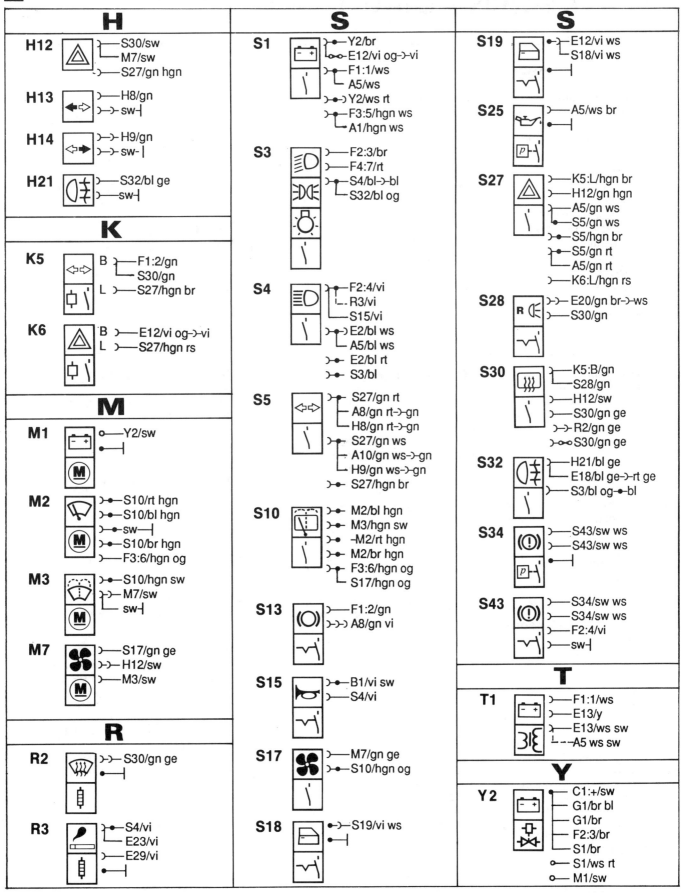

H

H12
- S30/sw
- M7/sw
- S27/gn hgn

H13
- H8/gn
- sw

H14
- H9/gn
- sw

H21
- S32/bl ge
- sw

K

K5
- B
  - F1:2/gn
  - S30/gn
- L
  - S27/hgn br

K6
- B
  - E12/vi og-vi
- L
  - S27/hgn rs

M

M1
- Y2/sw

M2
- S10/rt hgn
- S10/bl hgn
- sw
- S10/br hgn
- F3:6/hgn og

M3
- S10/hgn sw
- M7/sw
- sw

M7
- S17/gn ge
- H12/sw
- M3/sw

R

R2
- S30/gn ge

R3
- S4/vi
- E23/vi
- E29/vi

S

S1
- Y2/br
- E12/vi og-vi
- F1:1/ws
- A5/ws
- Y2/ws rt
- F3:5/hgn ws
- A1/hgn ws

S3
- F2:3/br
- F4:7/rt
- S4/bl-bl
- S32/bl og

S4
- F2:4/vi
- R3/vi
- S15/vi
- E2/bl ws
- A5/bl ws
- E2/bl rt
- S3/bl

S5
- S27/gn rt
- A8/gn rt-gn
- H8/gn rt-gn
- S27/gn ws
- A10/gn ws-gn
- H9/gn ws-gn
- S27/hgn br

S10
- M2/bl hgn
- M3/hgn sw
- M2/rt hgn
- M2/br hgn
- F3:6/hgn og
- S17/hgn og

S13
- F1:2/gn
- A8/gn vi

S15
- B1/vi sw
- S4/vi

S17
- M7/gn ge
- S10/hgn og

S18
- S19/vi ws

S

S19
- E12/vi ws
- S18/vi ws

S25
- A5/ws br

S27
- K5:L/hgn br
- H12/gn hgn
- A5/gn ws
- S5/gn ws
- S5/hgn br
- S5/gn rt
- A5/gn rt
- K6:L/hgn rs

S28
- E20/gn br-ws
- S30/gn

S30
- K5:B/gn
- S28/gn
- H12/sw
- S30/gn ge
- R2/gn ge
- S30/gn ge

S32
- H21/bl ge
- E18/bl ge-rt ge
- S3/bl og-bl

S34
- S43/sw ws
- S43/sw ws

S43
- S34/sw ws
- S34/sw ws
- F2:4/vi
- sw

T

T1
- F1:1/ws
- E13/y
- E13/ws sw
- A5 ws sw

Y

Y 2
- C1:+/sw
- G1/br bl
- G1/br
- F2:3/br
- S1/br
- S1/ws rt
- M1/sw

KEY TO WIRING DIAGRAMS

COMPONENT CODE

The Component Code consists of a letter and number. The letter identifies the component group and the number identifies the specific component.

A - Assemblies
B - Transducers
C - Capacitors
E - Lamps, Miscellaneous
F - Protective Devices
G - Generators
H - Warning Devices
K - Relays
M - Motors

N - Regulators
P - Meters/Gauges
R - Resistors
S - Switches
T - Transformers
V - Semi-conductors
W - Spare Cables
X - Connectors
Y - Solenoids

COLOUR CODE

bl	=	blue	rs	=	pink
br	=	brown	rt	=	red
be	=	beige	sw	=	black
el	=	cream	vi	=	violet
ge	=	yellow	ws	=	white
gn	=	green	hbl	=	light blue
gr	=	grey	hgn	=	light green
nf	=	neutral	rbr	=	maroon
og	=	orange			

ABBREVIATIONS

ABS Anti-lock braking system
AC Air conditioning
AED Automatic enrichment device
AT Automatic transmission

A Assemblies
A1 Radio/stereo unit
A5 Instrument panel
A8 Rear lamp assembly, left
A10 Rear lamp assembly, right

B Transducers
B1 Horn (single or LH)
B3 Fuel gauge tank transmitter
B4 Coolant temperature transmitter

C Capacitors
C1 Battery

E Lamps, Miscellaneous
E1 Headlamp LH
E2 Headlamp RH
E5 Side lamp LH
E6 Side lamp RH
E7 Tail lamp LH
E8 Tail lamp RH
E9 Number plate lamp (single or LH)
E10 Number plate lamp RH
E11 Panel illumination lamp/s
E12 Interior lamp/s front
E13 Distributor
E18 Rear fog lamp (single or LH)
E20 Reversing lamp (single or LH)
E21 Reversing lamp RH
E23 Clock
E29 Cigarette lighter lamp
E33 Clock lamp

F Protective Devices
F1-F30 Fuse box

G Generators
G1 Alternator

H Warning Devices
H1 Ignition warning lamp
H2 Main beam warning lamp
H3 Stop lamp LH
H4 Stop lamp RH
H5 Oil pressure warning lamp
H6 Indicator warning lamp (single or LH)
H7 Indicator warning lamp RH
H8 Indicator lamp LH front
H9 Indicator lamp RH front
H10 Indicator lamp LH rear
H11 Indicator lamp RH rear
H12 Emergency lamps warning lamp
H13 Indicator repeater lamp LH
H14 Indicator repeater lamp RH
H21 Fog warning lamp rear

J Relays
K5 Indicator relay
K6 Emergency lamps relay

M Motors
M1 Starter motor
M2 Wiper motor
M3 Washer motor
M7 Heater blower motor

N Regulators
N1 Voltage regulator
N2 Voltage stabiliser

P Meters/Gauges
P3 Fuel gauge
P4 Coolant temperature gauge
P7 Tachometer

R Resistors
R2 Heated rear window
R3 Cigarette lighter

S Switches
S1 Ignition/starter switch
S3 Main lamp switch
S4 Dip/main/flash switch
S5 Indicator switch
S10 Rear wipe/wash switch
S13 Stop lamps switch
S15 Horn switch
S17 Heater/AC motor switch
S18 Courtesy lamp switch LH front
S19 Courtesy lamp switch RH front
S25 Oil pressure warning lamp switch
S27 Emergency lamps switch
S28 Reversing lamps switch
S30 Heated rear window switch
S32 Rear fog lamps switch
S34 Brakek pressure warning lamp switch
S43 Brake warning lamp test switch

T Transformers
T1 Ignition coil

Y Solenoids
Y2 Starter solenoid

Body & Fittings

INTRODUCTION . . . . [1]

The Mini body fittings are all fairly simple and easy to work on for the DIY mechanic. Access to all the components is easy and no problems should be encountered if the removal and installation instructions in this chapter are followed carefully.

The body panels are all welded in position and therefore replacement of these is beyond the scope of this manual.

TOOLS & EQUIPMENT . . . . [2]

In addition to the tools listed under Basic Tools & Equipment in BASIC PROCEDURES, the following items will be required to carry out some of the operations detailed in this section:

- A selection of Philips and crosshead screwdrivers – for removing body fittings.
- A pop rivet gun and rivets – for replacing the wheel arch extensions.

BONNET . . . . [3]
Removal (Fig.N:1)
1. Open the bonnet and support in the fully open position.
2. Mark the position of the hinges in relation to the brackets on the bonnet panel to assist realignment when refitting. This can be done by either scribing round the hinges or using chalk.
3. Undo the four hinge retaining nuts and washers, and spring the hinges from the bonnet brackets.
4. Unhook the support stay and lift the bonnet panel away from the car, taking care not to damage the surrounding paintwork.

Installation

Install the bonnet in the reverse order of removal, using the marks made previously, to align the panel.

Do not fully tighten the hinge nuts until the bonnet is correctly aligned with the surrounding panels.

BONNET LOCK . . . . [4]
Replacement — Except Clubman & 1275 GT (Fig.N:2)
1. Open the bonnet and support with the stay.
2. Remove the ignition shield (if fitted).
3. Unhook the slider catch return spring.
4. Undo the two cross-head retaining screws from the lock assembly.
5. Lift off the upper guide plate and manoeuvre the lock

assembly out from behind the wiring loom, below the bonnet landing panel.
6. Install the lock assembly in the reverse order of removal.

Replacement — Clubman & 1275 GT (Fig.N:3)

Replacement of the bonnet lock fitted to Clubman and 1275 GT models follows the same procedure as described for standard Saloons with the exception that the ignition shield is left in position as it is attached to the engine in this case.

BOOT LID . . . . [5]
Removal (Fig.N:4)
1. Disconnect the number plate lamp wiring.
2. Undo the screws retaining the support cables to the lid.
3. Support the weight of the lid and undo the two nuts and washers securing each hinge to the boot lid.
4. Carefully lift the lid from the hinges, taking care not to damage the paintwork.
5. If a new lid is to be fitted, remove the number plate lamp as described in GENERAL ELECTRICS and pull the sealing rubber away from the edge of the panel, carefully easing out each of the spring clips.
6. Remove the handle and lock assembly as described in the following section.

Installation

Install the boot lid in the reverse order of removal, using new clips for the sealing rubber and new packing pieces between the hinges and the lid. Before the hinge nuts are fully tightened the lid should be carefully closed to check its alignment with the surrounding panels.

BOOT LID LOCK & HANDLE . . . . [6]
Removal (Figs.N:5 and N:6)
1. Undo the four cross-head screws securing the lock assembly to the boot lid and withdraw it from the square shank of the handle.
2. Undo the two nuts and washers securing the 'T' handle and withdraw it together with the rubber gasket.
3. Prise off the spring clip and remove the two flat washers and the wavy washer to release the yoke (2,Fig.N:6).
4. Using a fine pin punch, tap out the lock barrel retaining pin and withdraw the barrel from the 'T' handle.
5. Push out the locating pin (3,Fig.N:6).

Installation

Reassemble and install the lock assembly in the reverse order of removal, ensuring that the actuating pin on the lock barrel engages with the slot in the locking pin and that the mechanism, with the exception of the lock barrel, is greased before installation.

DOORS & HINGES — FRONT .... [7]

The door hinges on all Mk 1 and Mk 2 Saloons and all Van and Pick-up versions are of the external type. Mk 3 Saloons have concealed hinges, but in both cases the removal of the doors/hinges is a straightforward job.

The most common problem with the hinges is pin wear, in which case the only satisfactory answer is to fit new hinges.

Removal — Mk 1 and Mk 2

1. Undo the two cross-head screws retaining the check strap to the kick panel and remove the reinforcing plate.
2. With the aid of an assistant supporting the weight of the door, undo the four nuts and washers from behind the front wing and release the hinges from the body.
NOTE: These nuts are exposed to dirt and water thrown up by the wheels and will therefore be corroded and difficult to undo, however if the hinge is not being replaced it can be left in position on the body and detached from the door panel as described below.
3. Ease out the end trim pads from the door and carefully flex the main trim panel across the middle so that it can be manoeuvred out of the door pressing.
4. Support the weight of the door and undo the nuts and washers from the hinges and lift the door away from the body.

Removal — Mk 3

1. Remove the split pin from the check strap clevis pin and withdraw the pin from the strap.
2. With an assistant supporting the weight of the door, undo the four hinge securing nuts and reinforcing plates from behind the door pillar (these are accessible from within the wheelarch).
3. Lift the door away from the body.
4. Remove the door trim panel, as described later in this section.
5. Undo the four cross-head screws securing the hinges to the door and remove them.

Installation — All Models

Installation of both types of door is a reversal of the removal procedure, but before fully tightening the hinge nuts the alignment of the door in relation to the surrounding panels should be carefully checked.

REAR DOORS — ESTATE & VAN .... [8]

Replacement

1. Undo the cross-head self-tapping screws and remove the rear door pillar trim panel.
2. Undo the nut and bolt securing the door check strap and remove the trim.
3. Undo the two nuts and bolts securing each of the door hinges to the pillar.
4. Lift the door away from the body.
5. Install the door in the reverse order of removal and check the alignment before fully tightening the hinge bolts.

DOOR TRIM PANEL .... [9]

Removal (Fig.N:7)

1. Undo the cross-head screw securing the window winder handle and remove the handle.
2. Undo the cross-head screw and remove the interior lock handle.
3. Undo the two screws securing the door pull.
4. Using the blade of a screwdriver, lever the door lock lever plastic moulding away from the door panel.
5. Ease the trim panel clips away from the door at the sides and along the lower edge.
6. Pull the panel down and away from the locating channel along the upper edge.
7. Remove the trim panel from the car.

Installation

Install the trim panel in the reverse order of removal.

DOOR LOCKS & STRIKER PLATE .... [10]
Door Lock — Mk 1 & Mk 2 — Removal (Fig.N:8)
1. Undo the cross-head screw and remove it from the end of the square handle shaft.
2. Slacken the cross-head screw clamping the interior handle (if fitted).
3. From the outside pull the exterior handle through the lock and interior handle.
4. Undo the three screws securing the lock assembly to the inner door panel and remove the lock.

Installation

Install the door lock in the reverse order of removal, ensuring that the interior handle is fitted in the correct position and that the rubber sealing gasket is in position.

Door Lock — Removal — Mk 3 (Fig.N:9)
1. Remove the door trim panel as previously described.
2. Undo the screws securing the interior handle to the inner door skin.
3. Undo the screws securing the lock operating lever to the inner door skin.
4. Undo the four cross-head screws securing the lock assembly to the rear edge of the door.
5. Pull the lock assembly from the door and prise off the spring clip from the lock operating lever link rod.
6. Prise off the spring clip securing the interior handle operating rod to the lock.
7. The door lock can now be removed from the car.

Installation

Install the door lock in the reverse order of removal, ensuring that the exterior handle lock lever engages with the lock pin (4,Fig.N:9).

Replacement — Striker Plate (Fig.N:10)

1. Lever out the blanking cover from the rear of the 'B' post.
2. Undo the two cross-head screws (2,Fig.N:10) and remove the outer plate and the inner striker plate (3,Fig.N:10).
3. Install the striker plate in the reverse order of removal and align with the door lock before fully tightening the retaining screws.

DOOR EXTERIOR HANDLE .... [11]

Removal of the door exterior handle on Mk I and Mk 2 cars is described in the relevant Door Lock Removal section of this chapter.

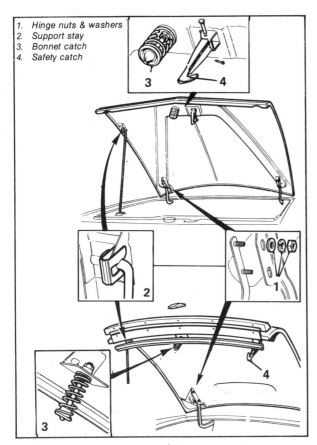

1. Hinge nuts & washers
2. Support stay
3. Bonnet catch
4. Safety catch

Fig. N:1 Removing bonnet panel

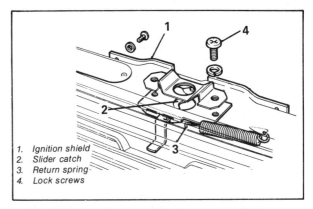

1. Ignition shield
2. Slider catch
3. Return spring
4. Lock screws

Fig. N:2 Removing bonnet lock — except Clubman & 1275 GT

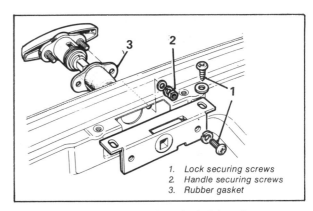

1. Lock screw
2. Return spring
3. Locating cup
4. Slider catch

Fig. N:3 Removing bonnet lock — Clubman 1275 GT

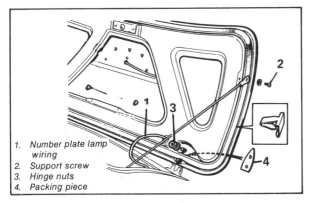

1. Number plate lamp wiring
2. Support screw
3. Hinge nuts
4. Packing piece

Fig. N:4 Removing boot lid

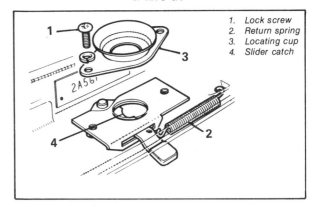

1. Lock securing screws
2. Handle securing screws
3. Rubber gasket

Fig. N:5 Removing boot lock & handle

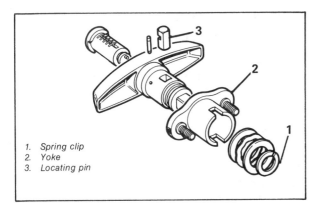

1. Spring clip
2. Yoke
3. Locating pin

Fig. N:6 Exploded view of boot handle

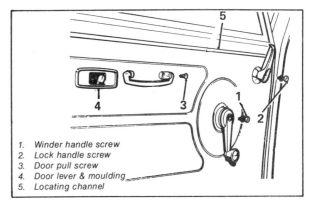

1. Winder handle screw
2. Lock handle screw
3. Door pull screw
4. Door lever & moulding
5. Locating channel

Fig. N:7 Removing door trim panel

Removal — Mk 3 (Fig.N:11)

1. Remove the door trim panel and lock assembly as previously described.
2. Undo the two screws securing the exterior handle, one is accessible through the aperture in the inner door skin and the other is fitted through the trailing edge flange of the door.
3. Remove the handle from the door together with the gasket.
4. Prise off the clip from the rear of the lock barrel and withdraw the barrel with the aid of the key (Fig.N:12).
5. Undo and remove the small screw from the retaining plate and remove the push button, return spring and washer.

Installation

Reassemble the lock and install the handle in the reverse order of removal, ensuring that the lock operating link engages with the lock barrel lever.

DOOR WINDOW GLASS . . . . [12]
Sliding Type — Removal (Fig.N:13)

1. Undo the cross-head screws and remove the two window catches, sealing rubbers and threaded bosses.
2. Pull off the weather strip from the front edge of the rear sliding window glass.
3. Undo the screws securing the sliding channel to the top of the door frame.
4. Slide both windows into the middle of the channel and pull the sliding channel and metal catch strip away from the door.
5. Remove the sliding window glasses from the channel.

Installation

Install the window glasses in the reverse order of removal ensuring that the front glass is positioned on the outside.

Removal — Winding Type (Fig.N:15)

1. Remove the door trim panel as previously described.
2. Undo the four screws securing the window winder mechanism and ease the plate away from the sealing compound which will hold it to the door panel.
3. Temporarily refit the winder handle and wind the arms to the top of their travel.
4. Slide the winder mechanism forward and detach the rear arm from the glass channel. Slide the mechanism rearwards and detach the front arm from the forward glass channel.
5. Support the door glass with a block of wood placed between the bottom edge of the glass and the aperture in the inner door skin.
6. Prise off the outer sealing strip and the inner finisher from the top edge of the door.
7. Lift out the window glass by tilting it and withdraw from the outside of the frame.

Installation

If a new glass is being fitted, the lifting channel will have to be transferred. Measure and note the location of the two lifting channels and then tap them away from the glass using a block of wood, being careful not to distort the channel.

Place the new glass with the bottom edge uppermost, on a piece of wood and tap the channels into the measured position using a soft faced mallet.

Refit the window and regulator mechanism in the reverse order of removal.

CENTRE CONSOLE . . . . [13]
Removal

1. Disconnect the battery earth lead.

2. Undo and remove the console securing screws.
3. Pull off the radio knobs and finishers and unscrew the spindle nuts.
4. Pull the console rearwards and select top gear.
5. Undo the radio mounting screws and push the set clear of the console.
6. Disconnect the wiring harness from the clock and the cigar lighter.
7. Unplug the speaker lead from the radio.
8. Release the gear lever grommet and lift the console out of the car.

Installation

Install the console in the reverse order of removal, reconnect the battery earth lead and reset the clock.

FASCIA TOP RAIL COVER . . . . [14]
Replacement (Fig.N:16)

1. Unscrew the fresh air outlet retaining ring and remove the moulded binnacle (Fig.N:14).
2. Twist the air outlet valve anti-clockwise and remove it from the fascia.
3. Repeat the operation for the opposite side.
4. Carefully peel the door sealing rubbers away from the 'A' posts in the region of the fascia top rail.
5. Manoeuvre the left-hand parcel tray liner trim away from the fascia.
6. Undo the four securing nuts and lift off the fascia top rail cover.
7. Install the cover in the reverse order of removal.

SEATS . . . . [15]
Front — Replacement (Fig.N:17)

1. Undo the two bolts securing each of the hinges to the front face of the floor cross member or remove the pivot bolts if fitted.
2. Release the seat tipping safety catch and lift out the seat.
3. Install the seat in the reverse order of removal.

Rear — Replacement (Saloon)

1. Lift up the front edge of the cushion and pull it out from below the backrest. On later models, unscrew the cushion retaining strap screws which also retain the backrest.
2. Open the boot lid and undo the two screws securing the backrest to the rear parcel shelf.
3. Lift up the backrest, unhook it from the front edge of the parcel shelf and remove it from the car.
4. Install the seats in the reverse order of removal, ensuring that the backrest is located firmly on the parcel shelf lip and the cushion/backrest retaining screws are refitted (later models).

Replacement — Estate

1. Hinge up the cushion into the upright position.
2. Undo the two bolts securing one of the hinges to the cross support bar.
3. Slide the opposite hinge away from the hinge pin and lift the cushion out of the car.
4. Fold the backrest down flat.
5. Undo the four cross-head screws securing the two 'flap' type hinges and lift out the backrest assembly.
6. Install the seat components in the reverse order of removal.

REAR QUARTER WINDOW — SALOON . . . . . [16]
Replacement — Saloon (Fig.N:18)

1. Undo the two screws securing the 'over centre' catch to the rear quarter panel.
2. Undo the two screws securing the hinges to the 'B' post.

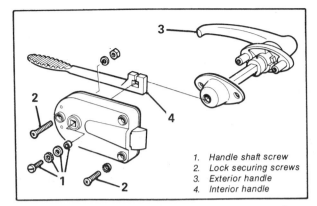

1. Handle shaft screw
2. Lock securing screws
3. Exterior handle
4. Interior handle

Fig. N:8 Door lock & handle components Mk 1 & Mk 2

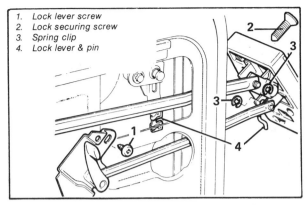

1. Lock lever screw
2. Lock securing screw
3. Spring clip
4. Lock lever & pin

Fig. N:9 Door lock & hinges — Mk 3

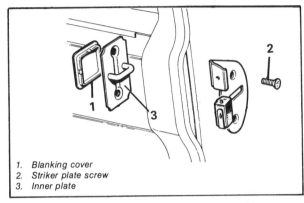

1. Blanking cover
2. Striker plate screw
3. Inner plate

Fig. N:10 Removing striker plate assembly

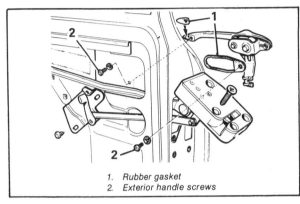

1. Rubber gasket
2. Exterior handle screws

Fig. N:11 Removing exterior door handle

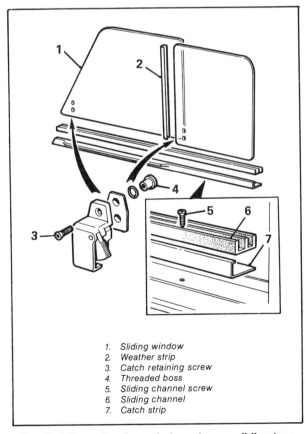

1. Sliding window
2. Weather strip
3. Catch retaining screw
4. Threaded boss
5. Sliding channel screw
6. Sliding channel
7. Catch strip

Fig. N:13 Removing door window glass — sliding type

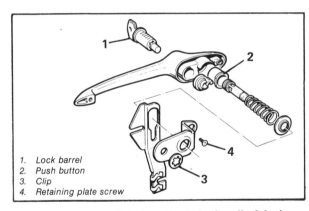

1. Lock barrel
2. Push button
3. Clip
4. Retaining plate screw

Fig. N:12 Exploded view of exterior handle & lock

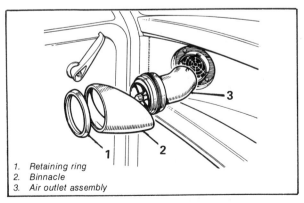

1. Retaining ring
2. Binnacle
3. Air outlet assembly

Fig. N:14 Removing fascia air outlet

3. Lift out the quarter window assembly.

REAR SIDE WINDOW — ESTATE .... [17]

1. Carefully prise the cant rail trim away from the securing clips.
2. Undo the screw securing the locking peg (fixed windows only).
3. Undo the screws securing the upper and lower sliding channels to the body.
4. Undo the screws securing the front and rear glazing channels to the body and remove both channels.
5. Slide both window glasses as far forward as possible.
6. Ease down the rear end of the upper sliding channel and pull it rearwards from body.
7. Tilt the upper edge of the glasses away from the body and lift them out.
8. Lift out the lower sliding channel.
9. Install the windows and channels in the reverse order of removal.

SEAT BELTS .... [18]

NOTE:When the seat belts have been in use in a vehicle which has been involved in an accident with a severe impact, the complete belt assemblies must be replaced, including the centre stalks.

Front Belts — Replacement (Fig.N:19)

1. Undo the nut and bolt securing the inertia reel to the companion box, and note the position of the large flat washer and sleeve.
2. Undo the lower belt mounting bolt and note the position of the nylon washers, spacer and fibre washer.
3. Unclip the plastic cover from the upper belt mounting.
4. Undo the upper mounting bracket bolt and remove it together with the two nylon washers, the spacer and the fibre washer.
5. Pull the rubber sleeve up the flexible stalk and undo the floor mounting bolt.
6. Remove the stalk with the bolt, spacer and fibre washer.

Installation

Install the seat belts in the reverse order of removal, taking care to fit the spacers and washers in the correct positions. Tighten the mounting bolts to a torque of 2,5 kg m (18 lb ft).

Rear Belts — Replacement

1. Lift out the rear seat cushion.
2. Remove the rear seat backrest as previously described.
3. Undo and remove the bolts and spring washers securing the belt mounting brackets.
4. Install the belt in the reverse order of removal, ensuring that the long section of the belt is fitted to the mounting nearest the centre of the car.
5. Tighten the mounting bolts to a torque of 3,5 kg m (25 lb ft).

WHEEL ARCH EXTENSIONS .... [19]

Replacement

The wheel arch extensions are secured to the body by pop-rivets. To remove an extension, drill through the head of each rivet and pull the extension off.

When installing, make sure that the back of the extension and the corresponding bodywork are clean and that the rivet holes are clear of swarf and old rivets. Secure the extension with new pop rivets.

CORROSION & BODY REPAIR .... [20]

The paint on your Mini is an important part of the total protection against rusting. Regular checking of the paintwork for damage is important. Damaged paintwork should be attended to as soon as possible to prevent the formation of rust.

Stone chipping and scratches are the most common blemishes and can easily be remedied. Look for bubbling or flaking of the paint or underbody sealant underneath the wheel arches, along the sills, and any points where a joint is made between the panels.

Before carrying out any paint repairs on your car always clean the car and make sure that it is dry. Warm temperatures are important for successful paint repairs, try and carry ⟨ repairs when the temperature is at least 15°C (60°F).

Your Mini may be fitted with a service plate in the engine compartment which gives details of the paint colour code number – see HISTORY & IDENTIFICATION for the location of the plate.

When buying touch-up paint always use the colour code number if possible to ensure that you get the right colour.

Some of the aerosol paints now available come complete with abrasive paper, filler and a touch-up brush and are well-suited for small paintwork repairs.

Minor Stone-chip Damage

If stone chips have occurred when the paint surface has been damaged, but the paint film has not been penetrated down to the body metal, then simple touching in with a brush is sufficient.

Use a sharp penknife or small modelling knife to scrape off any dirt or polish which may be in the paint chip. Take care not to remove paint at the bottom of the hole or metal may be exposed (A,Fig.N:20).

Thoroughly stir the paint in the touch-up can to make sure that the pigments are fully mixed. Insufficient mixing will always result in a colour matching problem.

Touch in the damaged areas using the small brush in the lid of the paint can or a small artists brush (B,Fig.N:20). Build up the paint until the repair is just proud of the surrounding paint surface.

Allow the paint to dry thoroughly before using a light cutting compound to polish the surface of the repair. Use a soft rag and apply the compound sparingly. Finish off with a wax polish.

Chips or Scratches

If the damage has penetrated through to the metal, then a more extensive repair will be necessary to prevent rusting under the paint.

Scrape the damaged surface clean and bevel off the chipped edges. Apply some rust remover to the exposed metal and leave to react.

Apply a suitable primer with a small brush and build up the level of paint, using several thin coats rather than one thick layer. When the primer is thoroughly dry, apply and finish the top coat.

Flaking Paint

Before starting repairs, clean the surrounding paintwork of dirt and polish using soft rubbing compound. Remove any paint flakes and rub the affected area down using wet and dry paper,

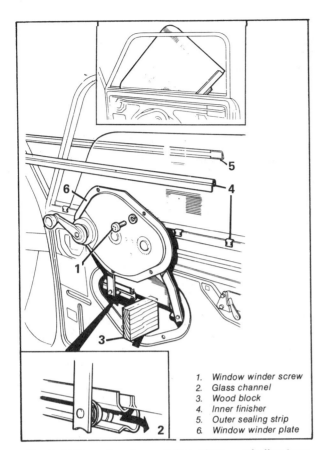

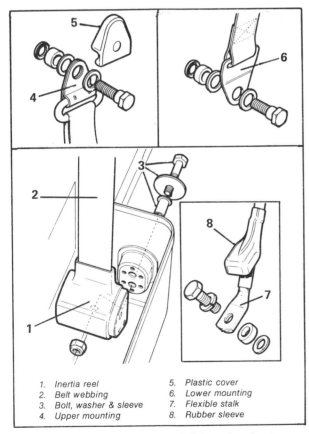

1. Window winder screw
2. Glass channel
3. Wood block
4. Inner finisher
5. Outer sealing strip
6. Window winder plate

Fig. N:15 Removing door window glass — winding type

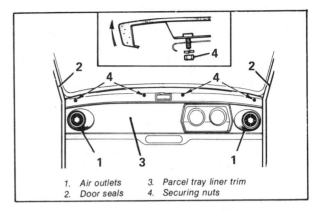

1. Air outlets
2. Door seals
3. Parcel tray liner trim
4. Securing nuts

Fig. N:16 Removing fascia top rail cover

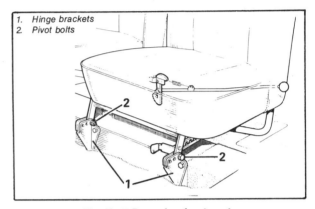

1. Hinge brackets
2. Pivot bolts

Fig. N:17 Removing front seat

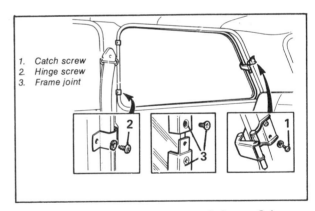

1. Catch screw
2. Hinge screw
3. Frame joint

Fig. N:18 Removing rear quarter window — Saloon

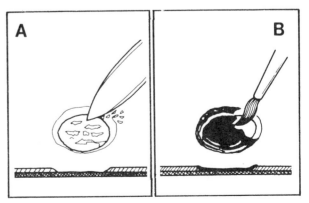

1. Inertia reel
2. Belt webbing
3. Bolt, washer & sleeve
4. Upper mounting
5. Plastic cover
6. Lower mounting
7. Flexible stalk
8. Rubber sleeve

Fig. N:19 Inertia reel seat belt layout — front

Fig. N:20 Cleaning & touching — in paint chips

used wet, until the surface is smooth and the edges of the surrounding paint have been 'feathered' or tapered off.

If the surface of the metal is rust pitted, it must be treated with a rust remover/inhibitor. An application of zinc based primer will help to prevent any further rusting.

Mask off the surrounding area with newspaper and masking tape to keep overspray from the undamaged paintwork.

Shake the primer aerosol for at least one minute to make sure that the paint is throughly mixed. Spray the primer moving the can over the repair area, keeping the nozzle approximately 20-30mm (8-12 in) from the surface. The first coat can be 'dusted' on by moving the aerosol quickly. On the second coat, the aerosol can be moved more slowly, putting more paint on to the surface. The previous 'dust' coat will help key the second coat. Do not allow the paint to get too thick or it will sag and run.

When the primer has dried it should be lightly rubbed down using 500 grade wet and dry paper to remove any dirt and blemishes and to provide a key for the colour coats.

Any dust from the flatting operation should be wiped off the primer coat, using a tack rag, before starting to apply the colour coats.

Spray the colour coats in the same manner as the primer, allowing each coat to dry for at least ten minutes before applying the next coat.

Rust

We all recognise rust when it starts to appear around parts of the car body. Leave it untreated and it will spread and eventually produce holes which will not only weaken the car body, but drastically reduce the car's value as well.

The only way to beat rust is to prevent it forming in the first place, or at the very least, slow it down by making sure that any parts where the paint has been chipped off are touched-up as soon as possible.

All Mini models have rustproofing measures applied at the factory which should last for several years. However, the complete underbody should be checked at least once a year to make sure that the protective layer has not been damaged. To do this, the car will have to be thoroughly cleaned underneath using a high pressure hose, or the car steam cleaned.

Examination will now show up any suspect areas where additional rustproofing protection is required. There are various underbody rustproofing kits on the market designed specifically for the DIY motorist which are easy to apply.

These should be used after the offending rust area has been sanded down and all traces of corrosion removed.

Undersealant

Applying underbody sealant is a dirty job so be well prepared with old clothes, gloves and a hat. The car should be raised and supported on axle stands – see BASIC PROCEDURES.

The surface to be treated must be clear of any foreign matter. For good application of underbody sealant use a cheap paint brush. It is important that the sealant used will remain flexible and will not chip or flake at a later date. Care should be taken not to cover moving parts such as driveshafts, handbrake linkages, etc, as well as the radiator which must be left uncovered. If necessary mask these areas first. The rustproofing used in the beams and box sections should not require retreatment except after any repair work.

Accessories

INTRODUCTION . . . . [1]

Various accessories are available specifically for the Mini which can be added according to your needs. The most comprehensive accessory selection naturally comes from Unipart who supply the original optional accessory equipment for the Mini. In this chapter we give fitting instructions for the more popular items, as listed above, although the instructions will also be useful if your car already has a particular accessory fitted and you wish to change or remove it, when selling the car for example.

When removing or installing any electrical accessory, make sure that the battery earth lead is disconnected first. This will avoid the possibility of any short-circuits if another component has to be disturbed or disconnected.

TOOLS & EQUIPMENT . . . . [2]

Other than those tools listed under Basic Tools & Equipment in BASIC PROCEDURES, the only items needed in order to carry out all the operations detailed in this chapter are:
- A pair of wire strippers/cutters - for making wiring connections to wire ends.
- A pair of crimping pliers - for attaching connectors to wire ends.
- A test lamp or multi-test meter - for electrical circuit testing.
- A sharp knife - for cutting trim material.
- An electric drill, various drill bits and a centre punch - for drilling holes for mounting screws and bolts.

RADIO & SPEAKER FITTING . . . . [3]
Radio Fitting (Fig.O:1)
The following instructions describe the installation of a radio using the Unipart fitting kit, part number GCA 1001.
1. Disconnect the battery earth lead.
2. Locate the two mounting holes in the underside of the parcel tray (1,Fig.O:1).
NOTE:It may be necessary to peel back the trim before the left-hand hole is visible.
3. Using the existing holes as a guide, drill through them with a 10 mm (25/64 in) dia. drill bit.
4. Slide the triangular mounting plate up behind the parcel shelf rail until the two studs can be fitted through the two enlarged holes.
5. Place the radio mounting bracket over the three studs of the triangular plate, and fit nuts and washers to the front studs.
6. Fit a self-adhesive foam pad to the top, rear edge of the radio casing, and another pad to the rear support bracket.
7. Connect the battery supply to the radio using one of the following connections, depending on the particular wiring harness fitted to the car in question:
a) If there is a green/white lead, on the left-hand side of the steering column, terminating in a black plug, connect this to the battery supply lead on the radio.
b) On cars not fitted with a combined steering lock/ignition switch, the radio supply lead should be connected to the spare terminal on the ignition switch.
The switch is located in the middle of the switch panel and is accessible once the heater control panel has been lowered – see COOLING SYSTEM.
c) On cars fitted with a combined steering lock/ignition switch, the radio supply lead should be connected to the main lighting switch. Remove the heater control panel and disconnect the brown/blue wire from the switch and, using a 'piggy back' connector, connect the radio supply lead and the brown/blue wire to the switch terminal. Refit the heater control panel.
8. Install a 2 amp fuse in the supply lead fuseholder.
9. Connect the aerial and speaker leads to the radio.
10. Fully extend the aerial and reconnect the battery earth lead.
11. Tune the radio to a weak station around 200m medium wave and use a very small screwdriver to adjust the aerial trimmer screw until maximum volume is obtained. The aerial trimmer screw may be accessible, either through the top casing, or adjacent to the tuning control spindle at the front of the set, depending on the make and model.
12. Fit the radio to the mounting bracket using the spindle nuts and faceplate at the front, and the mounting bracket at the rear.
13. Check the operation of the radio with the engine running and if any interference is evident, fit suppressors as necessary – see Suppression.

Speaker Installation — Saloon (Fig.O:2)
1. Route the speaker lead from the radio position to the centre line of the bulkhead (positioning the lead to avoid interference with pedal movements) then down to the floor tunnel (underneath the floor covering) and alongside the tunnel to the front seat floor stiffener panel.
2. Route the lead under the front seat floor stiffener via the shallow pressing in the floor running under the stiffener, and along the floor tunnel to the rear seat.
NOTE:On some models it may be necessary to use a piece of stiff wire to pull the speaker lead through the stiffener.
3. Temporarily lift out rear seat cushion.
4. Drill a 16 mm (5/8 in) dia. hole through the front section of the rear seat pan, 127 mm (5 in) to the rear of the front edge on the centre line of car. Route the speaker lead through this hole using the grommet provided.
5. Drill another 16 mm (5/8 in) dia. hole below the rear seat squab through the rear bulkhead into the luggage compartment, 38 mm (1.5 in) up from the seat pan on the centre

line of the car. Route the speaker lead through this hole using the grommet provided.

6. Pass the lead through the cable clips on the side of the petrol tank.

7. Locate the speaker holes provided in the centre of the metal panel of the rear parcel shelf (Fig.O:2).

NOTE:On some models, a sheet of felt wadding is attached to the underside of the rear shelf. The wadding must be cut away to expose the speaker holes and to clear the speaker chassis.

8. Cut away the sections of trimmed pad which are visible through the two larger holes.

9. Pierce the four holes for the speaker bezel studs through the trimmed pad.

10. Connect the lead to the speaker.

11. Fit the bezel and speaker to the parcel shelf as shown in Fig.O:2 and secure with fixings provided.

12. Secure the speaker lead to the floor, tunnel, seat pan etc., with the self adhesive tape provided.

13. Refit the rear seat cushions.

Speaker Installation — Clubman & 1275GT (Fig.O:4)

1. Remove the directional face level air vent from the passenger side of the fascia by unscrewing the plastic outer rim and removing the vent cowling. Disengage the vent pipe by twisting it half a turn anti-clockwise and then withdrawing it (Fig.O:3).

2. Unclip a section of passenger side rubber door seal, and break the adhesive bond between the end of the parcel tray trim panel and the post. Release the other end of the trim panel by easing the side flap out from behind the rim of the instrument nacelle, and remove the panel completely by bowing it outwards sufficiently to clear the underside of the fascia top rail.

3. Mark and cut out a 16 mm (⅝ in) dia. hole in the trim panel, to the dimensions shown in Fig.O:4.

4. Pierce four 4 mm (⁵⁄₃₂ in) dia. fixing holes in the trim panel, using the speaker as a template (Fig.O:4).

5. Fit the spring clips (supplied) to the speaker support board, and assemble the speaker and mounting components to the trim panel.

6. Connect the lead to the speaker, and route the lead down through the demister pipe hole at the rear of the parcel tray to the radio position.

7. Refit the trim panel/speaker assembly and air vent in the reverse order of removal.

Stereo Speakers Installation — General (Fig.O:5)

1. Remove the interior trim panel from the door or side panel after removing the door handle, window winder, etc – see BODY & FITTINGS.

2. Where possible, select a position on the trim panel that coincides with a suitable hole in the metal door panel.

3. Ensure that the speaker magnet is clear of the window winding mechanism and that the speaker grille is clear of the window winder and door handles.

4. Using templates, pierce four 3 mm (⅛ in) dia. fixing holes and cut the 127 mm (5 in) diameter centre hole.

5. When there is a clearance hole in the metal panel behind the fixing holes, secure the speaker to the trim using four No. 6 x 1.25 in screws and flat nuts.

6. If any of the fixing holes are backed by metal, drill a 2 mm (⁵⁄₆₄ in) dia. hole and secure the screw to the metal panel without using the flat nut.

7. The water proof cowl must be positioned at the top of the speaker.

8. If there is no suitable hole in the metal door panel, cut the door trim panel and using this as a template, cut and drill corresponding holes in the metal door panel.

9. Before securing the speaker, drill a 9 mm (⅜ in) dia. hole in the leading edge of the door and a corresponding hole in the door pillar, unless suitable holes exit.

10. Fit the rubber grommets provided to these holes, and route the speaker lead from the radio or tape player position through these grommets to the speaker position.

11. Attach the leads to the speaker and secure the speaker door trim etc., ensuring that the speaker lead is clear of the window winding mechanism.

AERIAL .... [4]

1. Mark and drill a 22 mm (⅞ in) dia. hole in the left-hand side front wing to the dimensions shown in Figs.O:6 or O:7.

2. Drill a 14 mm (⁹⁄₁₆ in) dia. hole through the wing valance from the engine side of the car as indicated in Fig.O:8.

NOTE:Ensure that the air ducting hose under the wing is clear of the drilling area.

3. Scrape around the underside of the aerial hole to reveal bright metal in order to ensure a good earth connection. Failure to do this may result in aerial-borne interference being transmitted to the receiver.

4. Pass the aerial upward through the aerial hole and secure into position, taking care to position any keyhole or locking device for easy access.

5. Route the aerial lead through the valance hole into the engine compartment and fit the grommet supplied.

6. Feed the aerial lead through the grommet in the engine compartment bulkhead (3,Fig.O:8). From inside the car, locate the aerial plug through the demister pipe hole in the underside of the front parcel tray, and draw the lead to the radio position.

NOTE:On some vehicles it may be found necessary to pull back the sound proofing material to locate the grommet in the engine bulkhead.

SUPPRESSION .... [5]

It is important in the interests of efficient suppression, to scrape to bare metal, each point at which an earth connection is made.

1. Fit a 1 mfd capacitor to the 'SW' terminal on the ignition coil. Earth under the coil mounting bolt.

2. Where the alternator is fitted with a yellow identification mark on the alternator cap, no further suppression is required to this component.

3. Where an alternator without a yellow identification mark is fitted, connect a 1 mfd. suppressor capacitor to the output terminal of the alternator as follows:

a) Pull off the wiring plug connection on the alternator back plate.

b) Undo the two moulded cover securing screws and detach the cover.

c) Route the fly lead of the capacitor through the slot in the moulded cover and, ensuring that associated wiring is not disturbed, connect the lead to the spare ³⁄₁₆ in terminal blade attached to the main output terminal on the alternator.

d) Refit the moulded cover and reconnect the wiring plug to the alternator.

e) Earth the capacitor mounting clip under the alternator rear fixing bolt.

4. On vehicles fitted with a dynamo fit a 1 mfd. capacitor to the output (large) terminal on the dynamo. Earth under the dynamo mounting bolt.

5. Electric fuel pump models – fit a 1 mfd. capacitor to the supply terminal (white lead) on the petrol pump (located under the left-hand rear of the body). Connect the small tag of the earthing lead to the earth terminal on the petrol pump. Earth the large tag of the lead and capacitor to the bolt on the pump mounting bracket.

6. Connect the small tag of the other earthing lead to the small cheese head screw on the terminal end plate (motor body) of the

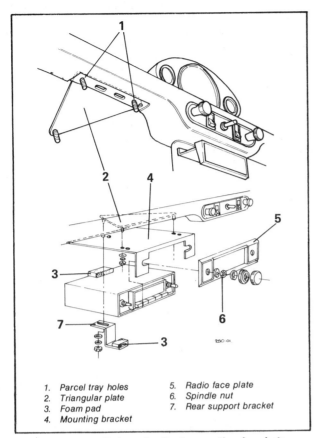

1. Parcel tray holes
2. Triangular plate
3. Foam pad
4. Mounting bracket
5. Radio face plate
6. Spindle nut
7. Rear support bracket

Fig. O:1 Installation of radio & mounting brackets

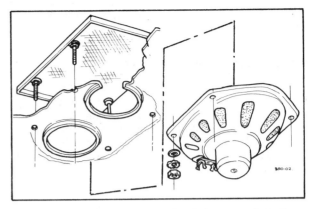

Fig. O:2 Installation of speaker below parcel shelf

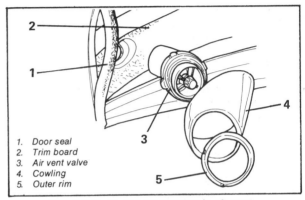

1. Door seal
2. Trim board
3. Air vent valve
4. Cowling
5. Outer rim

Fig. O:3 Exploded view of fascia air vent

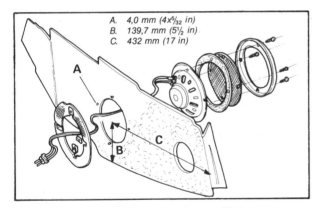

A. 4,0 mm (4x⁵/₃₂ in)
B. 139,7 mm (5½ in)
C. 432 mm (17 in)

Fig. O:4 Installation of speaker — Clubman

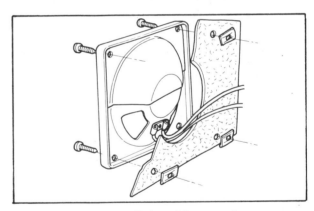

Fig. O:5 Installation of door speaker

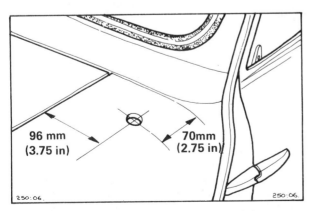

96 mm (3.75 in)
70mm (2.75 in)

Fig. O:6 Aerial positioning — 850/1000 Saloon

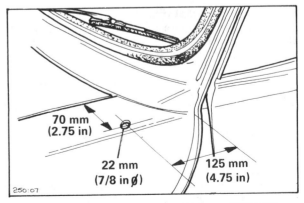

70 mm (2.75 in)
22 mm (7/8 in ⌀)
125 mm (4.75 in)

Fig. O:7 Aerial positioning — Clubman/1275 GT

windscreen wiper motor. Earth the other end of this lead to the gusset plate immediately forward of the wiper motor, where a hole should be provided.

TOWBAR & LIGHTING SOCKET . . . . [6]

The following instructions relate to the Unipart GTT 125 towbar kit which is available from all Unipart stockists and most good accessory shops. It is designed to spread towing loads evenly through the body shell without fouling the rear sub-frame.

The height of the coupling bracket is below the normal standard, and this is necessary to enable the coupling ball to clear the boot lid when it is lowered.

Towbar Fitting (Fig.O:10)

1. Raise and support the rear of the car – see BASIC PROCEDURES.
2. Remove the rear bumper – see BODY & FITTINGS.
3. Position the clamp strip (7,Fig.O:10) above the rear body flange and over the centre hole.
4. Mark and drill two holes through the flange for the 8 mm ($\frac{5}{16}$ in) dia. bolts (8,Fig.O:10).
5. Position the main bracket assembly (1,Fig.O:10) under the floor, and bolt the rear frame to the body flange and clamp strip.
6. Push the forward end up against the floor panel and drill two holes (6,Fig.O:10) for the 10 mm ($\frac{3}{8}$ in) dia. retaining bolts.
7. Bolt the forward end of the towbar to the floor using the strengthening plate (4,Fig.O:10), and the two spacer tubes (5,Fig.O:10). The bolts have large flat washers above the floor panel.
8. Drill two holes, for the 10 mm ($\frac{3}{8}$ in) dia. mounting bolts, up through the rear body valance and through the spare wheel well floor (10,Fig.O:10).
9. Position the short spacer tube between the towbar and the valance, the long tube spacer between the floor and the valance and the stiffening plate (9,Fig.O:10) on top of the floor. Fit the bolts, nuts and washers.
NOTE:The four spacers tubes are all slightly different lengths and must be positioned correctly – see Fig.O:10.
10. Refit the bumper to the body flange.
NOTE:If difficulty is experienced in refitting the nut to the centre bolt, it may have to be pulled down slightly into the countersunk recess in the stiffening strip (7,Fig.O:10).
11. Bolt the coupling ball mounting bracket (2,Fig.O:10) in position and fit the coupling ball. On Clubman and 1275 GT models, a 19 mm ($\frac{3}{4}$ in) spacer and longer bolts will be required to clear the bumper.
12. Fully tighten all the mounting bolts.
13. It is recommended that all the bolts are retightened after approximately 50 miles of towing.

Fitting — Lighting Socket (Fig.O:11)

Obviously if you are going to fit a towing bracket and ball hitch to your Mini then you will also have to fit an electrical socket so that the trailer or caravan can be wired to the car's electrics. A lot of DIY mechanics will tackle the most complicated of mechanical repairs but fight shy of anything to do with the electrical system. However the fitting and wiring of a two bracket wiring kit is straightforward provided the job is carried out methodically and with care.

The following text describes the fitting of a complete Unipart (Transflash) wiring kit. A complete wiring kit comes with all the fittings, leads and connectors.

Fitting a heavy duty flasher unit is unnecessary with this unit as the kit includes its own 'slave' flasher which is capable of handling hazard warning lights and repeater flashers, if fitted.

The kit described includes a supplementary socket, fitted with connections for charging an auxiliary battery, powering a refrigerator, operating a reversing lamp as well as the panel warning light.

1. The Transflash relay should be mounted with terminals facing downwards. Position it near the rear end of the car in the boot, adjacent to the wiring harness. Take care that the relay is not mounted in a position where accidental damage is likely to be caused by loose baggage.
2. An additional warning light on the fascia is required to indicate that the complete vehicle flasher system is working and that any bulb failure is indicated. Locate a suitable position for the trailer warning light on the fascia, in good view from the driver's seat, and to balance with the other instruments, or fit an auxiliary bracket and mount it under the fascia.
3. Check that the lighting and flasher circuits are working correctly. If there are any faults, correct them before proceeding. Then disconnect the battery.
4. Strip about 50 mm (2 in) of the cable outer sheath from one end of the multi-core cable, taking care not to damage the insulation on any of the wires.
5. Strip 13 mm ($\frac{5}{8}$ in) of insulation from the ends of the exposed wires. Twist the strands of each wire together.
6. Connect the wire to the socket terminals in accordance with the colour code. The terminal numbers are marked on the socket. Check that each wire is firmly connected and that frayed wires do not bridge two terminals.
7. Strip a short length of outer sheath from the free end of the cable. Grip the bunch of wires with a pair of pliers and hold the black sheath with the other hand. Pull with the pliers and, at the same time, allow the hand to slide slowly down the sheath towards the socket. Repeat a few times until the sheath slides along the wires against the socket as far as it will go.
8. Finally insert the cable through the centre hole of the rubber gasket, slide the gasket along the cable until it fits snugly against the socket flange.
9. Thread the end of the multi-core cable into the centre hole in the socket mounting plate for the wire, and pull the cable through. When the socket is in position against the plate, the end of the sheath should remain through the hole to protect the wires. Attach the socket to the mounting plate with the three bolts, nuts and washers provided. The socket should be mounted with the hinge uppermost.
10. Fit the mounting plate to the vehicle between the towing bracket and the towbar. Lead the end of the multicore cable into the vehicle boot through any convenient existing hole, or directly into the body through a 13 mm ($\frac{1}{2}$ in) dia. hole drilled through the bodywork behind the bumper.
11. Fit the rubber grommet into the hole and thread the cable through. Smear grease on the cable if it is tight in the grommet. From inside the boot, pull the cable gently to take out the slack. Wrap insulation tape round the cable adjacent to the grommets to prevent the loop of cable from hanging loose. Carefully strip all the black outer sheath from the end of the cable inside the vehicle, leaving only 1 in of sheath projecting through the grommet.
12. Connect the Transflash wiring harness as shown on the wiring diagram (Fig.O:9).

Pin no	Colour	Function
1 (L)	Yellow	Left-hand indicator
2 (54G)	Blue	Supply from rear fog lamp switch
3 (31)	White	Earth
4 (R)	Green	Right-hand indicator
5 (58R)	Brown	Right-hand side & tail lamps
6 (54)	Red	Stop lamps
7 (58L)	Black	Left-hand side & tail lamps
(58b)	Red/Brown	Towing vehicle rear fog lamps

Connections to the original wiring harness can be made by Scotchlok connector. See the Wiring Diagrams section for tracing the lead location and colours. When connecting the rear fog lamps however, the cable to the rear fog lamps should be cut. Join the cut end of the rear fog lamp cable, which leads to

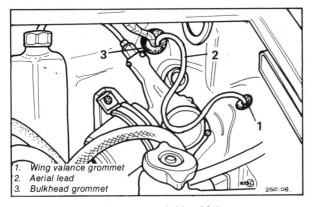

1. Wing valance grommet
2. Aerial lead
3. Bulkhead grommet

Fig. O:8 Routing aerial lead into car

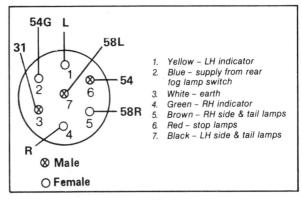

1. Yellow – LH indicator
2. Blue – supply from rear fog lamp switch
3. White – earth
4. Green – RH indicator
5. Brown – RH side & tail lamps
6. Red – stop lamps
7. Black – LH side & tail lamps

⊗ Male
○ Female

Fig. O:9 Towbar socket connections

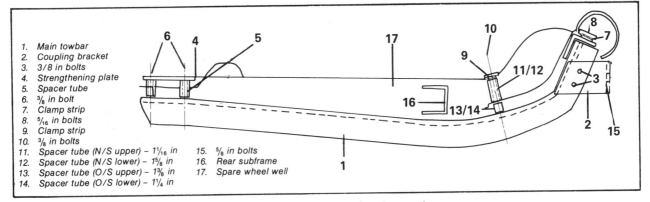

1. Main towbar
2. Coupling bracket
3. 3/8 in bolts
4. Strengthening plate
5. Spacer tube
6. ³⁄₈ in bolt
7. Clamp strip
8. ⁵⁄₁₆ in bolts
9. Clamp strip
10. ³⁄₈ in bolts
11. Spacer tube (N/S upper) – 1¹⁄₁₆ in
12. Spacer tube (N/S lower) – 1⅝ in
13. Spacer tube (O/S upper) – 1⅜ in
14. Spacer tube (O/S lower) – 1¼ in
15. ⅝ in bolts
16. Rear subframe
17. Spare wheel well

Fig. O:10 Sectional view of towbar & mounting

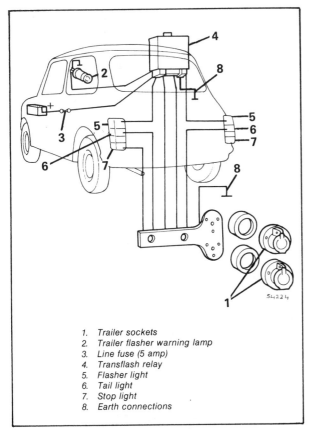

1. Trailer sockets
2. Trailer flasher warning lamp
3. Line fuse (5 amp)
4. Transflash relay
5. Flasher light
6. Tail light
7. Stop light
8. Earth connections

Fig. O:11 Unipart/Transflash wiring diagram

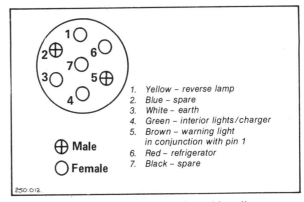

1. Yellow – reverse lamp
2. Blue – spare
3. White – earth
4. Green – interior lights/charger
5. Brown – warning light in conjunction with pin 1
6. Red – refrigerator
7. Black – spare

⊕ Male
○ Female

Fig. O:12 Supplementary socket wiring diagram

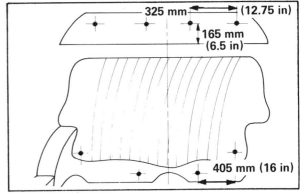

Fig. O:13 Safety seat anchorage points — Saloon

the switch, to the blue lead in the multi-core cable (from 54G on socket). Using the red/brown lead supplied connect terminal 58b on the socket to the remaining cut end leading to the vehicle rear fog lamps.

13. If a supplementary socket is to be fitted, follow the same procedure to fit the socket. A double socket mounting plate will be necessary. Connect the wiring harness to the socket as shown in the illustration (Fig.O:12). The spare terminals can be connected as desired, noting that no single pin must carry more than 16 amps.

Before using the sockets for towing, check the system.

1. Check all the connections and then reconnect the battery. Note that, if the flasher wiring or rear wiring is not correctly connected, there is a possibility that the flasher unit could be burnt out due to a short circuit.

2. Check that the trailer or caravan wiring is connected to the plug according to the 7-pin plug and socket connections. Rewire the plug if the wires are incorrectly connected. (Caravans are often wired by caravan agents and not by the manufacturers, and are not always wired to the British and I.S.O. Standard).

3. Connect the caravan or trailer to the vehicle, and fit the trailer plug into socket on the vehicle.

4. Switch on the vehicle side lights. The vehicle side and rear lights should illuminate, together with the caravan/trailer rear lights, and the rear numberplate light on both should also be illuminated.

5. Switch on the ignition and operate the vehicle foot brake. The stop lights on the vehicle, and on the trailer, should all illuminate together.

6. Operate the vehicle flasher switch to indicate left turn. The left-hand flashers at the front and rear of the vehicle, and at the rear of the trailer, should all operate together. Also the new warning light should operate alternately with the vehicle warning light. Repeat for turning right.

7. Disconnect the trailer plug from the socket and operate the vehicle flasher switch for turning left. The new warning light should cease to function. Check that the vehicle flashers at the front and rear operate satisfactorily. Repeat for right turn.

Fault Finding

1. If the warning indicator lamp does not flash when indicators are being used:
Check
a) That the 7 pin plug is firmly connected to the socket.
b) The live feed including the fuse to the Flash-Master unit.
c) The earth tag connection on the Flash-Master unit.
d) The indicator lamp for bulb failure and also the earthing tag.
2. If the indicator warning lamp fails to flash when using right-hand flashers:
a) Check right-hand flasher bulb on towed vehicle, and the wiring from the 7 pin plug.
b) Check wiring connection to Flash-Master unit, right terminal tag. Conversely, check the left-hand flasher bulb and Flash-Master unit tag if warning lamp fails to flash when indicating to the left.

CHILD SAFETY SEAT . . . . [7]

Only by fitting a child safety seat or harness, secured firmly to the car structure, can a child have a good chance of surviving a severe road accident without injury. Furthermore, with the child safely in position at the rear of the car, a driver can concentrate on the road with less distraction, while the child can enjoy the ride in safety and comfort.

There are many types of baby seat and cot restraints on the market and it is essential to the child's safety that a unit be fitted which meets the required safety standards. The Unipart child safety seat fulfils these requirements and can be easily fitted by

the DIY mechanic. It is suitable for carrying a child weighing between 9-18 kg (20-40 lb) and aged between 9 months and 5 years, depending on size. The seat must only be fitted to the rear and it is recommended that it should be positioned behind the driver so that the driver's view in the rear mirror is not obstructed.

The safety seat is fixed to the car at four anchorage points using adjustable straps to obtain the correct position. The child is held in the seat by a harness that can be used in one of two alternative positions depending on the size of the child.
NOTE:Whenever holes are drilled through the body, the area behind the panel to be drilled must be checked carefully to avoid the possibility of drilling through brake pipes, fuel pipes, or wiring harnesses.

Fitting — Saloon (Fig.O:13)

1. Remove the rear seat cushion as described in BODY & FITTINGS.
2. Bolt the lower seat straps to the anchorage points built in to the floor pan (Fig.O:13).
NOTE:Early cars, not fitted with anchorage points, must have mounting holes drilled as follows:
Mark the floor pan just below the bottom edge of the seat back rest so that two holes can be drilled 30-60 cm (12-24 in) apart and equidistant of the proposed centre line of the safety seat.
Carefully check behind the panel to be drilled for brake pipes, fuel pipes or wiring harnesses. Drill two 18 mm ($^7/_{16}$ in) dia. holes and fit the lower belt mountings using the tapped anchorage plates.
3. Drill two holes in the parcel shelf, 30-45 cm (12-18 in) apart and equidistant of the proposed centre line of the safety seat.
4. Fit the upper anchorage straps using the tapped anchorage plates.
Fit the safety seat to the upper anchorage straps by clipping the free end of the each strap to the hook on the side of the safety seat, ensuring that the spring clip returns to its original position.
5. Adjust the length of each strap so that the seat hangs vertically.
6. Hook the safety seat to the lower anchorage straps and ensure that the spring clip on the hook returns to its original position.
7. Adjust the length of the lower straps so that the seat hangs vertically, but do not overtighten them.
8. Refit the seat cushion, ensuring the adjusting length of the strap protrudes between the back rest and cushion. Adjust the length of the anchorage straps until the safety seat nestles firmly into the rear seat back rest.

Fitting — Estate (Fig.O:14)

1. Drill the lower anchorage points and fit the attachment straps as described for the Saloon.
2. Mark the position for the mountings on the load space floor so that they are 30-45 cm (12-18 in) apart and make an angle of no more than 45 deg. (Fig.O:15). Check the underside of the floor to ensure that the holes will be clear of any brake pipes, fuel pipes or wiring harnesses.
3. Drill two 18 mm ($^7/_{16}$ in) dia. holes and bolt the upper anchorage straps in position.
4. Fit the safety seat to the anchorage straps as described for the Saloon.

Adjusting (Fig.O:16)

1. Adjust the child harness to suit the individual child by slackening off the two shoulder strap adjusters which are located behind the seat on either side.
2. Place the child in the seat and bring the crotch strap between the childs legs and slot the crotch bracket over the

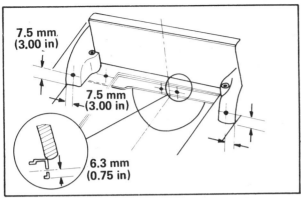

7.5 mm (3.00 in)

7.5 mm (3.00 in)

6.3 mm (0.75 in)

Fig. O:14 Safety seat anchorage points — Estate

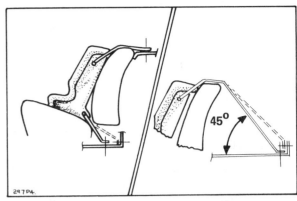

45°

Fig. O:15 Child safety seat mounting

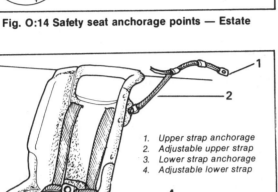

1. Upper strap anchorage
2. Adjustable upper strap
3. Lower strap anchorage
4. Adjustable lower strap

Fig. O:16 Safety seat strap layout

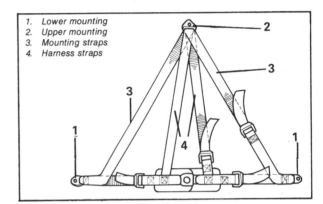

1. Lower mounting
2. Upper mounting
3. Mounting straps
4. Harness straps

Fig. O:17 Child safety harness layout

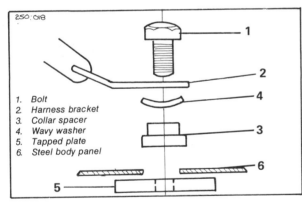

1. Bolt
2. Harness bracket
3. Collar spacer
4. Wavy washer
5. Tapped plate
6. Steel body panel

Fig. O:18 Exploded view of anchorage components

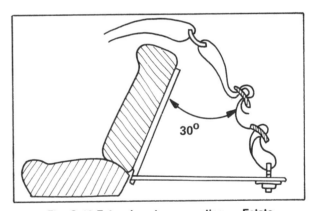

30°

Fig. O:19 Extension strap mounting — Estate

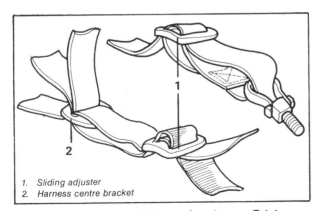

1. Sliding adjuster
2. Harness centre bracket

Fig. O:20 Attachment of extension strap — Estate

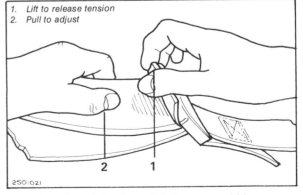

1. Lift to release tension
2. Pull to adjust

Fig. O:21 Adjusting safety harness webbing

tongue of the buckle, then push home the tongue into the release buckle. A positive click will be heard and will indicate that the buckle is secured. If there is any doubt that the buckle is fully engaged, pull firmly on either side of the buckle as a test.

3. Take out the slack by pulling the free ends of the webbing through the shoulder strap adjusters until a tight but comfortable restraint is imposed on the child.

4. The hip straps must be fastened around the child's hips and not the abdomen.

5. Before removing the child from the seat it is good practise to slacken off the shoulder straps. This means that the harness must be readjusted before it is used again, and this ensures correct fitting even when extra clothing is worn. The buckle has been designed to minimise the possibility of the child inadvertently releasing it, and it may be found necessary to exert a slight pull on the tongue when the release button is pressed.

CHILD SAFETY HARNESS . . . . [8]

The following fitting instructions refer to the Unipart child safety harness, part number GSS 207 and the extension strap kit, part number GSS 208 for Estate cars, where applicable.

Fitting — Saloon

1. Remove the rear seat cushion and mount the lower strap fixing brackets to the anchorage points or drill holes as necessary – see Child Safety Seat.

2. Remove the parcel shelf trim pad and drill an 11 mm ($7/16$ in) dia. hole in the shelf panel, positioned centrally between the two floor mounting points.

3. Bolt the top anchorage to the shelf using the tapped anchor plate as shown in Fig.O:18.

4. Adjust the belts as described later in this section.

Fitting — Estate

1. Fit the lower harness straps to the floor as described for the Saloon above.

2. Select a mounting point behind the rear seat on the steel floor panel, so that the extension strap makes an angle of approximately 30° with the seat back (Fig.O:19).

3. Ensure that the underside of the panel is clear of brake pipes, petrol pipes and the wiring harness.

4. Drill an 11 mm ($7/16$ in) dia. clearance hole through the floor and mount the shackle bolt using the tapped anchorage plate supplied with the main harness kit (Fig.O:18).

5. Thread the webbing of the extension strap through the slot in the upper harness bracket from the underside and then through the adjuster (Fig.O:20).

6. Adjust the extension strap, using the sliding adjuster, until any excessive slack has been taken out.

Do not overtighten as final adjustments are made with the main harness as described under Adjustment – All Models below.

Adjustment — All Models

1. Pull the slack webbing through the adjuster buckle in the outer diagonal harness strap until the straps are as tight as possible against the seat backrest. This will prevent any possibility of the seat moving forward if the car is involved in an accident.

2. To adjust the harness for the child, place the lap strap round the lower pelvic region, making sure that the comfort pad is positioned correctly, and fasten the buckle.

NOTE:A positive 'click' will be heard when the tongue has engaged securely in the buckle. Engagement can be checked by pulling the webbing on both sides of the buckle.

3. Pull the loose ends of the lap strap adjusters outwards until the strap is a tight but comfortable fit.

4. Adjust the shoulder straps by pulling the free end of the webbing through the adjuster situated near the main buckle.

Technical Data

GENERAL DIMENSIONS - mm (in) ....[1]

Length:
Mini Saloon 3054 (120.23)
Clubman Saloon 3166 (124.65)
Mini Estate & Van 3299 (129.88)
Clubman Estate 3402 (134.00)
Pick-up 3315 (130.50)
Width – all models 1415 (55.71)
Height (unladen):
Saloons 1346 (53.00)
Estate, Van & Pick-up 1359 (53.50)
Wheelbase:
Saloons 2036 (80.16)
Esate, Van & Pick-up 2138 (84.18)
Track – Front:
All models – except 1275 GT (pre 74) 1205 (47.44)
All models – except 1275 GT (74 on) 1215 (47.50)
1275 GT & Mini (84 on) 1239 (48.75)
1275 GT – Denovo tyres 1230 (48.37)
Track – Rear:
All models – except 1275 GT (pre 74) 1164 (45.82)
All models - except 1275 GT (74 on) 1178 (46.37)
1275 GT & Mini (84 on) 1204 (47.43)
1275 GT – Denovo tyres 1200 (47.25)
Turning circle:
Saloons .... 8.70 m (28.5 ft)
Estate, Van & Pick-up .... 8.80 m (29.0 ft)
Ground clearance (unladen, '84 on) .... 159 mm (6.25 in)
Ground clearance (unladen, pre '84) ...... 167 mm (6.50 in)

Kerb weight (average) - kg (lb)

Mini saloon - Manual 630 (1390)
Mini saloon – Automatic 650 (1440)
Mini saloon – Hydrolastic 660 (1460)
Clubman saloon 670 (1480)
Estate, Countryman & Traveller 680 (1500)
Van & Pick-up 600 (1320)
Maximum towing weight:
Saloon 407 (895)
Estate, Van & Pick-up 305 (671)
Maximum vehicle loading:
Equal to 4 persons plus 48 kg (106 lb) of luggage 318 (700)
Maximum roof rack load 40 (90)

NOTE:Any loads that are carried on a roof rack or a downward load from a towing hitch must be included in the maximum loading figure.

ROUTINE MAINTENANCE ....[2]

Specified Lubricants

Engine/gearbox oil (inc.automatic) Multigrade 10W/30, 10W/40 to
MIL-L-2104B or A.P.I. SE or SF specification
Grease points .... Multi-purpose lithium grease N.L.G. 1/2
Steering rack .... BP Energrease/FGL Fluid grease
Anti-freeze   Unipart Universal or equivalent to BS 3151 or 3152
Brake fluid .... Unipart Universal or equivalent to
FMV SS 116 DOT 3 or SAE J1703 spec.
Fuel octane:
848 cc & 998 cc 91
998cc ('82 on) & 1275 97
1098 cc 95

Capacities - litres (pints)

Engine oil (inc. filter):
Manual 4,83 (8.5)
Automatic 5,0 (9.0)
Cooling system:
With heater 3,55 (6.25)
Without heater 3,00 (5,25)
Steering rack .... 100 cc (0.18)
Fuel tank – litres (gals):
850, 1000 & Clubman 25 (5.5)
850 from VIN 691247 .... 34 (7.5)
1000 from VIN 701402 .... 34 (7.5)
Clubman from VIN 689970 .... 34 (7.5)
Estate, Van & Pick-up 27,3 (6.0)
1275 GT 34 (7.5)

Anti-Freeze Concentration

Protection to:
-19°C 33⅓%
-36°C 50%

Anti-freeze Specific Gravity:

50% solution 1.075
45% solution 1.068
40% solution 1.061
30% solution 1.047
20% solution 1.032
10% solution 1.017

Battery Specific Gravity:

Fully charged 1.280
Half charged 1.200
Fully discharged 1.120

Tyre Pressures (cold) - bar (lb/in²)

Normal Load	Front	Rear
520x10 crossply	1,7 (24)	1,5 (22)
145 SR 10 radial	2,0 (28)	1,8 (26)
145/70 SR 12	2,0 (28)	2,0 (28)
155/65 SF310 Denovo	2,0 (28)	1,8 (26)
165 HR70x10	1,7 (24)	1,8 (26)
Fully Laden	Front	Rear
520x10 crossply	1,7 (24)	1,7 (24)
145 SR 10 radial	2,0 (28)	1,8 (26)
145/70 SR 12	2,0 (28)	2,0 (28)
155/65 SF 310 Denovo	2,0 (28)	1,8 (26)

TUNE-UP ....[3]

Compression Pressures - bar (lb/in²)

850/1000 cc (1962-76) 10,5 (150)
850/1000 cc ('76 on) 12,0 (170)
850/1000 cc – Auto. (1965-74) 11,25 (160)
850/1000 cc – Auto. (1974-76) 10,5 (150)
850/1000 cc – Auto. ('76 on) 12,0 (170)
1100 cc ('74 on) 11,6 (165)
1275 GT ('69 on) 12,3 (175)

Valve Clearances (cold) - mm (in)

Inlet & Exhaust 0,3 (0.012)
Spark plugs (City, HLE, Mayfair '82 on):
Make/type .... Champion RN9Y or Unipart GSP263
Electrode gap 0,9 (0.035)
Tightening torque .... 2,5 kg m (18 lb ft)
Spark plugs (All other models):
Make/type .... Champion N9Y or Unipart GSP163
Electrode gap 0,64 (0.025)
Tightening torque .... 2,5 kg m (18 lb ft)

Idle Settings
850 cc Engines:

Trans.	Year	Carb.	Type Idle Speed	Idle CO %
Manual	1959-72	HS2	500	-
Automatic	1965-69	HS4	650	-
Manual	1972-74	HS2	800	3,4-4,5
Manual	1974-76	HS4	800	3,5-4,5
Manual	1976-80	HS4	750	3 max.
Manual	1976-80	HS4	750	3,5-4,5

1000cc Engines:

Manual	1967-72	HS2	500	-
Automatic	1967-74	HS4	650	-
Manual	1972-74	HS2	800	3,5-4,5
Manual	1974-76	HS4	750	3,5-4,5
Manual	1976-	HS4	750	3 max.
Automatic	1976-	HS4	750	3 max.
Manual	1976-78	HS4	750	3,5-4,5
Automatic	1976-78	HS4	750	3,4-4,5
Manual	1982-	HS4	650	2,5±1

1100cc Engines:

Manual	1974-76	HS4	750	3-4,5
Manual	1976-78	HS4	750	3 max.
Manual	1976-78	HS4	750	3-4,5

1275cc Engines:

Manual	1969-72	HS4	650	-
Manual	1972-76	HS4	750	3-4,5
Manual	1976-77	HS4	850	3 max.
Manual	1976-77	HS4	850	3-4,5
Manual	1978	HS4	750	3 max.

Ignition Timing
848cc Engines:

Special Ver.	Year	Distri. serial number	Static	Dynamic
97 octane	1959-72	40768, 41026, 41411	TDC	3/600
91 octane	1959-72	40767, 41007, 41410	7°	10/600
Automatic	1965-69	41134, 41242, 41251,41417	3	6/600
	1972-74	41026, 41411	TDC	19/1000
SU-HS2	1974-76	41569, 41570	9	14/1000
SU-HS4	1974-76	41570	6	11/1000
	1976-	41417, 41767	-	7/1000

998cc Engines:

	1967-72	40931, 41030, 41412	5	8/600
Van/Pick-up	1967-72	41007, 41410	7	10/600
Automatic	1967-74	41134, 41242, 41417	4	6/600
	1972-74	41254, 41412	5	11/1000
SU-HS2	1974-76	41246, 41418	10	13/1000
SU-HS4	1974-76	41418	4	7/1000
	1976-78	41418, 41793	-	7/1000
	1978-82	41406, 41765	-	8/1000
	1982-	Lucas 41882/Duce. 5252	-	8/1500

1098cc Engines:

	1974-76	41246, 41418	9	12/1000
	1976-78	41418, 41793	-	12/1000

1275cc Engines:

	1969-72	41257, 41419	8	10/600
	1972-76	41257, 41419	8	13/1000
	1976-78	41419, 41768	-	13/1000

Distributor

Contact breaker gap .... 0,35-0,4 mm (0.014-0.016 in)
Dwell angle:
Lucas 25D4 .... 60°±3°
Lucas 45D4 (non-sliding contacts) .... 51°±5°
Lucas 45D4 (sliding contacts) .... 57°±5°
Ducellier .... 57°±2°30'
Lucas 59D4 .... 54°±5°
Ducellier 59D4 .... 57°±2.5°
Rotor arm rotation .... Anti-clockwise
Firing order .... 1 – 3 – 4 – 2

ENGINE ....[4]

Engine Identification Code
Mini 850 .... 8MB/85H
Mini 1000 .... 99H
Mini 1100 .... 10H
Mini 1275 GT 12H

General Specifications - mm (in)
8MB/85H Engine:
Capacity .... 848 cc
Bore 62,94 (2.478)
Stroke 68,26 (2.687)
Compression ratio .... 8.3:1 (8.9:1, auto 1965 to 74)

Pistons - mm (in)
Clearance of skirt in cylinder:
Top 0,066-0,081 (0.0026-0.0036)
Bottom 0,015-0,030 (0.0006-0.0016)
Number of rings .... 4 (3 compression, 1 oil control)
Width of ring grooves:
Top, second & third 1,805-1,843 (0.0715-0.0725)
Oil control 3,213-3,238 (0.1265-0.1275)
Piston pin bore 15,867-15,872 (0.6245-0.6247)
Oversizes available 0,254; 0,508; 0,762; 1,016
(+ 0.010; + 0.020; + 0.030; + 0.040)

Rings - mm (in)
Compression rings:
Fitted gap 0,178-0,305 (0.007-0.012)
Ring to groove clearance 0,038-0,089 (0.0015-0.0035)
Oil control ring:
Fitted gap 0,178-0,305 (0.007-0.012)
Ring to groove clearance 0,038-0,089 (0.0015-0.0035)

Crankshaft - mm (in)
Journal diameter 44,46-44,47 (1.7505-1.751)
Minimum regrind diameter 43,45 (1.7105)
Bearing clearance 0,025-0,068 (0.001-0.0027)
Crankshaft endfloat 0,025-0,127 (0.001-0.005)
Big-end bearings:
Crankpin journal diameter 41,28-41,29 (1.6254-1.6259)
Minimum regrind diameter 40,27 (1.5854)
Bearing clearance 0,025-0,064 (0.001-0.0025)

Camshaft - mm (in)
Camshaft endfloat 0,076-0,178 (0.003-0.007)

Valves - mm (in)
Valve spring free length 41,27 (1.625)
Inlet valve:
Stem to guide clearance 0,038-0,064 (0.0015-0.0025)
Seat angle .... 45°
Exhaust valve:
Stem to guide clearance 0,051-0,076 (0.002-0.003)
Seat angle .... 45°
Valve guide height 'X' .... 13,72 mm (0.54 in)

Oil Pump - mm (in)
Type .... Hoborn-Eaton rotor type or Concentric
Inner to outer rotor clearance .... 0,152 (0.006) max.
Outer rotor to housing clearance ...... 0,254 (0.010) max.
Rotor endfloat .... 0,127 (0,005) max.
Warning light switch pressure .... 0,4-0,7 bar (6-10 lb/in²)
System pressure:

Running	4,22 kg/cm² (60 lb/in²)
Idling	1,05 kg/cm² (15 lb/in²)
Relief valve opening pressure	4,22 kg/cm² (60 lb/in²)
Relief valve spring free length	72,64 mm (2.86 in)

99H Engine:

The following information gives only the points of difference from the 8MB/85H engine and should be used in conjunction with the proceeding specifications.

Capacity	998 cc
Bore	64,588 (2.543)
Stroke	76,2 (3.000)
Compression ratio:	
HC	8.3:1 (8.9:1, auto 1965 to 74)
LC	7.6:1
1982 on	10.3:1

Pistons - mm (in)

Clearance of skirt in cylinder:

| Top | 0,060-0,085 (0.0022-0.0033) |
| Bottom | 0,010-0,026 (0.0004-0.0014) |

Width of ring grooves:

| Top, second & third | 1,638-1,663 (0.0645-0.0655) |

Rings - mm (in)

Compression rings:

| Ring to groove clearance | 0,051-0,102 (0.002-0.004) |

10H Engine:

The following information gives only the points of difference from the 8MB/85H engine and should be used in conjunction with the specification for the 8MB/85H models given previously.

8MB/85H models given previously.

Capacity	1098 cc
Bore	64,58 (2.543)
Stroke	83,72 (3.296)
Compression ratio	8.5:1

Pistons - mm (in)

Clearance of skirt in cylinder:

| Top | 0,05-0,08 (0.0021-0.0033) |
| Bottom | 0,013-0,040 (0.0005-0.0015) |

Width of ring grooves:

| Top, second & third | 1,638-1,663 (0.0645-0.0655) |

Rings - mm (in)

Compression rings:

| Ring to groove clearance | 0,051-0,102 (0.002-0.004) |

Oil control – fitted gap:

| Rails | 0,305-0,711 (0.012-0.028) |
| Side springs | 2,54-3,81 (0.10-0.15) |

Valves - mm (in)

| Valve spring free length | 49,78 (1.96) |

Inlet valve & exhaust valve:

| Stem to guide clearance | 0,040-0,080 (0.0015-0.0025) |

12H Engine:

The following information gives only the point of difference from the 8MB/85H engine and should be used in conjunction with the specification for the 8MB/85H models given previously.

Capacity	1274.86 cc
Bore	70,61 (2.78)
Stroke	81,28 (3.2)
Compression ratio:	
HC	8.8:1
LC	8.0:1

Pistons - mm (in)

Clearance of skirt in cylinder:

| Top | 0,070-0,114 (0.0029-0.0045) |
| Bottom | 0,031-0,056 (0.0012-0.0022) |

Width of ring grooves:

| Top, second and third | 1,230-1,250 (0.0484-0.0494) |
| Oil control | 4,001-4,003 (0.1578-0.1588) |

Rings - mm (in)

Compression rings – fitted gap::

| Top ring | 0,28-0,41 (0.011-0.016) |
| Second and third | 0,20-0,33 (0.008-0.013) |

Oil control ring:

| Fitted gap, rails & side springs | 0,254-1,02 (0.010-0.040) |

Crankshaft - mm (in)

Main bearings:

Journal diameter	50,83-50,84 (2.0012-2.0017)
Minimum regrind diam.	49,78 (1.9605)
Big end bearings:	
Crankpin journal diameter	44,44-44,46 (1.7497-1.750)
Minimum regrind diam.	43,44 (1.7102)

Tightening Torques - kg m (lb ft)

Camshaft nut	8,9 (65)
Clutch spring housing to pressure plate setscrews	2,2 (16)
Coolant temperature transmitter	2,2 (16)
Connecting rod big-end:	
Bolts	5,1 (37)
Nuts	4,6 (33)
Crankshaft pulley bolt	10,3 (75)
Cylinder head nuts	6,9 (50)
Additional nuts on 1275 GT	3,5 (25)
Cylinder side cover (99H engine)	0,5 (3,5)
Driving strap to flywheel setscrew	2,2 (16)
Flywheel centre bolt	15,5 (112)
Flywheel housing bolts and stud nuts	2,5 (18)
Gudgeon pin clamp screws (850 only)	3,2 (24)
Main bearing bolts	8,7 (63)
Manifold to cylinder head nuts	1,9 (14)
Oil filter head nuts	1,9 (14)
Oil pipe banjo	5,3 (38)
Oil filter bowl centre bolt	1,9 (14)
Oil pump bolts	1,1 (8)
Oil relief valve cap nut	5,9 (43)
Rocker cover	0,5 (3,5)
Rocker shaft bracket nuts	3,2 (24)
Spark plugs	2,5 (18)
Sump drain plug	3,5 (25)
Timing cover to front plate:	
¼ in dia. U.N.F. bolts	0,7 (5)
⁵⁄₁₆ in dia. U.N.F. bolts	1,7 (12)
Water outlet elbow nuts	1,1 (8)
Water pump bolts	2,2 (16)

ENGINE ELECTRICS ....[5]

Battery (Lucas, unless otherwise stated)

Polarity	Type	Capacity (at 20hr rate)
Positive earth	BLT/BTZ 7A	34
Positive earth	BT/BTZ 7A	43
Negative earth	Pacemaker A7	30
Negative earth	Pacemaker A9	40
Negative earth	CLZ/CL 7	34
Negative earth	Exide 6VTP9-BR	35
Negative earth (1275 GT)	Pacemaker A9	40
Negative earth (1275 GT)	Pacemaker A11/9	50
Negative earth (1275 GT)	C/CZ 9	43

Dynamo

Type	Lucas C40
Rated output	22 amp
Minimum brush length (protrusion)	6,5 mm (0.25 in)

Alternator

Type	Lucas 11AC
Rated output	43 amp
Minimum brush length (protrusion)	4 mm (0.15 in)
Type	Lucas 16ACR
Rated output	34 amp
Minimum brush length (protrusion)	8 mm (0.30 in)
Type	Lucas A115
Rated output	45 amp
Minimum brush length (protrusion)	10 mm (0.4 in)

Starter Motor

Type	Lucas M35J/M35G
Minimum brush length	8 mm (0.3 in)
Commutator thickness	2 mm (0.08 in)

Distributor

Mini 850 – 1976 on:

Type	Lucas 45D4
Serial number:	
Non-sliding contacts	41417
Sliding contacts	41767
Condenser capacity	0.18-0.24 mfd
Centrifugal advance – vacuum pipe disconnected:	
Decelerating check	24-28° at 4800 rpm
	18-22° at 2800 rpm
	12-16° at 1600 rpm
	0-4° at 800 rpm
No advance below	300 rpm
Vacuum advance:	
Starts	76,2 mm Hg (3 in Hg)
Finishes	381 mm Hg (18° at 15 in Hg)

Mini 1000 – 1976-1978:

Type	Lucas 45D4 or Ducellier
Serial number:	
Non-sliding contacts	41418
Sliding contacts	41793
Condenser capacity	0.18-0.24 mfd
Centrifugal advance – vacuum pipe disconnected:	
Decelerating check	14-18° at 4000 rpm
	9-13° at 2400 rpm
	6-10° at 1500 rpm
	0-1° at 900 rpm
No advance below	800 rpm
Vacuum advance:	
Starts	152 mm Hg (6 in Hg)
Finishes	356 mm Hg (16° at 14 in Hg)

Mini 1000 – 1978:

Type	Lucas 45D4 or Ducellier
Serial number:	
Non-sliding contacts	41406
Sliding contacts	41765
Condenser capacity	0.18-0.24 mfd
Centrifugal advance – vacuum disconnected:	
Decelerating check	23-27° at 4800 rpm
	16-20° at 2500 rpm
	8-12° at 1600 rpm
	0-4° at 700 rpm
No advance below	300 rpm
Vacuum advance:	
Starts	76 mm Hg (3 in Hg)
Finishes	24° at 330 mm Hg (13 in Hg)

Mini Clubman 1098cc – 1976-78:

Type	Lucas 45D4 or Ducellier
Serial number:	
Non-sliding contacts	41418
Sliding contacts	41793
Condenser capacity	0.18-0.24 mfd

Centrifugal advance – vacuum pipe disconnected:	
Decelerating check	20-24° at 6000 rpm
	14-18° at 4000 rpm
	9-13° at 2400 rpm
	6-10° at 1500 rpm
	0-1° at 900 rpm
No advance below	800 rpm
Vacuum advance:	
Starts	152 mm Hg (6 in Hg)
Finishes	16° at 356 mm Hg (14 in Hg)

1275 GT – 1976-1978:

Type	Lucas 45D4
Serial number:	
Non-sliding contacts	41419
Sliding contacts	41768
Condenser capacity	0.18-0.24 mfd
Centrifugal advance – vacuum pipe disconnected:	
Decelerating check	18-22° at 4000 rpm
	11-15° at 2800 rpm
	6.5-10° at 2100 rpm
	4-8° at 1600 rpm
	0-3° at 800 rpm
No advance below	300 rpm

Ignition Coil

Make/type:	
All except 1275 GT & Mini 1000 1982 on	Lucas LA12
1275 GT	Lucas 15C6
Mini 1000 (1982 on)	AC Delco 9977230 or 520035A
Primary resistance at 20°C (68°F):	
Lucas LA12	3.2-3.4 ohms
Lucas 15C6	3.2-3.4 ohms
AC Delco	1.2-1.5 ohms
Consumption – ignition on:	
Lucas LA12 & 15C6	3.9 amps
Ballast resistance – AC Delco	1.3-1.5 ohms

Tightening Torques - kg m (lb ft)

Alternator adjusting link to alternator	1,2 (9)
Alternator adjusting link to front plate	3,7 (27)
Alternator bracket to crankcase	2,2 (16)
Alternator pulley nut	3,9 (28)
Dynamo pulley nut	2,2 (16)
Alternator top fixings	2,2 (16)
Distributor clamp setscrew	2,2 (16)
Starter motor to flywheel housing	3,7 (27)

COOLING SYSTEM ....[6]

Coolant capacity:	
With heater	3,55 litres (6.25 pints)
Without heater	3,00 litres (5.25 pints)
Thermostat (standard):	
Pre '76	82°C
'76 on	88°C
Pressure cap:	
Pre 1974	0.9 bar (13 lb/in²)
1974 on	1.05 bar (15 lb/in²)
Water pump drive belt tension:	
Max. deflection	13 mm (0,5 in)

Tightening Torques - kg m (lb/ft)

Water pump bolts	2,2 (16)
Water outlet elbow nuts	1,1 (8)
Coolant temperature transmitter	2,2 (16)

FUEL SYSTEM ....[7]

Fuel Pump

Pressure test:	
Suction minimum	152 mm (6 in Hg)

Pressure maximum .... 0,28 bar (4 lb/in²)

Carburettor Specifications

Year	SU Type	Identification No.	Needle
850 engine, manual transmission:			
1959-1972	HS2	-	FB
1972-1974	HS2	AUD 449	AAV
1974-1976	HS4	AUD 611	ABS
1976-1980	HS4	FZX 1043 1142, 1143, 1064	ADH
850 engine, auto. transmission:			
1965-1969	HS4	-	AN
1000 eng., manual traansmission			
1967-1972	HS2	-	GX
1972-1974	HS2	AUD 509	AAV
1974-1976	HS4	AUD 679	ABX
1976	HS4	FZX 1044 1146, 1147	ADE
1976-1978	HS4	FZX 1065	ADE
1982-	HS4	FZX 1415	AAC
1000 engine, automatic transmission			
1967-1974	HS4	-	AC
1974-1976	HS4	FZX 1044 1146, 1147	ADE
1976-1978	HS4	FZX 1065	ADE
1100 engine, manual transmission			
1974-1976	HS4	AUD 508	ABP
1976-1978	HS4	FZX 1045, 1160, 1161, 1066	ABP
1275 engine, manual transmission			
1969-1972	HS4	-	AC
1972-1976	HS4	AUD 567	ABB
1976-1977	HS4	FZX 1046 1047, 1165	ABB
1978	HS4	FZX 1174	AAT

Fast-Idle Speed - rpm

850 engine, manual transmission
1959-1972 900
1972-1976 1100-1200
1976-1980 1200
850 engine, automatic transmission
1965-1969 1050
1000 engine, manual transmission
1967-1972 900
1972-1976 1100-1200
1976-1982 1300
1982- 1100
1000 engine, automatic transmission
1967-1974 1050
1974-1976 1100-1200
1976-1978 1200
1100 engine, manual transmission
1974-1976 1100-1200
1976-1978 1200
1275 engine, manual transmission
1969-1972 1050
1972-1976 1100-1200
1976-1978 1300
Piston spring colour (all carbs) .... Red
Jet size .... 3 mm (0,09 in)

CLUTCH & GEARBOX ....[8]

Clutch - mm (in)

Make .... Borg & Beck or Verto (1982 on)
Type .... Diaphragm spring (coil springs on early type)
Operation .... Hydraulic

Diaphragm spring colour:
850/1000 cc .... Brown
1100 cc .... Green
1275 cc .... Blue
Return stop clearance:
Early type (non adjustable throw-out stop) 1,52 (0.060)
Later Borg & Beck (adjustable throw-out stop) 0,50 (0.020)
Later Verto (throw-out stop at cover end) 6,5 (0.260)

Transmission - mm (in)

Primary gear endfloat 0,1-0,18 (0.004-0.007)
Primary gear shim range 2,79-2,84 (0.110-0.112)
　　　　　　　　　　　　　　　2,84-2,89 (0.112-0.114)
　　　　　　　　　　　　　　　2,89-2,94 (0.114-0.116)
　　　　　　　　　　　　　　　2,94-2,99 (0.116-0.118)
　　　　　　　　　　　　　　　2,99-3,04 (0.118-0.120)
Idler gear endfloat 0,10-0,18 (0.004-0.007)
Idler gear thrust washer range ... 3,35-3,37 (0.132-0.133)
　　　　　　　　　　　　　　　3,40-3,42 (0.134-0.135)
　　　　　　　　　　　　　　　3,45-3,47 (0.136-0.137)
　　　　　　　　　　　　　　　3,50-3,53 (0.138-0.139)
Final drive bearing pre-load 0,25-0,50 (0.001-0.002)
Bearing pre-load (bearings marked THRUST') 0,10 (0.004)
Laygear endfloat 0,05-0,15 (0.002-0.006)
Laygear thrust washer calculation:

Use thrust washer no.

Laygear measured gap	3-synchro	4-synchro
3,18-3,22 (0.125-0.127)	88G 325	22G 856
3,25-3,30 (0.128-0.130)	88G 326	22G 857
3,32-3,37 (0.131-0.133)	88G 327	22G 858
3,41 (0.134)	88G 328	22G 859

1st motion shaft circlip calculation:

Measured gap	Use circlip no.
2,43-2,48 (0.096-0.098)	2A 3710
2,48-2,54 (0.098-0.100)	2A 3711

3rd motion shaft bearing shim calculation:

Measured gap	Use shims totalling
0,13-0,15 (0.005-0.006)	0,13 (0.005)
0,15-0,20 (0.006-0.008)	0,18 (0.007)
0,20-0,25 (0.008-0.010)	0,23 (0.009)
0,25-0,30 (0.010-0.012)	0,28 (0.011)
0,30-0,35 (0.012-0.014)	0,33 (0.013)
0,35-0,38 (0.014-0.015)	0,38 (0.015)

Tightening torques - kg m (lb ft)

Flywheel housing nuts and bolts 2,5 (18)
Clutch pressure plate to flywheel (Verto) 2,5 (18)
Flywheel retaining bolt 15.5 (112)
Clutch spring housing to pressure plate (Borg & Beck) ... 2,2 (16)
Driving strap to flywheel 2,2 (16)
Third motion shaft bearing retainer screws 1,8 (13)
First motion shaft nut 20,7 (150)
Third motion shaft nut 20,7 (150)
Transmission case to crankcase 0,8 (6)
Transmission drain plug 3,5 (25)
Transmission case studs – ⅜ in dia. UNC 1,1 (8)
Transmission case studs – 5/16 in dia. UNC 0,8 (6)
Transmission case stud nuts – ⅜ in UNF 3,4 (25)
Transmission case stud nuts – 5/16 in UNF 2,5 (18)
Bottom cover set screws – ¼ in dia. UNC
(change-speed tower) 0,8 (6)
Final drive crown wheel to diff. cage 8,3 (60)
Driving flange to differential nut .... 9,6 (70) align to next split pin hole
End cover bolts (differential housing) 2,5 (18)

AUTOMATIC TRANSMISSION ....[9]

Type .... Automotive Products AP4
Kickdown up-shift speeds:
1-2 25-33
2-3 37-45

3-4	49-57

Kickdown down-shift speeds:

4-3	47-39
3-2	39-31
2-1	26-18
Kickdown crank gauge rod	6 (0.25)
Brake band adjustment (nut to lever)	1,02 (0.040)
Converter output gear endfloat	0,099-0,16 (0.0035-0.0064)
Thrust washers	see CLUTCH & GEARBOX data
Idler gear endfloat	0,1-0,18 (0.004-0.007)
Thrust washers	3,3-3,32 (0.13-0.131)
	3,35-3,37 (0.132-0.133)
	3,4-3,42 (0.134-0.135)
	3,45-3,47 (0.136-0.137)
	3,5-3,53 (0.138-0.139)
Input gear pre-load	0,025-0,07 (0.001-0.003)
Shim thickness	0,07 (0.003)
	0,3 (0.012)

Tightening torques - kg m (lb ft)

Transmission case:

5/16 in	2,6 (19)
3/8 in	4,1 (30)
Converter centre bolt	15,5 (112)
Converter 6 centre bolts	2,9 (21)
Converter housing nuts, bolts	2,5 (18)
Input shaft nut	9,7 (70)
Servo unit bolts	2,3 (17)
Valve block nuts	1 (7)
Kickdown control assembly	0,7 (5)
Transmission case to crankcase	1,7 (12)
Governor mounting plate bolts	1,8 (13)
Drain plug	3,5 (25)

STEERING .... [10]

Front wheel alignment to 1976	1,6 mm (1/16 in) toe-out
Front wheel alignment from 1976	parallel±1,5 mm (1/16 in)

Rack pinion pre-load - mm (in)

Mk 1 cars	0,05 (0.002)
Mk 2 cars	0,05-1,13 (0.002-0.005)
Mk 3 cars on	0,025-0,076 (0.001-0.003)
Shim thickness	0,06 (0.002)
	0,13 (0.005)
	0,25 (0.010)
Standard washer thickness	1,52 (0.060)

Rack damper setting – mm (in):

Mk 1 cars, flat spring	0,05 (0.002)
Mk 1, Mk 2 cars, coil spring	0,05-0,013 (0.002-0.005)
Mk 3 cars on	0,05-0,013 (0.002-0.005)
Inner ball joint articulation	0,36-0,59 kg m (32-52 lb in)
Pinion pre-load	0,17 kg m (15 lb in)
Ball pin centre dimension (Mk 2 on)	1056 mm (41.64 in)

Tightening Torques - kg m (lb ft)

Steering column clamp	1,7 (12)
Bracket to parcel shelf	1,9 (14)
Steering arm to swivel hub	4,3 (33)
Steering rack mounting bolts	1,7 (12)
Steering wheel nut	4,8 (35)
Track rod ball pin nut	3 (22)
Track rod end locknut	5,3 (38)

FRONT SUSPENSION .... [11]

Suspension type:

'Dry' type	Rubber cone springs with hydraulic shock absorbers
'Wet' type	Hydrolastic displacers

Suspension trim height (Hydrolastic) – mm (in):

NOTE:Trim height is measured from wheel centre line to underside of wing opening, with car in unladen condition and a maximum of 4 Imp Galls (18.2 litres) of petrol in tank. Adjust system pressure to obtain specified height.

Clubman, 1275 GT	343±9,5 (13.5±0.375)

All models except Clubman & 1275 GT

Early type front	330±6,35 (13±0.25)
Early type rear	343±6,35 (13.5±0.25)
Later type front	321±6,35 (12.625±0.25)
Later type rear	333±6,35 (13.14±0.25)
Swivel hub ball joint preload	0,05 mm (0.002 in)
Swivel hub ball joint shims available in – mm (in):	0.05 (0,002), 0.08 (0,003)
	0.13 (0,005), 0.25 (0,010), 0.51 (0,020)

Tightening Torques - kg m (lb ft)

Road wheel nuts (steel wheels)	6,4 (45)
Road wheel nuts (alloy wheels)	5,1 (37)
Driveshaft U' bolts	1,4 (10)
Hub ball joint socket	10,3 (75)
Hub ball joint nut to arms	5,3 (38)
Hub nut (align to next split pin hole)	8,3 (60)
Disc brake models	21 (150)
Lower arm shaft nut	4,5 (33)
Upper arm shaft nut	7,3 (53)
Tie rod to body	3 (22)
Tie rod to arm	2,6 (19)

REAR SUSPENSION .... [12]

Wheel alignment	3,2 mm (0.125 in) toe-in

Tightening Torques - kg m (lb ft)

Hub nut (align to next split pin hole)	8,3 (60)
Radius arm pivot shaft nut	7,3 (53)

BRAKES .... [13]

Front Drum Brakes - mm (in)

Minimum shoe lining thickness	2 (0.08)
Drum diameter	178 (7)
Cylinder bore diameter	24 (0,94)

Front Disc Brakes - mm (in)

Fitment 1275 GT, Mini 25 & all models Oct '84 on:

Disc pad minimum thickness	3,0 (1/8)

Brake disc diameter:

Up to 1974	191 (7.5)
1974 on	214 (8.4)
Caliper bore diameter	51 (2)

Rear Drum Brakes - mm (in)

Minimum shoe lining thickness	2 (0.08)
Cylinder bore diameter	19 (0.75)
1275 GT, 1974 on	13 (0.5)

Master Cylinder - mm (in)

Bore diameter	18 (0.7)

Tightening Torques - kg m (lb ft)

Disc brake caliper bolts	5,3 (38)
Disc to drive flange	5,8 (42)
Rear backplate to arm	2,8 (20)
Master cylinder PDWA end plug	4,5 (33)
Pressure failure switch	1,9 (14)
Compensating valve end plug	3,6 (26)
Master cylinder reservoir mountings	0,7 (5)
Inertia valve end plug	6,4 (45)

GENERAL ELECTRICS .... [14]

Fuses

No	Rating	Circuit

Positive earth cars, 1959-1967:

1 ....35 amp ....Control box (-1964)
Starter solenoid (1964-)
2 ....35 amp ....Horn
Interior lamp or
Parcel shelf lamp
3 ....35 amp ....Ignition coil
Ignition switch
Fuel pump
4 ....35 amp ....Stop lamp switch
Flasher unit
Fuel gauge or
Instrument voltage stabiliser (1964-)

Negative earth cars, 1967-1976:

1 ....35 amp ....Starter solenoid
Lighting switch (alternator)
Hazard warning unit
2 ....35 amp ....Horn
Interior lamp
Headlamp flasher
3 ....35 amp ....Ignition coil
Ignition switch
Fuel pump
Oil pressure warning lamp (dynamo)
4 ....35 amp ....Stop lamp switch
Instrument voltage stabiliser
Flasher unit
Wipe switch (dynamo)
Heated rear window

Negative earth cars, 1976 on:

1 ....35 amp ....Ignition coil
Ignition switch
2 ....35 amp ....Flasher unit
Stop lamp switch
3 ....25 amp ....Starter solenoid
Lighting switch
4 ....25 amp ....Headlamp flasher switch
Brake failure warning lamp
5 ....25 amp ....Starter switch
Radio
6 ....25 amp ....Wiper motor
Wiper switch
Heater switch

7 ....15 amp ....Lighting switch
8 ....15 amp ....Panel & instrument
lamps

Replacement Bulbs

Function	Wattage	Fitting
Sealed beam	60/45	Integral
Front lamps:		
Indicator	21	Bayonet
Park	5	Bayonet
Park, sealed unit	5	Capless
Indicator repeaters	21	Bayonet
Rear lamps:		
Indicator	21	Bayonet
Brake/park	21/5	Bayonet
Fog	21	Bayonet
Reversing	21	Bayonet
Number plate, Saloon	6	Festoon
Number plate Van, Pick-up	5	Bayonet
Interior lamps:		
Courtesy light	6	Festoon
Switches	0.75	Screw
Panel lamps	2.2	Screw
Headlamps		
Bulbs	45/40	Spring clip
Sealed beam	60/45	Integral
Front lamps:		
Indicator	21	Bayonet
Park	5	Bayonet
Park, sealed unit	5	Capless
Indicator repeaters	21	Bayonet
Rear lamps:		
Indicator	21	Bayonet
Brake/park	21/5	Bayonet
Fog	21	Bayonet
Reversing	21	Bayonet
Number plate, Saloon	6	Festoon
Number plate Van, Pick-up	5	Bayonet
Interior lamps:		
Courtesy light	6	Festoon
Switches	0.75	Screw
Panel lamps	2.2	Screw

Index